THE ARTS OF MANKIND

EDITED BY ANDRÉ MALRAUX
AND GEORGES SALLES

SCIENTIFIC CONSULTANT : ANDRÉ PARROT

Studios and Styles of The Italian Renaissance

ANDRÉ CHASTEL

Studios and Styles of the Italian RENAISSANCE

TRANSLATED BY JONATHAN GRIFFIN

ODYSSEY • NEW YORK

49 548

Library of Congress Catalog Card Number : 66-18997

Printed in France

Published 1966 by arrangement with Editions Gallimard.

Odyssey Books, New York,
Trade Division of Western Publishing Company, Inc.

CONTENTS

To Roberto Longhi

duca signor e maestro

nel campo della pittura italiana.

PREFACE: THE 'BOTTEGHE'

To reach the heart of Renaissance artistic activity, it is necessary, within the geographical and social framework established by the centres, to reconstitute the history of the studios, or workshops. The fifteenth century in Italy is the age of the *botteghe*. These ressembled small factories, run by firms, with directors and assistants; and we may take as typical what we know of Verrocchio's studio, with its coming and going of apprentices, the responsibilities that devolved upon Lorenzo di Credi when the master was in Venice in 1483, the list of work done, and the ways in which the difficulties of carrying out the orders were overcome. Their customers were extremely varied, but among them the city authorities and the churches predominated, and to meet their demands the *botteghe* undertook many jobs, not all by any means equally remunerative. Insignificant or showy, all the commissions amounted, more or less, to supplying some painted or sculptured monument and erecting it in its place,—that is, they involved fitting and decorating. No tomb went without its framework, no altarpiece without its mount, no ceremonial chamber without its marquetry *spalliere*. The workshop included carpenters, gilders and carvers of mouldings. Giuliano da Sangallo began by making wooden models of stalls or palaces and carving frames for Botticelli's *tondi*, before he went on to direct the building work at Poggio a Caiano and Santa Maria delle Carceri. This continuity between all the different aspects of artistic activity gives fifteenth-century art in Italy a character all its own: it retained a strong flavour of the workmanlike, however impressive the reputation, influence and pretentions of the masters.

The second half of the Quattrocento can be considered as the period when cross-fertilization, proliferation, specialization and conflict appeared most clearly among the *botteghe*. The journeys of Gagini from Lombardy to Sicily, of Antonello to Naples and on to Venice, come to mind; or again, the expansion of the 'school' of Schiavone and of Verrocchio's studio. But in addition we must imagine, at each place they stopped, a regrouping of forces—the arrival of auxiliaries, a recourse to local practitioners and the establishment of a complete organization, small by modern standards but capable of surviving the departure of the 'masters'. So it was at Rome with the men employed on the monumental tombs under Innocent VIII, at Padua with

1 - E. DE' ROBERTI. GRIFFONI ALTARPIECE (DETAIL): THE FIRE. VATICAN LIBRARY.

Donatello's collaborators, in the Marches with Crivelli's assistants... The concept of the 'building-yard', in its full sense, is essentially complementary to that of the studio, or workshop, which must not be regarded as an independent cultural centre.

In each city of note we find competing *botteghe*. The fact needs stressing. A studio worked as a small clan, complete with its own supporters, faithful clients and publicity. But there were far stronger differences of nature, culture and taste than this implies; and between the *milieux* (and corresponding classes) of their customers the conflict of tendencies was often much more marked than is usually thought. One centre might comprise two or three studios, whose function and ambition were often quite distinct. People knew what to expect from the studio of Neri di Bicci, a good reliable house for the requirements of monasteries: to go to Botticelli or to Filippino was another matter. At Siena there was a gap of the same order between the normal production of Sano di Pietro and that of Neroccio or Benvenuto di Giovanni. In Liguria and Piedmont there was Massone as opposed to Braccesco or even the Breas: a well-organized export business was the reward and complement of facility. Even in the great houses of Venice or Florence—in that of the Bellinis for example (Vasari later stressed, not without malice, its well-conducted commercial side) and that of the Ghirlandaios—a certain amount of inferior but lucrative production was tolerated. The career of Perugino, commuting between Perugia and Florence and expanding his business in all directions, illustrates unforgettably the price exacted of art by success in commerce. Only when all this is realized can we understand the difference in quality between works produced at the same time. The ordinary *botteghe* were as closely geared to sales as the others: their output was large. Account books and 'log-books' of some of these enterprises—those of Maso di Bartolommeo, of Neri di Bicci, and others—have come down to us: the volume of their business is as remarkable as the care they took to respond effectively to the desires of their customers, who wanted a moderate modernism. We are here at a quasi-industrial level. At this level the Renaissance was characterized by a slow, regular perfecting of formulae, brought out discreetly, adopting certain interesting innovations with a delay of ten, twenty or thirty years; and the importance of such artists as Piero della Francesca, Tura, Liberale, Rizzo or Bramante showed in the smooth and regular vulgarizations of their styles. In Florence the process can be followed clearly,—the way in which the minor studios approached the moment when, under cover of the *piagnone* fashion, attachment to 'tradition' (that is, to a deliberate archaism) was recommended to the suppliers of religious art.

Those artistic experiments which arrest our attention with their originality —and by which we are tempted to mark out the phases of a great period—presuppose both clients and artists anxious to escape from the banal and anonymous. In the period under review, one finds the Duke of Urbino or Lodovico il Moro tirelessly seeking out architects or painters capable of accomplishing great things for them, while men like Giuliano da Sangallo, Verrocchio or Leonardo are on the look-out for the Maecenas who will enable them to give their full measure. The swift comings and goings of certain important artists from one centre to another are rather surprising, but certainly signs of vitality: these were 'polyvalent' masters, who could, at need, found an architect's or a sculptor's studio and, in any case, brought with them 'modernity'. But it was the reign of initiative and of the unforeseen. The case of Bramante is revealing: a native of Urbino (and born in 1444), he must, one supposes, have worked as a decorator in Federico's palace; but he escaped from there—in what circumstances is unknown—to Lombardy, where we find him practising by turns as painter and as architect. His Bergamo frescoes (*c.* 1477) have come down to us incomplete and mutilated; but they are indispensable for an understanding of Bramante's decisive contribution, described by a sixteenth-century critic as '*gran prospettivo come creato da Piero della Francesca*'. His architecture, in the church of Santa Maria presso San Satiro, was a painter's architecture; but as he got to know the palaeo-Christian masterpieces in Milan, and as he came into contact with Rome, he was led beyond that pure 'perspectivist's' vision. In short, Bramante developed ceaselessly as he passed from milieu to milieu: at each stage he created a definite movement, but then detached himself from it—so much so that the last works of one of the masters most typical of the end of the Quattrocento must be considered as falling within the High Renaissance.

Thus the concept of studio or workshop must not be made too rigid, but must take into account the mobility—nomadism, it may perhaps be called—of men of powerful individuality. They brought in that element of chance and the unforeseeable which is part of all living history. Because of their zig-zag careers, our final picture of this period of great initiative is inevitably, to a large extent, dominated by an impression of stir, of movements crossing and meeting. It is in the light of these facts that the play of exchange and competition and the moments of activity and success enjoyed by the studios should be viewed: all these developments must be studied in context and then the feeble years and the times of intensity will appear like the slack and the taut sections of a vibrating string. We have tried to distinguish the concrete manifestations of each of the main artistic categories: there are 'situations' proper to each centre; but the moments of effervescence and initiative constitute the 'events' of art history, which bring life to the 'situations'. They are like isothermal lines, in relation to which the workshops, major or minor, and individuals take their place. The centres are seen as sometimes 'in phase', sometimes not; and there emerges an image of the peninsula's activity that appears all the more coherent since its consequences are to be found throughout the Western world. Italian art took shape as it passed through these intermingled and concurrent actions. All the studios had a share in an effort of affirmation which extended over the whole of Italy. What is revealed to us is Italy, the Great Workshop, '*Officina italiana*'.

André Chastel

PART ONE

Il dissegno di
Col campanil del

I

ARCHITECTURE

THERE was abundant building activity in most of the Italian cities during the fifteenth century. Many of the buildings were designed to display the 'modern' effects, side by side with others that remained faithful to the norms of the Trecento. But examples of concerted schemes of modern building were rare, and were to remain the exception throughout the Renaissance. No important new city was founded except Pienza, the city of Pius II: built by B. Rossellino from 1459 onwards in an Albertian spirit, this is a city on a ridge, with its axis expanding, towards the north, into the market place and, towards the south, into the noble trapezoidal piazza bordered by buildings of a counterbalanced design. In the centre of this piazza the cathedral rises between two open spaces—the scale being set by a monumental well-head on the right, and, still more, by a pavement that gives rhythm and unity to the composition. The whole looks exactly like the realization of some ideal prospect; and like the *vedute* of the painters or the inlayers, it possesses an optimum viewpoint.

In Tuscany there were plans for rebuilding Poggio Imperiale (near Poggibonsi, about 36 miles from Florence on the way to Siena), and work was done on this between 1484 and 1495, but it remained only a beginning. At Ostia a small, well-ordered quarter was built around Giovanni da Sangallo's fortress. In Emilia the Marchese Gian Lodovico began rebuilding Cortemaggiore on a quadrilateral plan. The largest enterprise was that of Ercole d'Este at Ferrara: it is a an exceptional example of town-planning. Within a circuit of fortifications the embellishment of which was never completed, the master plan divides the new quarter like a draughtsboard; this new

2 - ANON. VIEW OF FERRARA (DETAIL).
MODENA, STATE ARCHIVES.

3 - PIENZA, CATHEDRAL, FAÇADE.

quarter takes over from the old quarter massed about the cathedral and castle, and in it each main crossing was provided, first of all, with a palace serving as a monumental landmark. But the old quarter retained its privileged ascendency, and the new prospects, for ever spectacular and useless, lead into an inert zone. This accounts for the impression one gets there of—in M. Butor's phrase—'real fragments of a dream city'. The desire for town planning was widespread in the fifteenth century, but it resulted more often in the straightening out of streets and the partial rebuilding of pre-existing blocks than in the creation of new quarters. A good example is that of Rome, in which Sixtus IV laid down a new street plan, centred on the Castello Sant'Angelo and later completed by the Via Giulia.

Fifteenth-century town-planning was essentially the composition of open spaces, the designing of piazze and other places for human commerce. The mediaeval tradition of the piazza was still alive, but—in conformity with the most ancient Mediterranean traditional plan—the central meeting-place of a city was still placed within a framework of buildings with porticoes, as, for instance, in the case of Faenza's long rectangular piazza, or those of Ascoli and Imola, or again that of Vigevano, on which Lodovico il Moro lavished such care, with its long horizontal lines broken by the tower of the city hall and by the church façade occupying the missing side of what would be a quadrilateral portico (the whole possesses a remarkable simplicity and is perfectly calculated for the enhancement of the open space, the meeting-place). The Piazza Contarena at Udine, which is later (1448-1533), aims at complex effects with its varying levels, fountains and loggias. The now recognized predominance of the piazza with the tendency to surround it with a continuous colonnade belongs to the end of the fifteenth century, and its complete development, in the following century, can be seen in the Piazza di San Marco. Giuliano da Sangallo's fine project for a semi-enclosed piazza with two arms to link the Medici Palace in Rome with the Piazza Navona is a late example. The distinctive buildings of Northern Italian cities are the colonnaded loggias with their brilliant decoration based on classical Antiquity.

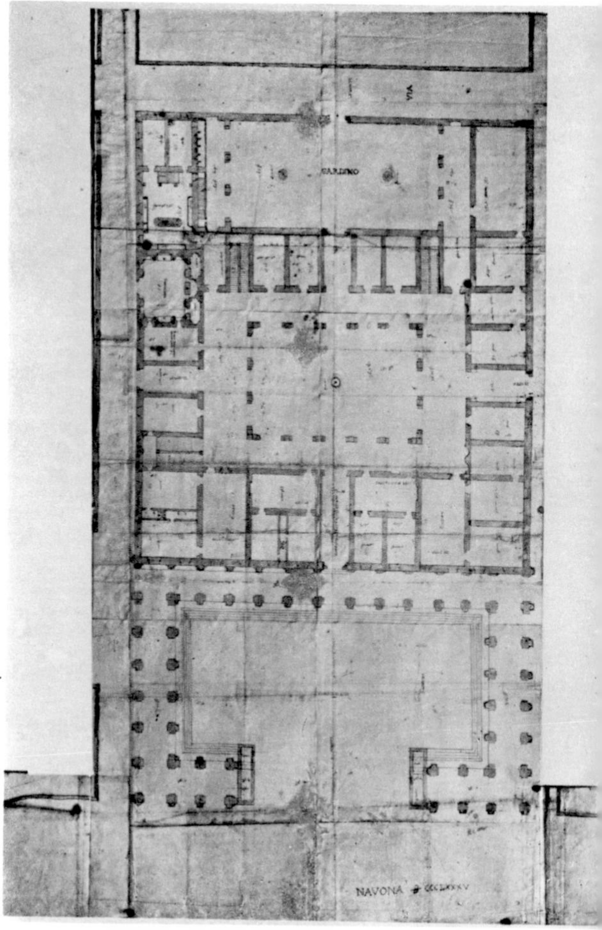

4 - G. DA SANGALLO. PROJECT FOR A PALACE LINKED TO THE PIAZZA NAVONA — FLORENCE.

5 - F. DI GIORGIO. IDEAL PIAZZA — BERLIN-DAHLEM, STAATLICHE MUSEEN, GEMÄLDEGALERIE.

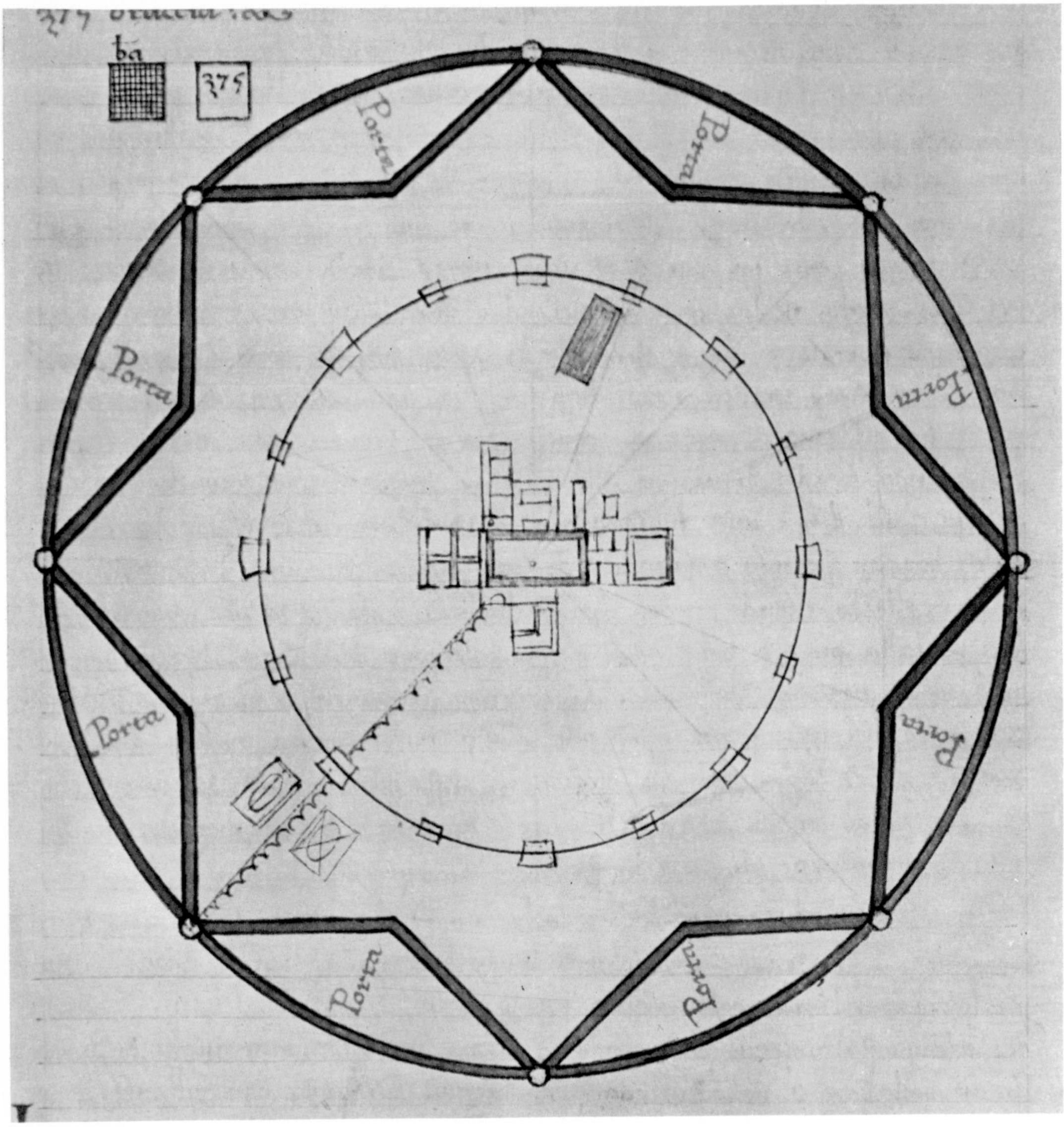

6 - FILARETE. PLAN OF THE SFORZINDA — FLORENCE, BIBLIOTECA NAZIONALE.

The idea of the city implied an articulation of various quarters within an enclosed space, and so the circular plan still seemed the most convenient way of designing a city and allocating its various parts: it gave the feeling that the city was a complete entity, an organism, a human unity. But at the end of the century this type of plan acquired a much more definite value from the development of the radial street-plan and the requirements of fortification. Filarete did not hesitate to inscribe the plan of Sforzinda, with its central piazza and its symmetrical parts within a circle; and Francesco di Giorgio distributed about the city centre—crowned by a *tempietto*—radiat-

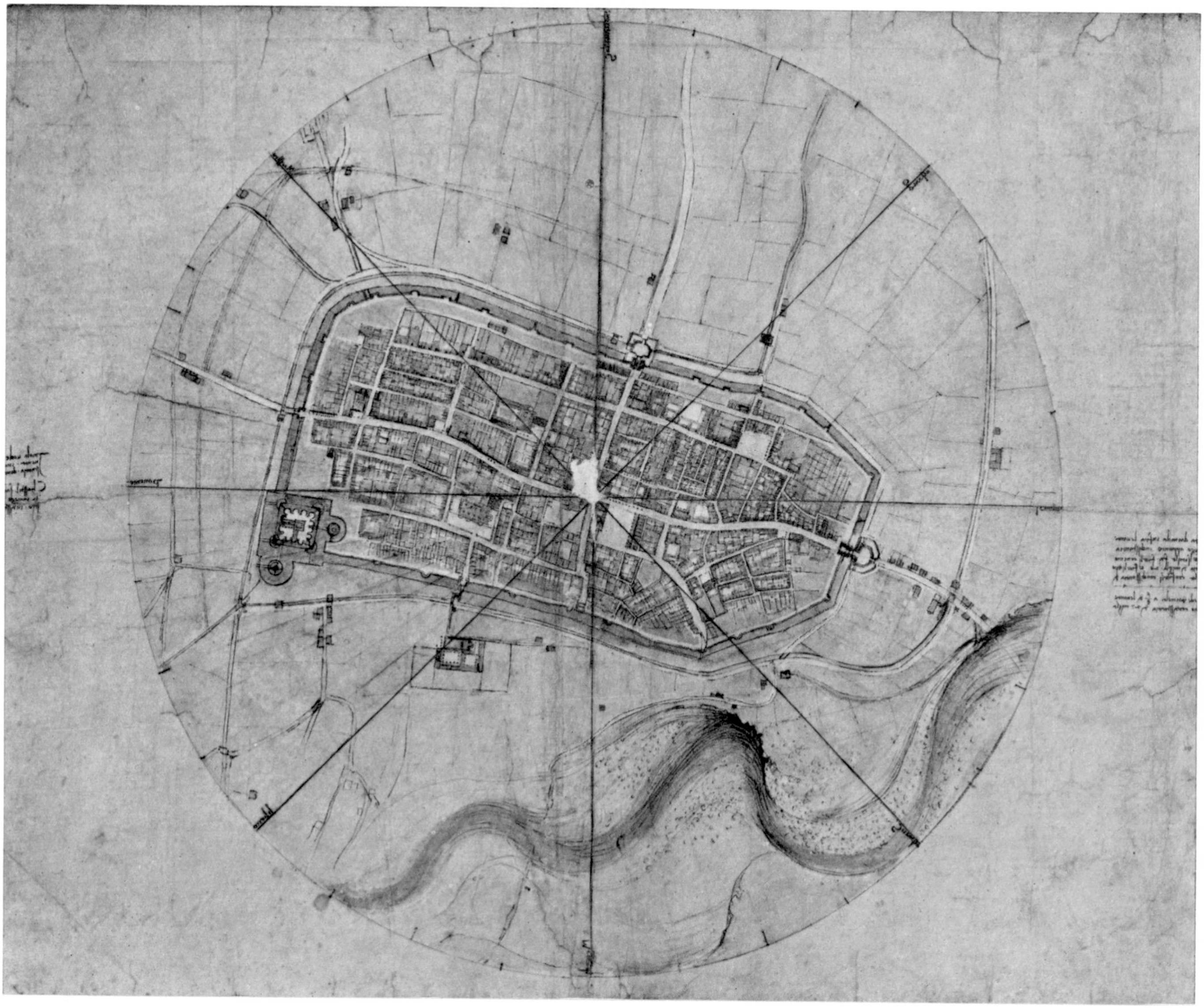

7 - LEONARDO DA VINCI. PLAN OF IMOLA — WINDSOR CASTLE, ROYAL LIBRARY.

ing avenues intersected by parallel streets or by a long spiral way. Such a scheme had both a social value, enabling the hierarchical elements (church and palace) to be stressed, and a technical value, making it easier to find one's way. So Leonardo thought that a city like Milan, if it was to be clearly intelligible, must be surrounded by a circumference whose centre would be the cathedral; and similarly, in 1502, the rectangular city of Imola was inscribed by him within a circular plan, where the radii made the placing of the various parts easier. The circular scheme was recommended as a help to topographical measurement.

At the same moment, regular polygonal forms were attracting more and more attention in the field of fortification, and these considerations were to have distant but important repercussions on Renaissance town-planning. The famous architects of that time usually served as military engineers—Bramante and Leonardo in the service of Lodovico il Moro, Giuliano da Sangallo in that of Florence, Francesco di Giorgio in that of Urbino. And the whole system of city defences was again *sub judice*, now that artillery was beginning to upset the habits of war. The superiority of Charles VIII in 1494 was above all due—the point has been made often enough since Michelet—to the fact that no wall could resist his cannons. That the problem was given high priority is evident: no longer was there a treatise on architecture without a special 'book' on fortification. The solutions proposed are the more interesting since in this case Antiquity could not be of any help. Francesco di Giorgio reminds his readers of this in his *Trattato*, in which the new principle is announced: 'The strength of a fortress depends more on the quality of its plan than on the thickness of its walls.' The idea of flankers, making it possible to command any breach, is already in evidence, and its logical application, the triangular bastion (replacing the round tower) had already—it seems—been thought of by Francesco, at least in drawings, before Sanmicheli began systematically equipping fortified cities with it. These requirements confirmed the authority of the radial plan, which is given such an important place in Francesco's treatise. The city that would conform to the new ideas of war would have to be disposed in depth: the height and thickness of the walls were less important than the articulation of the defences. Hence a new application of the centre-based radial plan with a centre: this still had its power as a symbol, and it now began to govern the distribution of the parts. It is to be found in all the architects' treatises—in Alberti's with more stress on the social requirements of urban organization, in Francesco di Giorgio's on the geometrical figuration of the plans and their military function, in Filarete's on the interest of the expressive forms. All were aware that an ideal 'city', must be thought out, so as to illuminate the future.

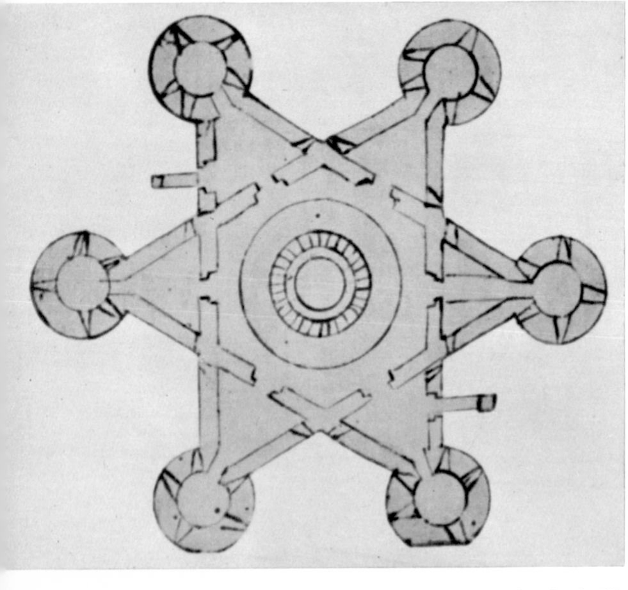

8 - G. DA SANGALLO. PLAN FOR A STAR-SHAPED FORT — SIENA, PICCOLOMINI LIBRARY.

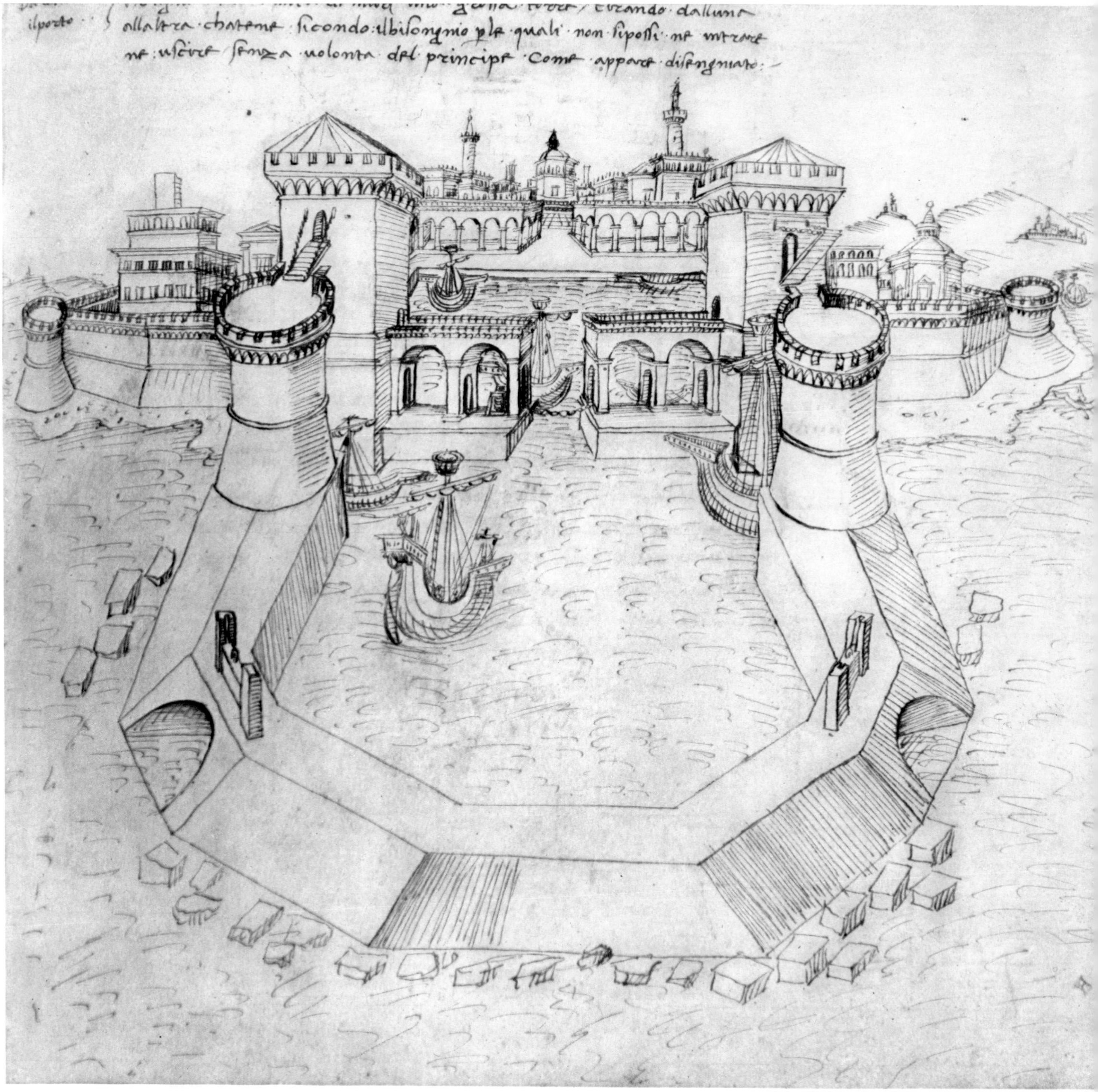

9 - FRANCESCO DI GIORGIO. HARBOUR AND DOCKS OF A LARGE TOWN — FLORENCE, BIBLIOTECA NAZIONALE.

FESTIVAL AND UTOPIA

THAT it was also the period of fictional architecture is not surprising. In painting, and even in relief carving, representations of plans and buildings acquired such amplitude and variety that, by themselves, they form an impressive chapter in the history of monumental art. It was long thought that these were anticipations, designs confirming the general need to renew the urban setting, the scene of men's lives. To the dream cities which the Gothic painters and illuminators had loved to arrange along the horizon (and of which Pisanello produced a last version in the church of Sant'Anastasia in Verona) the Florentines, beginning with Masaccio, had opposed the piazzas, loggias and façades of their own city, the purpose being to give topicality to the *storie* of major painting. This reform took place just when the achievement of perspective was transforming relations between painters and architects: painting was, in short, on the point of being able to expound architectural problems, anticipate them and try them out in abstract forms. Yet during the second half of the fifteenth century there persisted, in the painted architectural settings, a principle of fantasy which forces us to look for another explanation.

In these inventions one finds not only the desire to articulate ideal forms in space, but also the impulse to compose marvellous and impossible edifices. It has been observed that a great many of these compositions —loggias, shrines, temples, etc.—accompany either romantic scenes (especially on the *cassoni*) or dramatic episodes taken from the Bible or from the Golden Legend (especially on the predella panels). These subjects, borrowed from courtly romance or pious biographies, recur in the

10 - AMADEO. SCULPTED PANEL: THE FLAGELLATION. BERGAMO, COLLEONI CHAPEL.
Shaded for demonstration. See list of illustrations.

II - MASO FINIGUERRA. PICTURE-CHRONICLE. CECROPS AND THE TOWN OF ATHENS — LONDON.

sacre rappresentazioni and in the stage entertainments that were becoming more and more common in Florence, Rome, Milan and Naples. Emile Mâle has established the connection between the general development of iconography in the direction of pathos, and the spreading influence of the theatre of the mystery play. It becomes tempting to wonder whether the articulation of space in Italian painting after 1450-1460 was not of theatrical origin. Still more definitely, in the pictures of Uccello and of some of the popular painters the presence of conventional palaces, of 'mansions', of false mountains —in fact, of decorative accessories—is clearly perceptible: as soon as space in painting is amplified, the picture becomes a kind of stage action, in which the artifice of perspective now makes possible a fully controlled production. Can it be that the illusionism of the pictures had the same resources and the same limits as that of the theatre of the time?

If the architectural settings in late Quattrocento pictures are stage sets, or an imitation of these, does not this by itself explain their specific power of ennoblement and enhancement?

12 - GIOVANNI MARCANOVA. PALACE FAÇADE — MODENA, GALLERIA E MUSEO ESTENSE.

It is incontestable that the perspective terracing and the regular distribution of more and more ornate buildings give the architecture in the paintings an artificial, theatrical effect. From this it is easy to see what made this type of setting for the *storie* so successful, but there is not enough concrete evidence about its connection with theatrical production in practice. The machine invented by Brunelleschi for the *sacra rappresentazione* of the Annunciation had nothing of ideal architecture about it: it was a high scaffold with a circular 'sky'—it was indeed kept, carefully repaired and re-used up till the end of the century. What we know of the mysteries from their texts and the descriptions of them suggests that there were fixed structures: the colonnades, temples, etc., required for the presentation of the saints and angels provided no depth greater than that of a platform—they were simply façades and shrines set down side by side. They were, in short, a simultaneous décor, as in the countries of Northern Europe, and in them the only sign of the Mediterranean *all'antica* style was the abandonment of Gothic in the arcades and pediments. This is the type of architectural setting to be found on the *cassoni* of 1440-1450 and continued by such painters as Gozzoli: it scarcely goes beyond Trecentesque models. The archaizing art of the *cassoni* was no doubt related to the production of the *sacre rappresentazioni*, but it is evidence of their traditionalist and inert character. In it perspective is far from being exploited with all the imagination that is to be seen, for instance, in the fresco paintings. The strange *Assumption* by Gerolamo da Vicenza (1488) is almost the only instance of theatrical arrangement: the Madonna is borne on a kind of luminous globe adorned with angels, above an extremely high altar. The colours are very bright, and the whole of this vertical machinery is placed in a kind of flagged enclosure opening on the countryside. The setting stands apart from the central scene.

Not all painting was attuned to the theatre. True, Leonardo da Vinci, when he was at Milan, introduced new devices to the theatre, but these were not so much architectural effects as fantastic inventions, like the mountain that opened to reveal, behind its slopes, Pluto's Hades. And indeed it is fairly clear from the documents that Leonardo's concern was not confined to the settings, but extended to the porticoes, galleries and other temporary structures required for jousts and processions. The theatre in the Quattrocento was only a special aspect of the festival.

13 - G. DA VICENZA. DORMITION AND ASSUMPTION OF THE VIRGIN — LONDON, NATIONAL GALLERY.

This conception seems indispensible for an understanding of that peculiar mixture of realism and the marvellous which was so striking a quality of many of the architectural settings in Quattrocento pictures. In the city calendars there was a constant alternation of liturgical festivals and secular festivals, and these exchanged their resources: they had a definite effect on social life and on planning by causing the temporary metamorphosis of the city. The festival had two sides to it, a static and a dynamic, a time when it was still and a time when it was in movement; and both of these aspects affected architectural invention. In its mobile form, as procession and cavalcade, the love of triumphal chariots caused these to be given a definitely monumental quality. As for the static part of the festival, the stands and loggias embellished with fine textiles and enriched with statues and emblems provided an opportunity for displays of original architecture. So the real town became a town of fiction: Renaissance man achieved his desired self-projection especially in adopting classical dress. The fascination with *tempietti*, with domed edifices, is well attested in the early sixteenth-century triumphal entries, but it is reasonable to suppose that it was already widespread as early as 1475-1480. There was, in fact, round about those dates, a fairly general recourse to the hexagonal loggia or tabernacle —of which, it is true, most of the examples are to be found in paintings. These small structures occur both in ideal representations, where they serve as temples of honour, and in the illustrations of popular mysteries, like those of *Santa Guglielma*, *Santa Appolonia*, etc. (published in Florence after 1480 with woodcuts). These modest

14 - S. BOTTICELLI. MIRACLE OF ST ZENOBIUS — DRESDEN, GEMÄLDEGALERIE.

15 - ANON. FLORENTINE. TRIUMPH OF BACCHUS AND ARIADNE (DETAIL) — LONDON, BRITISH MUSEUM.

engravings suggest that the motif was probably introduced into stage productions; but if so this came from its use in other circumstances. The stage concentrated the two new features brought in by the festival—the chariot with its *tableau vivant*, and the box of honour.

Confirmation for this point of view may be found in the frequency with which, in the pictures of this time, noble edifices with somewhat ambitious decoration appear superimposed on the piazzas and houses of the familiar city. The contrast between the 'ideal' architecture of the festival and that of reality could not be expressed more clearly than it is in Botticelli's picture (Dresden Museum) in which the Miracle of St Zenobius takes place under a portico set down in the middle of a city

16 - JACOPO DA MONTAGNANA. TRIPTYCH (DETAIL): ANNUNCIATION — PADUA.

Shaded for demonstration.
See list of illustrations.

square. Such a portico figures constantly in those sacred scenes which are dominated by the static but impressive order of the formal 'presentations'. Most pictures of the Annunciation painted after the middle of the century show the Virgin enclosed in a portico-like shrine, and the singularity of this—which is the singularity of festival trimmings—is stressed by its placing in the urban scene. Montagnana's *Annunciation* is an eloquent example of this: its huge *tempietto* entablature and its architectural blocks divided by dark columns, contrasting with the sculptural rope-work and fluting, jut out into the street with the houses of the citizens receding into the distance. The same place of honour, treated in the form of a loggia, appears in countless *sacre conversazioni*: Filippino, in the *Madonna between St Martin and St Catherine* which he painted in about 1488 for Tanai di Nerli and his wife at Santo Spirito, has placed the figures within a loggia dominating the town. The effect may have been borrowed from the Flemish, but the analogy with the stands and places of honour of the festivals is striking.

This position of painted architecture half-way between spatial research and the minor magic of the festival enables us to understand better how it was often, as Sir Kenneth Clark has remarked, 'in advance of anything that architects proper had accomplished...; it was bolder, more complex and closer to classical models.' Sometimes the architecture in paintings perpetuates older models, as, for instance, in the *tondo* of the meeting between Solomon and the Queen of Sheba, in which an Emilian craftsman has elaborated on the theme of the 'princely encounter' under a portico, so popular ever since Ghiberti's Baptistry doors.

17 - FILIPPINO LIPPI. VIRGIN AND CHILD WITH SAINTS AND DONORS — FLORENCE, SANTO SPIRITO.
Shaded for demonstration. See list of illustrations.

But with this we may contrast an astonishing *tondo* of the *Nativity*, perhaps by Botticini, where all the magic of which painted architecture is capable, is fully displayed. The group is placed within a ruined temple, as was now common (Francesco di Giorgio, as we have seen, even made this temple into a triumphal arch, the better to bring out the 'representative' value of the architectural setting); the image of the classical world makes itself felt with all its grandeur in the broken pilasters and gaping vaults; the candelabra stand out in relief against a golden background; and a black and gold pavement stretches to the central altar. There is gilding everywhere. The shattered temple carries the suggestion of a splendid building, alone worthy of the royal scene. At the same time the regular recession of the flagstones stresses the axiality of the composition, which carries on its influence into the surrounding space and even into the landscape. Starting from a simpler composition by Botticelli, the painter has exploited all the powers of suggestion inherent in architecture—ruins, colours, structure.

The Venetian variations on the theme of imaginary buildings were no less interesting, and, as we have seen, the architectural settings depicted by Gentile Bellini and Carpaccio introduced a new note of exoticism. Venetian painters remained to some extent faithful to topographical landmarks which had come, more or less by convention, to signify Rome, Byzantium or Alexandria—and even corrected these from recent prints. But they did not forbid themselves the use of improbable inventions that gave the architectural setting its utmost power—as when Mansueti, at the Scuola di San Marco, showed in cross-section, and so treated as a portico, a kind of basilica with a nave and six aisles, highly convenient for the arrangement of his groups of figures. Yet it was earlier, in about 1470, and in Central Italy that, stimulated by various things, including the memory of Domenico Veneziano, the example of Piero della Francesca and a certain propensity towards the charms of the imaginary, the painters indulged in particularly felicitous variations that have become part of the whole impression left by that century. Bright colours exquisitely toned were brought in to diversify the harmonious and regular spatial

18 - FERRARESE SCHOOL. SOLOMON AND THE QUEEN OF SHEBA — HOUSTON, MUSEUM OF FINE ARTS.

Shaded for demonstration.
See list of illustrations.

19 - ANON. ITALIAN. THE ADORATION OF THE KINGS — CHICAGO, ART INSTITUTE, M.A. RYERSON COLL.
Shaded for demonstration. See list of illustrations.

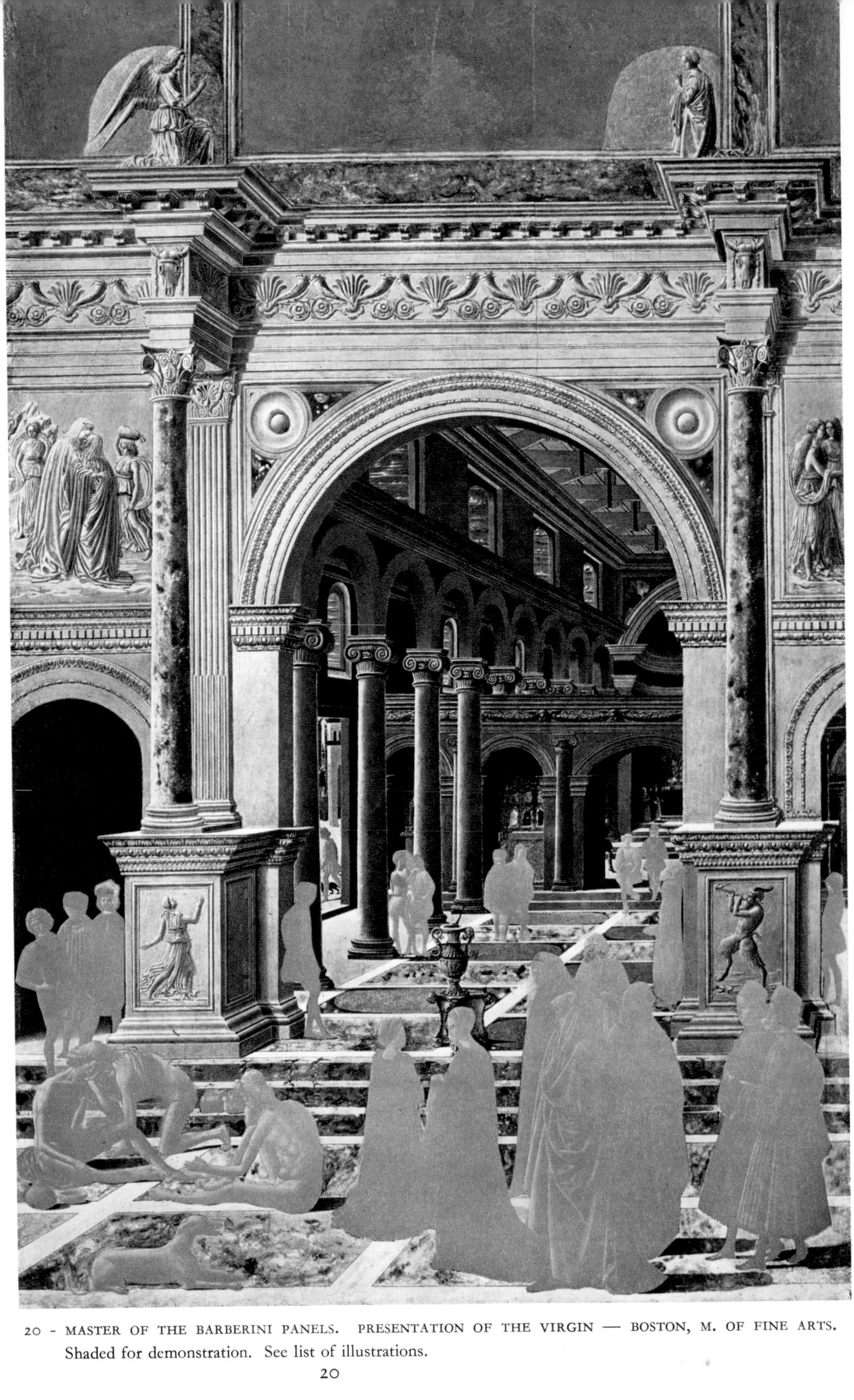

20 - MASTER OF THE BARBERINI PANELS. PRESENTATION OF THE VIRGIN — BOSTON, M. OF FINE ARTS.
Shaded for demonstration. See list of illustrations.

21 - PERUGINO. MIRACLES OF ST BERNARDINO. RAISING OF THE STILL-BORN CHILD — PERUGIA, NATIONAL GALLERY.
Shaded for demonstration. See list of illustrations.

compartments obtained by combining the effects of depth and axiality with those of frontality and arrangement in tiers. The two Barberini panels (Boston Fine Arts Museum, and Metropolitan Museum, New York), which may very well be by a painter from the Marches who was as familiar with Urbino as with Perugia (Giovanni da Camerino, according to F. Zeri), are the great triumphs of this art, with their clear divisions into galleries and screens. The other summit is the series of the *Miracles of St Bernardino* at Perugia, painted chiefly by Perugino and Fiorenzo di Lorenzo in 1473. Great play is made, as in stage designs, with architectural chromaticism and with openings that distribute the light. The structures are given the maximum ornamentation that is tolerable, and they are complete examples of the picturesque style, yet with a strictly selected formal vocabulary that stresses its freedom from everything Gothic. This spacious and colourful architecture was one of the remarkable creations

22 - F. DI GIORGIO. (ATTR.) ARCHITECTURAL PERSPECTIVE (DETAIL) — BALTIMORE.

of the fifteenth century; it was a dream world, which must once more be given its rightful place, for it was one of the period's original charms. It gave life to the whole sector of miniature painting, and continued to excite men's imaginations through the descriptions in the *Hypnerotomachia*, which bring together archaeological detail, geometry and colour and treat them with equal veneration. The results of this taste were not confined to painting: the Oratory of St Bernardino at Perugia, like the palaces on the Grand Canal and the Colleoni chapel at Bergamo, remind us that architecture itself could move in the same direction: but in this case painting is an irreplaceable witness.

The influence of this taste is no less clear in pictures whose whole direction, one feels, is away from it, towards that pure order, that sober and unadorned plastic effect which began to regain strength from 1480 onwards. This tendency was perhaps related to the successes of the marquetry versions of architecture, whose whole value depended on geometry. In any case the connection comes out clearly on those *cassoni* and *spalliere* panels which, enclosed in a frame of carved wood, represent majestic abstract architectural structures, made up of porticoes and flagged pavements, articulating both the axial drive and the lateral extension with a tranquil authority and a kind of intellectual certainty that carry complete conviction. The same role was assumed by the few surviving paintings that are entirely devoted to abstract architecture, the most famous of which are at Urbino, Baltimore and Berlin. These compositions, well calculated to expound the properties of perspective, can hardly be later than the end of the fifteenth century: they take us back to the circles of Francesco di Giorgio or Giuliano da Sangallo. They offer arrangements of urban space in which we find both probable buildings and sketches for stage sets, together

23 - FRANCESCO DI GIORGIO (ATTR.) ARCHITECTURAL PERSPECTIVE — BALTIMORE, WALTERS ART GALLERY.

within an ideal city. Productions on the stage may later have been derived from them, and in the sixteenth century they or similar models helped in the realization of Vitruvian settings, but there is no ground for considering them as stage designs from the start. Their significance was a different one: the strictly centred and framed organization of these pictures clarifies the piazza as the preferred field for architectural thinking in the fifteenth century.

The increasing use of imaginary architecture in the paintings and relief carvings of this period went with a more and more definite awareness of the 'representative values' of architecture, and was indeed its consequence: if historical and religious scenes were to be given the most monumental settings possible, this was because—as the humanists and chroniclers never ceased repeating—architecture was identical with civilization itself. Civilization asserted itself through the presence of great archetypes, like the Temple of Jerusalem, or through historical references such as were conveyed by the pyramids, triumphal arches and temples. Now that culture was again drawing men's attention to the Mediterranean masterpieces, their glamour enhanced that of architecture. Monumental grandeur seemed the guarantee of social vitality. This conviction encouraged the princes to build, and led some of the Popes to place the monumental rebuilding of Rome high among the interests of the Church. In presenting the testament of Nicholas V, Giannozzo Manetti frankly asserted the apologetic value of architecture: it helped, he said, to demonstrate the Faith by the permanence of its witness[1]'. The great ages—no one now doubted—were those that had built much and powerfully.

1. See Notes, p. 351.

25 - BOTTICELLI. THE PUNISHMENT OF KORAH, DATHAN AND ABIRON (DETAIL) — VATICAN, SISTINE CHAPEL.

24 - BENOZZO GOZZOLI. THE BUILDING OF THE TOWER OF BABEL (DETAIL) — PISA, CAMPO SANTO.

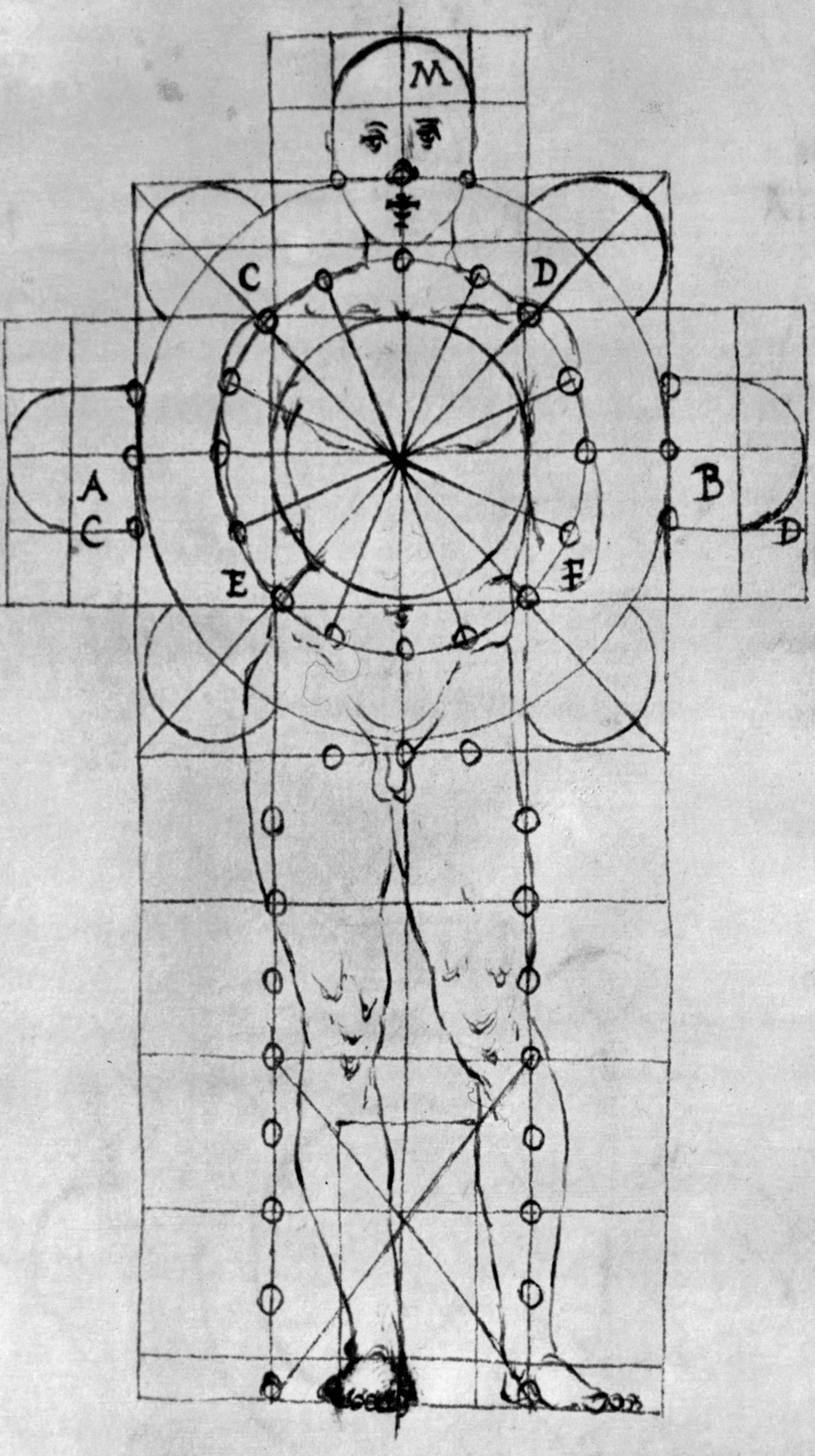
M
C
D
A
C
B
D
E
F

THEORY AND PRACTICE

In the second half of the Quattrocento there appeared a great many writings on architecture and architects' drawings and statements. Several main preoccupations emerged from these; research into the mathematical laws, the perfecting of forms on classical lines, and sometimes (as in the case of Leonardo da Vinci in about 1490) the analysis of the conditions of stability and sound structure. Yet it is hard to make out how these agree, or even how they connect. One has still the impression that the intellectual initiatives of the innovating architects were leading them in directions whose issue was not always clear. No coherent and constant relations between practice and theory can be observed: anonymous practitioners—and there were many of these—applied rules, ancient or recent, which the learned architect did not formulate; he intrepidly asserted 'self-evident truths' which the builder could not see how to exploit. 'It is a great thing to carry an architectural work through to its conclusion,' wrote Alberti at the beginning of his second book, and his intention was not merely to remind readers of the nobility of architecture: while stressing the value of the achievement, he also meant, it seems, to recall with a sigh the agonies of leaving works unfinished —agonies with which his career was strewn—and the material difficulties of all kinds that lay in wait for the architect. Two of Alberti's most notable enterprises were only rebuilding—the redesigning of the church of San Francesco at Rimini *all'antica*, and the *alla Toscana* treatment of the façade of Santa Maria Novella. The latter was completed, but the former was broken off short. Alberti's famous letter to Matteo de' Pasti, in which he

26 - FRANCESCO DI GIORGIO. STUDY OF PROPORTIONS — FLORENCE, BIBLIOTECA NAZIONALE.

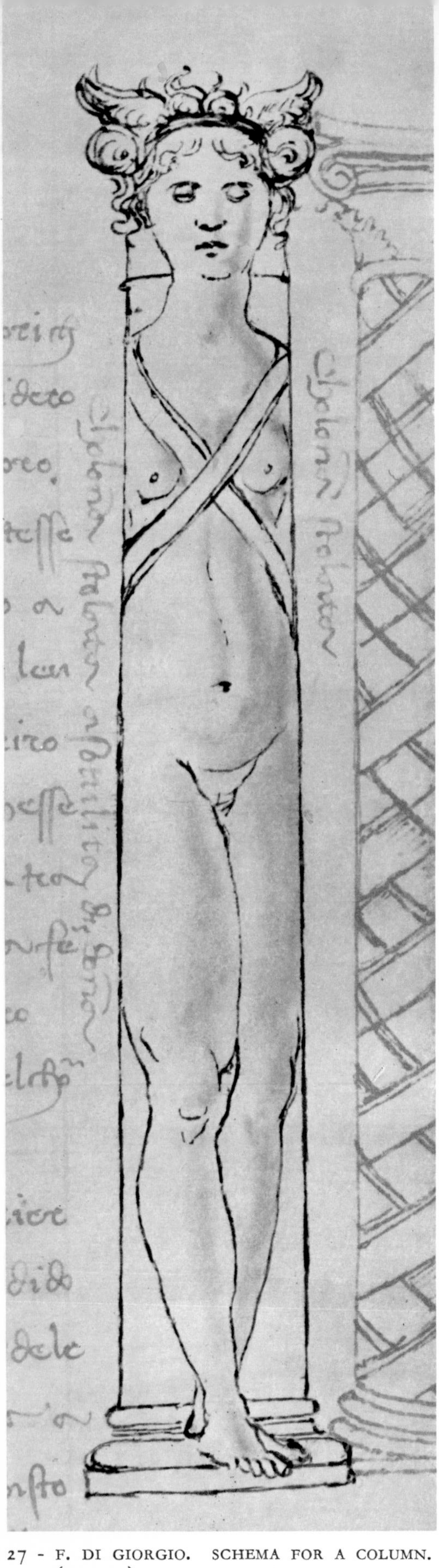

27 - F. DI GIORGIO. SCHEMA FOR A COLUMN. (DETAIL) — TURIN, BIBLIOTECA DEL RE.

insists that any alteration of his plans 'would untune the whole of that music,' is enough to show the difficulties of remote control, as this was practised by the humanists.

In agreement with the philosophers of humanism, Alberti, Francesco di Giorgio and Leonardo kept repeating that architecture must obey mathematical principles[2]. They put forward types of proportions which ought to be realized. Yet we do not possess, for any building of this period, a figured plan or a dimensional design that fully explains the combination of the parts and shows the process that was followed. The search for symmetry and the recourse to triangles and diagonals are so obvious that a system (that of Thiersch) for restoration of the method has been proposed, and seems very acceptable—it brings out the relations between the parts of the compositions; but there is no ground for stating that it gives us the way they were actually built, and Wittkower has reminded us of the danger of mistaking a result for a cause. The most that can be said is that architects seem not to have started from closely defined principles; they mixed intuition with calculation. It was no doubt to proclaim the validity of this overall impression that the building was constantly described as an 'organism,' and its parts as 'living beings.' We get a lively feeling of the beauty of the forms deployed in space, but the formulation of their relations is a tentative one. Alberti confessed this in a somewhat exceptional passage, in which he noted the gap between the architectural vision and its realization: 'I can say of myself that I have often formed in my mind ideas of buildings that have given me a wonderful delight, yet when I work them out into lines I discover that in the parts which please me most there are serious errors which must be corrected. On a second examination of the design, in translating it into numerical proportions, I am struck by and ashamed of my own inadequacy. Finally, when I have turned my design into a model and re-examined its elements, I sometimes find that I am mistaken, even in the numbers.'

The new architecture proceeded from a strict attention to the rhythms of space, of which walls, framework and other structural elements all gave evidence. A building was a kind of mathematical mesh, a transparent cage of harmonic relationships, giving the mind an abstract satisfaction; hence the importance of the painted 'ideal view', and the difficulties—and surprises—encountered in its realization. All the mason did was to submit to a sketch, which there was no question of his modifying. The use of a wooden *modello* soon acquired an increasing

28 - LEONARDO DA VINCI. STUDY IN PERSPECTIVE FOR THE ADORATION OF THE KINGS — FLORENCE.

importance: Sangallo, trained as a joiner, was a specialist in it. This practice established not only a new estimation of the importance of having a complete and final conception before execution, but also the primacy of the optical effect. As Burckhardt says, 'composition based on ratios devised for the eye is the very seed of the Renaissance.' When these were found, the 'architectural idea' was ready. This was a return to one of the favourite practices of Mediterranean art.

But there is no need to infer from this a conflict between effect and the requirements of structure. It would be an old error to repeat Choisy's dictum that 'The Renaissance in Italy implied no more than a reform in the system of ornament,' and that in France 'it was to meet with an obstacle in the very system of traditional building.' For, while there is one kind of architecture that aims at expressing the structure, there is another whose purpose is the organization of the external and interior space by the play of precise elements and their relationships—which has nothing to do with applied embellishment, or with the naïve idea of ornament that is sometimes held. The reproach that the Renaissance

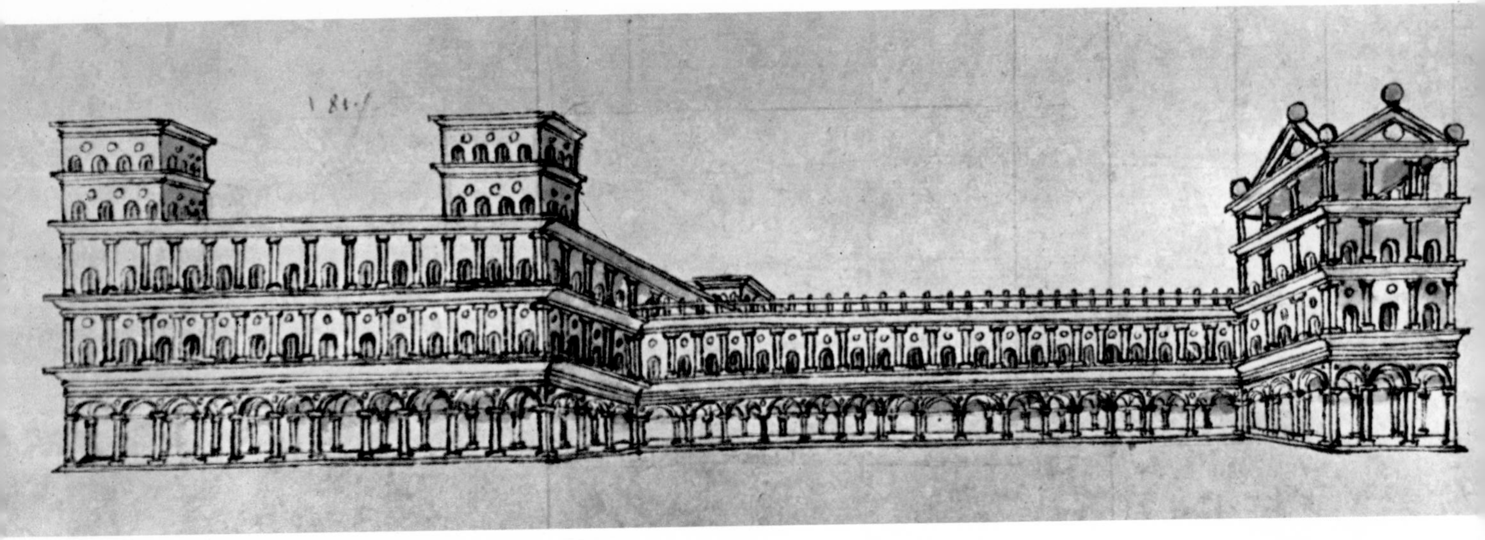

29 - FILARETE. EXTERIOR OF A CASTLE — FLORENCE, BIBLIOTECA NAZIONALE.

30 - PIETRO DA RHO. DOORWAY: PALAZZO STANGA (DETAIL) — PARIS, LOUVRE.

innovators levelled against 'the Gothic', as they knew it in the peninsula, was precisely that it was not 'true' architecture, but goldsmiths' work gone mad, devoid of the necessary order and articulation. It was against a hand-to-mouth architecture, carried out by addition and juxtaposition of bits, that the new architecture took its stand. Filarete, in Book VIII of his *Treatise*, about columns, observes that there are still to be seen too many buildings 'made by masters ignorant of the proportions and forms required'. He adds: 'It is true that in some places in Italy people have begun to appreciate and apply the more precise modular system of the ancients, so that [the columns] look quite different from those that have been used during the last hundred or two hundred years or more and are still used by the incompetent.' As he saw it, the moderns were the ignorant Gothic practitioners: the serious principles came from the *antichi*, who were coming to life again through the modern innovators—first and foremost Brunelleschi, who had been dead twenty years. Filarete wrote in about 1465, just when the general effort was being made throughout Italy to convince princes and prelates of the interest of the revolution that was going on. In support of his thesis he cites the new palace in the Via della Vigna Nuova (the Rucellai Palace) and certain buildings ordered by the Lord of Mantua '*a uno suo castello insù il Po*'. These were the examples to follow.

What mattered most was the repertory of forms—the *arco tondo*, rectangular bays, pilasters and columns. Filarete shows a marked impatience with the Gothic vocabulary of broken arches and flowered motifs. Speaking of bridges, he tries to find a reason for the decadence that caused the great examples to be abandoned: it was, he thinks, the invasion by foreign styles and their imprudent acceptance by weak-minded generations—'*questo uso e modo anno avuto ... da' tramontani, cioè da Tedeschi e da Francesi.*' The imported style was not architecture, it was goldsmiths' work (tabernacles and censers) or fantastic paintings, blown up to giant size. This was a polemical line that had come to stay: Filarete was preaching the Tuscan gospel to people who had to be converted. The Milan of the Sforzas must not be a continuation of the Milan of the Viscontis; the enormous cathedral and the Certosa, founded by these to assure their glory must be rectified before completion. Thus the most highly individualized attack on the Gothic *moderni* and the most imperious pleading in favour of the *antichi* came from so ambiguous an interpreter of the modern forms as Filarete—yet he did not hesitate to range himself with Brunelleschi and Alberti[3].

Throughout the period the ancient orders, though constantly invoked, were treated with an involuntary casualness. Doric was exceptional, Ionic rare and a more or less accurate Corinthian served as a basis for innumerable variations. The candelabrum-column, which is a fantastic interpretation, was to prevail with a surprising freedom. The feeling that each of the orders is a complete system and should govern the style employed did not yet exist. The column and the pier were only motifs. Architectural composition tended towards two distinct types:

31 - URBINO, DUCAL PALACE, WINDOW WITH TWIN BAYS.

32 - URBINO, DUCAL PALACE, DOORWAY LEADING TO THE THRONE ROOM.

in one the bays or isolated openings in the form of little aedicules with triangular or curvilinear pediments stand out from the surface of the wall: in the other the openings framed between columns and bands are set close together without any interval. After 1460 the two methods tended to become opposed: the former came to prevail in Tuscany —the small church of San Francesco al Monte by Cronaca and the substantial building of Santa Maria del Calcinaio at Cortona are examples of it; the second was to prevail in the North. In both cases the reference to classical antiquity was still a summary one, but the lines and projections sometimes give it definition. The introduction of these motifs made possible regular compositions that could be easily harmonized by means of diagonals and tracings: the illustrator of the *Hypnerotomachia* in due course gave some examples, and later Serlio would collect others from the work of Peruzzi. It seems almost beyond doubt that the habit of calculating architectural forms in accordance with a system of proportions became widespread among architects at the end of the fifteenth century. The writings of Pacioli suffice to show the splendid two-fold illusion that attracted them to this—the illusion of formulating beauty scientifically, and that of working in unison with Antiquity: that is to say, dominating at one and the same time both nature and history.

Yet to describe the situation in the Quattrocento simply in terms of a maturing of these discoveries would be fallacious: the revival of interest in the properties and surface effects of materials, and the many experiments that resulted from this, are equally characteristic of the period. The originality of the architectural work done after 1460 lies precisely in the combination—which, though paradoxical, gradually became general—of abstract requirements with picturesque inventions. A marked return to polychrome effects and to resourceful ornamentation proves that liberation from the older formulae had released a profound zest for all aspects of the art of building. The peninsula had at its disposal a vast range of possibilities, with its splendid limestone, its variety of hard and soft stones, and brick. Venice is inconceivable without Istria stone, Florence without the *pietra forte* and the grey *pietra serena*, Rome without travertine. The modern movement of the Renaissance was not a phase of negligence in this respect. Burckhardt noted that 'just as Florence is the city of rustication, so Venice—assured and calm, attuned to luxury and therefore to the use of precious materials, and habituated to mosaics—is the city of inlaid decoration.'

33 - CREMONA, PALAZZO STANGA. COURTYARD, TERRACOTTA DECORATION.

34 - B. DA MAIANO AND CRONACA — FLORENCE, PALAZZO STROZZI, FAÇADE.

35 - VENICE, PALAZZO DARIO, FAÇADE.

36 - BRESCIA. SANTA MARIA DEI MIRACOLI, FAÇADE.

The contrast between the Palazzo Strozzi in Florence (after 1489), with its pronounced rustication and Pietro Lombardo's Palazzo di Dario in Venice (about 1480), with its base of Istrian stone, its fragments of ancient 'violet' and its panels of porphyry, is both extreme and typical. But it only became as clear as this at the end of the century: in the years around 1450 to 1460 the use of inlay on buildings had not lost all its attraction for Florence and Tuscany, and it was then that Filarete went to Venice on behalf of Francesco Sforza to lay out for him a palace on the Grand Canal that was never finished, of which (as we have already mentioned) there survives a lower course heavily rusticated in the best Tuscan style; it was after 1480 that the distinction became plain to view, between an austere Tuscany and a City of the Doges whose taste ran to polychrome exteriors with plentiful inlay. For thirty years, experiments were made on a large scale with the most diverse materials. The animation of the surface by means of reliefs is marked, for instance, in the case of the Madonna di Galliera (1491) at Bologna, where the donors unfortunately insisted on the use of grey *masegna*, a local material that is friable. The two methods, relief carving and inlay work, are found in combination at Santa Maria dei Miracoli in Brescia (*c.* 1500). This was so general a feature that it led, in Tuscany, to the use of glazed terracotta (by the successful method which the della Robbias practised for lunettes and tympana), and in the provinces that had no good quarries and were too far from the mountains for the transport of rich materials to be economic, there grew up a fashion for friezes and terracotta medallions. This veneer architecture produced some rich and fascinating masterpieces, of a kind that did not reappear in the sixteenth century.

37 - BOLOGNA, SANTA MARIA DI GALLIERA, FAÇADE.

THE PALACE AND THE VILLA

In the middle of the century the idea of the town house had not yet taken final shape, even in Tuscany. There were three competing formulae—that of Brunelleschi (the plan he made for Cosimo was considered too grandiose), that of Michelozzo who produced the adaptable solution (in the palace in the Via Larga, 1444-1459) and that of Alberti (in the Palazzo Rucellai). The features which tended to become general for the *casa signorile* (or palazzo) were the massive cube or parallelepiped (making possible the majestic isolation of the residence), the rythmical ordering of the storeys (with or without explicit separation of bays), and the inner courtyard or *cortile* (a secular variant of the cloister, embellished with loggias or, at least, a colonnade on the ground floor level). This simple, rather abstract scheme made it possible to give the patrician residence aloofness without causing a violent break with the alignment of the street. The Florentines persisted in it for half a century, and did not dare to stress the main uprights of the building and the frames of the bays on the outside too strongly, still less to open up loggias between them. Comparison between the Palazzo Gondi (built after 1490) and the plans which Giuliano da Sangallo conceived on such generous lines for Naples or Rome shows clearly that his imagination was ready to break with the Tuscan norms, but that in Florence itself he conformed to these, for convention still forbade an escape from them. Other cities which, after 1460, welcomed the new formula with interest, had not the same scruples: in them the problem of the palazzo soon fired men's imaginations, and at the end of the century, in many cases, the situation was reversed—the

38 - MICHELOZZO — FLORENCE, PALAZZO MEDICI-RICCARDI.

39 - MILAN, CASTELLO SFORZESCO, AERIAL VIEW.

most interesting enterprises were no longer Tuscan.

In Milan the palace of the Medici Bank, presented to Cosimo by Francesco Sforza in 1462, was entirely rebuilt, no doubt on directives supplied by Michelozzo, the architect of the Medicis, and with the assistance of Filarete, who gives a detailed description of it in his *Treatise*. The formula was clearly a popular one: Michelozzo was invited in 1463 to direct the rebuilding of the Palazzo dei Rettori at Ragusa, and in 1464 he even signed a contract for work in Chios. The presence of the new palazzo in Milan became fully significant when the Castello was being extended—its feudal and military conception being at the opposite pole from that of the *casa* of the Medicis. This makes more revealing the effort to give a modern

40 - MICHELOZZO, DOORWAY TO THE MEDICI BANK — MILAN, ARCHEOLOGICAL MUSEUM.

style to the fortress, which lay right outside the city and stood out impressively against the horizon. Everything in it is colossal: with its round towers framing its long fortified façade and with its central tower known as the clock tower standing well back, it really looks like one of the fantastic compositions of Filarete or of Francesco di Giorgio. This formula too was a successful one: it proliferated as far as the Kremlin. The castles of Mantua and Ferrara were far from undergoing a similar modernization—how far may be seen if one considers the innovations, such as the Sala delle Asse, and the embellishments, such as the Ponticella (a suspended gallery), with which the castle of Lodovico il Moro was enriched in the time of Bramante and Leonardo.

41 - URBINO, AERIAL VIEW.

The castle of Urbino is a building that crowns a height, a gigantic mass welded firmly to the city. Its most striking effect lies not so much in its plan as in the size of its wall, and the openings in it and—on its upper level, in the articulation of the courtyards and of the blocks of building next to the cathedral. From 1450 onwards the old fortress of the Montefeltros underwent a series of modifications which were interrupted by the Duke's death in 1482: the two most important of these followed the arrival of Luciano Laurana and that of Francesco di Giorgio (whose contract was signed in 1468); in addition, apart from the prolonged visits of Piero della Francesca and Alberti, something must have been due to Federico himself—the men of letters sing the praises of his competence, perhaps to excess. For twenty years Urbino was a privileged place. The *cortile*, with its distinct frames to doors and windows (which recur throughout the palace), is the first great monumental

42 - L. LAURANA - URBINO, DUCAL PALACE, COURTYARD.

example of the kind; the façade with its superimposed loggias between the round towers, harmonizing perfectly with the landscape, belongs to a different conception. The castles of the Montefeltros were outside the current formulae: at Urbino the Tuscan *cortile*, treated with the utmost strictness, is boldly inserted into a mass not intended for it; at Gubbio the *cortile*, the continuous layout of the rooms and the imposing *studiolo* recur, making it a small-scale replica of the Urbino palace-fortress. And indeed the eastern slope of the Appenines is dotted with *castelli* built for Federico, among them the Rocca di Sassocorvaro.

These castles crown high positions in a remarkable manner, reminiscent of the countless fortified manors which have dominated the hills of Italy since the Middle Ages. A massive silhouette, oblique salients and their foundations mark them out as works of the Renaissance, though their coping, contrary to the 'flamboyant' French

43 - THE 'ROCK' OF SASSOCORVARO.

châteaux of the fifteenth century, is far from elegant. The preoccupation with defence counted for more than decorative display, and the architect-engineers of the period 1475-1500 had to consider what plans were most appropriate. The invention of the triangular bastion in place of the circular tower was conceived apparently by Francesco di Giorgio, at least in theory and on paper, before Sanmichele built his fortifications in the North. It was the logical conclusion to the idea of defending the flanks, allowing control over all the sides of a polygon. This principle emerged, naturally enough, at the moment when a practical solution was being sought for the articulation of structural blocks, and it was precisely in the

44 - THE 'ROCK' OF MONDAVIO.

Trattato of Francesco di Giorgio that we find the idea first put forward: 'the strength of a castle depends less on the thickness of the walls than on the quality of its design'. The application of this idea was a slow process in the art of fortification, though its consequences for town planning have already been pointed out.

The association of palazzo and stronghold makes Urbino an exceptional case: juxtaposition of the two types is more frequent. This is to be found in Milan and in other great cities, especially Naples. The destructions and transformations that have taken place may easily obscure for us the amplitude of these southern buildings. The palace of Diomede Carafa (1466) has a system of 'Cata-

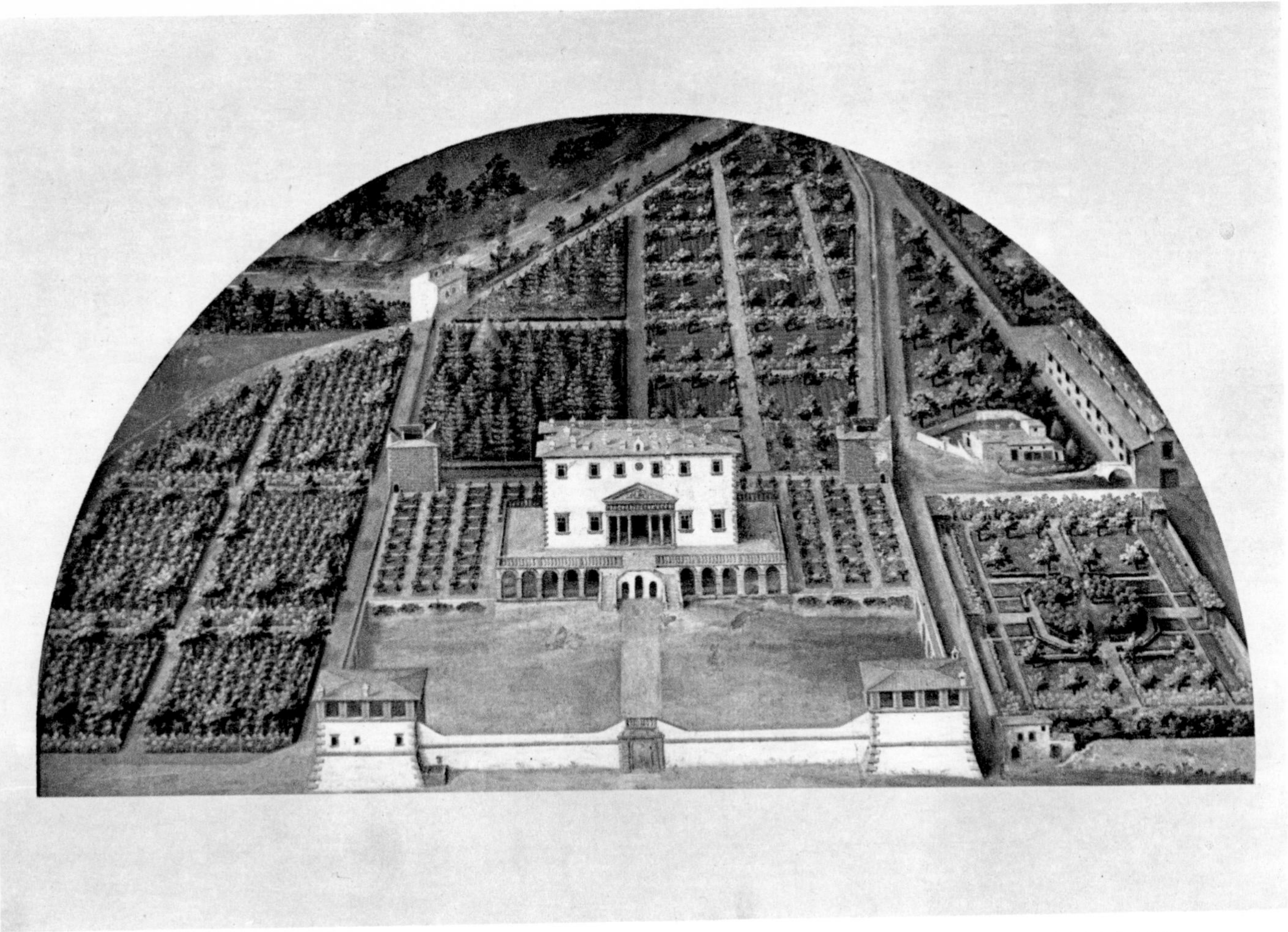

45 - UTENS. THE MEDICI VILLA AT POGGIO A CAIANO — FLORENCE, TOPOGRAPHICAL MUSEUM.

46 - UTENS. THE MEDICI VILLA AT CAFAGGIOLO. FLORENCE, TOPOGRAPHICAL MUSEUM.

lan' arches and decoration on the inside, and on the outside a doorway of classical design; the same is true of the Palazzo Cuano (1464-1490), where Florentine architects were certainly used; and the palace of the Sanseverino family (princes of Salerno) at the heart of the town was a spectacular building, with its diamond façade (of which more will be said later). The fortress of the Castelnuovo, in spite of its triumphal archway, no longer satisfied Ferdinand II: in 1488 Giuliano da Sangallo brought him an imposing model for a building in the shape of a square with sides 190 metres long; it was to include a rectangular courtyard with steps and surrounding colonnades, a vast chamber with a barrel vault, and a great many rooms symmetrically disposed as at Poggio a Caiano. This was unquestionably the last word of that particular type: Sangallo's plan, when compared with no less complex designs by Francesco di Giorgio, makes it quite clear

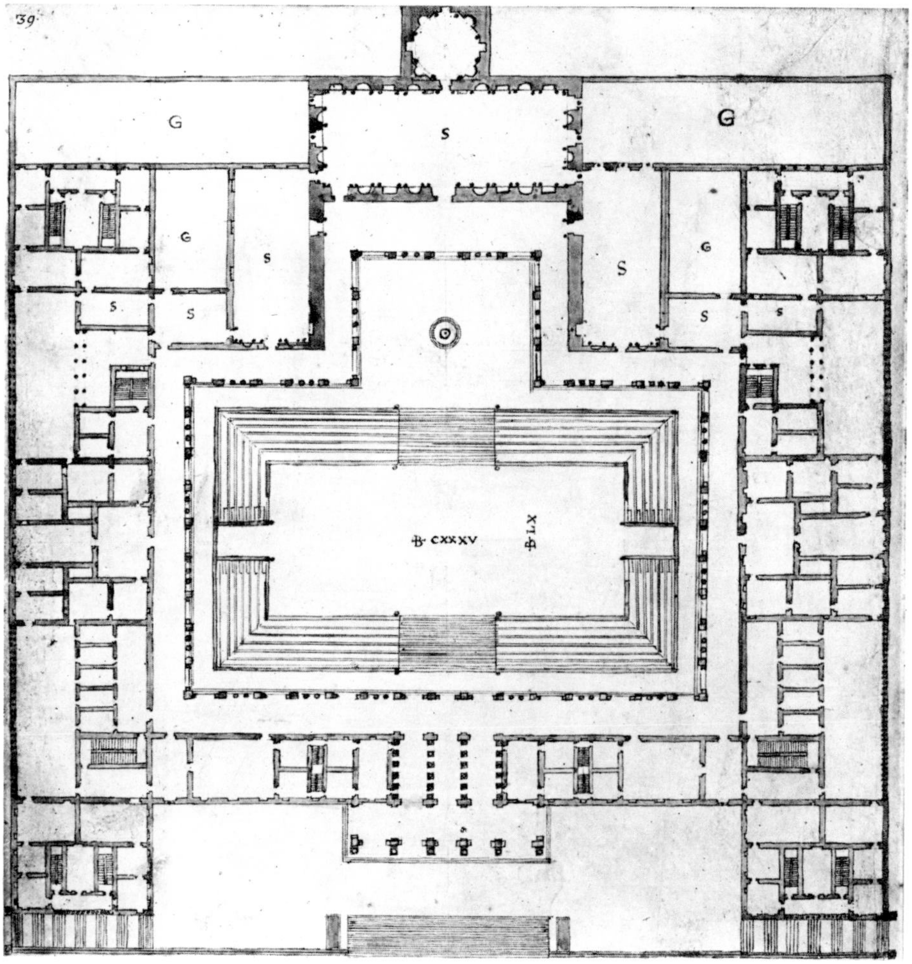

47 - GIULIANO DA SANGALLO. PROJECT FOR THE CASTLE OF FERDINAND OF ARAGON IN NAPLES, PLAN — VATICAN LIBRARY.

that the idea of this huge layout came from a study of classical models, especially of the Roman Baths, in which there were many rooms and in which internal communication was restricted. Both these architects anticipated in their designs a much more coherent planning of the inside of a building, with rooms joined together to form regular suites, which might be repeated symmetrically: the rooms ceased to be determined only by the *cortile*. Sangallo's plan, therefore, marks an important date. Though not carried out, it was so well-known that it deserves to be considered as an essential stage in the evolution which led to Palladio. When one remembers that, at the same moment, Prince Alfonso, Ferdinand's brother, was having a villa of revolutionary design built near the city gates (the villa of Poggio Reale), it becomes clear that round about 1490—Naples was a centre of capital importance for the future of civil architecture.

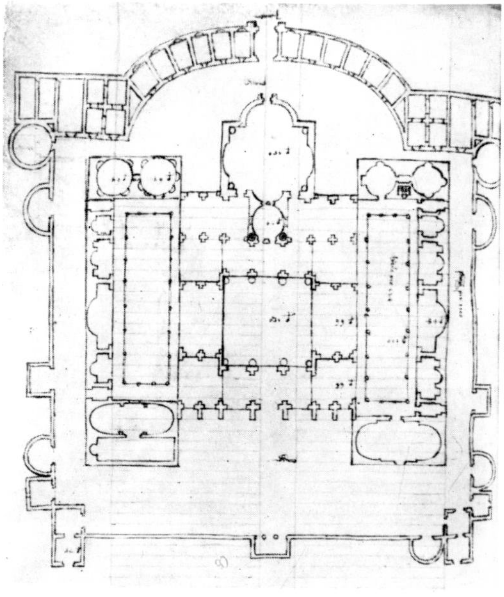

48 - F. DI GIORGIO. THERMAE — TURIN, BIBLIOTECA DEL RE.

49 - ROME, PALAZZO DELLA CANCELLERIA, FAÇADE.

At that moment there was something of a return to the ideas and taste of Alberti—not in Florence, but in Rome, and, finally, in Venice. Following the ambitious (and interrupted) work on the palace of San Marco, many patrician residences were built, but without any notable imaginative effort : plain courtyards, robust and simple adornments. Yet in Rome, at the time when Giuliano's brother, Antonio da Sangallo, was working there the desire for a grand effect and the return to a vertical rhythm through the use of bays, made the Palazzo Riario (or Cancelleria) highly significant. In it Alberti's forms are amplified to a

50 - ROME, PALAZZO DELLA CANCELLERIA, COURTYARD.

Roman scale. An inscription on one of the windows on the Corso shows that this façade is late (1511); but the palace was lived in as early as 1489, and its eastern face and the courtyard must have existed, at least in part, at this date. The extension to the south and to the west, back to the Via del Pellegrino, probably dates from the years 1489-1495. The inner courtyard is not free from a certain clumsiness, but the ordering of the façade, for the first time in Rome, is carried through with solemnity.

In Emilia, adaptation of local conventions was rather rapid. At Bologna, Imola, Ferrara and other places a

51 - BOLOGNA, PALAZZO BEVILACQUA, FAÇADE.

predilection for treating the *cortile* in two storeys is notable, with large-scale arcades on the ground floor level and small ones above—for instance in the Fava and Bevilacqua palaces at Bologna and the Scrofa palace at Ferrara. At the same time there was a new treatment of external ornamentation, thanks to the use of terracotta which was now becoming widespread from the Alps to the Adriatic. In Venice there was no room for the development of great *cortili*, and architectural effects on the grand scale were excluded; but the Palazzo Corner-Spinelli shows Mauro Coducci's almost unprecedented

52 - VENICE, PALAZZO CORNER-SPINELLI.

53 - VENICE, PALAZZO VENDRAMIN-CALERGI, FAÇADE.

54 - VERONA, PALAZZO DEL CONSIGLIO, LOGGIA.

interest in the regular distribution of openings, and the Palazzo Vendramin exemplifies a decided adaptation of the Albertian rhythm to the Venetian formula: the *bifora* is fitted in to a stylar elevation, and this makes possible a distribution of the openings in the façade that, as in the older traditional buildings, places the central loggia between two wings; the cornice completes and closes the composition, which is perhaps the most elaborate offered by the fifteenth century. Here it is not Gothic but the ancient fund of palaeo-Christian style that carries the weight of the invention.

After 1460 the design of façades acquired an importance commensurate with the desire (already noted) to enliven the look of the city and to express the building externally. The municipal loggias at Bologna, Brescia, Verona, Padua and Lucca have two or three groups of windows above a portico storey, the whole being defini-

55 - NAPLES, PALAZZO SANSEVERINO, FAÇADE.

tely framed by pilasters placed upon one another and by a cornice which, in Verona, becomes a support for statues. The palazzi observe greater severity, the ground floor remaining closed in and having bosses that stress the effect of hardness. In general the Quattrocento was still characterized by an effect of flatness and by respect for the surface; the forms on this are as though written, incised and adorned with graphic motifs. This is true of the Palazzo Riario in Rome, as well as of the Palazzo Rucellai: the façade is not treated as a plastic body. But in about 1470, as a consequence of the increased search for expression, we begin to meet with diamond-point bosses, the use of inlay and the vogue for features made of terracotta. Since the diamond points made their appearance as early as 1470 in the southern provinces (for example, on the façade of the Palazzo Sanseverino in Naples, the work of Novellus da Sancto Lucano, later incorporated in the church of the Jesuits), it has been thought that the formula came from Catalonia and reached Italy through Aragon. This type of external decoration spread, in fact, to Northern Italy after 1480: on the Palazzo Bevilacqua in Bologna (1481-84), the bosses have simple diagonals across them, and the same recurs on the Palazzo Trucchi-Raimondi at Cremona (1496). To these must be added the Rio di Palazzo façade of the Doge's Palace (*c.* 1480) and the Palazzo dei Diamanti at Ferrara (*c.* 1491). Diamond-point bosses made their appearance in Rome towards the end of the century on the lower storey of the Palazzo Santa Croce—or, more exactly, at the bottom of the square tower at the corner of the Via del Pianto. Several late Quattrocento houses of merchants in Rome (Vicolo del Governo Vecchio, Via degli Amatriciani) were adorned with a painted imitation of this motif. This formula even recurs in Russia, in the Kremlin.

The cutting of these regular facets gave a new elegance to the stone-work, just when inlay panels and applied relief-carvings were also becoming frequent. In Venice Commynes was struck by the use of gilding —which was soon forbidden by law: this added fresh surface effects to the polychrome decoration in which Venetians had delighted for centuries and which was acquiring a new lease of life at a moment when the Tuscan forms had to be assimilated. Results were surprising: in the Palazzo Vendramin the shadows of the loggia intervene amidst medallions and relief-carvings. Lastly, in Emilia and in the region north of the Apennines, where marble was as rare as the grey stone of Tuscany, the new spirit showed itself in the spread of applied terracotta ornamentation.

56 - FERRARA, PALAZZO DE' DIAMANTI.

57 - MICHELOZZO — CAREGGI, THE MEDICI VILLA.

The most remarkable new development in the last third of the fifteenth century was the rapid evolution of the villa. From the Trecento onwards the country house and the town house had gone together as complementary necessities. The country house took its meaning from the surrounding estate, which it interpreted, just as the palace was related to the quarter or block, which it dominated. In Italy as in France, by the middle of the century, the fortified manor was beginning gradually to lose its defensive characteristics; to appreciate the importance of the years 1470-80 in this respect one has only to compare Cosimo's Careggi, still traditional and closed, with the new-style villa of Poggio a Caiano. Alberti (*De re aedificatoria*, IX, 4) criticized the manor closed in upon itself. Crescenzio (reprinted in 1471) also described this style. Were the innovators simply overcoming a traditional practice? It has recently been pointed out that the renewal of the forms of the villa must have come from Venice where had persisted, as a devitalized vestige of late Antiquity, the practice of building small and regular edifices in which the ground floor lay open, having a portico sometimes surmounted by a loggia; only

58 - G. DA SANGALLO. THE MEDICI VILLA AT POGGIO A CAIANO.

one of the façades was stressed by means of ornamental bays. We are here at the opposite pole from the residence that is essentially a courtyard enclosed by walls. The single façade, which particularly suited Venice, tended to be ordered in the form of a gallery—or double gallery—between two masses that gave it stability and might even look like lateral towers—as in the case of the Fondaco dei Turchi (built in about 1250 by Palmieri, modified by the Duke of Ferrara in 1381, and taken over by the Ottoman merchants in the seventeenth century). After 1450-1460 minor buildings of this kind became common on the mainland, and J. Ackerman has raised the question whether the principal villas of the late fifteenth century should not be considered as developments originated by the Venetian formula (which in fact went back to an ancient Mediterranean type). Lorenzo de' Medici's Poggio a Caiano (begun in about 1480), Innocent VIII's Belvedere in the Vatican (on which work was begun in 1484) and Poggio Reale (built in about 1490 for Alfonso of Aragon on the outskirts of Naples) are all applications of the scheme of the portico between two masses. The

59 - BALDASSARE PERUZZI. VILLA CHIGI DELLE VOLTE — VATICAN LIBRARY.

final stage of this evolution was the Farnesina; it was built from 1508 to 1511 for Agostino Chigi by the Sienese architect Baldassare Peruzzi, and he had already experimented with the formula in about 1500, in the Villa Chigi delle Volte near Siena. It seems quite clear that these original experiments were connected. While Giuliano da Maino was building the villa for Alfonso, Giuliano da Sangallo, having already built Poggio a Caiano, presented a design for a palace to Ferdinand of Aragon in 1488, in the name of Lorenzo de' Medici. As for the Belvedere, its architect is not known for certain: Vasari strangely attributes it to Antonio Pollaiuolo; Jacomo da Pietrasanta is considered more likely; but the Tuscan origin seems plain and is significant. Lastly, the connection between Poggio Reale and the Farnesina finds proof in a drawing by Peruzzi himself, which indeed gives valuable help in reconstituting the plan of the building. To judge from the major works of the period, the modern form of the villa seems to have been a Tuscan interpretation of an ancient type handed down by Venice and adapted to the new taste.

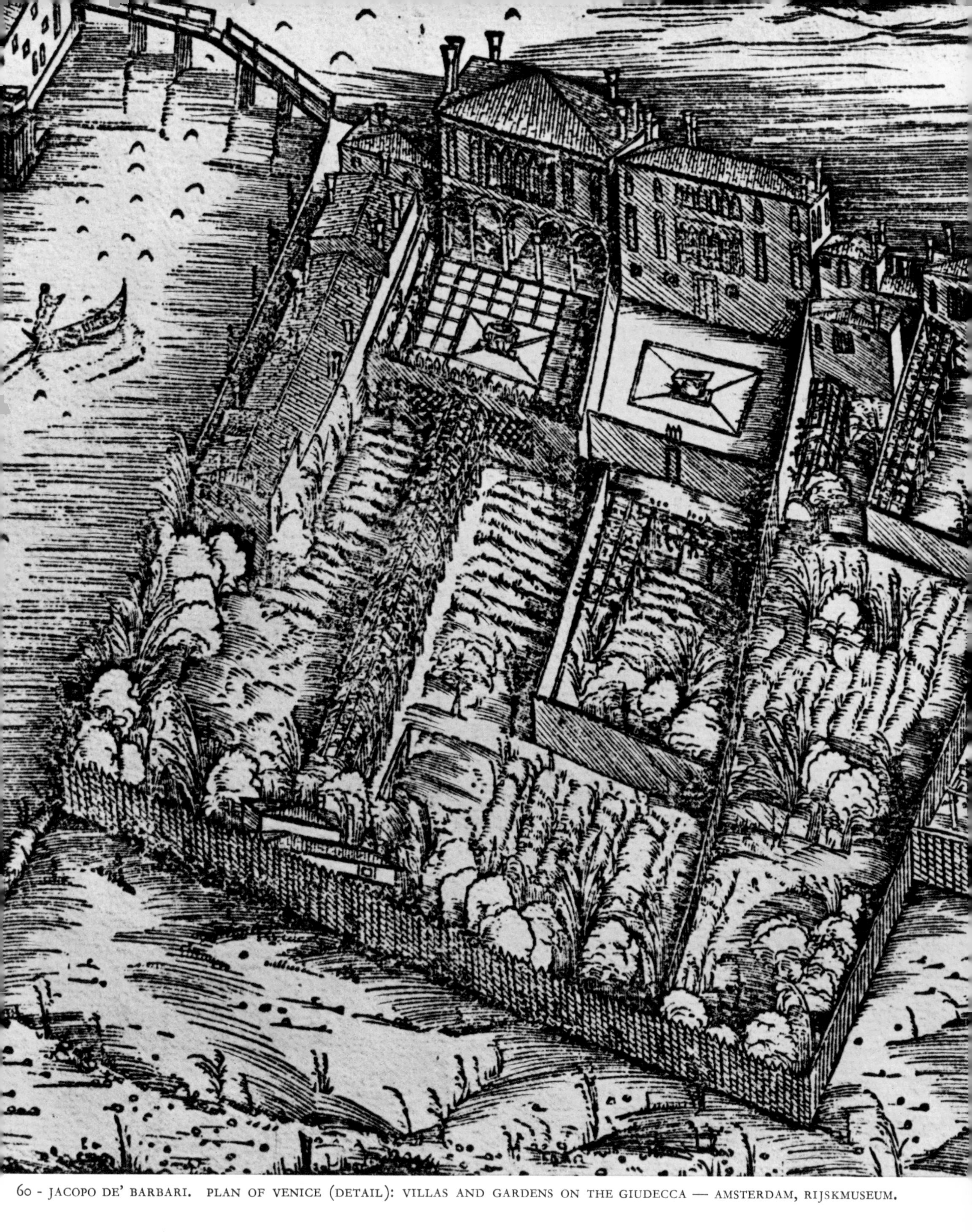

60 - JACOPO DE' BARBARI. PLAN OF VENICE (DETAIL): VILLAS AND GARDENS ON THE GIUDECCA — AMSTERDAM, RIJKSMUSEUM.

This makes the difference all the more significant. Poggio a Caiano is solid in volume, but it stands on a kind of pedestal in the centre of large gardens, and is treated as a country palace: the inner courtyard is replaced by a huge barrel-vaulted chamber, and the façade exhibits a second feature taken from Antiquity in the shape of an Ionic portico which opens like a loggia between two symmetrical and severe masses. This effect is far more marked in the Belvedere: here the villa, crowning a hill, has three storeys, one of which is a loggia fully deployed between two lateral blocks standing well forward. It was the first villa of this type in Central Italy since Antiquity; the predominance of the gallery, the inner portico and the decoration of frescoes add to the experiment all the resources of illusionism. The composition of Poggio Reale has to be reconstituted, and for this we have Peruzzi's drawing, the summary description by M.-A. Michiel and the simplified plan published in Serlio (Book III). It was the most complete example of the three, for there were now not one but four façades, and the indented quadrilateral of Poggio a Caiano had become a whole consisting of four towers bound together by four systems of colonnades which gives on to a sunken inner courtyard (12 m × 16 m). This formula, which was quite new, was admirably suited to a villa designed as a pleasure residence and setting for festivities, where banquets and balls could take place in the *cortile*. Certainly the openings on the outside were not as numerous as the arches of the arcades, but the axis of the courtyard was prolonged by loggias giving on to the garden. A comparison with the design for the palace for Ferdinand is revealing in that it underlines the significance of the courtyard with colonnades. On the outside, the framing by the four corner towers and the opening on to the garden created an original effect, which was destined to have an immense future in Western architecture[4].

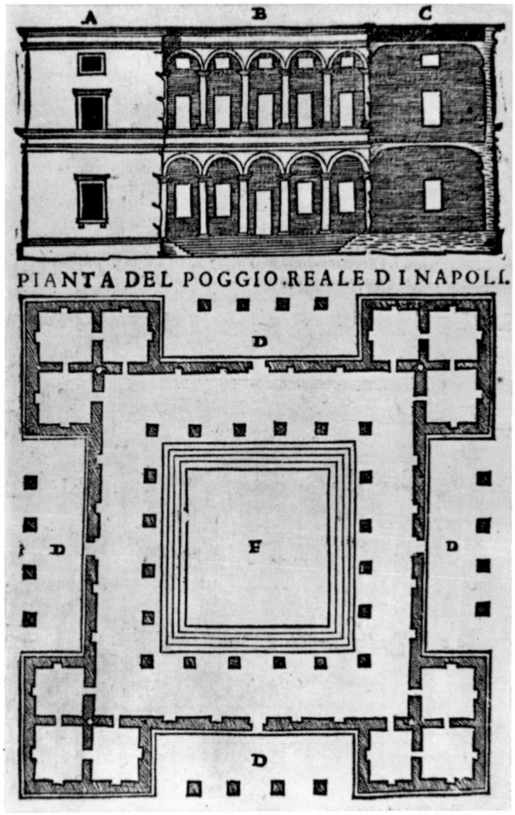

61 - POGGIO REALE. PLAN AND ELEVATION.

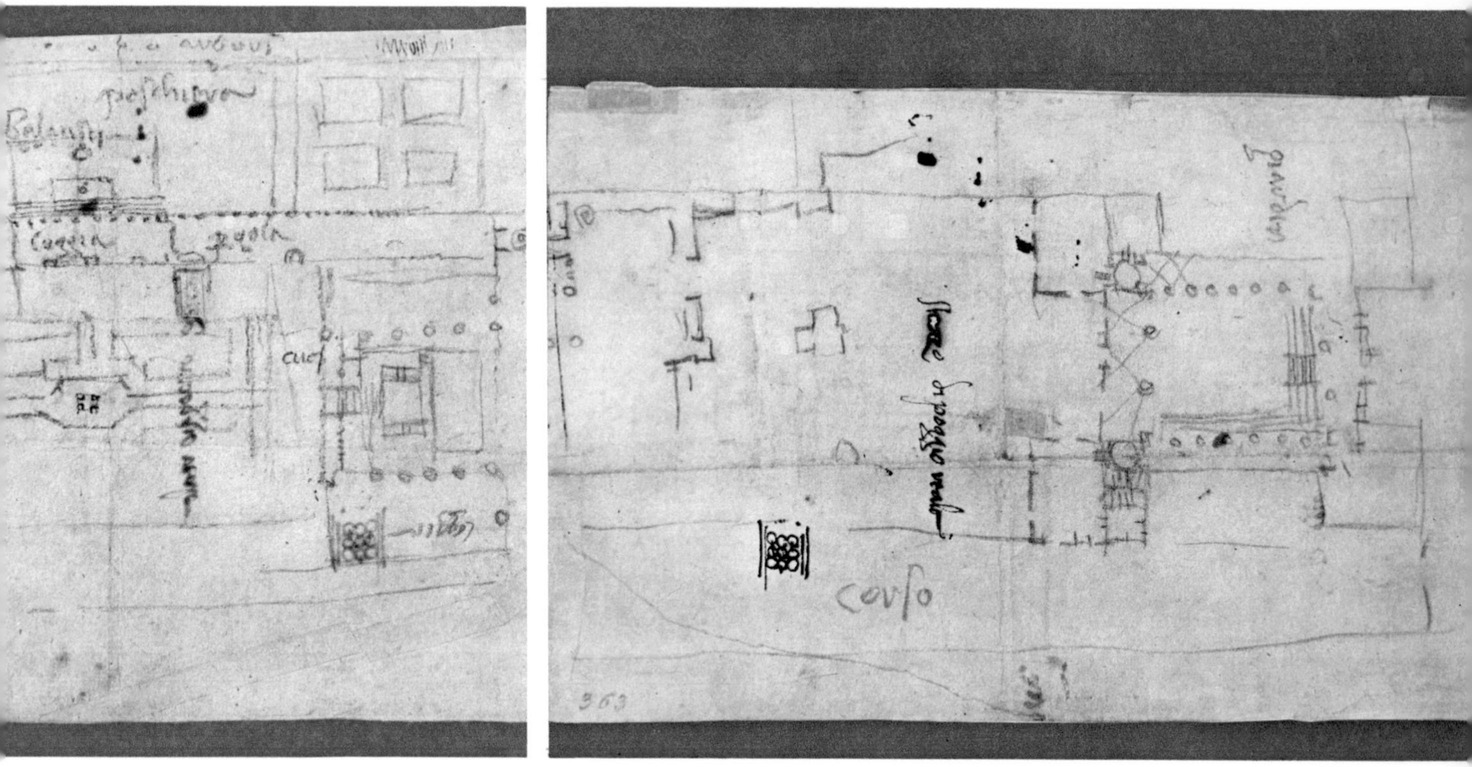

62 - B. PERUZZI. POGGIO REALE, PLAN — FLORENCE, UFFIZI.

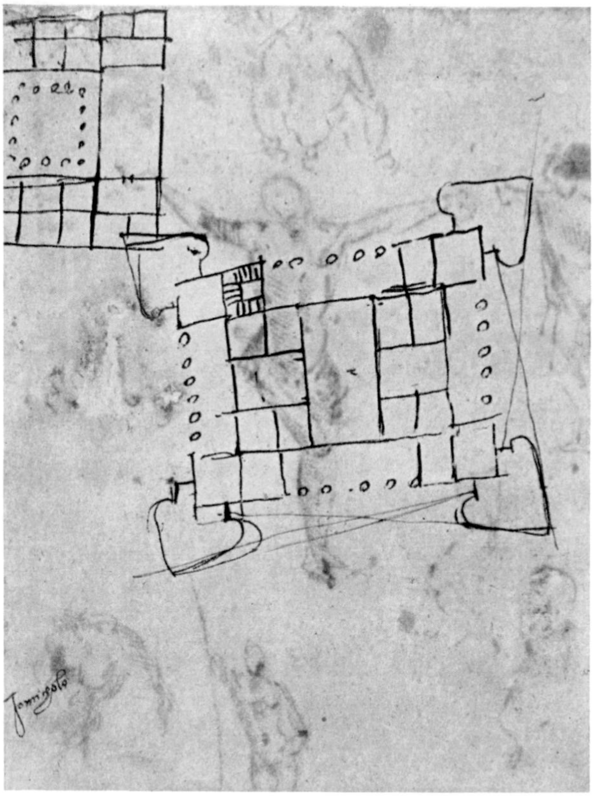

63 - FRANCESCO DI GIORGIO. PROJECT FOR A PALAZZO. FLORENCE, UFFIZI.

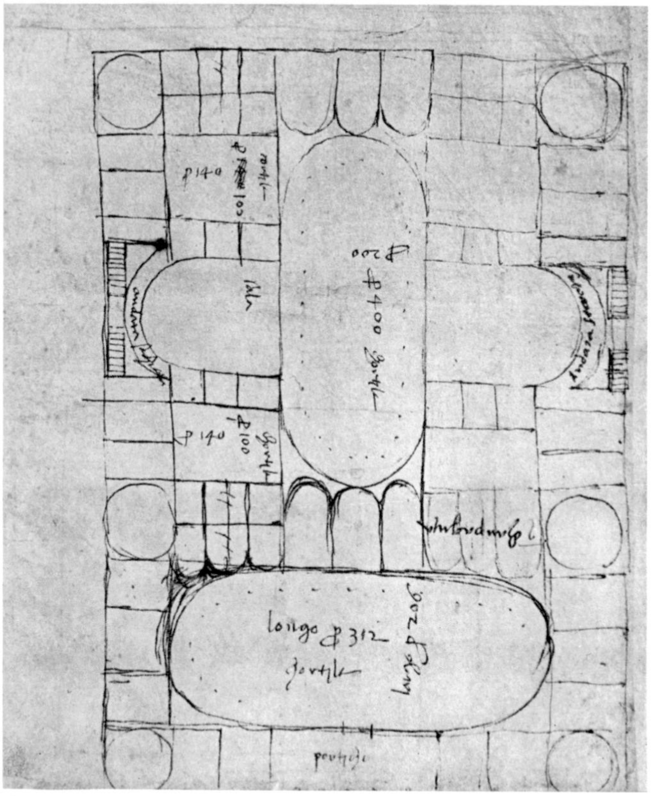

64 - FRANCESCO DI GIORGIO. PROJECT FOR A LARGE VILLA — FLORENCE, UFFIZI.

IOHANES·ORICELLARIVS·PAV·F·AN·SAL·MCCCCLXX

THE CHURCH: FAÇADE AND CENTRAL PLAN

ARCHITECTURE can be studied both from the inside and from the outside: it creates both space and volume. The Italian architects of the fifteenth century could not have defined these double requirements without at the same time discovering the difficulties of the problem. In treating the building as a plastic volume and in concentrating on the organization of the exterior masses, the innovators tended to detach the building from its urban context: this led them to devise an ideal town, an imaginary city, as the setting for their compositions. But in the existing town they became hesitant and after 1460 one could notice more and more frequent uncertainty over the problem of the façade. This problem is in fact bound up with town planning, and in Italy it was always strongly felt to be so: if many church builders in the fourteenth and fifteenth centuries were apparently in difficulties over the shaping of the façade and even left it unfinished (as that of San Lorenzo still is and that of Santa Maria dei Fiori long remained), this was no doubt because they hesitated to give the front of the church the desired amplitude. They did not think it sufficient to translate to the outside the interior divisions of the building, to treat the façade as a cross section, filled in and ornamented: in Italy the purpose of the façade was not to express the building, but to give it its proper value in its surroundings. The example of the Gothic cathedrals, with their deep porches and their vast wealth of sculpture, could not be followed in a country where importance was attached to 'exterior space', where the façade was required to bind the building to the neighbouring space and to contribute to the shaping of that space.

65 - ALBERTI. FLORENCE, SANTA MARIA NOVELLA, FAÇADE.

67 - MODENA, SAN PIETRO, FAÇADE.

68 - FERRARA, SAN FRANCESCO, FAÇADE.

66 - FLORENCE, SAN LORENZO, FAÇADE.

69 - LUGANO, SAN LORENZO, FAÇADE.

After 1460-1470 there was a general effort to find a way out of the difficulty. In Baccio Pontelli's group of churches in Rome (Sant' Agostino, Santa Maria del Popolo) and in those of San Francesco at Ferrara and San Pietro at Modena, a kind of minimum solution is seen, in which a central two-storey mass is crowned by a pediment and joined to the wings by small sloping walls or by volutes, the divisions being stressed by bands and by flat pilasters. The façade of Santa Maria Novella (finished in 1470) was of this type, apart from the ornamental inlay. As soon as this simplified formula was left behind, the choice between the panel façade and the portico façade arose. The former consisted of a single rectangular screen with two or three equal storeys: the *Madonna di Galliera* at Bologna, full of niches and flat pilasters, and the small

74 - VENICE. SANTA MARIA DEI MIRACOLI.

75 - VENICE, SAN ZACCARIA, FAÇADE.

76 - MANTUA, SANT' ANDREA, FAÇADE.

The portico façade was a return to the projecting porch, to the plastic mass, and its aim was to graft on to the church a composition *all'antica*. In about 1450, at Rimini, Alberti had firmly transferred the triumphal arch to a church front, and had intended to complete the composition, at the upper storey, with a curvilinear pediment enclosing a window; and towards 1470, in the church of Sant' Andrea in Mantua, he amplified the porch to such an extent that it became difficult to link it with the nave, which he covered with an enormous arch framed by a three-storey structure. In 1497, in the Abbiategrasso,

77 - BRAMANTE, STUDY FOR SANTA MARIA PRESSO SAN SATIRO, MILAN — PARIS, LOUVRE.

Bramante took up again the idea of a huge arcade grafted on to the façade; but already in 1480, in a design for San Satiro, he had hit on a more complete solution, that of a true façade having a central porch inscribed within a three-storey structure: this recalls the modest scheme of B. Pontelli, (already mentioned), but integrates into it classical supports and the triumphal arch idea. It was the forerunner of the Palladian solutions.

From this it is clear how far ideas had ripened by the time—after 1512—fresh thought was being given in Florence to the question of a façade for San Lorenzo. The

78 - CARADOSSO. ST PETER'S, ROME. LONDON, BRITISH MUSEUM.

79 - G. DA SANGALLO. TRIUMPHAL ARCH OF FANO (DETAIL) — VATICAN LIBRARY.

designs of Giuliano da Sangallo seem to contain all the elements—the rhythm given by the pedestalled double columns framing the entrance arcades and in the central part the addition of a storey with pediment. The problem had become interesting again, and it was at this point that Michelangelo took it up afresh. But now an ambitious conception made its appearance—that of framing the façade, in its strictest sense, with its two storeys, between two four-storey belfry towers: this is what Bramante had proposed in 1506 for St. Peter's, Rome, at least if we may judge from Caradosso's medal. Sangallo was not indebted to Bramante: the idea of this grouping seems to have been drawn from certain city gates of Antiquity, in which the triumphal arch is supported by two towers. Giuliano had taken his design from the gate at Fano (Vatican, Cod. Barb. 4424, fol. 21 v°). He may even have derived from this source the idea of the façade that forms part of a city layout—the idea of that type of large-scale spectacular composition which suddenly makes its appearance at the beginning of the sixteenth century.

The irresistible and widespread success of the central plan in the second half of the Quattrocento would be enough, by itself, to establish the amplitude of the architects' ambitions, the degree to which their speculations had advanced and the rise in them of a more exigent and precise awareness. The rules of the liturgy did not favour the centralized ground plan—or indeed any high degree of homogeneity in the interior space. In a circular or polygonal building the position of the altar becomes a problem: if it is placed in the middle, at the centre of the circle, it is given full value within a whole, but it is in the way; also to have only one altar is not practical in churches where many masses have to be celebrated. It seems clear, also, that the central plan conflicted with the recently acquired habit of arranging the inner space of a church in accordance with the laws of perspective: the nave, with its convergence on the lines of recession, yielded an image that possessed equilibrium and conformed to the modular ideal. No building with a central plan can easily be put into perspective; and the success of the formula seems to evidence a strong interest in the specific property of architectural masses, that is, in the two-fold power of the building to create an inner space and an outer volume, both of which should be striking. There is no clearer instance of the liberation from those Gothic habits that were still able to survive even in the revised basilical plan. In any case, there were now a great many attempts to realize the new form, first on a small scale,

80 - BANNER. VIEW OF SAN LORENZO, MILAN.

and in such church annexes as baptistries, chapels and sacristies, and then in whole churches, treating them as architectural entities. They led, finally, to the idea —a surprising one—of giving the mother-church of the Christian world, St Peter's, Rome, a Greek cross plan different from that of the basilica of Constantine.

But in fact palaeo-Christian and Romanesque precedents were not lacking. To mention only the most familiar instances, San Lorenzo in Milan, with its large cupola set upon a cube, the octagonal Baptistry in Florence, and Santa Costanza in Rome with its annular plan, provided examples which could be, and were, taken up again, as the drawings of Leonardo, Sangallo and Francesco di

81 - MASO FINIGUERRA. PICTURE-CHRONICLE: THE TEMPLE OF THEMIS — LONDON, BRITISH MUSEUM.

Giorgio prove beyond doubt. There was also the conviction, widespread among the humanists and archaeologists, that the pagan temple, like the early church, was by preference a sanctuary with a central plan. In Rome Santa Costanza and San Stefano Rotondo were thought of as pagan edifices readapted for Christian worship. There are countless examples of the recourse to circular *tempietti* for depicting the place of sacrifice, like the shrines of classical times, and at the end of the century the *Hypnerotomachia* added to this the sanction of a symbolic commentary, treating the sanctuary of Venus Physizoë as a structure built in imitation of the Cosmos. There was a similar tendency to show the Temple of Jerusalem—for instance in the backgrounds of pictures of the Marriage of the Virgin—as a polygon surmounted by a dome and framed by porticoes: this was the form given it by Perugino (in his picture, dating from 1500, in the Caen Museum) and by Raphael. Already in his *Remission of the Keys*, in the Sistine Chapel, Perugino had made brilliant use of what amounts to a model of an ideal edifice, whose octagonal ground plan is extended into a cross by four porticoes and is crowned by a dome.

The predilection for this kind of composition is thus connected with a widened conception of architecture: the central plan was thought by virtue of its simplicity, to possess a universal validity. Yet it was so difficult to use in isolation that the odd idea of grafting a rotunda on to a nave was not rejected; indeed it enjoyed some credit for a time after 1470. Michelozzo had tried it in 1450 at the Annunziata in Florence, and Alberti was to take it up again in 1470. Francesco di Giorgio worked out several plans of this type, which from the outside give the appearance of a basilical building and a high rotunda juxtaposed (Florence, Uffizi, drawing no. 1691 a). He also drew a generalized version of the formula, with rotundas at the ends of three of the arms of a basilical plan. Bramante, as we shall see, gave attention to the idea of associating two forms and so, a little later, did Siloé, the architect of Granada Cathedral.

In his work as an architect, Brunelleschi had so compellingly restored the central ground plan to a place of honour that its success in the fifteenth century is to some extent a measure of his influence. Having set the example of the inner space enhanced by a cupola on pendentives in the annexe—the Old Sacristy—to San Lorenzo in Florence, he wanted to use the idea in a complete building; but work on the hexagon of Santa Maria degli Angeli, which he began in 1434, was interrupted in 1437 never to

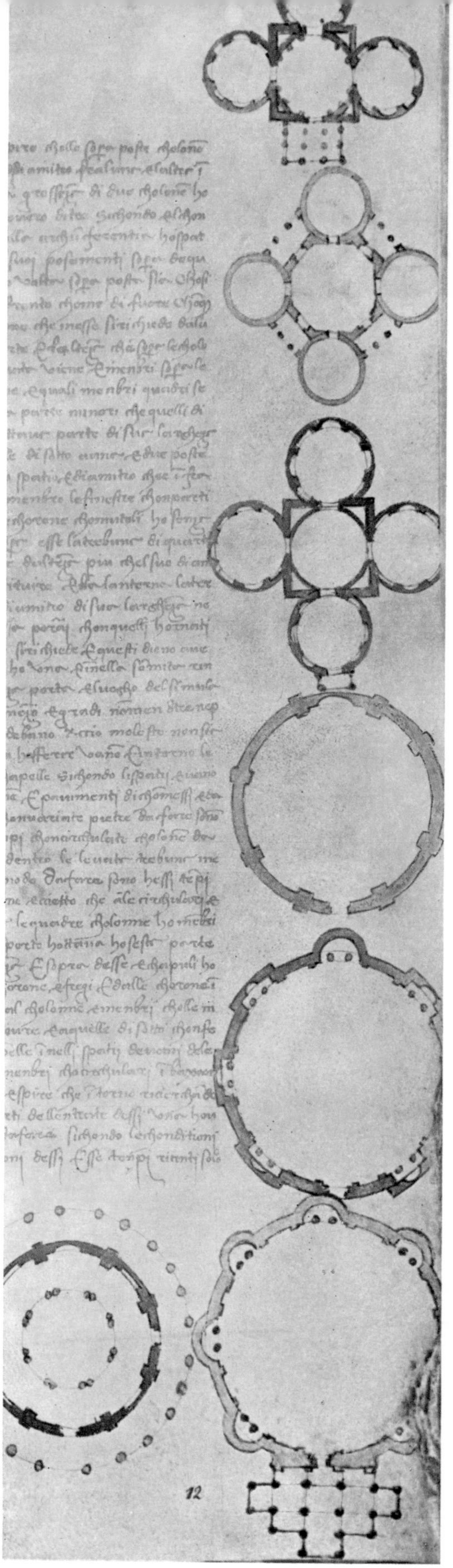

82 - FRANCESCO DI GIORGIO. BUILDINGS ON A CENTRAL PLAN — FLORENCE, BIBL. LAUREN.

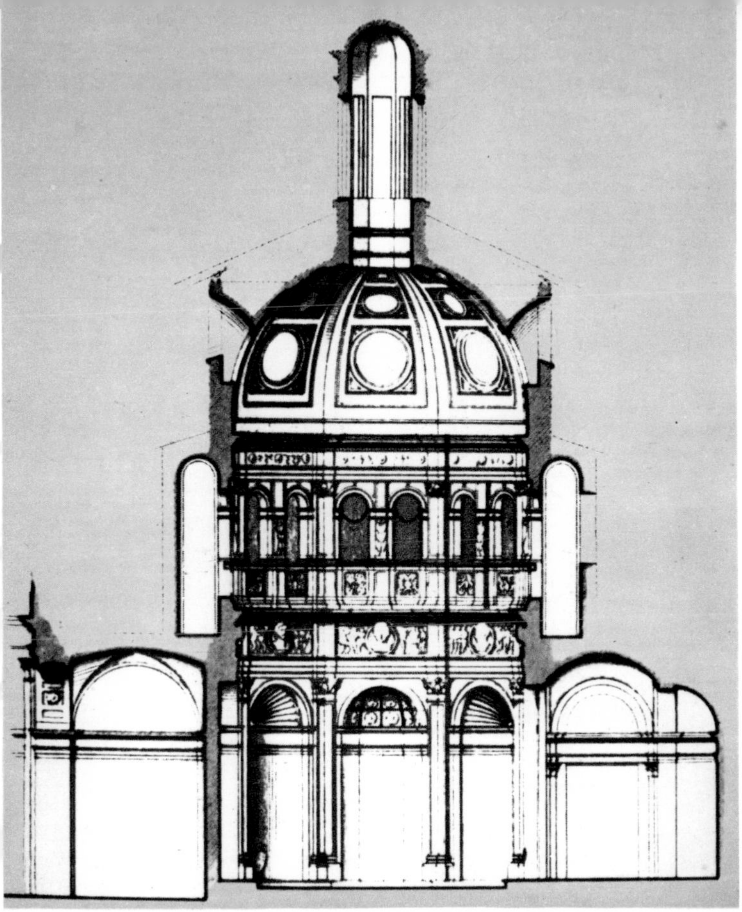

84 - MILAN, SANTA MARIA PRESSO SAN SATIRO, SECTION.

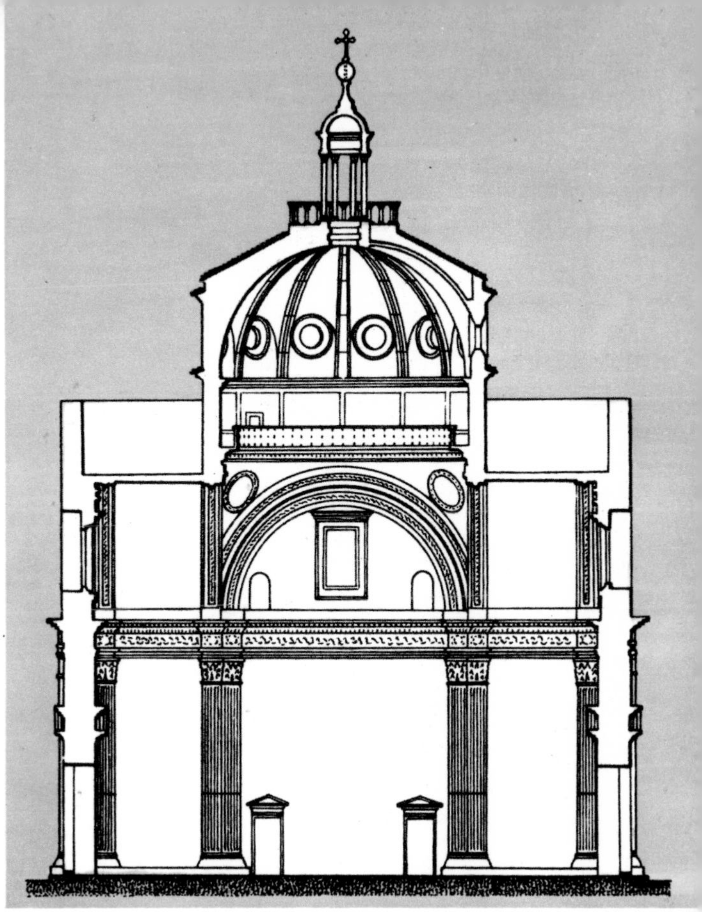

85 - PRATO, SANTA MARIA DELLE CARCERI, SECTION.

be resumed. Yet this composition was later studied by Sangallo in a famous drawing which dates from about 1480-1485, and the articulation of the chapels was noted by Leonardo in ms. B. (*c.* 1490). When, in about 1460, architecture throughout Italy was tending towards new forms, the prestige of the Old Sacristy dominated the horizon, its influence was seen in the mausoleum-chapels, like that of the Cardinal of Portugal in the church of San Miniato al Monte and the Portinari chapel in Milan. This was also the moment when, in Mantua, Alberti—perhaps as his answer to the unfinished hexagon of Santa Maria degli Angeli—conceived the regular Greek cross plan of San Sebastiano; the building, as he conceived it, was never finished (work on it was still going on in 1499), but was far enough advanced in 1473 for Cardinal Francesco di Gonzaga to allude to it then in a well-known letter to his father, in which he affects to wonder whether it is a church, a synagogue or a mosque. This provides sufficient evidence of how original the *all'antica* central plan appeared, and of the resistance it encountered.

Each province was anxious to hark back to its regional types, and adherents to the new programme favoured the revival of palaeo-Christian or Romanesque forms.

83 - MILAN, SANT' EUSTORGIO, PORTINARI CHAPEL.

86 - CREMONA, BAPTISTRY.

87 - LODI, SANTA MARIA L'INCORONATA, ELEVATION.

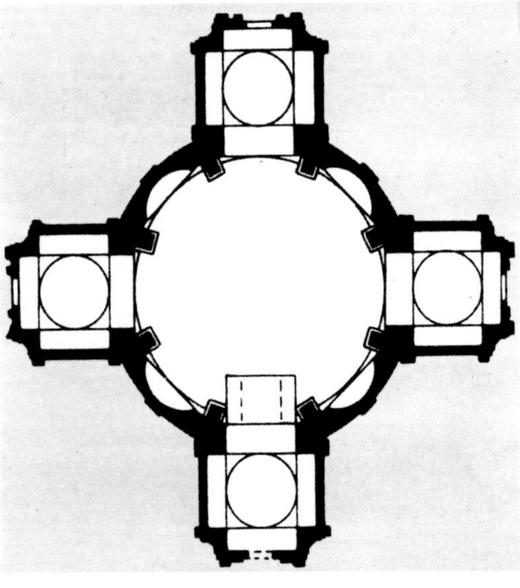

88 - CREMA, SANTA MARIA DELLA CROCE, PLAN.

The case is particularly clear in Lombardy: from the outside, the Portinari chapel appears framed by four small towers, bringing to mind the analogy with the fourth-century church of San Lorenzo in Milan, which architects were beginning to regard with fresh eyes. The palaeo-Christian scheme of the dome framed by four towers, or *pentapyrgion*, came back into favour for a long time. It is in this spirit that in 1470 or thereabouts Filarete made his drawing of the temple of Zogalia, one of his projects for ideal churches, and Amadeo supplied his designs for the façade of Bergamo cathedral and for the Colleoni funerary chapel. In the following years another ancient device gained ground among architects, that of the polygonal or round baptistries of the Romanesque period (at Biella, Asti, Cremona, Parma and elsewhere), adorned on the outside with galleries, and on the inside with blind

89 - CREMA, SANTA MARIA DELLA CROCE

90 - MILAN, SANTA MARIA DELLE GRAZIE, CLOISTERS.

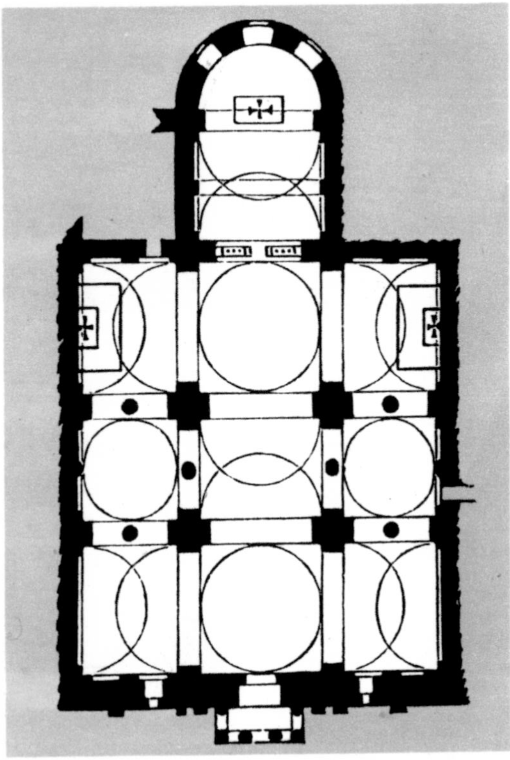

91 - BRESCIA, SANTA MARIA DEI MIRACOLI, PLAN.

arcades. Bramante took the baptistry (or sacristy) of Santa Maria presso San Satiro as the opportunity to give fresh force to this style (from 1482 to 1486). The principle was adopted in Battagio's sanctuaries at Lodi (after 1488) and Crema (design, *c.* 1493), and in that of Santa Maria Campanova (*c.* 1500). Some churches that have a nave were designed with a polygonal choir, for instance, as early as 1482-1485, Santa Maria della Croce by Battagio, and in 1492 in the church of Santa Maria delle Grazie (the church of the Dominicans which was to be the mausoleum of the Sforzas), Bramante grafted the huge central plan *tribuna* or choir on to the end of the Gothic nave. The cathedral of Pavia, about which the great specialists were consulted in 1488, was conceived as the ultimate expression of the modern formula: its Latin cross plan issues into a choir that is designed as a central plan structure, evolving the huge hollow of its space under a dome 310 feet high. In Venice the church of San Giovanni Crisostomo (built by Coducci from 1497 to 1504) presents an overt return to the Byzantine plan, a Greek cross enclosed in a square. And in Brescia, Santa Maria dei Miracoli was designed, in 1488, as a brilliant variation on

92 - GIULIANO DA SANGALLO. TEMPLES ON A CENTRAL PLAN PLAN AND ELEVATION — FLORENCE, UFFIZI.

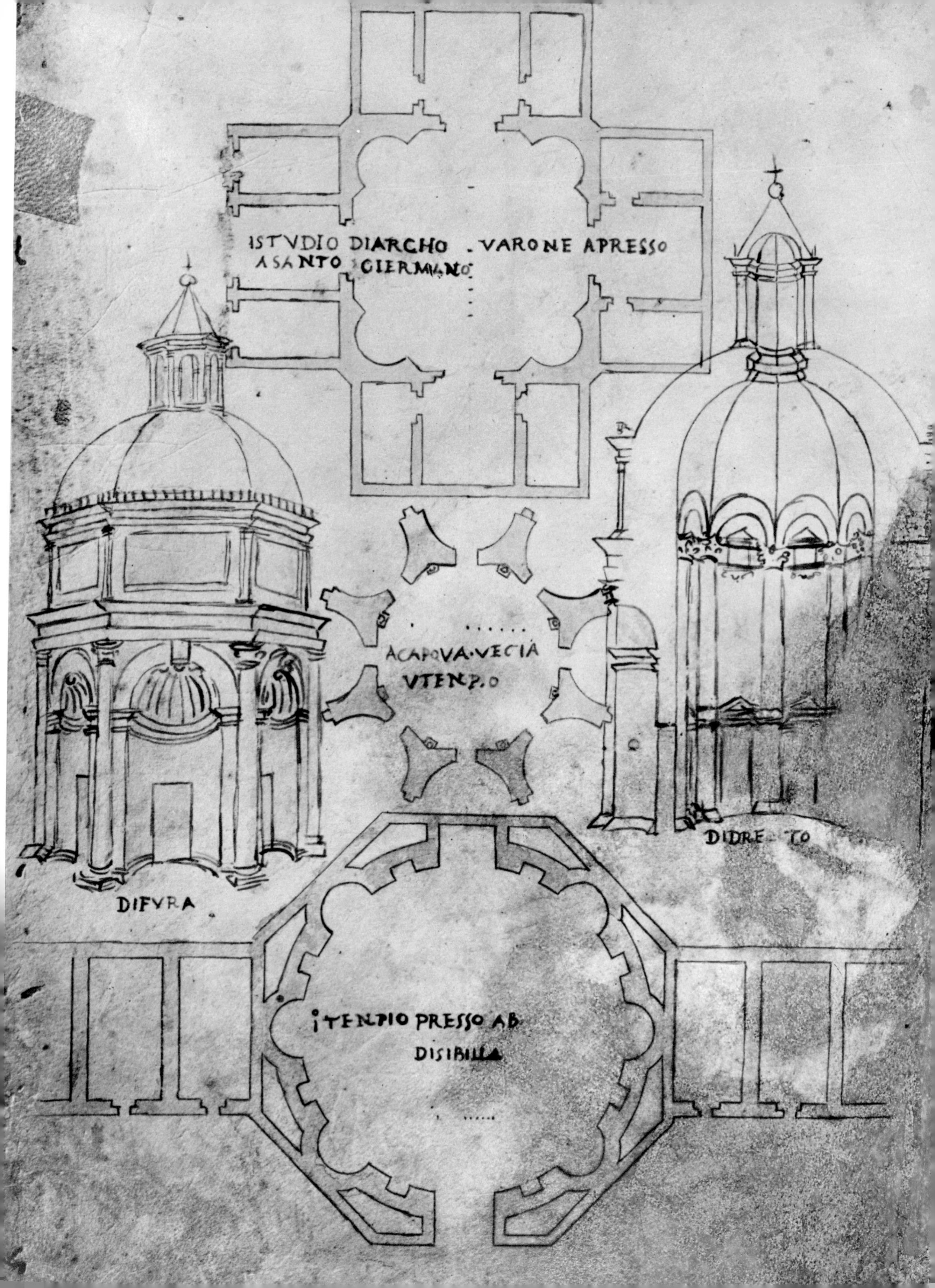
ISTUDIO DIARCHO . VARONE APRESSO
ASANTO CIERMANO
ACAPQUA.VECIA
UTENPIO
DIFURA
DIDRETTO
ITENPIO PRESSO AB
DISIBILLA

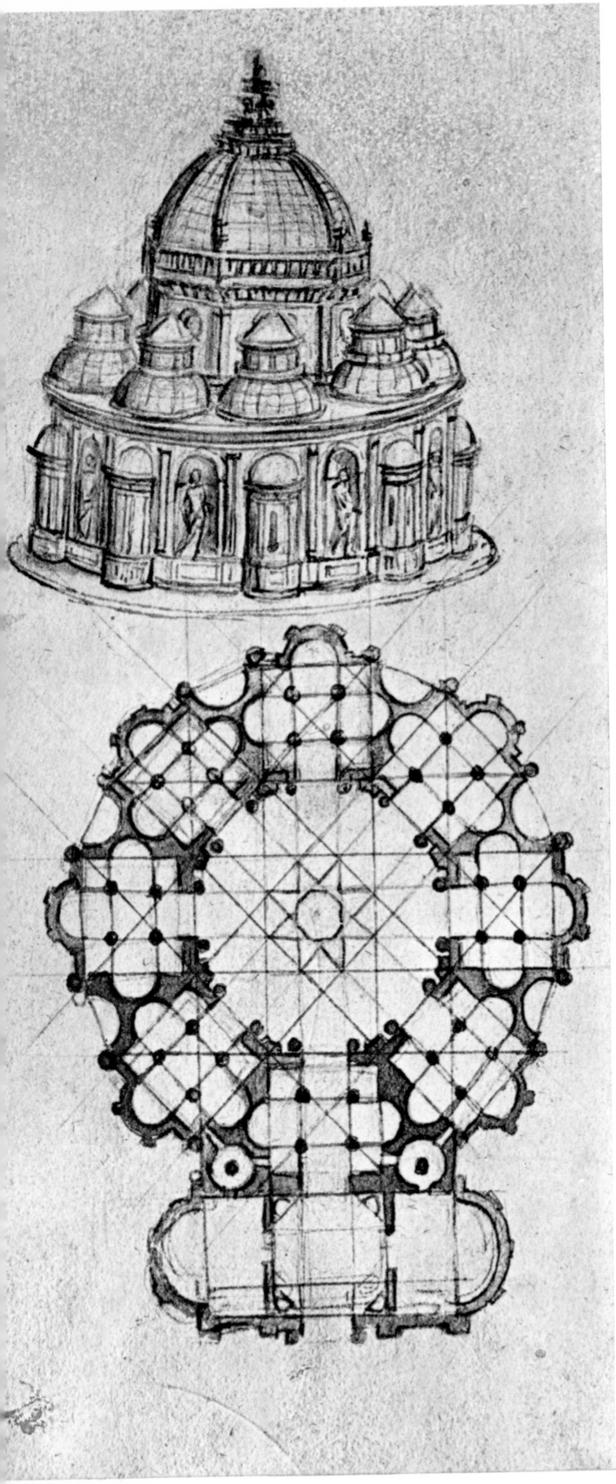

93 - L. DA VINCI. BUILDING ON A CENTRAL PLAN, PLAN AND ELEVATION — PARIS, INSTITUT.

the central plan, with an alternation of domes and barrel vaults. This makes it the more touching to observe the loyalty of Tuscany to its own ancient models: at Prato, Giuliano da Sangallo built Santa Maria della Carceri (1485-1491) on a splendidly ample Greek cross plan quite distinct from the Venetian type: the embellishments respect the wall surfaces, which are unbroken by niches or passages. The octagonal sacristy of Santo Spirito in Florence, for which the *modello* was supplied at the end of 1489, was finished by Cronaca: it is a play of structural members admirably stressed by the *pietra serena*. The theme of the clearly articulated octagon recurs in the Madonna dell' Umiltà at Pistoia (begun in 1492), which Sangallo helped design.

The central plan, brought into favour by cultural considerations, produced the masterpieces of the period, and seems never to have been approached with so much interest and ingenuity. If further confirmation of its privileged position were needed, the speculations of Leonardo would suffice. Leonardo was drawn towards architecture from 1481-1482 onwards, but it was in about 1488-1490 that this interest of his showed itself in practical work, for instance on the *tiburio* (covering of the crossing) of Milan cathedral, and at Pavia, as well as by his participation in architectural commissions. It was then that he wrote (in ms. B) his sketch for a *Trattato* on architecture, dominated by the problem of the central plan. Leonardo approached this from the point of view of a technician and systematizer. The upshot of these studies was a complete vindication of the dome, which became—by virtue of the volumes it engendered when seen from outside, and of the new articulation it imposed on the interior—the key factor in architecture. And so the return of the Quattrocento to the central plan brought into eminence a principle of monumental art, a certain way of bringing a building to a climax, which answered both to the requirements of town planning and to the need for monumental enhancement. The choice of the central plan for the new St. Peter's became inevitable: it seemed that no other structure could possibly be suitable. The vindication, once and for all, of the centralized domed building was the most explicit conclusion reached by the Quattrocento.

94 - VITTORE CARPACCIO. THE PRESENTATION AT THE TEMPLE (DETAIL) — FLORENCE, UFFIZI.

II

SCULPTURE

MONUMENTAL SCULPTURE

THE situation of Italian sculpture in the years around 1460 cannot be described without taking Donatello as the starting-point, and yet the sequel—in contrast with what happened in architecture—cannot be reduced simply to the spread of the Florentine motifs and the reactions it provoked. For at that time there flourished certain types of sculpture and certain formulae that owed nothing to Donatello's influence. There were many competing centres for sculpture, and in the case of painting this was soon even more marked. Nevertheless Donatello was certainly a national figure—as Piero della Francesca was in painting. Remaining active to his death in 1466 at the age of eighty, he passed through Rome, Padua and Siena, in each case stimulating the local community of sculptors and provoking interesting reactions. After the middle of the century we meet with the work of his pupils—of Andrea dell'Aquila and Antonio di Chellino in Naples (in 1455), of Vecchietta in Rome and Siena, of Bertoldo and Bellano in Florence (until Bellano returned to Padua). Donatello's great and admirable characteristic is his insistence on the plastic totality. He was all energy: in his work the monumental requirement certainly dominated, reviving interest in large-scale compositions like the equestrian statue, but it was bound up with an assertion of temperament, whose aim was to give statues and relief carvings an unprecedented animation. His creations were impressive; not everyone understood them. Sometimes they provoked both in connoisseurs and in the public a kind of mistrust, due to the feeling of being dwarfed by a rare power, by that *terribilità* which Michelangelo alone,

95 - DONATELLO. SANTA GIUSTINA — PADUA, THE 'SANTO'.

half a century later, would prove capable of mastering once more.

The Italian Quattrocento is dominated by the two antithetical personalities of Donatello and Piero della Francesca. Before 1460 they had said the essence of what there was to be said, by both affirming, values of a monumental style. Both reached out beyond their own arts. Donatello's violence left its mark on a whole field of painting, and without him it would be difficult to imagine the 'expressionist' development which modified, in Padua, Mantua and Ferrara, the noble forms that came from Piero. As for Piero, his work had a commanding influence both on the pure art of Laurana, that master of marble, and on the 'cubist' marvels of marquetry, and through these he explains a whole style of sculpture which soon limited and attenuated the Donatellism of the years around 1450. Here, therefore, one can perceive the opposition not merely of two Italian inclinations and of two outstanding men, but also of two distinct lines of inspiration.

The rivalry between sculpture and painting had not yet made its appearance: we must wait till the end of the century to find those scholastic discussions on the primacy of one or the other, which were in part stimulated by Leonardo and were soon taken up again by Castiglione in the *Cortegiano*. The question whether sculpture, as the art of total relief, includes and surpasses painting, or painting, as the art of 'simultaneous' harmony, is the more perfect imitation of nature (to which sculpture is merely a first approximation), had not yet come to the fore. But the concern with plasticity excited Italian sensibility: Alberti having written a treatise on painting, *De pictura* (1436), Ghiberti (who died in 1455) composed a long treatise in which sculpture, and before all else the art of working in bronze, was put forward as the principal art. Its content, under cover of the *all'antica* vocabulary and formulae, is commonplace, amounting to an insistence on *simmetria* (the harmony of proportions). In about 1460 a *libellus de arte fusoria* was in circulation: written by a humanist, Porcelio Pandone, it confirms the importance attached by thinking men of that time to bronze as a material for great art.

The technique of casting bronze required a stable and well organized workshop, especially for large-scale works[5]. In the decade 1460-1470, practically the only ones available were those of Antonio Pollaiuolo and of Verrocchio: these were in competition for nearly twenty years.

96 - DONATELLO. THE RESURRECTION (DETAIL). FLORENCE, SAN LORENZO, RIGHT PULPIT.

98 - DONATELLO. CRUCIFIXION (DETAIL) — FLORENCE, SAN LORENZO.

97 - DONATELLO, CHRIST IN LIMBO (DETAIL).
FLORENCE, SAN LORENZO.

99 - DONATELLO. PENTECOST (DETAIL) — FLORENCE, SAN LORENZO.

It was a field in which the Florentines long remained dominant. In the studios, both of Pollaiuolo and of Verrocchio, the goldsmiths' and silversmiths' art was practised, and both of them were to have a share in the completion of the silver altar for the Baptistry (between 1477 and 1480). This activity had its importance, for the finishing of sculpture in bronze is mainly a question of polishing and chiselling. But nobody was able to follow up all the new lines opened by Donatello: in particular, he was the first to practise the *non finito* technique. Vasari notes this, at the beginning of a famous passage on the virtues of *furor* or inspiration. On his return from Padua in 1452, Donatello went to Siena, and then, suddenly, on to Florence: in both places he imposed (or tried to impose) his new style—in Florence with the San Lorenzo pulpit ordered by Cosimo in 1461. In this new style the forms are deliberately made to retain the look of a sketch and, though less closely interwoven, are more firmly massed

100 - DONATELLO. THE ENTOMBMENT (DETAIL) — FLORENCE, SAN LORENZO.

and seem to quiver under the light. The panel representing the *Martyrdom of St. Lawrence*, which is dated 15 June 1465, is in the condition intended by the artist: it confirms the final direction taken by Donatello towards a style where enriched, syncopated and even convulsive forms receive a treatment now utterly free from the conventional. It is possible, by comparison, to evaluate the work of his assistants on these panels—that of Bellano in the finishing of the *Pentecost*, and that of Bertoldo in the *Entombment*, the former more angular, the latter more linear (G. Previtali). The San Lorenzo pulpit represents a crucial moment—the meeting of three styles or, at least, of three potentialities. After 1466, Bellano went to Rome and then to Perugia, before returning to Padua where the somewhat laborious roughness of his style was confirmed. At the end of the century his pupil, the young Riccio, had no difficulty in surpassing him with his relief carvings, his astonishing 'Paschal candlestick' (1506)

101 - DONATELLO. MARTYRDOM OF ST LAWRENCE (DETAIL) — FLORENCE.

104 - ANON. PADUAN. PIETA WITH THE VIRGIN AND ST JOHN — WASHINGTON, NAT. GALLERY.

105 - B. BELLANO. SAMSON DESTROYING THE TEMPLE (DETAIL). PADUA, THE 'SANTO'.

106 - ROMAN ART. STATUE OF MARCUS AURELIUS — ROME, CAPITOL.

and the bronze bibelots which he made fashionable. Bertoldo, a master of the small-scale relief carving and the statuette, continued till 1491 to provide the small change of the great Donatellian style. Wavering between fine chiselling and graphic effects with highly polished modelling, he did not assume the responsibility of a *non finito* style; where it occurs in his work it is merely a survival from the imperfect casting of certain pieces. The only artist who seems to have understood Donatello's spirit and was able to treat his 'atmospheric' relief with the necessary delicacy was the Sienese, Francesco di Giorgio. Donatello's final style was not, and hardly could be, followed up.

The pride of place held by the bronze door in the minds of the 1440 generation now passed to the equestrian statue. The aim was to rival the Marcus Aurelius in Rome, the Regisole in Pavia and the horses of St. Mark's. The monument to Niccolò d'Este in Ferrara (set up in 1451) and to Gattamelata in Padua (set up in 1453) provided examples that arrested the attention of the powerful.

107 - DONATELLO. THE HORSE TRAINER — FLORENCE, SAN LORENZO.

108 - VITTORE CARPACCIO. THE DISPUTE OF ST STEPHEN (DETAIL) — MILAN, BRERA.

109 - A. VERROCCHIO. THE COLLEONI MONUMENT — VENICE

112 - ANTONIO POLLAIUOLO. STUDY FOR THE SFORZA MONUMENT — NEW YORK, PRIVATE COLL.

In 1479 Pollaiuolo supplied Lodovico il Moro with proposals and with a drawing, in which Francesco Sforza is seen in armour, on a horse that rears above the vanquished enemy. This was a general type later taken up by Leonardo in the huge *cavallo* which he modelled in 1493 (it was destroyed in 1501, and never cast). In 1491, on the invitation of the Venetian Senate, Verrocchio undertook the monument to Colleoni, completed by the caster A. Leopardi. Antonio Pollaiuolo constantly returned to the idea of an equestrian statue; there is a letter from him to Virginio Orsini, which says, 'I would have liked to make a statue of you on a bronze horse, to render your fame eternal' (1494).

The bronze tomb was less common, but here too the Florentines tried out all the possibilities of monumental sculpture. In San Lorenzo, Verrocchio composed his tomb of the Medicis, in which the combination of marble sarcophagus and metal claws makes a splendid effect (1472), and Pollaiuolo created the powerful slab-shaped tomb of Sixtus IV in St. Peter's (finished in 1493).

Finally, there was a place for bronze statues and, even more, for metal panels carved in low relief, as part of the decoration of certain chapels: Vecchietta's *Christ* for Santa Maria della Scala and Antonio Lombardo's *Saints* for the Zen Chapel in St. Mark's are fine examples in the two precisely opposite styles, the violent and the cold.

Used in these different ways the bronze figure acquired greater freedom of movement, but it was still far from being emancipated from the architectural frame: Verrocchio's *St. Thomas*, deliberately overflowing the niche, was a piece of exceptional boldness. The equestrian statue, it is true, tended to isolate the block formed by it, and to make the whole effect depend upon its jutting mass and silhouetted outline, yet it formed part of that expanded frame, the city square. The statues gained from having a building or an archway as background. Harmony is obtained by a hair's breadth in the case of the *Baptism*

113 - G.F. RUSTICI. ST JOHN THE BAPTIST PREACHING — FLORENCE, BAPTISTRY, NORTH DOOR.

of Christ group by the north door of the Baptistry (1506-1509) which may be considered as the last word of the fifteenth-century bronze workers and of the Verrocchio style. The whole seems detached in empty space; and yet, in reality, the Baptistry as a whole sustains and includes it; the figures, though accentuated till they become types, are admirably balanced, and one has no difficulty in accepting Vasari's statement that Rustici, when working on them, took the advice of Leonardo (who was living in his house in 1507).

114 - VECCHIETTA. CHRIST — SIENA, SANTA MARIA DELLA SCALA.

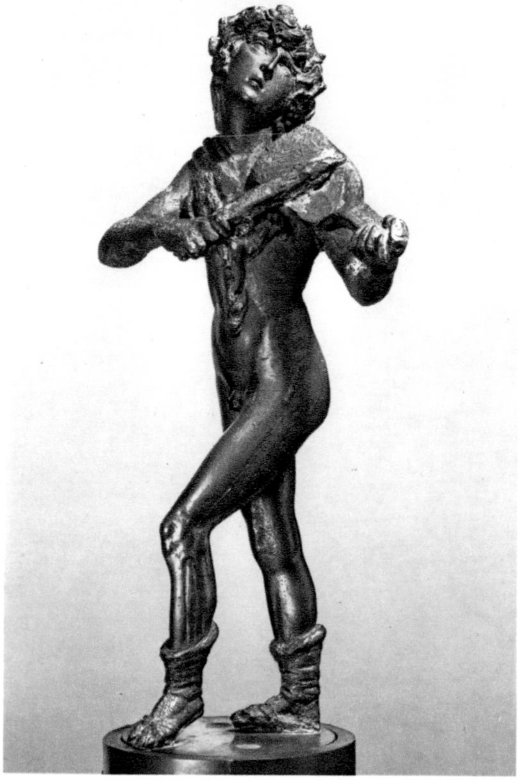

116 - BERTOLDO. ORPHEUS — FLORENCE, BARGELLO.

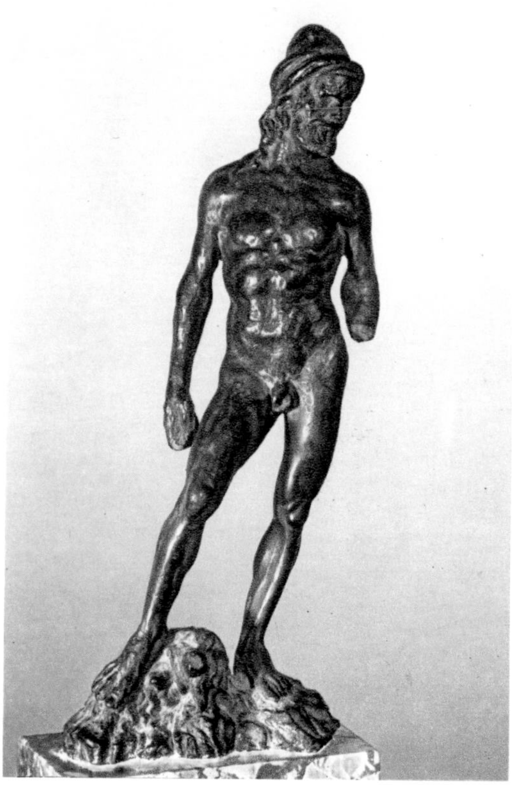

117 - A. POLLAIUOLO (ATTR.). DAVID. NAPLES, MUSEO DI CAPODIMONTE.

Apart from the works on a monumental scale, a noteworthy new development at the end of the Quattrocento was the fashion for small bronzes, statuettes or little plaques. Hardly any bronze plaques earlier than 1470 are known, other than those designed for an oratory or for a shrine (such as the *Flagellations* by Vecchietta and Francesco di Giorgio), and hardly any statuettes except those crowning a holy water stoop or a fountain (such as Verrocchio's famous *putto*). After 1480 the fashion suddenly spread from the North—more precisely from Padua, where Riccio recreated the naturalistic bibelot, following the example of Antiquity. In Florence Bertoldo was at hand to produce small allegorical plaques on commission for the humanists and other eminent men, and to supply statuettes like the *Orfeo* (or Arion) of the Laurentian collection, which may be regarded as a reply to Riccio's deliciously chiselled *Arion*. The personal emblem became naturally associated with the bibelot to be offered: for Ercole d'Este many statuettes of Hercules were made, including the *Hercules on Horseback* by Bertoldo (at Modena) and the *Hercules with the Club*, directly imitated from Antiquity.

118 - ANDREA RICCIO. ARION — PARIS, LOUVRE.

5 - FRANCESCO DI GIORGIO. FLAGELLATION OF CHRIST. PERUGIA, NATIONAL GALLERY OF UMBRIA.

119 - ANTICO. VENUS — VIENNA, KUNSTHISTORISCHES MUSEUM.

120 - ANON. PADUAN, GNOME RIDING A SNAIL — PARIS, LOUVRE.

To group the whole output under Padua and Florence, distinctive though they were, would be an oversimplification. The plaques made in Florence were elegant, vague, somewhat confused. Mantua must be given the doubtful credit of having produced Pier Jacopo Alari (or L'Antico), with his many small figures of Apollo, Venus or Hercules in bronze heightened with gold and silver. Padua specialized in bibelots (vases, inkstands, brackets, etc.) that were complicated and faunesque, with comic intertwinings of satyrs, shell motifs, and goat-footed demigods. In the years around 1500 the success of these daring miniatures was only beginning. Riccio worked from 1507 to 1516 on the extraordinary Paschal candlestick for the Santo, which finally gave status to the extravagances of the new style through a spectacular large-scale work. But the incredible *Gnome riding a Snail*

121 - ANDREA RICCIO. SATYR — FLORENCE, BARGELLO.

had already had the honour of being often copied, and scholars have traced the *Figure riding on a Tortoise* to an inventory of 1496. The marketing of these bronze toys for princes and great ladies gave rise, as usual, to some earth-shaking reputations. In the *Saint Augustine*, which he painted for the Scuola degli Schiavoni in Venice, Carpaccio was not above adorning the *studiolo* of the Saint with some samples of *all'antica* statuettes. And Gauricus, the author of the treatise *De sculptura* (1504) places in a class by himself a certain Severo of Ravenna: besides a statue of St John the Baptist in the Santo, this sculptor was responsible for a dragon-inkstand (signed), a Pluto with dragon, etc., and indeed a whole group that was for long attributed to an anonymous 'Master of the Dragon.' This minor field of the bibelot did in fact satisfy the tendency to isolate the figure.

122 - ANDREA RICCIO — PASCHAL CANDLESTICK. PADUA, THE 'SANTO'.

The other noble material was marble. In it the more original sculptors palpably found inspiration; deference to Antiquity was apparently felt to be less imperative in marble than in bronze, and the authority of Donatello asserted itself less exclusively. The *De sculptura* contains a valuable list of the artists who were highly considered, and declares that the workers in marble were 'innumerable': among these it picks out Antonio Rizzo, Pietro Lombardi and his sons, Solari and the author of the doorway of Santa Maria dei Miracoli, placing them alongside Benedetto da Maiano, Andrea Sansovino and Michelangelo. In thus setting Venice and Florence upon opposite scales, Gauricus was correctly describing a situation that had been steadily taking shape.

123 - MINO DA FIESOLE. TOMB OF COUNT UGO OF TUSCANY — FLORENCE, BADIA.

In Florence the outstanding works in the second quarter of the century had been funerary monuments to the humanists, and of these Antonio Rossellino's tomb of the Cardinal of Portugal was both the peak and the evidence of approaching decline: what counts in it is not so much the structure as the atmosphere of the chapel as a whole. After 1460 a kind of hesitation appeared in the design of tombs in Florence. At the Badia, especially in the monument to Count Ugo, Mino da Fiesole produced a stylized version of the type associated with B. Rossellino. In the Sassetti tomb, where Giuliano da Sangallo arranged a porphyry sarcophagus under an arcosolium, Antiquity has provided the authority for an old solution, which is here given a learned and somewhat enigmatic piquancy. The only notable project for a tomb in marble was that for the Forteguerri monument at Pistoia: for this, in 1477, Verrocchio and Piero Pollaiuolo competed; Verrocchio's design was preferred, but after 1488, in spite of the intervention of Lorenzo di Credi, work was discontinued, and we must reconstitute the tomb in imagination if we would appreciate what John Pope-Hennessy has called 'its emotional tension communicated through the broken rhythms of a continuous plastic surface', which seems to lead straight on to Bernini.

124 - MINO DA FIESOLE. TOMB OF COUNT UGO OF TUSCANY (DETAIL): CHARITY — FLORENCE, BADIA.

126 - A. VERROCCHIO. ANGEL. MODEL FOR THE FORTEGUERRI TOMB — PARIS, LOUVRE.

125 - A. VERROCCHIO. FORTEGUERRI TOMB, MAQUETTE (DETAIL).
LONDON, VICTORIA AND ALBERT MUSEUM.

127 - PIETRO LOMBARDO. TOMB OF ANTONIO ROSSELLI. PADUA, THE 'SANTO'.

128 - ANTONIO RIZZO. TOMB OF THE DOGE NICCOLÒ TRON. VENICE, SANTA MARIA GLORIOSA DEI FRARI.

Just when the tomb was ceasing to be the most significant genre in Florence, it was becoming so in Venice. The Foscari tomb in the Frari, by A. Bregno (after 1475), was a direct adaptation of Florentine models, and, even more clearly, so was the tomb of Antonio Roselli in Padua, by Pietro Lombardo (1467). The opposite—or competing—styles of Antonio Rizzo's tomb of Niccolò Tron (Santa Maria dei Frari) and Pietro Lombardo's tomb of Pietro Mocenigo (SS. Giovanni e Paolo), both dating from 1476, show clearly the amplitude which the new theme had acquired by then. It came to its climax in the Marcello and Vendramin tombs, both of them in the church of the Dominicans, both of them from the Lombardi workshop, and both of them representing

129 - PIETRO LOMBARDO. TOMB OF THE DOGE PIETRO MOCENIGO. VENICE, SS. GIOVANNI E PAOLO.

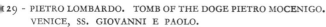

130 - P. AND T. LOMBARDO. THE TOMB OF ANDREA VENDRAMIN. VENICE, SS. GIOVANNI E PAOLO.

the last word in this development. Such close attention to the monumental theme was to be found nowhere else, not even in Rome. There the idea of a monument embedded in a wall, and treated as a large-scale shrine enclosing the sarcophagus, evolved very slowly, from the tomb of Cardinal Riario in the Santissimi Apostoli to the pairs of tombs in Santa Maria del Popolo.

The main concern of sculptors in Venice was not, as in Florence, with a coherent distribution of the total effect, but with the framing of the figures: Rizzo's and Pietro Lombardo's statues are prisoners of their niches; and even when, with Tullio Lombardo, the male and female saints in attendance had acquired the look of vestal virgins or Roman warriors, complete with toga

132 - P. LOMBARDO. TOMB OF THE DOGE PASQUALE MALIPIERO (DETAIL): VIRTUE — VENICE, SS. GIOVANNI E PAOLO.

I - ANTONIO RIZZO. TOMB OF NICCOLÒ TRON (DETAIL): VIRTUE — VENICE, SANTA MARIA GLORIOSA DEI FRARI.

133 - ANTONIO RIZZO. WARRIOR — VENICE, DOGE'S PALACE.

and breast-plate, and were placed between the supports of triumphal arches, this merely accentuated the stifling and odd feeling of the space so organized. In Venice sculpture still seemed oppressed by the architectural setting, and the elaborate large-scale works of the late fifteenth century have a tiresomely artificial effect. The likeness between the Tron tomb, with its elaborate marble structure, and Coducci's façades, has often been noted; but all the advantage lies with the latter. The two finest statues of fifteenth-century Venice, Rizzo's *Adam* and *Eve*, are not free-standing statues. They are lodged in the tall niches of the Foscari arch in the Doge's Palace and occupy their compartments with the same anthority as does Verrocchio's bronze *St. Thomas*.

134 - ANTONIO RIZZO. ADAM — VENICE, DOGE'S PALACE

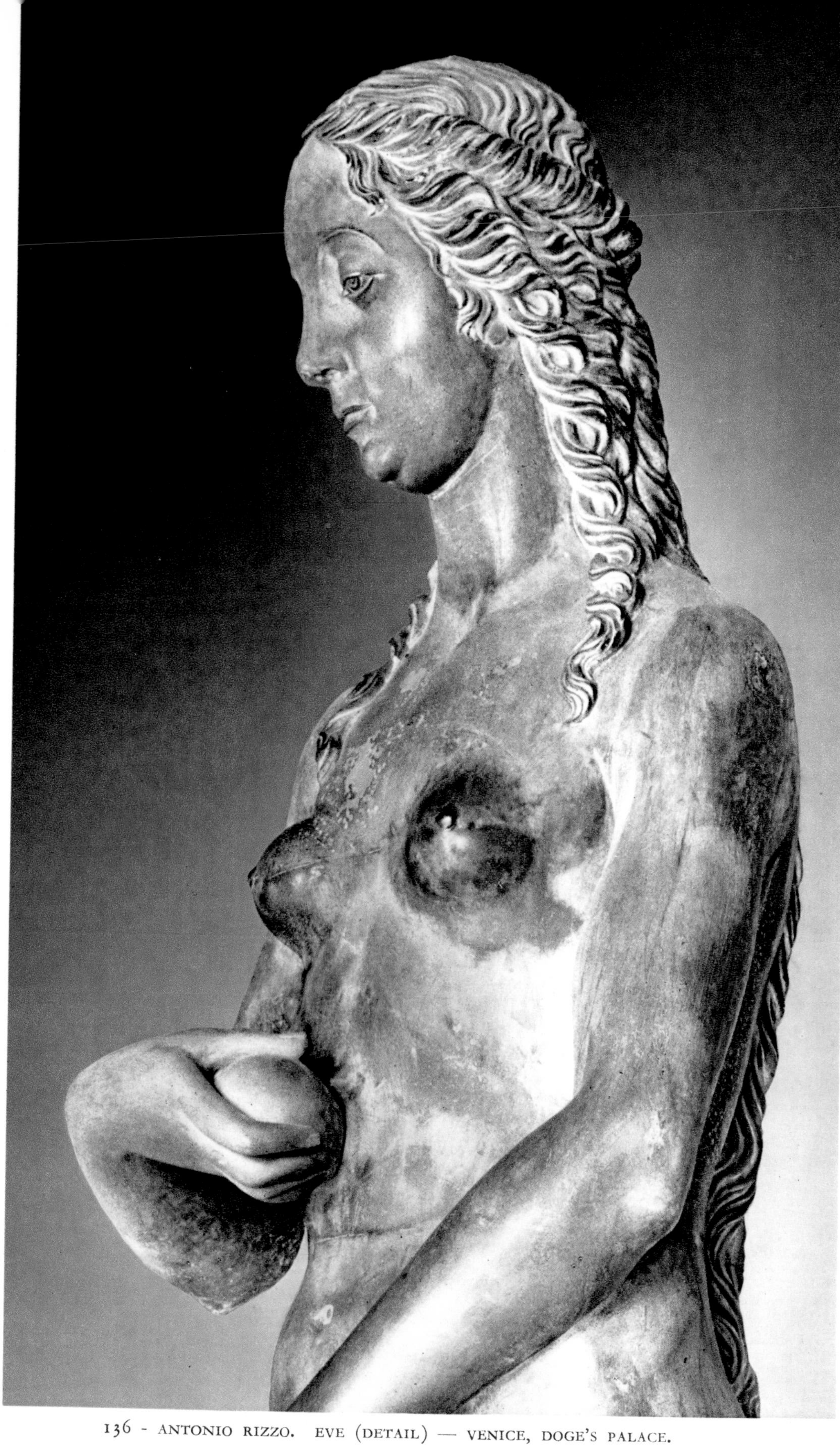

136 - ANTONIO RIZZO. EVE (DETAIL) — VENICE, DOGE'S PALACE.

135 - ANTONIO RIZZO. EVE (COPY) — VENICE, DOGE'S PALACE, FOSCARI ARCH.

137 - F. DI SIMONE FERRUCCI. TOMB OF BARBARA MANFREDI — FORLI, S. BIAGIO IN S. GIROLAMO.

138 - G.A. AMADEO. TOMB OF MEDEA COLLEONI — BERGAMO, COLLEONI CHAPEL.

In Rome also, tombs conceived as monuments in a wall were very numerous. They were executed by Lombard craftsmen familiar with Tuscan ideas, or by Florentines like Mino. In some of them there is an evident desire to produce a clear effect of classical Antiquity by means of monumental or structural details, but really successful examples are rare. There is nothing among them comparable to the bold line taken by Francesco di Simone Ferrucci, a pupil of Verrocchio, in the tomb of Barbara Manfredi at Forli (*c.* 1470): this forms a kind of mortuary chapel, not devoid of nobility, about the sarcophagus and the recumbent effigy, and here again the sculpture achieves unity with the architectural composition, the whole being a revealing example of what men could do with marble at the end of the fifteenth century. All the effect resides in the harmony between decorative parts and figure—or more precisely, between the structure, the play of ornament and the human elements.

It was in Lombardy, the home of decorative architecture, that intentions clarified. In the tomb of Medea

139 - G. C. ROMANO. TOMB OF G. GALEAZZO VISCONTI — PAVIA.

Colleoni at Bergamo a kind of festive animation prevails, due to the use of black and white squares and to the hanging draperies, which fit in so well with the rich and colourful architecture of the chapel. And certainly one of the most original tombs of the 1490s was that designed by Gian Cristoforo Romano for Gian Galeazzo Visconti. Here, for the first time (so it seems) a complete three-dimensional structure makes its appearance—an *arcus quadrifons* which encloses the sarcophagus and forms a two-storey shrine, in which all the sculptured parts are coherently distributed. The success of the new type proved enormous: in Rome it led to the first project for the tomb of Julius II; in France it inspired the royal monuments in Saint-Denis; in Milan also it produced Leonardo's extraordinary plan for the Trivulzio monument. Here the marble tomb forming a shrine or temple and the bronze equestrian statue surmounting it were associated with an unprecedented burst of power and ambition in the art of sculpture. Once again the history of an important genre culminated in a work that was not carried out.

140 - G.C. ROMANO. TOMB OF G. GALEAZZO VISCONTI (DETAIL) — CERTOSA DI PAVIA.

142 - STUDIO OF L. DA VINCI. HORSEMAN — BUDAPEST, MUSEUM OF FINE ARTS.

141 - LEONARDO DA VINCI. STUDY FOR THE TRIVULZIO MONUMENT. WINDSOR CASTLE, ROYAL LIBRARY.

143 - MICHELOZZO. THE MEDICI BANK, DOORWAY. MILAN, ARCHAEOLOGICAL MUSEUM.

144 - PIETRO LOMBARDO. ALTAR — CESENA, CATHEDRAL.

Any account of the activity of Italian sculptors after 1460 and of their attitude to monumental work would be inadequate if it neglected those ornamental compositions which formed part of the architecture. The doorway now became, as the staircase did later, one of the main themes of applied sculpture. It was given solemnity by the dimensions now required, and became the field for a proliferation of carving in which plane surface, surface texture and incrustation effect, all had scope. Its heyday passed when the door became a porch, acquiring a composition in depth, a salient structure and free-standing pillars.

The fifteenth century loved the pilaster, the flat part of which became a panel requiring decoration with swags or medallions: in Michelozzo's doorway for the Medici Palace in Milan (*c.* 1460), for instance, various forms of applied ornament—caryatids, corner medallions, relief carvings along the lintel—made their appearance, and they came to stay. There is, of course, a fine example of the classicizing doorway, using only floral and abstract decoration, at Urbino, in the entrance to the throne room. The arch and its curve are dispensed with, and we have the strict scheme of the rectangular ceremonial door. There were soon innumerable ornamental variations on this theme, including some of the outstanding successes of Italian sculpture. In Lombardy motifs of all sorts were taken up again and treated in relief, so that the swags were enlarged and twisted and adorned with miniature figures, masks, vases, etc. Forms were suddenly amplified and given fresh life. The tortured column became a candelabrum. A Corinthian volute would be transformed into a dolphin or a cornucopia. The doorway to the Palazzo Stanga, by Pietro da Rho and his assistants, became a kind of medal-cabinet, a list of heroes, panel by ornate panel. Sculpture moved in everywhere, drawing a strange 'dynamic' effect from metamorphoses and minglings of the stock themes.

In the doorway to Como cathedral, carved after 1491 under the direction of Tommaso Rodari, the candelabrum-column rests on four lions which serve as base—an old Romanesque device revived. There are countless instances of these sustained and closely-packed compositions, some of which, it must be admitted, have a surprising vitality. Inevitably Bologna produced a version in terracotta, with relief carving of a delicate liveliness: in the Corpus Domini chapel the virtuosity of the execution is such that it has been attributed to a medallist, Sperandio.

45 - PIETRO DA RHO. DOORWAY TO THE PALAZZO STANGA. DETAIL) — PARIS, LOUVRE.

146 - T. RODARI. DOORWAY (DETAIL) — COMO, CATHEDRAL.

147 - VENICE. SCUOLA DI SAN GIOVANNI, STAIRCASE. 148 - TOSCANELLA. LUDOVISI CHAPEL.

The buildings of the Scuola di San Giovanni Evangelista in Venice—the seat, as we have seen, of a particularly active brotherhood—illustrate the attractiveness and effectiveness of this type of work. In the courtyard there is a screen-like partition with doorway, made by Pietro Lombardo's workshop in 1481. The fluted pilasters stand out against the walls, and the carved reliefs are confined to the architectural members. Twenty years later Coducci went much further, with the monumental stairway of the Scuola: here he introduced two slender columns to receive the arch, some light swags and small rosettes on the plain parts, and the whole structure receives life from the carving which communicates, so to speak, antiphonally from arch to arch. Three typical achievements are the chapel of St. John the Baptist in the church of San Lorenzo in Genoa (executed slowly, from 1441 to 1496), the Ludovisi chapel at Toscanella (1486) and the choir

149 - VENICE. SANTA MARIA DEI MIRACOLI, CHOIR.

150 - MILAN. SANTA MARIA PRESSO SAN SATIRO, CHOIR.

of Santa Maria dei Miracoli (after 1481): the slightly awkward screen of the first, the superb arch of the second and the stage-like form of the third are so many different ways of enclosing the sanctuary with precision. Sculpture takes full advantage of the clear containment of the forms, for the effect derives all its meaning from an axial vision and demands a fixed viewpoint. This was a kind of optical play very dear to the Quattrocento; the opposite kind of illusion is represented by the choir of Santa Maria presso San Satiro. Each of these structures owes its peculiar rhythm to the quality of the carved reliefs, of the panelling, of the inlay work, niches and medallions. It would be inexact to say that the sculpture contributes to the effect, for this is clearly shaped as a whole by the quivering life of the ornamentation and its harmonious distribution. At the end of the fifteenth century relief carving was one of the most active factors in monumental art.

BUSTS AND PAINTED STATUES. WOOD AND TERRACOTTA

To express the grandeur of Antiquity as forcibly as possible, Gauricus said that in Rome, in former days, the imaginary population *(populus fictus)* of statues had equalled the living one. Modern Italy was still far behind that. There were, after all, not very many equestrian statues; and free-standing statues on columns—though there were fine examples at the entrance to the *piazzetta* in Venice and another, recent one, in the Florence market-place in the shape of Donatello's *Dovizia*—were also rare. On the other hand, there was an increasing demand for busts and, in general, sculptured portraits, which had become a Tuscan speciality. Savonarola's anger was roused by this profane use of art, and he condemned a number of portraits to the fire. After 1470 a remarkable two-fold reversal took place: mouldings taken from the life came in again, along with what John Pope-Hennessy calls 'an interpretative element', which was a novelty in the sculptured bust. Naturalism and stylization were the two complementary aspects of the emancipation of this genre. Certain figures by Antonio Rossellino, such as his *Giovanni Chellini* (Victoria and Albert Museum), and by Benedetto da Maiano, such as his *Pietro Mellini* (Bargello), illustrate very clearly this two-fold effect of the classical model and of the mask, both of which contribute to the peculiar shaping of these works achieved by cutting off the arms below the shoulders, by the distinctive axes and by the relationship of full-face and profile. 'Truth to life' was sought both through a stressing of the facial features and through the general character

I - FRANCESCO LAURANA. BUST OF A YOUNG WOMAN. (DETAIL) — PARIS, LOUVRE.

152 - BENEDETTO DA MAIANO. BUST OF PIETRO MELLINI. FLORENCE, BARGELLO.

and balance of the forms. Almost the only artists to escape from this powerful idiom were Laurana, who subjected his busts of women to a kind of superstylization that carried Mino's calm geometry even further, and Verrocchio, with whom plastic intensity overcame the resist-

153 - ANTONIO ROSSELLINO. BUST OF GIOVANNI CHELLINI — LONDON, VICTORIA AND ALBERT MUSEUM.

ance of the portrait—as in his *Lady with the bunch of Flowers* (Bargello).

The importance attached to the lifelike and to an accurate rendering of the face may explain the success of the wax masks—based on an easily obtained mould and

154 - MINO DA FIESOLE. BUST OF NICCOLÒ STROZZI. BERLIN-DAHLEM, STAATLICHE MUSEEN.

mounted on a prepared neck-and-shoulders dummy—and of the portrait in painted wax, which developed simultaneously. The new fashion was preceded by the use of wax *ex votos*, of which there is evidence at the Annunziata; in the Benintendi family, son succeeded father as *ceroplasta*. This unexpected aspect of Florentine sculpture would have had its culmination in the coloured wax *Flora*, attributed to Leonardo, if this could still be considered an original by him: it was the subject of violent controversy in 1909 and 1910, when the Berlin Museum had just acquired it, and unfortunately it has turned out to be merely a modern adaptation of some Leonardesque picture of Flora, one of the fake Renaissance sculptures that became fairly common in the last century[6].

Wood-carving was still almost entirely confined to the church. It was usually intended to be gilded or painted, and was associated with the manufacture of picture frames, decorative settings, choir stalls, screens, and devo-

155 - ANDREA VERROCCHIO. BUST OF A LADY. FLORENCE, BARGELLO.

156 - FRANCESCO DI GIORGIO (ATTR.). ST CHRISTOPHER — PARIS, LOUVRE.

tional panels. It was a conventional branch of sculpture, in a craftsman's tradition. It rose to monumental groups of figures, or pairs of figures facing each other, in a few marginal regions only: first, in that of Siena, where there was still a demand for large-scale figures of the Virgin and the Angel of the Annunciation, and where the most eminent masters still produced some impressive pieces: Vecchietta his *St. Antony* (1475) and his *St. Bernard*, Francesco di Giorgio his *St. John the Baptist* (1464) and his *St. Christopher*; but also in the provinces of the eastern zone of the Apennines and of Northern Italy—Friuli, the Romagna and the Abruzzi. Here the old crafts were kept going by workshops whose members, in many cases, even came from abroad, especially from Germany. They specialized in the popular production of devotional groups, such as the *pietà*, and in the decoration of choir stalls with turned wood in a traditional style. One case among many is that of a 'German carver, Corrado Teutonico, at Cingoli near Josi; he was working from 1475 to 1490 at Arcevia, where he executed the Gothic choir stalls of S. Medardo' (W. Körte). As this example shows clearly (and plenty of others could be found to confirm it), provincial wood-carving long maintained a taste for draperies and attitudes—and probably a way of painting sculpture—still faithful to Trecentesque ideals; and it continued to supply picture frames, mouldings and panels that were also faithful to the lines, shapes, pointed arches and interlacings of the Gothic style. In Piedmont and Lombardy, as in the Abruzzi, the joiners still used the old patterns for choir stalls and sacristy cupboards. All this enhances the significance of the success achieved at such centres as Urbino, Florence and Verona, in creating a coherent vocabulary of decorative motifs that could stand up against the Gothic, and, more particularly, in making use of the possibilities of wood in the great intarsia schemes. This, as we have seen, reached its height between 1460 and 1510. It is a remarkable fact that the art of working in wood—in which Italy had not till then excelled—was one of the fields where the revolution in the style of ornamentation was realized.

Wood sculpture had always called forth a more or less hard and expressive treatment; and, when painted in bright colours, its effect was rustic and naïve. While this crude and angular style created a natural bond with some of the forms of Gothic beyond the Alps (where wood-carving was gaining ground and was inspiring masterpieces for which there was no equivalent in Italy), the

157 - NEROCCIO DI BARTOLOMEO LANDI. SAN BERNARDINO (DETAIL) — BORGO A MOZZANO, SAN JACOPO.

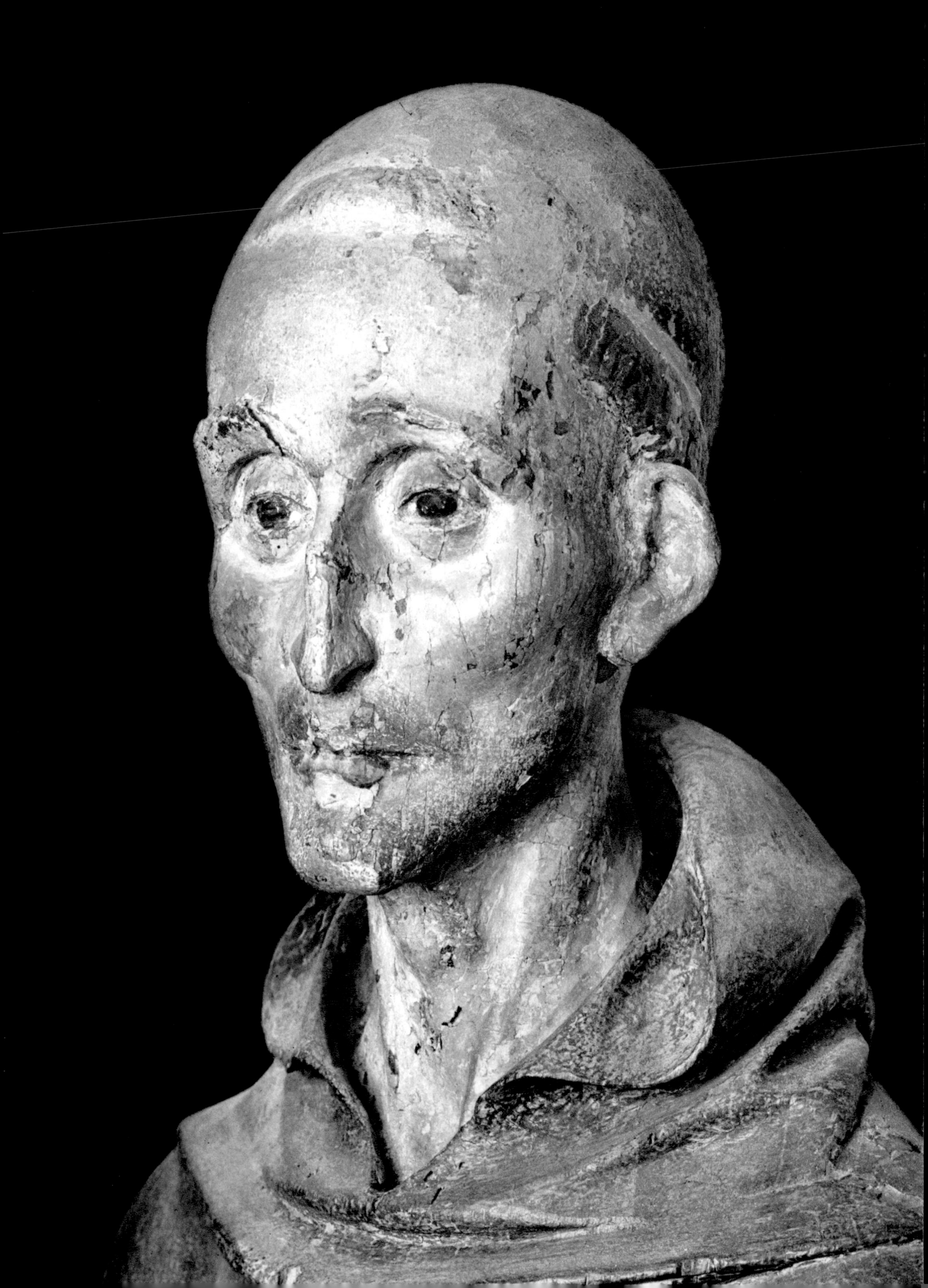

158 - G. MAZZONI. THE DEPOSITION — MODENA, SAN GIOVANNI BATTISTA.

art in the South tended to be distinguished by the use of colour. In the medium of terracotta, which was more favourable to plastic feeling both in statuettes and in ornamentation, the comparison is more interesting and more to the advantage of Italy. We have already seen how important terracotta became in certain Italian provinces, as a medium for ornamentation. It lent itself also to portraiture: when it was pigmented, its smooth surface became a skin, and a bust could easily be given that aggressive, 'speaking' character which was valued at this time. Some good examples have survived, but the bust of Lorenzo, known to us through several copies (one of which is in Washington), cannot be counted among them: to judge from its size—larger than life—and its somewhat grandiloquent effect, it is probably a sixteenth-century commemorative piece. Terracotta was sometimes used for groups of figures on a monumental scale, and between 1460 and 1495 there emerged several strange masterpieces whose likeness, not with Bavarian and Rhineland work, but with that of Burgundy and Languedoc, is remarkable and has often been pointed out: these are the treatment of the *Nativity* and of the *Descent from the Cross* (or *Pietà*) by Guido Mazzoni and by Niccolò da Bari. The travels of Guido Mazzoni are significant: he was at Busseto, Modena and Ferrara before being called to Naples (where in 1492 he produced the *Lamentation* for Santa Anna dei Lombardi); then in 1495 he went to France and worked at Saint-Denis. Niccolò da Bari came from Dal-

159 - GUIDO MAZZONI. FIGURE OF MOURNER:
ST MARY MAGDALEN — PADUA, MUSEO CIVICO.

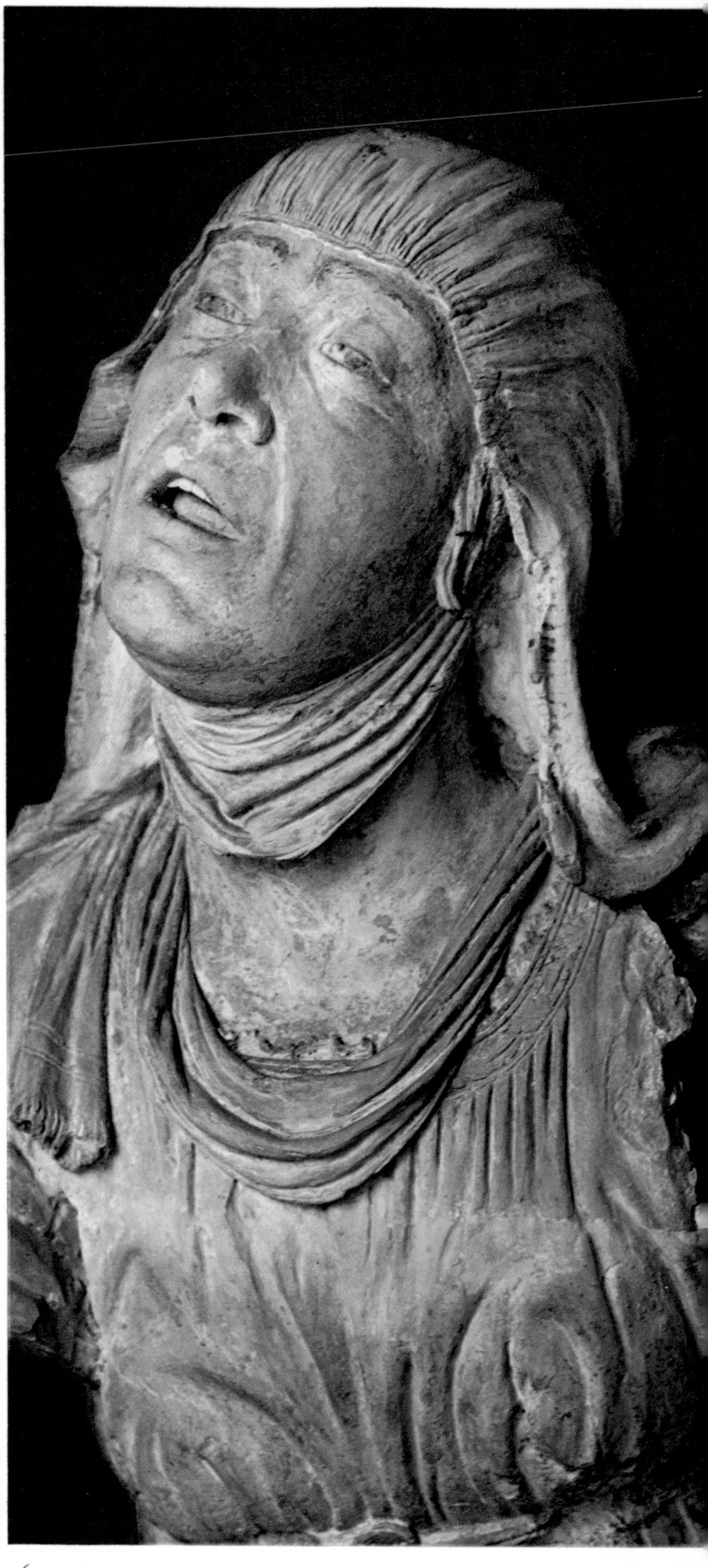

160 - GUIDO MAZZONI. FIGURE OF MOURNER:
HOLY WOMAN — PADUA, MUSEO CIVICO.

161 - NICCOLÒ DELL'ARCA. THE DEPOSITION — BOLOGNA, SANTA MARIA DELLA VITA.

matia, stopped for some time in Naples, then in France, and finally in about 1470 arrived in Emilia. The likeness between their work and French work is therefore not inexplicable; the disappearance of the colouring must have accentuated the difference, but even so the stature of the figures, the strongly stressed drapery and the excessively precise finish of the French sculptures in question recur fairly exactly in these works, though with the slight softening usually to be found in moulded sculptures by comparison with those carved in stone.

The calmest groups are those of the Northern countries: no *Entombment* produced in the Champagne district round about 1500 has the frenzied and tumultuous movement of the extraordinary *Pietà* in Santa Maria della Vita at Bologna (which probably dates from about 1485).

One must also bear in mind that Modena was a centre for the output of theatrical masks, and it is certain that Mazzoni worked on at least some of these.

162 - NICCOLÒ DELL'ARCA. THE DEPOSITION (DETAIL).
BOLOGNA, SANTA MARIA DELLA VITA.

163 - ANDREA DELLA ROBBIA. THE ARCHANGEL MICHAEL — NEW YORK, METROPOLITAN MUSEUM.

In Tuscany quite a different use was found for terracotta. It goes back to the collaboration between Luca della Robbia and Brunelleschi in about 1440 and to the enamelled terracotta medallions of the Pazzi chapel. When Luca's workshop, entrusted with the decoration of the ceiling of the Cardinal of Portugal's chapel, placed there the five large convex medallions on a green and yellow field, the fashion for brilliant yet gently pigmented sculptures became general in Tuscany. In the last third of the century the demand for overdoor lunettes, altar decorations, basins and other pieces in this treacherously smooth technique was large enough to occupy Andrea, Luca's nephew, and five of his sons: it was a branch of Florentine output in which, at the end of the century, decadence and success went together. The Santa Cristina altar at Bolsena and Giovanni della Robbia's basin under a large arch in the sacristy of Santa Maria Novella (1497) should be compared with Luca's elegant tabernacle at Peresola (1442): they demonstrate how enamelled terracotta could be made to imitate a wide range of structures and to envelop them in green garlands and pale blue panels. But this technique had the misfortune of being able to continue the gentle style of the 1450's till it reached the extreme of insipidity, losing the rather 'Attic' delicacy with which Luca had endowed it. Yet Andrea Sansovino succeeded once more in recapturing precisely this charm in his small figures when in about 1490 he composed the delightful blue and white frieze for the pediment of Poggio a Caiano. His success was in harmony with a classicizing and purist tendency that came into Italian sculpture as a whole, and to which we will return.

164 - LUCA DELLA ROBBIA. TEMPERANC
FLORENCE, SAN MINIATO AL MONT

LOMBARDS AND TUSCANS: NEO-CLASSICISM

THE stylistic evolution of Italian sculpture was now, on the whole, dominated by the interactions—or conflicts—that developed in the various regions between the Tuscan style and Lombard craftsmanship. To Gauricus, in 1504, Florence was '*semper harum artium mater*' he singles out for praise Rizzo and Bellano, but notes the inneffaceable memory which Donatello had left behind him. Florence was still the city of powerful, organized workshops, whose members were glad to join the service of illustrious clients elsewhere—as Maiano did in Naples, Pollaiuolo in Rome and Verrocchio in Venice, while Mino da Fiesole divided his activity between Florence and Rome. Agostino di Duccio developed his own style of very shallow relief in Rome, before carrying on his career in Perugia (*c.* 1460). These movements of the masters themselves did not exclude direct continuation of their influence through clever disciples like Civitali in Lucca or Francesco di Simone Ferrucci in Bologna and Forlì. By 1485, as a result of all these departures, Florence had begun to feel a certain drain on her resources, just before the young generation came into action—the generation which, with Andrea Sansovino, Rovezzano, Baccio da Montelupo and Michelangelo, all of them workers in marble, achieved the conception of the 'grand style'. Apart from the great bronze workers, the authority of the Tuscans came from a generally delicate and harmonious treatment of relief and from a precise and regular use of ornamental motifs. The spirit of Donatello was set aside in sculpture of this kind; with its attention fixed on slow rhythms, it always held the figure back on the brink of any excessively vital expressiveness. This is clearly shown by Desiderio's *Magdalen* in Santa Trinità, when compared with the splendid and cruel *Magdalen* made by Donatello for the Baptistry.

165 - AGOSTINO DI DUCCIO. ANGEL DRAWING A CURTAIN. RIMINI, TEMPIO MALATESTIANO.

166 - DONATELLO. ST MARY MAGDALEN — FLORENCE, BAPTISTRY.

167 - DESIDERIO DA SETTIGNAGNO, ST MARY MAGDALEN — FLORENCE, SANTA TRINITÀ.

168 - ANTONIO RIZZO. STAIRCASE — VENICE, DOGE'S PALACE.
Retouched photograph. See list of illustrations.

The most important success of the Lombards was in Venice and the North of Italy, where the Florentines had been dominant in the middle of the century. Decorative sculpture found a sturdy agent in Antonio Rizzo. After moving from Verona to Pavia, where he was working in 1465, he came to Venice, to be joined by Pietro Lombardo, who was settled in Padua in 1467, in 1474. These two men with their assistants soon transformed Venetian habits, and were themselves transformed. Their monumental tombs are not their most successful works: a better idea of how they assimilated the spirit of Venice and attained a new style of expression can be obtained, in the case of Rizzo, from the Scala dei Giganti (after 1491) and from the choir of Santa Maria dei Miracoli (1489). Those works did not pass unnoticed, and they were followed up by many others. In the years around 1490 Venice and the Veneto regained a place of honour, in this field as in painting. Indeed relief carving there soon took a precocious neo-classical turn.

Activity was no less intense in Lombardy itself, nor were the results less original. Unlike the Tuscans, the Lombards were attracted both by the instability and the depth of space, and this was the tendency that triumphed in the work of Amadeo and the Mantegazzas who vividly combined convoluted forms and spatial recessions.

169 - G.A. AMADEO (ATTR.) PULPIT (DETAIL): THE MARTYRS BEFORE THE EMPEROR CLAUDIUS — CREMONA, CATHEDRAL.

The same is true of the vocabulary of ornament; to measure the victory won by good taste and the insipidity of which it was the beginning, we need only compare Desiderio's or Mino's delicate tabernacles with the powerful *aediculum* in which Donatello placed his 1435 *Annunciation*. The repertory of ovolos and *rais de cœur* had become well established; the edges of the mouldings curved gently inwards; scales, dentils, palmettes, etc., were distributed with an ease, even an assurance, that readily grew monotonous; the crown on the outside face of the arch, the garlands on the lintel, the palmettes and the *putto*—the motif developed early in Tuscany as a facile means of introducing a slight animation—seemed all-sufficient. A discreet tinge of classical Antiquity was provided by the small shrines with pediments supported by pilasters or little fluted corinthian columns. In the relief carvings the axes of the composition and the folds of the draperies were always delicately adjusted to the frame as, for instance, in Benedetto da Maiano's pulpit for Santa Croce in Florence (*c.* 1472-1475). But the same sculptor adopted without hesitation motifs that had been tried out in the Mastrogiudici chapel of the Monte Oliveto at Naples, and in the San Bartolo chapel of the church of Sant' Agostino in San Gimignano. Antonio Rossellino also had been invited to Naples, and there (as at Santa Anna dei Lombardi) he reproduced for Maria of Aragon the exact scheme of the Cardinal of Portugal's tomb. And his example gave rise to the small school of Silvestro dell'Aquila in the Abruzzi. The way in which the Florentine ideas—fully evolved almost half a century back—were used till they were threadbare is clearly shown in the work of Matteo Civitali: he was responsible for that little masterpiece, the chapel of the Santo Volto in Lucca (1481), but also for the St Regulus altar (1484-5) in the same church, in which the combination of funerary monument and niches harks back to an old idea of Donatello's and is very ill-suited to the altar. It was clearly against the increasing formalization of relief carving that Verrocchio, as early as 1475, reacted by taking, in practically every genre a strong line against the fashionable *dolce stil*.

For generations Lombardy had been training masters of ornamentation and sending them out to all parts of Europe. Just when the Tuscans, taking the initiative, were raising the level of sculpture in most regions, the Lombards felt it necessary to react and attempted to reverse the situation. And so the great enterprises of Milan cathedral and the Certosa of Pavia—which for reasons of prestige the Milanese were unwilling to give up—became

170 - DOMENICO GAGGINI. LINTEL PORTRAYING FERDINAND OF ARAGON — LOS ANGELES, COUNTY MUSEUM OF ART.

the scenes of contradictory experiments. The taste for *quadratura*, for an overall formal scheme, inculcated by the visitors from the North, joined with the proverbial technical skill of the *tagliapietre* of the Lakes to produce a vivacious, ornate, rather facile style, which readily admitted new motifs. Round about 1470-1480 there was something like a revival of enthusiasm for the resources of relief carving and ornamentation among the craftsmen of Como, Bissone and Milan. They were soon propagating widely a vocabulary of motifs that was more confused, more pliable, but also more capable of piquant invention than that of the Florentines. The two often met and mingled.

So it came about that Domenico Gaggini worked in Genoa and then in Naples and Palermo. In Palermo he carved in honour of Ferdinand of Aragon an admirable doorway framed by astrological figures of Mars and Mercury. The Lombards were no less numerous and active in Rome, where, in the person of Bregno they won a kind of predominance, though this was interrupted by the arrival of various Tuscans, and was indeed often bound up with the spread of Mino's style—for instance in the tomb of Pietro Riario in the Santissimi Apostoli. The situation in Urbino, in about 1475, was more interesting. Domenico Rosselli, in his friezes of *putti* and of garlands, brought a partial return to the firm art of Agostino di Duccio, while Ambrogio Barocci of Milan represented the rich, almost luxuriant, Lombardo-Venetian style.

172 - AGOSTINO DI DUCCIO (ATTR.) VENUS (DETAIL) — RIMINI, TEMPIO MALATESTIANO, CHAPEL OF THE PLANETS.

174 - C. AND A. MANTEGAZZA. EXPULSION FROM PARADISE (DETAIL): ADAM AND EVE — CERTOSA DI PAVIA.

173 - A. MANTEGAZZA. THE LAMENTATION (DETAIL) — CERTOSA DI PAVIA.

176 - PIETRO DA RHO. ST JEROME — CREMONA, MUSEO.

Amadeo made his mark with the Colleoni chapel at Bergamo (after 1470), and in 1474 he obtained the commission to build and embellish half the façade of the Certosa of Pavia. His example was followed up by the Rodaris of Como and Briosco. His invention was full of vitality, and there is no doubt that it had a great effect on Lombard work. He was able to express his predilection for a space that is broken-up and dove-tailed with a superimposing of bevelled forms—a good example being his panel in half-relief for the church of San Imerio in Cremona (the fragment of the *arca* of San Arialdo, executed between 1481 and 1484). Cristoforo Mantegazza was working at the Certosa at the same time; he died in 1482, and his brother, Antonio, who lived on till 1495, showed a greater boldness, producing masterpieces of fragmented and nervous form. His *Pietà* in the Louvre, with the two figures belonging to it, is one of the peaks of 'expressionism', imbued with a powerful style.

75 - T. RODARI, AEDICULE WITH A STATUE OF PLINY THE ELDER — COMO, CATHEDRAL, FAÇADE.

177 - G.A. AMADEO (?). TYMPANUM (DETAIL): MEDALLION-BUST — CERTOSA DI PAVIA, SMALL CLOISTER.

With Cristoforo Solari (who returned to Lombardy in 1489 from a period in Venice) and Gian Cristoforo Romano (who was trained in Rome) there came, at the end of the century, a return to plastic firmness which attenuated the angular style, yet did not attain to classical definition which would have run counter to Lombard taste. Indeed the accumulation of means had now been carried so far that pieces of coloured marble and other stone were constantly inserted into the carved panels, and a simultaneous use of stone and terracotta was not found shocking. Already, in about 1480, in Pavia and in Cremona, the taste for medallions and for strong mouldings had come together with the fashion for terracotta. After the Sacristy of Santa Maria presso San Satiro, the new repertory had been created; it was spread by A. de Fonduli and Il Caradosso, and was widened further by Battagio. The courtyards of the Raimondi, Fodri and Stanga palaces in Cremona and of the Landi palace at Piacenza, all of them belonging to the last years of the century, have friezes with figures, medallions with busts, and ornaments

178 - T. LOMBARDO. BARBARIGO TOMB (DETAIL): ASSUMPTION OF THE VIRGIN — VENICE, CA' D'ORO.

repeated as though by stencils. An extreme case is the façade of Santa Maria dei Miracoli at Brescia, built from 1488 onwards: here all the architectural members are converted into complex plastic forms, and the whole is saturated with ornamentation, which harmonizes astonishingly well with the candelabrum-pillars and compartmented space of the interior.

Such were the upheavals of the Quattrocento. But just because of them there appeared, at length, forms that seem to be outside the framework of the century and to anticipate much later phenomena. Round about 1480 there came the affirmation of complete plasticity by Verrocchio, with the surprising impression he gives of a kind of pre-Baroque; and after 1490 neo-classical purism received a rapid statement from Tullio Lombardo, with his forecast of the cold and smooth style of all the later neo-classicisms. Both these men offered a clear and discouraging reply to all those manifestations of the years 1470-1480 which have sometimes been placed, for convenience, under the common heading of 'Gothic reaction'.

179 - ANON. FLORENTINE. IDEALIZED PORTRAIT OF SCIPIO — PARIS, LOUVRE.

180 - A. VERROCCHIO. LAVABO (DETAIL): CHIMAERA — FLORENCE, SAN LORENZO, OLD SACRISTY.

Verrocchio's ambition was to be a more complete Donatello. His career was not as long (instead of dying in 1488 he should have come back from Venice, as Donatello had come back after his experience in Padua), his work was more dispersed, and his attitude to classical Antiquity less firm; and yet one is struck by the force of his determination. His bold tomb for Piero de' Medici —marble and bronze together, in an eloquent and bare composition—was proof of a temperament determined to set a limit to the sweetness, however exquisite it might be, of his contemporaries. The lavabo in the adjoining sacristy is remarkable for the increased plastic power of the figures. In his impressive bronze statue of *St Thomas* he broke both with axiality and with the usual symmetry, and made it clear that sculpture was to be, first and foremost, mass and weight. The statue fills its space, the figure swirls to show its fullness—giving rise, in later art, to more and more frequent contortions—and its relief and its deep hollows seek to obtain a new collaboration from light. His *Scipio* relief combines these plastic properties with a fleshy modelling and with an incredible fantasy of ornament. He was aiming, at one and the same time, at Donatello's vigour and the subtlety of Desiderio: it is this total ambition, indeed, that makes Verrocchio's dreamy, thin David

184 - TULLIO LOMBARDO. TOMB OF P. MOCENIGO (DETAIL): ST MARK BAPTISING AMMIANUS — VENICE, SS. GIOVANNI E PAOLO.

relatively weak beside Donatello's hero. It is the contrary of a narrow classicism; if we wish to find analogies in the future, it is to the seventeenth century that we must go. The two-fold quality of energy and of smoothness suddenly broadened the repertory, and one can see very well the many links that, as the older writers have stressed, bound Leonardo to a master who was capable of enlarging so powerfully the range of sculpture.

Verrocchio's journey to Venice is evidence of his prestige, but he had no clear influence on the course of Venetian art. (The caster Leopardi did not hesitate to sign the Colleoni bronze.) The turn was taken in a different manner: as John Pope-Hennessy says, 'once the victory of Renaissance style was won, it was Venice and not Florence that achieved in sculpture the truer recreation of antiquity.' The field of sculpture was the only one in which the general idea of a 'return to Antiquity', and of bringing to life again the Mediterranean forms, was of unquestionable value. Here the gap between technical and cultural ambitions could be quite quickly closed. The grammar of ornament, as renewed by the masters, had systematized a type of setting—*tempietti* in the shape of small classical *aedicula*—which logically needed to house Roman soldiers and figures in togas. This was understood and straightforwardly carried out in the end by Pietro Lombardo; with him, and continuing after him, Tullio unhesitatingly clarified the types, isolated the figures and regulated forms and settings by one another.

185 - TULLIO LOMBARDO. ST MARK BAPTISING AMMIANUS (DETAIL) — VENICE, SS. GIOVANNI E PAOLO.

186 - TULLIO LOMBARDO. BACCHUS AND ARIADNE — VIENNA, KUNSTHISTORISCHES MUSEUM.

But perhaps the coldness of this style misleads us: at the time it seemed tender and delicate. The Vienna *Bacchus and Ariadne* was not a simple transposition of Roman reliefs. Tullio endowed them with an airy atmosphere that brings these full, smooth busts near to the melancholy, rounded figures of Giorgione. In a general way, Italian painting in the years 1490-1500 showed a parallel aspiration towards simplicity of effect, conscious elegance, economy and grace, which provokes comparison with the classicizing tendency in sculpture. Using means different from those of the Venetians, Andrea Sansovino (in the Volterra fonts), Rusticci and the young Florentine artists (soon to be dominated by Michelangelo) showed themselves equally anxious to bring together the complete plasticity, established in Verrocchio's work, and purity of style.

188 - GIORGIONE. PORTRAIT OF A YOUNG MAN — BERLIN-DAHLEM, STAATLICHE MUSEEN, GEMÄLDEGALERIE.

187 - MICHELANGELO. THE BATTLE OF THE CENTAURS.
FLORENCE, CASA BUONARROTI.

BERNARDINV
PICTORICIVS
PERVSINV

III

PAINTING

In the second half of the fifteenth century there was a tendency for the painter of a picture to introduce himself with less discretion than before. This was the moment when the signature began to be given prominence, in the form of the *cartellino*, a sheet of paper or a tablet bearing the artist's name or other information about the execution of the work[7]. Another frequent device was the insertion of the painter's own portrait in the right-hand corner of the composition, as, for instance, did Botticelli in his *Adoration of the Magi* (*c.* 1476) for the Medici. Lastly, portrait and inscription together might be presented on a panel or in a niche, as was done—somewhat exceptionally, it is true—by Pinturicchio at Spello (1502). These new devices, which became common after 1460, appear to signify a clearer awareness of personality; but in the main the purpose of these workshop 'labels' was to draw attention not only to the artist himself, but to the 'firm' directed by him.

The increasingly widespread habit of placing a small picture within the composition is interesting. Sometimes the painter introduced a specimen of his art, for instance by representing an altarpiece inside a chapel, as Pinturicchio did in the Piccolomini Library in Siena. Rondinelli, who seems to have been fond of exploiting this original device, depicts a Bellini-type Madonna of his own in his *Galla Placidia* (Brera), and Braccesco his own triptych in his *Miracle of St Andrew* (Musée de Cluny). In these cases the painter was giving a double demonstration of his technique and style. The intention is more subtle when the picture within the picture is representative of a style different from the painter's own:

189 - BERNARDINO PINTURICCHIO, SELF-PORTRAIT — SPELLO, SANTA MARIA MAGGIORE, BAGLIONI CHAPEL.

190 - MASTER OF THE BARBERINI PANELS. PRESENTATION OF THE VIRGIN (DETAIL) — BOSTON.
Shaded for demonstration. See list of illustrations.

in such cases the painter is making a regional or historical point by means of a type of art foreign to his. Thus in the Barberini *Presentation* (Boston Museum of Fine Arts) triptychs are somewhat unexpectedly introduced, apparently in order to fit in with the *all'antica*, or palaeo-Christian, style of the architectural setting. The same sort of purpose must be attributed to the mosaics which the Venetian painters from 1480-1485 onwards were so fond of inserting into the apse-shaped niches that serve as backgrounds to their Sacre Conversazioni—Giovanni Bellini, for instance, in the San Giobbe altarpiece, and many others after him.

Just as the extraordinary development of painted architectural settings and city views was bound up with the problem of monumental art, so it seems hard not to

191 - VITTORE CARPACCIO. LEGEND OF ST URSULA (DETAIL) — VENICE, ACCADEMIA.
Shaded for demonstration. See list of illustrations.

see in the insertions just described a sign of the importance now attached to pictures and of the attention now given to their presentation, to their place in the decoration of interiors, their contribution to the general effect. In the Northern countries the theme of St Luke painting the portrait of the Virgin had been used to magnify the 'sacred' value of art: the theme was rare in Italy. A picture of the Madonna on the Evangelist's easel does figure on the ceiling of the cathedral of Atri, painted in 1481 by Delitio, a veteran of the smooth and twining Gothic style, but this naïve way of stressing the painter's importance stands in contrast to the cleverness shown by Carpaccio, when he adorned the room of St Ursula's father with nothing but a small picture of the Madonna hanging on the wall—a modern 'icon'.

192 - PIERO DELLA FRANCESCA. STORY OF THE TRUE CROSS. DEATH OF ADAM (DETAIL) — AREZZO, SAN FRANCESCO

PIERFRANCESCAN PAINTING AND THE INFLUENCE OF SQUARCIONISM

FILARETE, who was well informed about what was going on in Central Italy as well as in the North of Italy, gives in his treatise (written in about 1465) a short list of the 'good masters in painting' at that moment. 'We have,' he writes, 'a Fra Filippo of Florence, a Piero of Borgho, an Andrea of Padua known as Il Squarcione, a Cosimo of Ferrara and, in addition, a Vincenzo of Brescia.'[8] Though Filarete here associates or confuses Andrea Mantegna of Padua and Squarcione, his picture of the Italian 'leaders' is a good one. Filippo Lippi was finishing the cycle of frescoes at Prato; the choir of San Francesco in Arezzo and the Eremitani Chapel had just established beyond question the glory of Piero 'dal Borgho' and of Mantegna; Cosimo Tura had decorated with allegories the Belfiore studio in Ferrara (1459-1463), worked on the Mirandola Library between 1465 and 1467, and was soon to take part, again in Ferrara, in painting the Palazzo Schifanoia frescoes; and Vincenzo Foppa —the Vincenzo who came 'from Brescia' and Bergamo— was employed at Sant' Eustorgio in Milan. This recapitulation should suffice to remind us of the grandeur attained by wall painting in the 1460-70 decade: it had never been more rich or more varied.

The best nourished, most complex and most monumental of the styles confronting one another at that moment was that of Piero della Francesca; it was also one that exerted the dominant influence in a zone stretching from Rome to Ferrara and skirting Tuscany. The reasons for its authority have been admirably expounded by several writers: in it definition of space and exaltation of the surface by means of fields of colour harmonized so firmly and convincingly as to make it the first modern 'synthesis.' Here we are concerned only with the consequences: during a short phase of the Quattrocento Piero became a kind of national figure. The powerful organization of his compositions proved useful to artists of the most varied kinds. It could serve as the basis for the romantic decorations of the *cassoni* and was even exploited

193 - PIERO DELLA FRANCESCA. STORY OF THE TRUE CROSS. DISCOVERY OF THE CROSS (DETAIL) — AREZZO, SAN FRANCESCO

194 - ANTONIAZZO ROMANO. STORY OF THE TRUE CROSS (DETAIL
ROME, SANTA CROCE IN GERUSALEMME.

195 - G. BIRAGO. NATIVITY OF THE VIRGIN. MODENA, BIBL. ESTENSE.

in miniature painting. But not in Tuscany. There is no sign in Florence, except in the work of Baldovinetti, of the response that might have been expected to the Arezzo masterpiece, for instance. The slight Pierfrancescan movement round about 1465 'was rapidly stifled' (R. Longhi). This is one of the paradoxes of the later part of the fifteenth century. Possibly, as the tense manner of Pollaiuolo was followed by the plasticity of Verrocchio, the Florentines felt that they had once and for all passed beyond the too exclusively monumental style of Piero. And yet, in about 1490, place had to be found for an echo of it, in the shape of the spacious art of Perugino and the vigour of Signorelli; in these cases, factors dissociated from the art of Piero evolved separately, and Florence took part only indirectly in their elaboration. The only evidence of a kind of regret among the Florentines is the work of Bartolomeo della Gatta. His early works are characterized by a fine painterly handling; in his *Nativity* (Vienna) and his *Annunciation* (Périgueux) he displays a seductive, somewhat minor assimilation of the art of Piero. This explains why, after Bartolomeo had worked in Rome, assisting Signorelli with the frescoes in the Sistine Chapel, his *St Francis receiving the Stigmata* at Castiglione d'Olona is so interesting—and indeed isolated.

196 - BARTOLOMMEO DELLA GATTA. ST JEROME — AREZZO. CATHEDRAL, SACRISTY.

197 - MELOZZO DA FORLÌ. CHRIST GIVING HIS BLESSING — ROME, PALAZZO DEL QUIRINALE.

In 1459, according to a document in the Papal archives, Piero della Francesca received 150 florins for painting. It was his first, or perhaps his second, stay in Rome. It has been impossible to establish the scale of this work, which was commissioned by Pius II and—according to Vasari—destroyed in the time of Julius II. Yet Piero's presence on this occasion opens an interesting vista. Fifteen years later Melozzo painted for Sixtus IV that solemn panel in the Vatican Library, in which space is magnified for its own sake; and a certain attraction towards grandeur continued, for example, in the work of Anto-

198 - MELOZZO DA FORLÌ. VAULT OF THE FEO CHAPEL (DETAIL): A PROPHET — FORLÌ, SAN BIAGIO.

niazzo Romano. Neither the 1480-1481 frescoes in the Sistine Chapel (with the exception of Perugino's *Remission of the Keys)* nor—indeed, still less—Pinturicchio's gilded and artificial compositions, were able to fulfil the aroused expectation: this was done only after 1507, by Raphael in the *School of Athens*, bettering even Perugino in the Sistine Chapel. Seen in this context, Melozzo's presence in Rome must be regarded as a more important fact than his few surviving works might lead us to think. His function in the Marches was to maintain the feeling for solemn volumes and for perspectives worked out for the sake of grandeur, not caprice. His contribution can be gauged by studying the cupola of the Feo Chapel in the church of San Biagio in Forlì, where the false vault on drums and the huge draped outlines of the seated prophets crowning the parapet create a massive overhanging effect of an admirable authority. There are reasons for believing that this was Melozzo's last work (between 1492-1495), finished (especially as regards the curved triangles) by Palmezzano.

In Umbria—or rather, in a zone extending from Arezzo to Perugia, to the villages of the Marches and to Urbino—the art of Piero della Francesca enjoyed complete authority for thirty years. It had achieved a lasting

199 - B. BONASCIA. PIETÀ WITH THE VIRGIN AND ST JOHN — MODENA, GALLERIA ESTENSE.

reconciliation of the contraries, by harmonizing Sienese smoothness with Florentine geometry, the full range of light colours with strictness in the forms. But the sturdy type of Piero's figures and the rustic *timbre* of his style could not fully control the Perugian masters. Those enchanting curls and folds, which Piero had allowed himself to shape in play, and which acted as a kind of border of refinement to his austerity, became to Bonfigli the essential; and preciosity is dominant in the affected elegance of Caporali and even in Fiorenzo di Lorenzo. The links between Piero and Perugino are more subtle: in the St Bernardino *Tavolette*, now attributed to him, the young Umbrian unquestionably owed what Longhi calls the 'milky quality of the light' to the San Sepolcro master.

Piero della Francesca—the point has been made above, with some insistence—represented more than a painterly 'manner': his style was in harmony with the aspiration of the architects and sculptors towards a definite nobility of rhythm. This, fairly precisely, is what Urbino seems to have stood for—especially when we restore to the art of that centre its doctrinal and humanistic context. Through the Lendinaras, as we have seen, this abstract style developed some of its remarkable properties in the field of marquetry. The style had a general value, and formed a kind of inner connection between several domains of Italian art. Its power, precisely, was that it could absorb contributions that seemed essentially foreign to it. The presence of Joos van Ghent and of Berruguete in Urbino reminds us of how important was the Flemish-Italian conjunction. After 1475 it acted as a stimulant, even to the exceptionally noble art of Piero.

The most remarkable changes that took place in Quattrocento painting were due to the meeting of the Pierfrancescan style with the Squarcionesque line of inspiration and with the Gothico-Byzantine formulae still prevalent in Venice. In the first case, the love for picturesque detail and the superabundance of effects might have been expected to annihilate the results of the 'monumental synthesis'; in the second, the vitrified handling and the mummification of the forms seemed bound to offer an unsurmountable obstacle to a broad and clear definition of space.

The art of the Ferrara masters achieved the paradoxical feat of bringing together Piero's monumental strength and Paduan fantasy. But in addition to Ferrara, which constitutes a special field, unexpected (though less astonishing) encounters of styles were taking place all over the northern part of Italy—as, for instance, in Bonascia's *Pietà* at Modena, the date of which is as late as 1485. Another and tendentious adaptation of the majesty of Piero's types was the late development in Lombardy of a taste for very large and clear-cut figures filling the wall spaces of buildings: the 'philosophers' painted in 1477 on the façade of the Palazzo del Pretore at Bergamo recall both Mantegna and the decorations of the Urbino *studiolo*. The attribution of these to Bramante is only provisional, but they are certainly by a painter to whom perspective and moderation were important, and who was influenced by Melozzo. The Casa Panigarola in Milan, a palatial town house, had eight figures—of warriors and poets: the warriors have far more strength than the Bergamo figures, though they do not attain sublimity; the grave, rather solemn arrangement comes from Melozzo. It is not likely that the *Argus* fragment (Castello Sforzesco) is by Bramante. Combining massiveness with capriciousness, and stressing the jutting consoles, they suggest rather, as Berenson was inclined to think, the more provocative art of Bramantino.

200 - BRAMANTE (ATTR.) FAITH — BERGAMO.

The style of Piero della Francesca was capable of inciting artists to produce robust forms and articulated space. It brought to life a whole series of works in which the feeling is one of strong figures standing out against a vigorously rhythmic background. But the pressure of this style ran into an opposite drive towards the singular, detailed and tormented; and the result was a multitude of interactions, the principal source of which must, it seems to us, have been in the North. The well-known passage by Roberto Longhi has rightly drawn attention to the inevitability of 'all that took place between Padua, Ferrara and Venice from 1450 to 1470, from the fiercest follies of Tura and Crivelli to the sorrowful elegance of the

201 - BRAMANTINO. ARGUS — MILAN, CASTELLO SFORZESCO.

ABIIT

202 - L. SCALETTI (ATTR.). THE VIRGIN AND CHILD — FAENZA, PINACOTECA CIVICA.

young Giambellino and to Mantegna's grammar of vigorous display; all this had its origin in that troupe of desperate vagabonds, sons of tailors, barbers, shoe-makers and peasants, which during those twenty years found its way to the studio of Squarcione.' The social origin of the disciples of Squarcionism was perhaps not always as humble as that, and it is not necessary to attribute to their art a revolutionary or anarchist basis; yet it is a remarkable fact that the lines which lead to the Venice of Jacopo Bellini, to the Mantua of Mantegna, to the Ferrara of Tura and even to the Milan of Foppa, can be arranged like the rays of a star about Padua, that centre of an 'expressionist' Renaissance.

The determination to frame the figures within niches, arches and heavy shrines covered with mouldings and broken up by swirling garlands of fruit and flowers; an untiring attention to sharp and broken forms, to cut gems, to coral and to metallic outlines; a propensity towards pathos, towards sorrowing faces and violent gestures, these were the constant elements of that archaeology-nourished 'expressionism,' the influence of which, through some well-known artists and numerous small fry, is beginning to be more clearly perceived. The links

ɔ3 - GIORGIO SCHIAVONE. THE VIRGIN AND CHILD — AMSTERDAM, RIJKSMUSEUM.

204 - SCHOOL OF SQUARCIONE. ANGELS CARRYING THE INSTRUMENTS OF THE PASSION (DETAIL). BERGAMO, ACCADEMIA CARRARA.

between Scarletti (who worked at Faenza from 1458 to 1495), Gregorio Schiavone (who remained tied to Padua) and Marco Zoppo (who moved on to Ferrara) sometimes seem inextricable. Crivelli's absurd and acid little *Madonna* of about 1460 (in the Verona Museum), which is like a Mantegna in miniature, adequately sums up the implacable authority of this line of inspiration. In Padua itself the (much altered) frescoes by Parentino and Angelo Zotto in the church of San Giustino (*c.* 1490) are representatives of the style—a loaded style that is all folds, wrinkles and puckerings; and Parentino's strange *Temptations of St Anthony* (in the Doria Collection,

205 - C. CRIVELLI. VIRGIN OF THE PASSION — VERONA, MUSEO CIVICO.

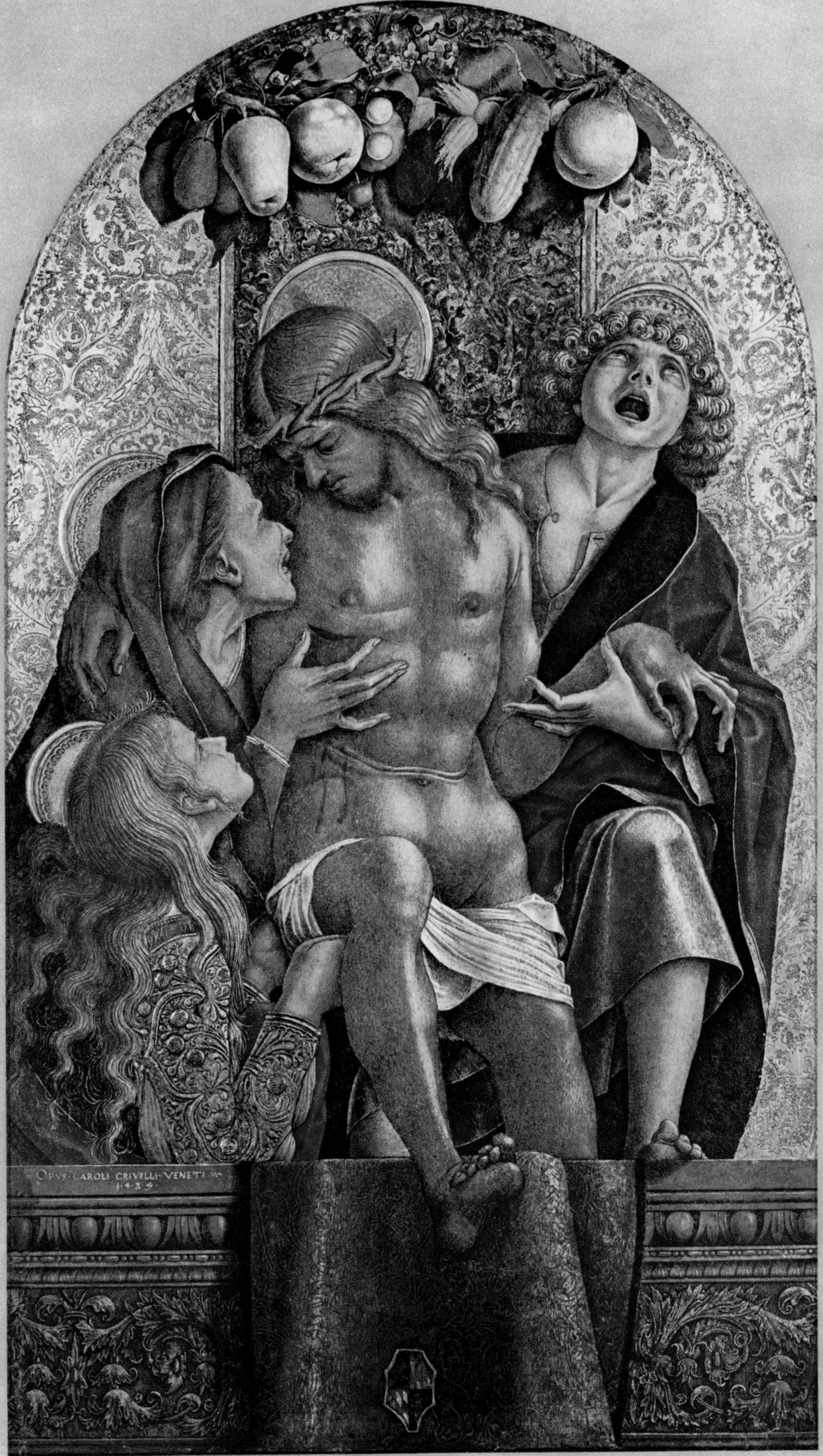
OPVS CAROLI CRIVELLI VENETI
1485

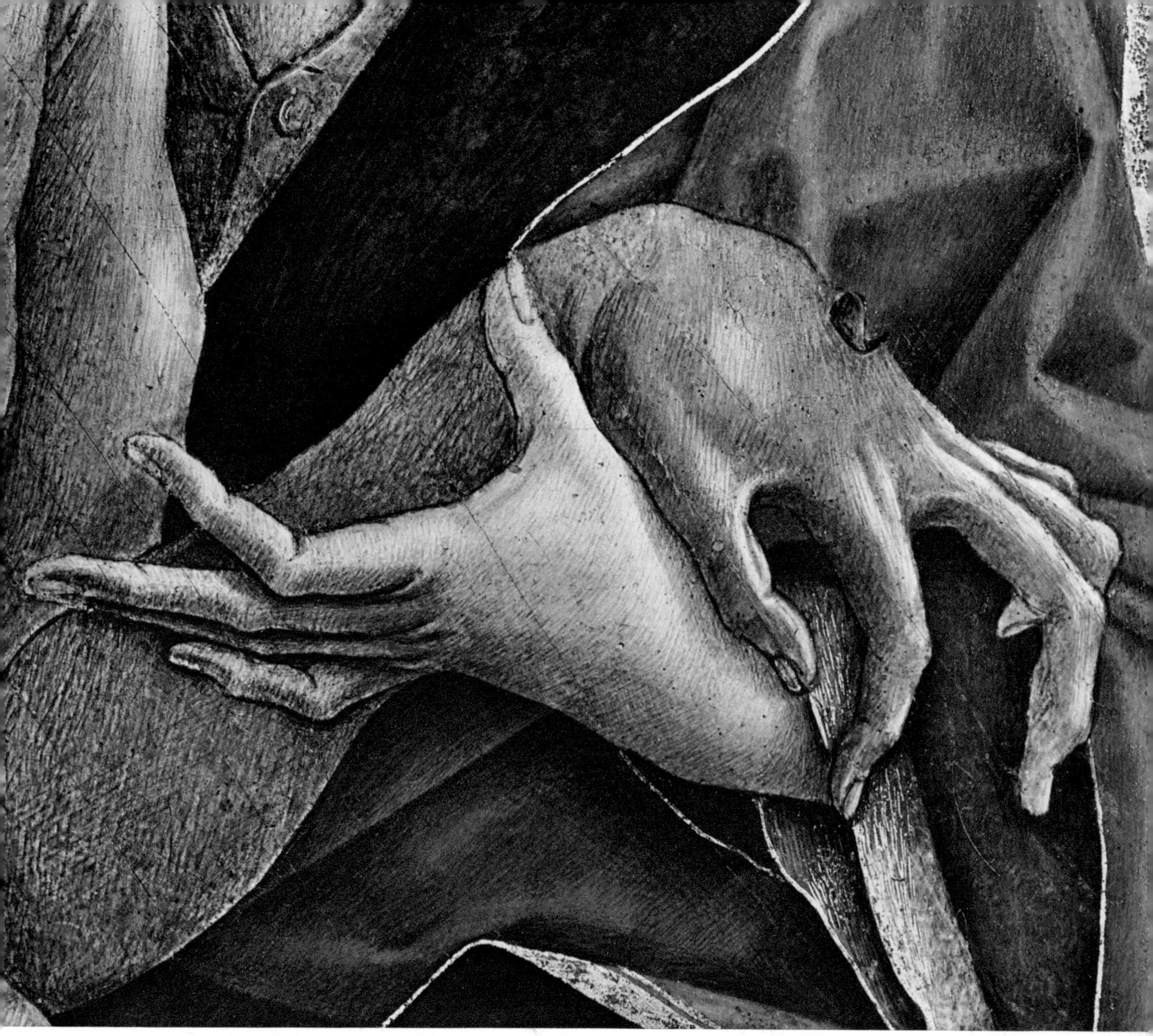

207 - CARLO CRIVELLI. PIETÀ (DETAIL) — BOSTON, MUSEUM OF FINE ARTS.

Rome) reveals something of its Nordic affinities. The term 'late Quattrocento neo-Gothic' or 'return to Gothic,' is inadequate to designate the range of this phenomenon of resistance to the monumental nobility of Piero della Francesca; Botticelli's linear sublety, which developed late in a kind of Florentine sealed chamber, has nothing in common with the harshness of the 'Squarcionesques', still less with Mantegna's military march and metallic uniforms—which themselves show so little harmony with the crystalline handling and the alternately sharpened and polished profiles of the Ferrarese.

206 - CARLO CRIVELLI. PIETÀ — BOSTON, MUSEUM OF FINE ARTS.

209 - F. DEL COSSA. THE MONTH OF APRIL (DETAIL): THE THREE GRACES — FERRARA, PALAZZO SCHIFANOIA.

208 - S. BOTTICELLI. THE BIRTH OF VENUS — FLORENCE, UFFIZI.

211 - GIOVANNI DI PAOLO. THE LAST JUDGEMENT. PARADISE (DETAIL) — SIENA, PINACOTECA.

In Siena the situation had grown much simpler. The outstanding painters were dead. 'As Sano di Pietro (1481) and Giovanni di Paolo (1482) confined themselves within a kind of separate style, the best Sienese painting of the second half of the century could not, in so far as it was Sienese, take its inspiration from anyone but Vecchietta. Neroccio di Bartolommeo, Francesco di Giorgio Martini and Benvenuto di Giovanni were actual pupils of his. Matteo di Giovanni also owes a great deal to him' (E. Carli). In point of fact Vecchietta was devoting himself more and more to sculpture, and Francesco di Giorgio was soon dividing his time between painting and other activities; Matteo di Giovanni alone seemed capable of clear compositions filled with nervous life, a good example being his *Massacre of the Innocents* in the church of Sant' Agostino (1482). Gradually paralyzed by Florentine gravity, which did not really suit it, Sienese painting

210 - VECCHIETTA. ASSUMPTION OF THE VIRGIN — PIENZA, CATHEDRAL.

212 - F. DI GIORGIO (ATTR.). CASSONE PANEL. THE RAPE OF EUROPA (DETAIL) — PARIS, LOUVRE.

213 - FRANCESCO DI GIORGIO. ANNUNCIATIO
SIENA, PINACOTECA.

QVANTVM·HOMINI·FAS·EST·MIRA·LICET·ASSEQVAR·ARTE
NIL·AGO·MORTALIS·EMVLOR·ARTE·DEOS·

214 - NEROCCIO DI BARTOLOMMEO DE' LANDI. PORTRAIT — WASHINGTON, NATIONAL GALLERY.

215 - NEROCCIO DI BARTOLOMMEO DE' LANDI. THE VIRGIN AND CHILD BETWEEN SAINTS (DETAIL) — SIENA, PINACOTECA

216 - LIBERALE DA VERONA. CASSONE PANEL. THE RAPE OF HELEN (DETAIL) — CAMPANA COLL.

217 - G. DA CREMONA. ADORATION OF THE MAGI. SIENA, PICCOLOMINI LIBRARY.

seems to have received the stimulus it needed from Liberale da Verona who arrived in 1466 and stayed till 1474, first at Monte Oliveto and then in Siena itself. His Paduan origin and his connections with the Squarcionesques have been established beyond doubt. Though he came to Siena to work on the choir books for the cathedral with Girolamo da Cremona, the *cassone* panel depicting the *Rape of Helen* (Le Havre) may be taken as representing the culmination of this stay in Siena, during which Liberale, having enriched the Sienese vocabulary, benefited in turn from the calligraphic and imaginative freedom still maintained, in some cases, by the pupils of Vecchietta. This enabled Liberale, when he went back to Verona, to produce a more poetic version of this youthful Squarcionism. It is he who seems to have been responsible for one of the most singular works of the period, the *Christ* in Viterbo cathedral (1472). The frontality of the central figure, surrounded by a half circle of saints rigorously distributed about the pedestal, and above all the arrangement of the two hands along perpendicular axes, forcibly remind us of Piero della Francesca.

218 - LIBERALE DA VERONA. CHRIST BETWEEN FOUR SAINTS — VITERBO, CATHEDRAL.

MURAL PAINTING AND PAINTING ON CANVAS

In the middle of the fifteenth century, mural painting was at its peak. It had a great past, of which men were acutely conscious, especially in Tuscany, and it was still considered the true medium of great art. The very difficulty of its technique contributed to its prestige; it was felt that the rapid execution necessary if a damp surface was to be covered quickly enough, must correspond to a grandeur of conception. Both these factors were soon to change[9].

After 1450 the technique of fresco painting began to alter. The under-tracing (known as *sinopia*)—that is to say, the squared enlargement of the drawing, made on the coarse plaster coating (or *ariccio*)—was replaced by a diagram imprinted on the coating through holes pricked in the cartoon; the pricks were called *spolveri*. This new practice made the work easier and reduced the part played by improvisation. According to E. Borsook, it made its appearance in the middle of the century, with the three painters who worked together at Sant' Egidio: Castagno, Domenico Veneziano and Piero. Castagno had already tried combining the use of fresco for the shadows with that of colour laid on *a secco* (*tempera*, clearly) for the draperies; mixed techniques now became more and more general, and experiments were carried out—by Baldovinetti, among others—with new methods of using oil paints along with the conventional media of wall painting—for instance, in the chapel of the Cardinal of Portugal. The aim was to combine the matt effect of watercolour with the transparent effects of oil. Disappointments were in store for Baldovinetti, as later for Leonardo.

Rational perspective had become, with Masaccio and his great Florentine successors, a satisfying and scrupulously controlled means of organizing space, of harmonizing and distributing the figures. A slight lowering of

219 - A. BALDOVINETTI. NATIVITY (DETAIL). FLORENCE, SS. ANNUNZIATA, CLOISTER.

220 - BENOZZO GOZZOLI. THE BUILDING OF THE TOWER OF BABEL. (DETAIL) — PISA, CAMPO SANTO.

221 - D. GHIRLANDAIO. SAINT FRANCIS RAISING A CHILD FROM THE DEAD — FLORENCE, SANTA TRINITÀ, SASSETTI CHAPEL.

the horizon line enhanced the figures; the progressive diminution of the landmarks in the picture made it possible to insert useful details methodically in the intervals between the foreground plane. The Florentines, following the course set by Gozzoli and Lippi, did not take advantage of the Pierfrancescan solution, by which the distribution of the light authorized bolder groupings, silhouettes and contours. The indefatigable Gozzoli was soon providing, at Pisa, a continuation of the easier style—animated, at least, by a frank recourse to architectural motifs. In the work of Ghirlandaio at San Gimignano, in the Sassetti chapel in Santa Trinità (Florence) in 1485, and then in Santa Maria Novella, problems of composition which go back to the Trecento are given a well thought-out conclusion: here with a kind of return to Masaccio, Gozzoli's picturesque space is replaced by an urban—or perhaps civil—space, which serves as a framework for the sacred scenes. One feels that restraint has been exercized, to avoid misusing the feigned space of the fresco, but also that the artist was anxious to vary his arrangements of motifs drawn from familiar buildings which seem here to suffice. Yet in this way fresco painting

222 - D. GHIRLANDAIO. FRESCOES. FLORENCE, SANTA MARIA NOVELLA.

223 - DOMENICO GHIRLANDAIO AND HIS PUPILS. THE VISITATION (DETAIL) — FLORENCE, SANTA MARIA NOVELLA.

224 - FILIPPINO LIPPI. FRESCOES — FLORENCE, SANTA MARIA NOVELLA, STROZZI CHAPEL.

225 - FILIPPINO LIPPI. MIRACLE OF ST PHILIP — FLORENCE, SANTA MARIA NOVELLA, STROZZI CHAPEL.

was losing its epic power. It could not, however, renounce the use of symbols and the task of heroicizing, and Filippino seems to have been the man most clearly aware of this. In the Strozzi Chapel of Santa Maria Novella he reacted in more ways than one against what Ghirlandaio had done in the nearby chapel: he simplified the arrangement in tiers, created original and unreal motifs for each *istoria*, and supplied the facing wall with a painted architectural framework quite foreign to the chapel's Gothic style. By so doing, he bore witness in his fashion to the difficulties—not to say the crisis—now troubling the fresco painters.

The two most remarkable series of frescoes of this period, after the Eremitani and the Arezzo cycle, were painted not in Tuscany, but in Ferrara and in Rome;

226 - UGO TOGNETTI. THE SISTINE CHAPEL BETWEEN 1448-1508.

they are those of the great room in the Palazzo Schifanoia (1458-1478) and in the Sistine Chapel (1481-2). In both cases the walls are divided by great horizontal bands, in which the *storie* form continuous cycles on a grand scale: one of them is the most solemn celebration in paint of the 'Months' and the order of secular life, while the other is a series of scenes from Scripture. In Rome the bringing together of Tuscan and Umbrian artists (they were set in more or less overt competition by Sixtus IV) enables us to appreciate the community of principles between Botticelli and Signorelli—both of them adepts at treating a subject in the form of a frieze—and the originality of Perugino, who gave first place to harmonious space and symbolic architecture. In Ferrara it

227 - (A) LUCA SIGNORELLI. THE LAST DAYS OF MOSES.

is not easy to assign the different artists their shares, though the month of *April* belongs to Cossa and *September*, it seems, to the young Ercole de' Roberti; but the conception of the whole is as brilliant as the execution is sure. The arrangement in tiers enabled the artists to display the allegories of the 'planetary children' (crafts and occupations corresponding to each planet) on the upper level, the 'works of the months' (in this case, the life of the court) on the lower, and to bind them together by the astrological symbols of the decans (subdivisions of the Zodiac) standing out against a dark ground. Even if the effects are overstressed, one is reminded that the examples supplied by Piero at the Palazzo Municipale (1449) were not far away.

227 (B) - SANDRO BOTTICELLI. THE PUNISHMENT OF KORAH, DATHAN AND ABIRON.

In the Sistine Chapel, as in the Salone dei Mesi, the painters were able to divide up the walls of rectangular chambers to suit their purposes. Usually, in the churches where they worked on commission from some religious foundation, their task was to adorn the walls of a chapel, sometimes inconveniently shaped. Yet, before Filippino in the Strozzi Chapel, the fresco painters do not give the impression of having been irritated by working in a space delimited by Gothic arches and groins. Normally they divided the wall into tiers of frescoes, as Giotto had done at Santa Croce. But now the use of regular perspective rendered this superposition as arbitrary as could be. In 1480 and thereabouts the painter most sensitive to the peculiar possibilities of perspective was

227 (G) - D. GHIRLANDAIO. THE CALLING OF ST PETER AND ST ANDREW.

227 (H) - COSIMO ROSSELLI. THE LAST SUPPER.

229 - S. BOTTICELLI. ANNUNCIATION — FLORENCE, SAN MARTINO DELLA SCALA.

Botticelli, whose *Annunciation* in the atrium of San Martino della Scala distributed with unusual virtuosity expressive voids within the strict network of his space. At the same moment Ghirlandaio was showing, in the refectory of the Ognissanti, his ability to adapt the lines of recession in his composition to the space of the room he had to decorate: the fresco is a noble continuation of the room. Leonardo adopted exactly the same principle for his *Last Supper* at Santa Maria delle Grazie, taking perspective as the basis for the main effect of the composition, which seems a reflection of the refectory itself. The fresco is adjusted precisely to its setting. Leonardo was so conscious of the necessity of this that, in notes written in 1492 or thereabouts, he formulated a vigorous criticism of the traditional way of painting: 'There is a general practice among painters of chapel walls that is open to serious criticism. They make a composition with buildings and landscapes on one plane, and then, higher up, another composition in which they change the pointview,

228 - S. BOTTICELLI. ANNUNCIATION (DETAIL). FLORENCE, SAN MARTINO DELLA SCALA.

230 - DOMENICO GHIRLANDAIO. THE LAST SUPPER — FLORENCE, OGNISSANTI.

and so on. It is absolutely stupid. On one and the same wall one finds four viewpoints. We know that the viewpoint corresponds to the spectator's eye, and if you desire to know how to represent the life of a saint in several episodes on one wall, I will explain it to you: you must place the foreground in relation to the eye of the spectator, then arrange figures and buildings in regular diminution over the hills and plains so as to unfold the whole story. The rest of the wall, up to the top, must be adorned with trees of dimensions proportional to the figures, or filled with angels, if they are suitable, with birds, with clouds...' (B.N. 2038, f° 16*a*). This condemnation applies to centuries of practice, including Masaccio and Piero; the Santa Trinità and

231 - LEONARDO DA VINCI. THE LAST SUPPER — MILAN, SANTA MARIA DELLE GRAZIE.

Santa Maria Novella cycles are not immune from it. In Leonardo's view, justification could be found only for unified compositions placed more or less on eye level, like the *Last Supper*, or established on a raised base, like the Umbrian cycles soon to be produced in the Cambio in Perugia and in the San Brizio Chapel in Orvieto.

232 - LUCA SIGNORELLI. FRESCOES — ORVIETO, CATHEDRAL, CAPELLA DI SAN BRIZIO.

233 - LUCA SIGNORELLI. THE LAST JUDGEMENT. THE DAMNED (DETAIL) — ORVIETO, CATHEDRAL.

234 - ANDREA MANTEGNA. LA CAMERA DEGLI SPOSI (DETAIL) — MANTUA, PALAZZO DUCALE.

Thus a change in the usual style of mural painting was dictated by the importance now accorded to the organization of perspective. But this requirement itself brought with it a new risk. In the Eremitani the *trompe-l'œil* effect, though strongly stressed in the lunettes, is still, in the arrangement of the painted architecture, corrected by the frontal façades and the distribution of the masses; and Melozzo's fresco in the Sistine Chapel adjusted itself to the shape of the interior without accentuating the element of illusion. Such was the rule in the Quattrocento. Filippino's final experiments, however, showed that this reserve would not be maintained for long; and the full play of *trompe-l'œil* effects had made its appearance in Mantua, simultaneously with another change in fresco painting. The decoration of the Camera degli Sposi at

Mantua, which was finished in 1474, is at one and the same time a celebration (as in the Palazzo Schifanoia) of typical scenes from court life with an inevitable insistence on portraits, the most complete display of *all'antica* pilasters and medallions yet seen, and a no less original essay in extending illusionist decoration over a whole room. The *trompe-l'œil* lunette of the ceiling and the landscape in the fresco on the left form part of a structure divided by architectural and decorative elements, into which the mantelpiece and bays are integrated; and since the unpainted parts of the wall were covered with decorated leather, the whole was a continuum—an imaginary yet habitable space. In the Belvedere Mantegna produced for Innocent VIII another development of the same conception: the *storie* were surrounded by a great blossoming of ornamental motifs and chiaroscuri, so that, according to Vasari, ceiling and walls made one think of miniatures rather than of fresco painting. This rather surprising genre of the *camera picta* was taken up again by Pinturicchio in the Basso della Rovere Chapel of Santa Maria del Popolo. It was, indeed, a genre with which *trompe-l'œil* effects were easily combined. It was continued in a flight of imagination that proved to be the most fantastic of that century—indeed the one that did most to undermine traditional methods: in the Sala delle Asse in the castle of Milan Leonardo succeeded, by transferring the foliage ornamentation of the Trecento to a painted trellis, in producing a naturalistic *camera picta*, a purely decorative *trompe-l'œil.*

But a more far-reaching initiative was taking place in Venice. The city of mosaics, of inlay and incrustation possessed hardly any frescoes, except those by Pisanello and Gentile da Fabriano in the Sala del Gran Consiglio and those by Castagno in San Zaccaria. The Mascoli Chapel in St Mark's, where the Renaissance style obtained a foothold, was carried out in mosaic (*c.* 1450). And then, in about 1480, when the Bellinis were entrusted with redecorating the Sala del Consiglio in the Ducal Palace, there came the substitution of canvas for wood as the support of the painting—and this in a large-scale scheme of a kind that could only, normally, be conceived in fresco. From that time onwards the important cycles in Venice—those for the Scuola of St John the Evangelist, of St Ursula, etc., were painted on canvas. Venice, having joined the main stream of Italian art scarcely half a century before, had not taken long to part company with it on a matter of capital importance. The consequences of this new support were immense.

235 - ANDREA MANTEGNA. SAINT EUPHEMIA. NAPLES, MUSEO DI CAPODIMONTE.

The reasons that precipitated recourse to the new support cannot yet be very clearly distinguished: they were numerous and diverse. The change took place slowly and at first interested only a limited number of artists. The oldest Italian painting on canvas that we know of is Mantegna's *Santa Euphemia* (Naples) which dates from 1454. His *Presentation in the Temple* (Berlin), which is perhaps not earlier than his Mantuan period (*c.* 1466), is painted on a canvas nailed to a pine-wood stretcher. Although Mantegna continued to paint often on *tavole* (that is to say, on wood) his work includes a remarkable proportion of paintings on canvas, and these are of all kinds. They range from the small devotional image, like the *Madonna with the Sleeping Child* (Berlin; *c.* 1460) to large compositions like the *Victory Madonna* (Louvre; 1496) or the *Madonna and Saints* (Castello Sforzesco, Milan; 1497). The colouring may be very lively (as it is in these late works or in the series of allegories painted for Isabella d'Este), or it may be reduced to monochrome, to chiaroscuro; and here again there are both small scenes, treated with astonishing delicacy and precision, like the *Samson and Delilah* (National Gallery, London), the *Abraham* and the *David* (both in the Kunsthistorisches Museum, Vienna), etc., and the very large canvases of the *Triumph of Julius Caesar* (Hampton Court; nine episodes), intended to be hung like tapestries [10]. This diversity in the use of canvas was, it should be stressed, the sign of an interest, probably also an experimental bent, peculiar to Mantegna: no equivalent is to be found in Italy at that date in the work of any other master, and so productive a workshop as that of Perugino does not seem to have gone in for it. On the other hand, the *Madonna* painted by Cossa for Bologna in 1474 is in tempera on fine canvas.

Most of the large-scale compositions on canvas dating from the last years of the Quattrocento, when they were a novelty, were decorative in purpose: canvas was convenient for work on this scale. The huge paintings by Cosimo Tura, his *St George* and his *Annunciation* (4.13 m. × 3.38 m.), were organ doors for the cathedral of Ferrara (they were removed in the eighteenth century); Botticelli's *Birth of Venus* (1.72 m. × 2.78 m.) was a mural decoration, no doubt the equivalent of a movable tapestry; but the commonest occasion for such paintings was the official historical commemoration, such as the set (the *Justice of Trajan* and *Legend of Herkenbald*) painted by Rogier van der Weyden for the Hall of Justice in the Brussels Hôtel de Ville after 1439, when he was official painter to the city. The earliest cycle on canvas traceable,

36 - ANDREA MANTEGNA. THE TRIUMPH OF CAESAR : IV. THE VASE BEARERS — HAMPTON COURT PALACE.

238 - COSIMO TURA. ANNUNCIATION — FERRARA, MUSEO DEL DUOMO.

37 - COSIMO TURA. SAINT GEORGE AND THE PRINCESS (DETAIL) — FERRARA, MUSEO DEL DUOMO.

239 - GENTILE BELLINI. MIRACLE OF THE HOLY CROSS (DETAIL) — VENICE, ACCADEMIA.

as far as we know, in Italy, was the great series of the *Storie di Gesù e di Maria* painted by Jacopo Bellini for the Scuola di San Giovanni Evangelista between 1453 and 1465 (it has vanished, but was still known to Sansovino and Ridolfi in the sixteenth and seventeenth centuries); then came Gentile Bellini's cycle for the Sala del Consiglio in the Ducal Palace in 1476 (destroyed by fire in 1577). The next was the *Triumph of Julius Caesar* by Mantegna who, according to Vasari (III, 156) 'having more facility and experience in painting on canvas... obtained permission to execute this work not in fresco but on canvas.'

The Mantegna-Bellini circle had thus a special responsibility for the innovation, painting on canvas. The great increase in the use of the new support for pictures, including large-scale cycles, was due to the Venetians, in the decade 1460-1470. And it is at the beginning of his *Life* of Jacopo Bellini that Vasari, in one of his usual helpful and aptly placed digressions, makes the necessary points about the new technique. After mentioning the cycle in the Scuola di San Giovanni Evangelista, he adds: 'This cycle was painted on canvas, as has almost been usual in this city in which, unlike others, painting is rarely done on panels of poplar wood (or *gattice*); this tree, which ordinarily grows on the banks of rivers and pools, provides a wood that is admirably suitable for painting and keeps its firmness when it has been treated. But in Venice panels are not made, or, if they are, then from pine wood, which the city receives in abundance thanks to the Adige, which brings it from Germany, not to speak of what comes from Slavonia. And so in Venice they have continued to paint on canvas, either because it admits of compositions of the size required, or because of convenience for despatching pictures without trouble or expense' (*Vitae*, III, 152). These practical reasons were certainly the real ones: canvas made it possible to paint huge surfaces; the paintings could be easily transported from place to place; and the artist was not obliged, as with fresco, to do the work on the spot.

Not only did the new support set the painter free from the rules and practices imposed by the craft of fresco painting, but the new technique ran directly counter to the most firmly established Tuscan practice. When Ghirlandaio and Filippino Lippi—not to mention Michelangelo—were still climbing on to scaffoldings *(ponti)* to paint on the fresh plaster, the Venetian artists were unrolling huge canvases in their studios. Carpaccio painted at his own convenience the *St Ursula* cycle (1490 onwards) with its beautifully proportioned scenes and then the *San Giorgio dei Schiavoni* cycle (1502 onwards) on, it is true, a rather small scale (approx. 140 by 210-350 cm.) The qualities required were not the same: the wall exacts a grand design thoroughly worked out, while painting on canvas admits of revisions and freedom of detail. Venice had no equivalent to the monumental cycles of the Quattrocento; its decorative series were pictures very much enlarged.

The use of canvas had other consequences that more closely concerned handling and the overall effect of a

240 - GENTILE BELLINI. LORENZO GIUSTINIANI — VENICE, ACCADEMIA.

picture. The first canvases, which were of extremely fine and close woven linen, needed to be prepared with smooth plaster, as the wood panels were, so that no far-reaching change in technique was yet produced—though in Mantegna's *grisailles* the grain of the canvas begins to show through. Yet it is difficult to avoid seeing a relation between the transformation of pictorial technique that took place in Venice round about 1500 and the new practice of painting on canvas. The new way of handling paint resulted from the combination of oil as a medium and canvas as support with another innovation, that of attacking the picture directly without a preliminary drawing.

241 - VITTORE CARPACCIO. THE LEGEND OF ST URSUL
(DETAIL) — VENICE, ACCADEMIA.

242 - V. CARPACCIO (ATTR.). DESIGN FOR A TRIPTYCH — COPENHAGEN, STATENS MUSEUM FOR KUNST.

THE AGE OF THE ALTARPIECE

The altarpiece was a privileged object in a church. Brought into prominence by being placed on the altar, at the centre of the perspective of the interior, its volume, articulation and style made it one of the essential factors of the building's inner space. If it was made to harmonize with the architecture, it irresistibly concentrated the effect of the latter. If the building and the altarpiece were not contemporary, the altarpiece attracted attention to itself by contrast. In either case, it was the main liturgical illustration within the church and indicated the patron saint. Its connection with the saint after whom church or chapel were named and the circumstances of the dedication were usually decisive in determining the organization, often the structure, of the altarpiece.

These observations apply generally throughout Italy, where the altarpiece had enjoyed an uninterrupted favour since the fourteenth century; but they are above all true of Italy at the end of the fifteenth century, when this favour reached exceptional proportions. It is perhaps safe to state that, if the Trecento witnessed the birth of the altarpiece and the second half of the Quattrocento its improvement, the most interesting innovation occurred after the decade 1450-1460: the great period of the genre, both in quantity and in quality, comes between 1470 and 1495.

The almost systematic breaking up of the altarpieces, which began as early as the eighteenth century, has created a great many unnecessary problems. Scholars have based their work on the modern idea of the *picture*, at the expense of the composition as a whole; pieces of a predella and, often, fragments cut from a panel have been judged as distinct works of art, each to be given an attribution and to have its separate qualities described. Interpretation of the style has been driven astray and identification of an altarpiece as a whole rendered hazar-

244 - COSIMO TURA. MADONNA SURROUNDED BY MUSIC-MAKING ANGELS — LONDON, NATIONAL GALLERY.

43 - COSIMO TURA. ROVERELLA ALTARPIECE. RECONSTRUCTION.

dous for lack of awareness that the altarpiece is a unity, a kind of artistic cell—that it makes its effect both as a structure and as a system of images, that it presupposes both a coherent articulation of space and light and a precise iconographic arrangement. For example, the Roverella altarpiece, painted by Cosimo Tura in about 1472-1475 for the Olivetan church of San Giorgio fuori le Mura at Ferrara, included the tall panel of the *Madonna* (National Gallery, London, 2.30 m. × 1.02 m.) and the huge lunette of the *Pietà* (Louvre, 1.32 m. × 2.60 m.) which suggest that the whole may have formed an enormous two-storey colonnade with a powerful perspective (M. Salmi); the right-hand wingpiece represents Sts Paul and Maurelius with the donor (Galeria Colonna, Rome); of the left-hand wingpiece there survives only a head of St George (San Diego Museum, California); and Roberto Longhi has suggested, very plausibly, that three medallions (Gardner Museum, Boston; Fogg Art Museum, Cambridge; Metropolitan Museum, New York) belong to the predella. Sts Benedict and Bernard, mentioned in early descriptions, are missing. This is a case where the structure —with its rising perspective, cold light coming from the right and its extraordinary harmony between the strange ornamental motifs, the folds of the draperies and the stature of the figures—is more eloquent than the detail. Another fifteenth-century specialist in great altarpiece structures was Crivelli, and the polyptych painted by him for the church of San Domenico at Ascoli Piceno (1476) has recently been reconstructed, after its fragments had long been confused with the débris of another altarpiece. To take a third case, in the important work completed by Perugino in about 1498 for the church of San Pietro in Perugia there were, gravitating about the *Ascension* and the *God the Father in Glory* (Lyon Museum), medallions and panels that make little sense and have little interest apart from the monumental complex.

Every altarpiece had a central panel with or without wings, and with or without a crown-piece constituting an upper storey. This also might be more or less divided up (in Italy the wings were rarely treated as folding wingpieces). There was also a frame, which might or might not allow room for small figures or medallions to be placed one above another within the lateral pilasters, and might or might not include a series of small narrative panels or medallions within the lower border (known as the predella). The great variety of schemes that is to be found resulted from the play of all these variants. Some schemes included also carved parts, and in some cases

245 - FLORENCE. SAN MINIATO AL MONTE, CHAPEL OF THE CARDINAL OF PORTUGAL.
Shaded for demonstration. See list of illustrations.

246 - NAPLES. MONTE OLIVETO, MASTROIANNI CHAPEL.

the painted panels and medallions were replaced by reliefs. The simplest case was that of the framed panel or *pala*, the most complex that of the polyptych, forming a scaffolding of many medallions and panels.

There are relatively few examples of altarpieces—painted and carved—that were conceived for a chapel contemporary with them and were made to harmonize closely with its architecture. In the funerary chapel to the Cardinal of Portugal in the church of San Miniato (1467), the frame made by the arch fits exactly round the altar and the panel by the Pollaiuolo brothers: designed as a tabernacle, it is surmounted by an *oculus* through which it becomes part of the architecture, and is flanked by majestic red curtains that bind it into the polychrome scheme of the chapel. In the Mastroianni Chapel of the Monte Oliveto in Naples, the carved altarpiece by Giovanni da Maiano is likewise inserted with precision into the wall as a whole, and the *oculus* which touches the architrave binds it closely to the architecture.

247 - BENOZZO GOZZOLI. MADONNA AND CHILD WITH SAINTS — CASTELFIORENTINO, SANTA MARIA DELLA TOSSE.

The case of the altarpiece painted in fresco and isolated simply by a frame that adjusts it to the altar, within a scheme that is also in fresco, is very rare. One example is the small tabernacle of the Madonna della Tosse, near Castelfiorentino, where the whole decoration was done by Gozzoli in 1484. Here the back wall is occupied by five angels, who support a heavy red curtain framing a frescoed altarpiece—a painting within the painting—of the Madonna between four saints. Perugino's decoration of the Chapel of the Conception in old St Peter's, Rome may have been another example; the work was done in 1479 and destroyed in 1509; an early sketch gives us an idea of it; from this the relationship of entrance arc, painted wall, and *aediculum*, emerges clearly. There are more frequent instances of the altarpiece being continued by elements painted in fresco—angels or

248 - GIROLAMO MOCETTO. FOUR SAINTS — VENICE, SS. GIOVANNI E PAOLO.

worshipping figures. In such cases the altarpiece becomes almost comparable to the stained-glass window, by virtue of the authority with which it presents, as this did, a sublime and apparently real world. The stained-glass window, like the altarpiece, glorifies hieratic and motionless figures, and makes use of a limited but powerfully articulated space within which there reigns a light that converts the tones into enamel colours. This, at least, was how altarpieces were interpreted in Italy in the years around 1470-1480. Many painters tried their hands at this branch of art, following the experiments made by Ghiberti, Castagno and others in the middle of the century. Domenico Ghirlandaio did so in Santa Maria Novella; and in Northern Italy Cossa at San Giovanni in Monte, Costa at San Petronio in Bologna, and Mocetto at San Giovanni e San Paolo in Venice.

As a counterpart to this, there was the isolated altarpiece, prominent on the altar and treated as a miniature building: an example is depicted in one of Pinturicchio's frescoes in the Piccolomini Library (Siena Cathedral). With Crivelli's edifices in tiers, or again the Treviglio *pala*, the isolated altarpiece becomes a huge screen, rather like a well-fortified castle.

There is something rather surprising in the continued success of these artificial schemes. In the cities of the Marches—where during forty years a great many inordinately complex examples were produced (at Ascoli Piceno, at Camerino and elsewhere) and sometimes a modest church contained several altarpieces—it may be explained as a local attachment, a deliberate provincialism. But the demand was no less firm in the advanced cities of Central or Northern Italy; there the most important workshops readily attacked the problem of the altarpiece. Every altarpiece has some local distinction. The central theme is determined by the saint to whom the church is dedicated or the circumstances of the donation. Subordinate to it, certain obligatory subjects form iconographic couples—Annunciation and Crucifixion, or Nativity and Lamentation—and these too are affected by regional predilections. The glorification of the Madonna is by far the most frequent theme, and the parade of saints surrounding this is itself governed by three or four considerations: the nature of the principal scene; the saint to whom the sanctuary is dedicated, together with its particular function (especially if it is served by an Order, whose protectors the painting will doubtless be required to exalt; sometimes also the donor may wish to introduce his patron saint, or the city to do likewise. On these principles an *a priori* examination of the Sant' Agostino polyptych completed by Piero in 1469 made it possible to foresee what the wing figures must be (M. Meiss) and then find them (Sir Kenneth Clark): they are St Augustine (Lisbon), St Michael (London), St John (Frick Collection, New York), and St Nicholas of Tolentino (Poldi-Pezzoli Museum, Milan). On a sheet of notes by Leonardo there is a diagram with names of saints, which allow us to identify a project for an altarpiece (1497) for Brescia.

As Burckhardt has rightly shown, the two decisive innovations in the history of the *pala* were: first, the treatment of the panel within an *ediculo*—that is to say, its arrangement within an architectural unit on a reduced scale, which might have pilasters, a pediment, etc., of gilded wood, allowing the (painted) figures to be disposed in depth; and secondly—a direct consequence of this arrangement—the regrouping of the Virgin and saints in a kind of timeless gathering, known as a 'Sacra Conversazione.' These two devices were already well established by the middle of the century and familiar almost everywhere. They were not, for all that, adopted by all artists, yet the great altar of the Linaiuoli for St. Mark's in Florence, for which Ghiberti was called in to work on the frame, goes back to 1433. In the fine altarpiece of Santa Lucia dei Magnoli (*c.* 1445) Domenico Veneziano was still rather unnecessarily combining background niches with a colonnade, and complicating his problem strangely with pointed arches. To compare it with the contemporary altarpiece by Giovanni d'Alemagna in Venice (1445) is interesting: the Venetian artist attempts to unify the space as a Gothic enclosure, heightened by bastardized flamboyant forms. In the triptych by the Erri brothers in Modena (1465) the central panel is emphasized by the throne of the Madonna, and the wings with their gold backgrounds seem imperfectly harmonized with it; but it should be observed that the Modena painters were in this case inspired by Piero's Perugia altarpiece, in which there is the same inequality of treatment as between wings and principal panel. This ceremonial architecture very soon tended to be drawn together in the form of a baldachino or a loggia, and at the same time the sacred figures, instead of being placed in lateral niches or arcades, tended to be arranged—with due attention to hierarchy—in the same space, which all the resources of the art of the festivals were employed to enhance, embellish and render monumental.

The *pala* was, above all, a royal presentation of the Madonna, and it was essential to make her throne as impressive as possible. For this purpose there was the baldachino to cover it. Either of these enabled the artist to insert, in the form of cypresses, roses and orange trees, an allusion to the exquisite beauties of nature: painting made use of such allusions with considerable taste between 1450 and 1470, with less after that. After 1470, in Italy, the decorative elements tended to take a vigorous architectonic form, and the space of the altarpiece became more monumental: in Piero's last picture, the *Montefeltro Altarpiece* (*c.* 1470), the niche has become an apse, and the ostrich egg hanging at its centre stresses its spatial properties. The baldachino became the dome of a central-planned building in the *San Casciano Altarpiece* (1475) by Antonello. In the North of Italy the two solutions were soon combined: the round arch of a central-planned build-

249 - FILIPPINO LIPPI. VIRGIN AND CHILD WITH SAINTS — FLORENCE, UFFIZI.
Shaded for demonstration. See list of illustrations.

ing is treated by Giovanni Bellini, in the *San Zaccaria Altarpiece* (1505), as an apse, and the jutting edges of capitals make the spectator feel that there is an arch above him.

The ideal edifice, or *tempietto*, a square building open on three sides, one of which coincides with the picture-plane, became the favourite device of the Venetians after 1475-1480. The niche or deep arched space retained its credit with the Florentines; thus in Botticelli's *St. Barnabas Altarpiece* (1488) the throne is set in the thickness of the wall, in a shallow round-arched vault scooped out of it, and a tent-like tabernacle is added.

250 - ERCOLE DE' ROBERTI. ALTARPIECE — MILAN, BRERA.
Shaded for demonstration. See list of illustrations.

The Ferrarese drew much more spectacular—and less well-balanced—effects from flights of steps and schemes of arches: in the *San Lazaro Altarpiece* (destroyed in Berlin in 1945) the Madonna is placed high up within a decorative construction even stranger than that of Tura's Roverella altarpiece; the throne is an architectural complex with a opening underneath it, disclosing distant landscapes. A degree of complexity and of learned extravagance was reached, which it would be hard to surpass: in the so-called *Ravenna Altarpiece* (in the Brera), painted by Ercole Roberti in about 1480, the device of the baldachino

251 - PERUGINO. POLYPTYCH — ROME, VILLA ALBANI.
Shaded for demonstration. See list of illustrations.

wins a clear victory, while again the raised platform of which the Ferrarese were fond lays open a wide view to the horizon.

The type of structure that developed concurrently with this, out of the polyptych with its juxtaposed compartments, was that of the colonnade, scanned at need by columns that provided the horizontal divisions. This made it possible to frame several groups within an arcaded system—a device used by Perugino in his *Albani Polyptych* (Rome) in 1491 (possibly 1482). The colonnade, viewed frontally and containing a series of enclosed bays,

252 - PERUGINO. POLYPTYCH (DETAIL): VIRGIN OF THE ANNUNCIATION — ROME, VILLA ALBANI.

supplied the sacred figure with a framing sky: this is the case with the Madonna in Perugino's huge and rather mediocre *Fano Altarpiece* (1497) in which the arcade rhythm gives the figures of the saints their places within the whole. It was also possible to lay out elaborate regular constructions in two or three storeys, with a fully worked-out perspective—illusionist lines of recession. In the *Treviglio Altarpiece* Zenale and Butinone, by taking up again Mantegna's idea of the *ediculo* with pilasters in his *San Zeno Pala* and extending this into many compartments enhanced by grilles and gilded ornamental motifs.

253 - B. BUTINONE AND B. ZENALE. POLYPTYCH — TREVIGLIO, SAN MARTINO.

254 - B. BUTINONE AND B. ZENALE. POLYPTYCH (DETAIL
ST MARTIN — TREVIGLIO, SAN MARTINO.

BEN DICTVS
S·NICOLAVS TOLEN

255 - A. MANTEGNA. MADONNA DELLA VITTORIA. PARIS, LOUVRE. Shaded for demonstration. See list of illustrations.

256 - G.B. CIMA DA CONEGLIANO. ALTARPIECE — VICENZA. Shaded for demonstration. See list of illustrations.

The combination of the Florentine formula, repeated monotonously by Ghirlandaio and his workshop, with the Ferrarese or Emilian method, took place unexpectedly in one of the earliest works of Cima da Conegliano, the *Vicenza Altarpiece* (dated 1489), in which the architecture, treated as a trellis, enfolds the Madonna, between the leafage of two orange trees. This enchanting image was not followed up: Cima returned to 'Sacre Conversazione' under arches or with landscape backgrounds. Venetian painting could wait no longer to call in sky and flowers: the stylistic methods of the Ferrarese inevitably did not suit it. Giovanni Bellini in his *Pesaro Altarpiece* (1475), had enhanced the luminous unity of the panel. And when Giorgione, in his *Castelfranco Altarpiece*, set his vistas of the Venetian mainland above the two saints and exalted landscape at the expense of architecture, the Quattrocento experiment was at an end.

257 - GIORGIONE. THE VIRGIN AND CHILD BETWEEN ST FRANCIS AND ST LIBERALE. CASTELFRANCO, SAN LIBERALE. Shaded for demonstration. See list of illustrations.

THE TURNING-POINT OF 1475. FLEMISH INFLUENCE AND THE RISE OF VENICE

Shortly after 1470 the whole of Italy seemed possessed by the need for a grand style. Tura's Roverella altarpiece, as we have seen, took the potentialities of Piero's style to the limit of resistance with the close-packed and hardened forms that were equally dear to him. And from 1472 to 1475, in Bologna, Cossa produced a series of major works, the *Madonna del Barracano*, the *Pala delle Osservanti* and the *Griffoni Polyptych*. In the last of these he placed a tall St Vincent Ferrer on a pedestal II—one of the first important examples of the tendency (of which more below) to magnify the individual figure in this way—and achieved for this church in Bologna a huge composition; its monumental quality goes a little too far in the direction of heavy forms, but these are redeemed by the vivacity of the predella—added later, it seems, by Ercole de' Roberti. This broad, hard and ornate manner met, indeed, with consideration and apparent approval in Venice, where Bartolommeo Vivarini, leaping ahead of his brother Antonio, composed his triptych for Santa Maria Formosa (1473), going on later to establish his talent firmly with his successful polyptych for San Giovanni in Bragora (1478).

In comparison, at that moment, the Bellinis seemed to have little to say. Jacopo had just died (1470), bequeathing to his *bottegha* at least as much uncertainty as guidance. Gentile's profile of Lorenzo Giustiniani (1465) contained no quality strong enough to contradict the authority of the sharp, close style. Giovanni was still under the influence of Mantegna's style—or, more precisely, of the vague Squarcionism which had gained ground in Venice. Crivelli, who had experienced the same influence fifteen years earlier and was now a voluntary exile, produced in

258 - F. DEL COSSA. GRIFFONI ALTARPIECE (DETAIL): ST VINCENT FERRER — LONDON, NATIONAL GALLERY.

259 - B. VIVARINI. POLYPTYCH — VENICE, SAN GIOVANNI IN BRAGORA.

1473 the huge polyptych for Ascoli Piceno, one of his masterpieces of precision and vigour. Thus in the North the situation seemed well defined. Mantegna himself, in 1474, finished the decoration of the Camera degli Sposi at Mantua, which achieved the conversion of the 'hard style' to secular decoration; from framing arches and garlands he went on to imitation vaults and domes, creating with them a vigorous setting for the scenes of contemporary life which followed the historical scenes.

Thus Mantua, Ferrara and Venice, taken together formed an impressive constellation in the years 1470-1475. Suddenly all the provincial, rather naïve products of Squarcionism were made to look old, and men were on the point of forgetting the impulse once given by that Paduan centre and by the somewhat legendary Squarcione, who in 1474 died at the age of seventy-seven, discredited by his law suits. It is, of course, true that he cannot be given credit for the nobility of tone that makes itself felt in Mantegna's processions of legionaries, for the kind of metamorphosis of male and female saints into precious stones that is achieved by Tura and Cossa, or for the graphic quality of Crivelli's gold threads and of his forms that seem like goldsmiths' work; the major virtues of the style dominant in those remarkable years have nothing to do with Squarcionism and its Gothic interpretation of the Renaissance. And yet his 'harsh manner'—to take up a phrase of Vasari's and use it without pejorative intent—did make its mark for a time: it even produced, shortly after the peak of its own growth, a certain res-

260 - CARLO CRIVELLI. POLYPTYCH (DETAIL) — ASCOLI PICENO, CATHEDRAL.

261 - S. BOTTICELLI. ADORATION OF THE KINGS — LONDON, NATIONAL GALLERY.

ponse in Florence. Botticelli, in the *Adoration of the Kings* commissioned from him by Zanobi del Lama (1475-1476), was still closely attached to the style of Lippi and Pollaiuolo; but in the series of portraits that followed this—the *Young Woman known as Simonetta* (Pitti Gallery, Florence, *c.* 1475) and the *Giuliano de' Medici* (Washington, 1478)—there is to be found an almost exclusive feeling for ridges and for line, a more graphic, less plastic feeling that was nourished from other sources. The *Primavera* (*c.* 1478), which is more diluted, and the *Saint Augustine* for the Ognissanti (*c.* 1480), which is more concentrated and more strongly coloured, exhibit the two ways in which it was possible for one of the most gifted Florentines of his generation to react to the great problem of the moment. These examples, coming in succession, have suggested the hypothesis of a kind of 'return to Gothic' in the years 1475-1490: this is supposed to be shown by the insistence with which the forms are broken up, the contours and folds interrupted, by the stress laid on expressive gesture, by the accumulation of

262 - S. BOTTICELLI. PORTRAIT OF A WOMAN — FLORENCE, PALAZZO PITTI.

263 - S. BOTTICELLI. PORTRAIT OF GIULIANO DE' MEDICI — WASHINGTON, NATIONAL GALLERY.

264 - S. BOTTICELLI. ST AUGUSTINE IN MEDITATION (DETAIL)
FLORENCE, OGNISSANTI.

266 - COSIMO TURA. ST JAMES — CAEN, MUSÉE.

details from all sources, perhaps also by the anti-realism of the colour. But chronology forbids us to group the original devices of the Ferrarese, firmly established by 1460, and the *bizzarie* of Filippino Lippi thirty years later; it is dangerous to apply 'neo-Gothic' to Italy after 1460, for the detachment from Gothic formulae hardly became general before then. Moreover, this undeniable reaction in favour of the accidents of form may very well have had different causes in Padua, in Venice and in Tuscany.

265 - S. BOTTICELLI. PRIMAVERA (DETAIL) — FLORENCE, UFFIZI.

267 - ERCOLE DE' ROBERTI. GRIFFONI ALTARPIECE (DETAIL). ST MICHAEL — PARIS, LOUVRE.

268 - FILIPPINO LIPPI. MIRACLE OF ST PHILIP (DETAIL) — FLORENCE, SANTA MARIA NOVELLA.

269 - PIERO DELLA FRANCESCA. MONTEFELTRO ALTARPIECE — MILAN, BRERA.

270 - PIERO DELLA FRANCESCA. MONTEFELTRO ALTARPIECE (DETAIL) — MILAN, BRERA.

This tendency to rewrite and reinterpret the monumental forms with an intensive animation and wealth of effect constituted an important modification of Piero's style and prepared the way for its extinction. Piero's last picture, the *Montefeltro Altarpiece*, probably dates from 1472, and was partly by assistants; the young Signorelli, in his *Flagellation* (*c.* 1475), shows a fine fidelity to the master's style, but it is already dramatized and somewhat forced. At this point everything was destined to be changed by an unexpected event that had considerable consequences, and which was destined, indeed, to consolidate

271 - ANDREA MANTEGNA. MARTYRDOM OF ST SEBASTIAN — PARIS, LOUVRE.

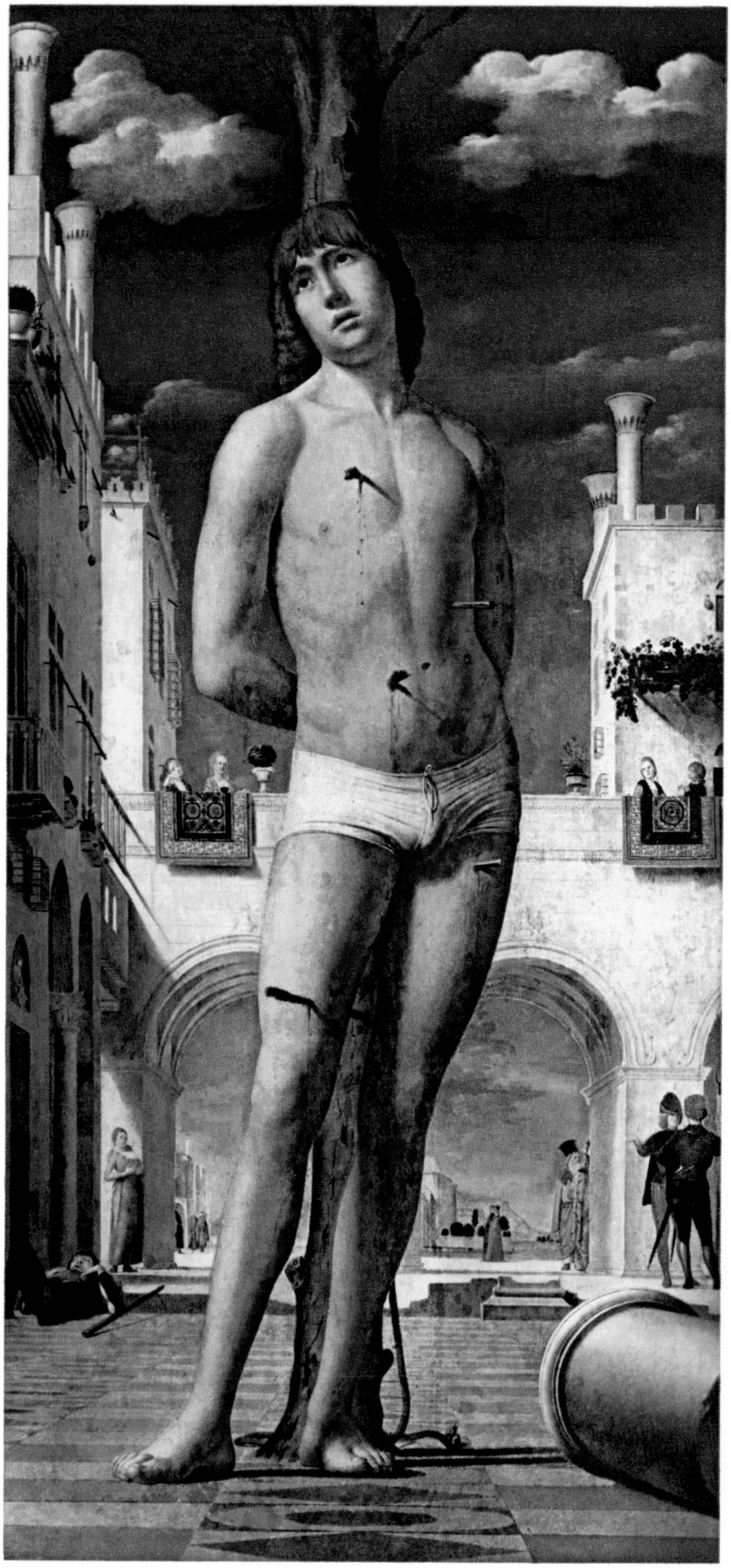

272 - A. DA MESSINA. MARTYRDOM OF ST SEBASTIAN — DRESDEN.

and give new life to one essential aspect of Pierfrancescanism: attention to colour, to its properties in space and to its action under a given light and in a given atmosphere. This attitude to colour, with the event that brought it to a head, makes the years around 1475 one of the main joints in the articulation of the history of modern painting. If we look for the places where resistance to the 'harsh' and broken up style made itself felt, we find that they are all either in the South or connected in some way with Piero's zone of influence: in Perugia, the rose-pink, lightweight, theatrical architecture of the *Life of San Bernardino* (1473) felicitously maintains the harmonious style, and in Rome, the already mentioned fresco by Melozzo for the Vatican Library confers upon space a remarkable dignity as a receptacle for light. But these manifestations needed to be confirmed; and now a southerner, Antonello da Messina, aroused, on his way from Naples to Venice, a new interest in colour treated as a means of bringing out light, no longer simply as a function of design. In addition, he stimulated pictorial technique by spreading Flemish procedures that were already familiar to southern artists. These things give his journey the significance of a reversal of style.

And indeed events now followed quickly. It seems likely that he visited Florence and there, slightly before 1475, excited a passing interest in the strong handling of paint; but it was in Venice, where he arrived in 1475 and in the following year produced a major demonstration in the form of his *San Casciano Altarpiece*, that Antonello confirmed at the psychological moment the new conclusions just reached, in the Pesaro altarpiece, by the young Giovanni Bellini, brought face to face with the example of Piero della Francesca. In a letter written in 1476 to Galeazzo Sforza, Pietro Bon declared that the work of Antonello 'promises to become one of the most brilliant, whether in Italy or abroad'. The reason for the Venetians to be so interested was that they now had before their eyes a new type of altarpiece. It was partly a development of Piero's final formula, that of the *Montefeltro Altarpiece*, with a unified architectural space, a rising perspective, and a throne raised very high as in many works by Mantegna.

The effect was instantaneous. The reconstitution of the altarpiece — mutilated in the seventeenth century—has indeed been facilitated by the paintings of Alvise Vivarini (*Altarpiece with Saints*, destroyed in 1945 in Berlin), of B. Montagna (*Madonna with four Saints*, *c.* 1480, Vicenza) and especially of Giovanni Bellini (the *San Giobbè Altarpiece* in particular), all of which were derived from it. But as

273 - A. DA MESSINA. SAN CASSIANO ALTARPIECE, RECONSTRUCTION.

274 - ANTONELLO DA MESSINA. SAN CASSIANO ALTARPIECE (DETAIL): ST NICHOLAS AND ST MARY MAGDALEN. VIENNA, KUNSTHISTORISCHES MUSEUM.

275 - ANTONELLO DA MESSINA. PIETÀ WITH ANGELS — VENICE, MUSEO CORRER.

276 - ANTONELLO DA MESSINA. ANNUNCIATION (DETAIL) — SYRACUSE, PALAZZO BELLOMO MUSEUM.

277 - ANTONELLO DA MESSINA. 'SALVATOR MUNDI' — LONDON, NATIONAL GALLERY.

278 - GIOVANNI BELLINI. STIGMATIZATION OF ST FRANCIS — NEW YORK, FRICK COLLECTION.

early as 1480, and in the years just after the death of Antonello, Giovanni Bellini was already developing those amber tones and that permeating, golden atmosphere which characterize his admirable *Transfiguration* (Pinacoteca, Naples); this atmosphere extended to the whole natural scene and took possession of the landscape in the extraordinary *San Francesco* (Frick Collection, New York). It was a style that made everything seem possible. In the field of the three-quarters bust and of religious themes like that of the *Salvator Mundi* (National Gallery, London) which now became popular in Italy, or like the *Crucifixion* (1475, Antwerp Museum), Antonello adapted Flemish techniques precisely to Italian sensibility, making progress from the ground prepared by Piero della Francesca. Giovanni Bellini reacted so quickly that he became the representative of the new style; he thus gained for himself the same kind of authority that Manet had among the moderns. The most active group seems to have formed itself about him, but it was not

279 - E. DE' ROBERTI. ALTARPIECE (DETAIL). MILAN, BRERA.

the only one capable of representing the new ideas: thus Carpaccio addressed himself to Antonello and perhaps to Giovanni; Cima moved from Vivarini to Antonello and Giovanni, and Catena followed suit. Quite a number of young painters rallied to the new flag—Palma, Previtali, Titian among them. Cariani took the 'warm' style to Bergamo, Bartolomeo Montagna to Vicenza. In a few years the authority of Mantegna and of the hard style was broken; and at one blow the artists who, like Bartolomeo Vivarini or Crivelli, had become set in the methods of 1470 (though Crivelli, in his admirable 1493 *Pietà*, could still add a final intensity to his style) became old-fashioned.

But one man had been still quicker, and had seized on the new potentialities with an imaginative force greater than that of the Venetians. This was the Ferrarese, Ercole de' Roberti—especially in the *Ravenna Altarpiece* (Brera), in which the tall female saint in red on the left, placed on the platform of the throne, is outlined against the sky with a new authority. Thus, as Roberto Longhi has put it, 'In about 1480 Ferrarese art succeeded, thanks to Ercole, in identifying itself with this fundamental Italian change of course, which had achieved for the first time a national unity—for the first time an agreement between North, Centre and South—in the meeting of Antonello and Giovanni Bellini on the basis of the "synthesizing moduli" of Piero della Francesca.' If we add that it was precisely between 1477 and 1488 that the (now destroyed) frescoes of the Garganelli Chapel in the church of San Pietro in Bologna were painted, there can hardly be any doubt that something important took shape between Bologna and Ferrara thanks to Ercole. Nothing equivalent to the San Pietro frescoes was produced during those ten years, at least not if we judge from the contemporary opinions that have come down to us. The deferential enthusiasm shown by Vasari was certainly inspired by Michelangelo, who spent several months in 1494 in Bologna and stated that Roberti's work was worth 'half Rome'. Through Bologna Ferrarese art was soon in communication with other centres, in particular with Florentine painting, which was then coming a little way out of its isolation. One of those who must be held to have played a part in these new alliances is Lorenzo Costa, one of the last stars of Ferrarese painting, which was now obliged to compromise [12].

Meanwhile Flemish painting had not only become known in Italy through intermediaries like Antonello: it had already found a foothold in Urbino, awakening the

280 - JUSTUS OF GHENT. INSTITUTION OF THE EUCHARIST — URBINO, NATIONAL GALLERY OF THE MARCHES.

interest of Piero della Francesca and his friends; in Florence and in Umbria, too, it had been assimilated by some of the best-known workshops. Though Federico da Montefeltro had no lack of architects and decorative sculptors, he ran short of painters when Piero della Francesca stopped working for him. Piero's diptych of the princely couple dates from 1469, and the *Sinigallia Madonna* from 1472. This seems to indicate the moment at which Piero gave up. The vicissitudes of the *Eucharist Pala*, commissioned by the Urbino Brotherhood of Corpus

281 - PEDRO BERRUGUETE. ARISTOTLE — PARIS, LOUVRE.

282 - PEDRO BERRUGUETE. SOLON — PARIS, LOUVRE.

Domini, dragged on for nearly ten years: in 1466 there had been negotiations about it with a Foligno painter, in 1467-8 with Uccello, who painted the famous predella, in 1469 with Piero; finally, in 1473-1475, payments were made for the central panel to 'Magistro Giusto da Gand dipintore', who had just been summoned to the castle by Federico. Vespasiano da Bisticci, the Duke's librarian, gives the reason—at first sight somewhat surprising—for this choice: 'Being very knowledgeable in matters of painting, and unable to find an Italian master who could paint in oils', the Duke 'finally approached a Flemish painter and had him come to Urbino'.

Apart from the Corpus Domini Pala, Justus of Ghent

283 - PEDRO BERRUGUETE. PIETÀ WITH ANGELS — MILAN, BRERA.

worked on the series of 'illustrious men' in the *studiolo*. But the authorship of the whole series cannot be attributed to him: examination of the panels shows that they are by at least two hands, and Justus's manner, so far as it is known from works that are certainly his, could hardly account for the whole. And indeed Justus disappears from the documents after 1475, which leaves him little time for work of wide scope; moreover, an entry made in April 1477 mentions the presence of a 'Pietro Spagnolo' at Urbino, while a passage written—much later, it is true—by Pablo de Cespedes (1604) precisely complements the evidence of Vespasiano da Bisticci with a mention of Pedro Berruguete working at the Ducal Palace.

CONFALONERIVS

285 - PEDRO BERRUGUETE (ATTR.). FEDERICO DA MONTEFELTRO AND HIS SON GUIDOBALDO — URBINO, NATIONAL GALLERY.

There were, therefore, not one but two foreign painters at Urbino, representing two aspects of Flemish style, the rich modelling of van Eyck and the precision of Rogier. But the most interesting of the Urbino pictures—the portrait of the *Duke with Guidobaldo*, the *Lecture* (Windsor Castle) and the panels of the *Liberal Arts* (of which only two survive, in the National Gallery, London)—can hardly have been painted by either of these two artists; the handling is unctuous and attentive to textures and light. While this indicates a painter who had reacted to the Flemish contribution—as Piero had just done in his *Sini-*

284 - UNIDENTIFIED MASTER. ALLEGORY OF MUSIC. LONDON, NATIONAL GALLERY.

286 - PIERO DELLA FRANCESCA. NATIVITY — LONDON, NATIONAL GALLERY.

gallia Madonna and, as regards both composition and landscape, in his *Nativity* (National Gallery, London) the feeling of space, the mastery of perspective and the control of the principal effect have, nevertheless, nothing Flemish about them. The whole mystery of the significance of Urbino in painting hangs on the discovery of the 'third man'; the names suggested so far, but unconvincingly, are those of Melozzo da Forlì and Giovanni Santi.

Piero's style itself contains important signs of borrowings from, or at least responses to Flemish painting, —of which Mantegna had already taken account. The *Sinigallia Madonna* is the second Italian example of a Ma-

287 - UNIDENTIFIED MASTER, LECTURE AT THE COURT OF URBINO. WINDSOR CASTLE, ROYAL COLLECTION.

donna depicted in a room (the other being that painted by Filippo Lippi in 1437,) and the *Montefeltro Altarpiece* is the first example of a 'Sacra rappresentazione' in a church interior; but both these themes had been familiar to Flemish art for the last thirty or forty years. Piero's innovations were not only iconographic: an increased attention to textures and other materials presupposes a more precise knowledge of the Northern masters. The strength of Piero's art was that it could assimilate, in its own way, the technique of oil painting, which was the glory of the art of Northern Europe. At the same moment Antonello was revealing this to Venice having probably stopped at Florence on the way. In Florence the technique of oil painting had been known since 1425-1430 and had received more serious consideration in about 1450, but it was now in the decade under discussion, finally tried out and put into practice[13]. The most alert reaction to it came, it seems, from Verrocchio's studio. Leonardo joined that studio in about 1464, and among his earliest notes there are recipes for varnish and for mixtures of colours—'*per fare olio buono a dipignere: una parte d'olio, una di prima di trementina e una di seconda*' (Cod. Atlanticus, 262 r° (e)). The 'finished' style practised in that studio and the striving after velvety effects in the work of Lorenzo di Credi, another pupil of Verrocchio, are significant.

288 - A. POLLAIUOLO. THE RAPE OF DEIANEIRA — YALE, ART GALLERY.

It was a real revolution; the *tempera* technique, with its matt surface and its wealth of tonality, was fundamentally called in question by the new method of laying on colour. The new way of painting led artists in a direction opposed to Italian habits, and even the art of fresco painting was in the end affected. Here too the end of the fifteenth century was a period of crisis. The challenge of Flemish painting reached its full force in about 1475-1485; and at this moment we find, in many different places, a rather chaotic evolution in landscape and in portrait painting.

Just when the great workshops were familiarizing themselves with the practice of oil painting, Flemish pictures were arriving in Italy. Chief among these—the one that attracted general attention—was the Portinari Triptych, sent by the Portinari firm to the church of Sant' Egidio in Florence. It is fairly easy to evaluate the effect of the Northern examples in such cases as Botticelli's *St Augustine*, or Ghirlandaio's *St. Jerome* in the Ognissanti; yet to reconstitute the sequence of artistic events and the production of the Florentine workshops during this period is a delicate task. One and the same picture, the *Tobias and the Angel* in the National Gallery, London, painted in about 1473, has been attributed in turn to Antonio Pollaiuolo, Domenico Ghirlandaio, Verrocchio, and finally to Perugino—who indeed seems to have been present in Florence between 1470 and 1475, working with Verrocchio. The *St Sebastian* by one of the Pollaiuolo brothers was painted in about 1475 for an oratory depen-

289 - ANTONIO POLLAIUOLO. THE RAPE OF DEIANEI
(DETAIL) — YALE, ART GALLERY.

290 - STUDIO OF VERROCCHIO. TOBIAS AND THE ARCHANGEL RAPHAEL — LONDON, NATIONAL GALLERY.

dent on the Annunziata. In the present state of our knowledge it is useless to try to determine whether the painter was Antonio or Piero; Vasari says it was Antonio, and there seems no reason why the best of the Pollaiuolesque pictures should not be attributed to this strong personality, beginning with the admirable *Apollo and Daphne* (London). The great panel of *Hercules and Deianeira* (Yale Art Gallery) is slightly later. All these are extremely ambitious works: they brought the relations between figure and landscape to the fore in Florence. In this context it is easier to understand the work done on the *Baptism of Christ* by Verrocchio: the picture was sketched out in *tempera*, and certain parts of it were then repainted in oil—parts of the landscape, in particular, by Leonardo. But it had been preceded by several works in which the same problem was attacked, notably the *Crucifixion* for the church at Argiano and the *Archangel Raphael with Tobias* (London). The way in which the figures are outlined and their harmonization with the ground, the horizon and the sky, are as different as possible in these two pictures, both of which are of

291 - STUDIO OF PIERO POLLAIUOLO. THE CRUCIFIED CHRIST BETWEEN ST JEROME AND ST ANTHONY — ARGIANO (VAL DI PESA), SANTA MARIA E ANGIOLO.

medium size and were painted between 1465 and 1470. In one of them the landscape is austere and sculptural like the saints for whom it is the setting; in the other the stones, like the clouds, simply accentuate and diversify the ornamental charm of sleeves, folds and hair. One and the same painter would be unthinkable: this is the parting of the ways between two tendencies. If (as certain similarities suggest) the second is given to Perugino, working under the influence of Verrocchio, it would be rash to attribute to him the first as well [14].

Though Florence was beginning to lose glamour and power after 1480-1485, the amplitude of the work accomplished there should none the less be noted—especially in Verrocchio's circle and by reaction against him. Some of the pictures that are most significant for the art of landscape were painted during this phase. They give permanent embodiment to two opposite attitudes: in contrast with Botticelli, who in his *Birth of Venus* and *Primavera* had resolved to reduce the landscape to its own symbol, Leonardo was to paint his *Virgin of the*

294 - S. BOTTICELLI. PRIMAVERA (DETAIL) — FLORENCE, UFFIZI.

Rocks (possibly begun in Florence, and finished after 1482) as an answer to the conceptions uppermost in Florence: the muted, blue-green medium of its cave has nothing in common with the then current forms of landscape, and that strange image had no perceptible echo till the end of the century. But already Perugino, in the so-called *Galitzine Triptych* (National Gallery, Washington), was conferring upon rocks and vegetation a rhythm that enabled him, through a softened light, to bend nature to the service of the figures. The relaxation had begun.

295 - LEONARDO DA VINCI. THE VIRGIN OF THE ROCKS — PARIS, LOUVRE.

296 - PERUGINO, APOLLO AND MARSYAS — PARIS, LOUVRE.

SUCCESS AND LIMITS OF THE 'DOLCE STIL'; REGIONAL REACTIONS

A comparison between Francia and (for instance) the ageing Ercole de' Roberti shows, as clearly as anything, the fall in tension that occurred in about 1495. It was a sign of the desire to attain smoothness of style at all costs. The ambitions of the Ferrarese artists were called in question, and the new tendency appeared plainly in Bologna, where Costa had taken over: his *Nativity* (Lyon) and the *Ghedini Pala*, painted for San Giovanni in Monte, demonstrated how far an artist was prepared to carry the increasing flexibility of the forms, the fear of being too explicit, and the relative importance accorded to the clear charm of the landscape.

The ambitious, sly Perugino was the strong man of this inclination towards sweetness, this cumulative exaltation of softness. It is hard to forgive the brilliant designer of the *Life of San Bernardino*, the painter of the *Remission of the Keys*, for the panderings and insincerities in which he indulged ceaselessly after 1490: they were due, at least in part, to his prodigious success. He directed simultaneously a workshop in Perugia and another in Florence. Here he became supreme, and in the end his *Dead Christ* unleashed the enthusiasm both of the nuns of Santa Chiara and of Francesco del Pugliese, a solid burgess who was a follower of Savonarola. The incontestable superiority of the master from Perugia lay in his power of scanning space with areas of emptiness, with harmoniously distributed silences, and in the irradiation of his pale colours; and, from the *Galitzine Triptych* (*c.* 1480) to the three compartments of the *Crucifixion* painted for Santa Maria Maddalena dei Pazzi (1493-1496) a growing assurance makes itself felt. The charming small picture of *Apollo and Marsyas* in the Louvre, which must still be given to Perugino and placed between those two works, marks the happiest and most coherent moment of the *dolce stil* that was now the fashion.

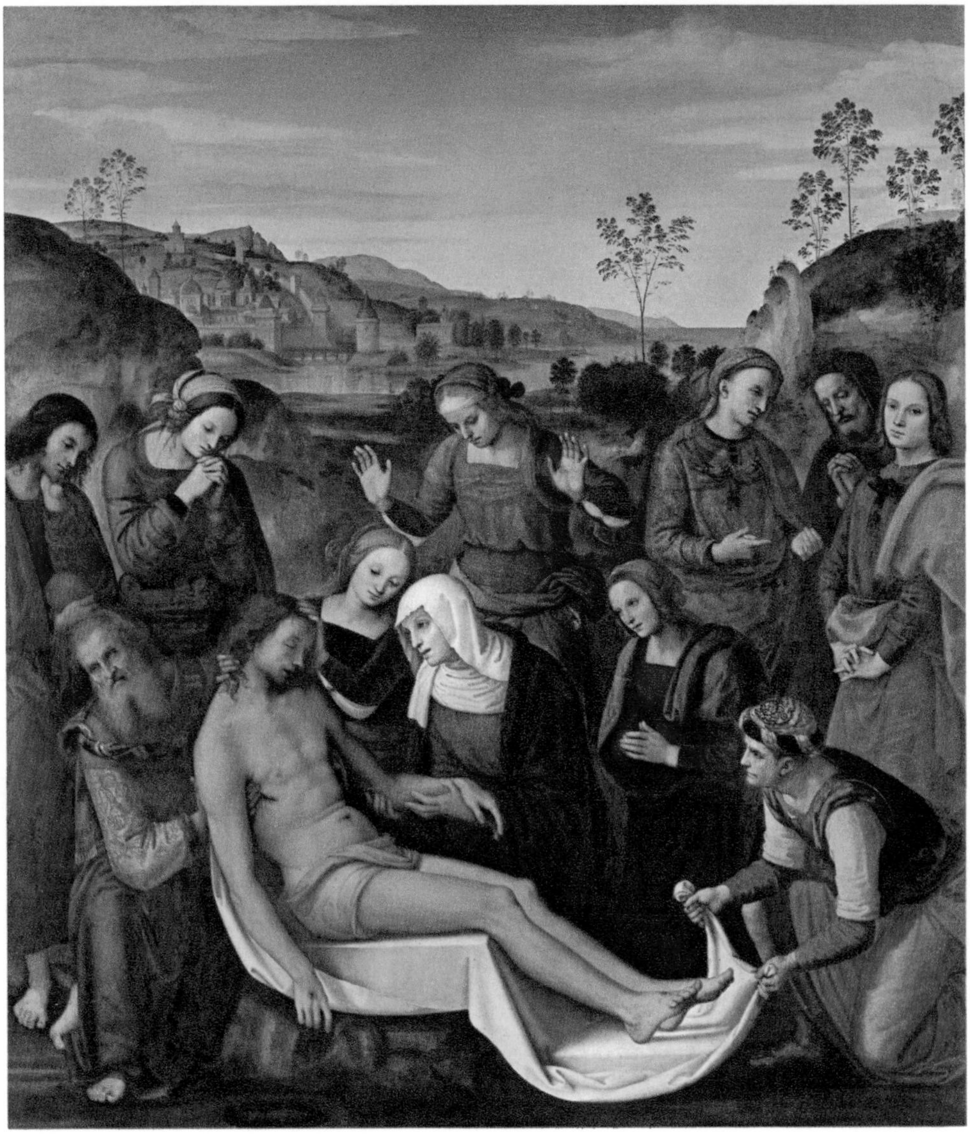

297 - PERUGINO. THE LAMENTATION. FLORENCE, PALAZZO PITTI.

Perugino was an Italian equivalent to Memling. His manner soon had the effect of diffusing mawkishness in the shape of these liquid-faced, misty-eyed male and female saints that the Florentines themselves were to find unendurable in fifteen years' time. In addition, Perugino's fame was seriously compromised by his negligence in the use of oil in some of his pictures; these began all too soon to show cracks through not drying properly. In 1503-4 it was possible for Michelangelo to attack him insolently in public and to denounce his art as *goffo* (inept).

298 - PERUGINO. THE CRUCIFIXION (DETAIL) — FLORENCE, SANTA MARIA MADDALENA DE' PAZZI.

All the same, the vogue of Peruginism was very great. It signified a check to the seething of forms, to ornament and to caprice; it swiftly ended the last lingerings of Squarcionism, as well as the tense romantic feeling of the Sienese and Tuscan narrative painters. It represented the final form of 'modernism,' the last word of the century.

In the years round about 1495 it was not Bramante or Leonardo who occupied the attention of Lodovico il Moro: Perugino was the man he wanted. Perugino was the artist called in to complete both Filippino's *Descent from the Cross* in Florence, and the allegorical cycle of the Mantua *studiolo*, which Mantegna had begun. Above all—and this is clearly stated by Vasari, whose tendency was to despise him and to consider him as merely the precursor of Raphael—Perugino was the Italian painter with the greatest authority in the West at the end of the century.

299 - PERUGINO. THE MARRIAGE OF THE VIRGIN — CAEN, MUSÉE.

300 - RAPHAEL. THE MARRIAGE OF THE VIRGIN — MILAN, BRERA.

302 - PIERO DI COSIMO. THE DEATH OF PROCRIS (DETAIL) — LONDON, NATIONAL GALLERY.

At that moment the demoralization of the Tuscan painters seems to have been fairly serious, even before the Savonarolan revolution, which was the political and religious expression of a malaise that went further. Leonardo had pulled out and gone to Milan: when he returned in 1501-2, it was to astonish his compatriots with output in an original style, which broke—or seemed to break—with the conceptions of the Quattrocento. With Verrocchio gone, Lorenzo di Credi had been carrying on the work of the studio with a maniacal precision, perfecting a technique of drawing and painting that was as sterilizing as it was meticulous. This was the moment of that artistic decline represented by the eclectic and limited Raffaellino. The most gifted of them all, Piero di Cosimo, oscillated between a quasi-Flemish realism heightened by subtle meanings (his *Nativity* is an attractive example) and freely fantastic compositions like his admirable series on prehistoric life—the revenge of a neurotic genius in his

301 - PIERO DI COSIMO. LEGEND OF PROMETHEUS (DETAIL). STRASBOURG, MUSÉE.

303 - PIERO DI COSIMO. HUNTING SCENE (DETAIL) — NEW YORK, METROPOLITAN MUSEUM OF ART.

304 - PIERO DI COSIMO. THE VIRGIN AND CHILD — PARIS, LOUVRE.

306 - RAFFAELLINO DEL GARBO. PIETÀ WITH SAINTS — MUNICH, PINAKOTHEK.

exasperation. The most intelligent, and the most uncertain, was surely Filippino Lippi, who 'had been deflected from his natural path by the relief-painting which Perugino's and Signorelli's use of oils had made possible, added to the achievements of Leonardian dynamism and luminism' (C. Gamba). The ambition to treat figures in the light and brilliance of nature, putting aside the usual architectural settings, was shown plainly, as early as 1486, in his *Virgin appearing to St Bernard;* a still more complete and less successful example is his *Christ appearing to his Mother* (*c.* 1495, Munich), which confirms the change of direction taken by the charming painter of Botticellian *cassoni* (the painter had been provisionally isolated by Berenson under the name Amico di Sandro). His work in Rome on the decoration of the Caraffa Chapel (1492-3) made him the painter-archaeologist *par excellence*, but he had also an impulsiveness and a feeling for fantastic settings—comparable to those of Piero di Cosimo—that render his frescoes in the Strozzi Chapel an irreplaceable manifestation of the anti-classical tendency at the end of the century that is frequently described as 'Quattrocento Mannerism'.

305 - FILIPPINO LIPPI. TABERNACLE (DETAIL): THE VIRGIN AND CHILD — PRATO, 'CANTO AL MERCATALE'.

307 - LUCA SIGNORELLI. TWO NUDES — CAMBRIDGE, FITZWILLIAM MUSEUM.

Far away, in Cortona—which he was never to leave again—Signorelli, having finished his cycle at Orvieto, and now forgotten by almost everyone, continued the doomed epic of the 'hard style.' Lorenzo di Credi, in so

308 - S. BOTTICELLI. PIETÀ — MUNICH, PINAKOTHEK.

far as the order of his output can be reconstituted, seems to have pushed steadily further his smooth manner and his striving for enamelled, polished forms without a speck of dust on them; but he was merely carrying on what he had learned from Verrocchio. And it is striking to see with what facility, after 1500, the veterans of the earlier workshops, as well as the younger artists, fell under the enchantment of the innovator Leonardo. For a few years Florence became once more a centre at which an artist could learn, and it was there that the young Raphael found his path. Paradoxically, the only artist capable of revitalizing the earlier 'virile' style was Botticelli: the complete proof of this is his impressive *Pietà* in Munich (which cannot be earlier than 1490, and dates probably from *c.* 1500)—simplified, monumental, and rejecting all recourse to landscape and to graciousness of colour. There occurred in Florence at that moment,

310 - S. BOTTICELLI. THE STORY OF VIRGINIA — BERGAMO, ACCADEMIA CARRARA.

like a sign of remorse, or at least of regret—what amounts to a return in force to the effort to embody architecture in painting. For forty years this had been developed almost everywhere else; but Florence had had no equivalent to the steep perspectives of Melozzo and the *ediculi* of Ferrara and Venice. It is strange to find a reinforcement of the architectural element in the last works of Botticelli, that painter who at the same time, in his drawings for the *Divine Comedy*, showed himself to be the one most capable of freeing himself from it. Thus the *Calumny* (1494, or perhaps 1496) re-establishes, in contrast to the woodlands of the tapestries, a framework consisting of a luminous temple; and in his *cassoni* panels —in the *Story of Virginia* (*c.* 1499, Bergamo), the *Story of Lucretia* (Gardner Museum, Boston) and in the series of the *Miracles of St Zenobius* (after 1500; London, Dresden, New York)—the story is authoritatively scanned by the buildings. These architectural settings, grey or heightened, may well have been due to the collaboration of Giuliano da Sangallo, or borrowed from models made by him. This merely makes the choice of them more remarkable.

9 - S. BOTTICELLI. THE DIVINE COMEDY. PARADISO, CANTO XXVIII.

311 - F. FRANCIA. MADONNA IN A ROSE GARDEN — MUNICH, PINAKOTHEK.

The vogue of the bland style came near to producing a disastrous insipidity in the art of Northern Italy. In Bologna, Mantua and Venice the page had been turned, and it is typical of this that in 1505 the Marchesa of Mantua, unable to find anyone else, sent for Perugino to complete the series of *studiolo* panels begun by Mantegna. And yet the relaxation does not account for everything: here and there it led to complementary manifestations which it is interesting to group together. Some concern for forms still existed. The stronger artists had understood that they must go back to 'masters' like Masaccio. In a good many painters there were superficial signs of a kind of formal recovery, harking back to the geometrism

312 - VITTORE CARPACCIO. MEDITATION ON THE DEAD CHRIST — BERLIN-DAHLEM, STAATLICHE MUSEEN.
Shaded for demonstration. See list of illustrations.

and the rigid axes of the years around 1470, for example in the group of Veronese artists led by Francesco Morone. The old Paduan attachment to dryness and to a complicated mineral decoration seemed still ready to spring to life again and to bring back with it a renewed aridity against the crystalline background which Antonello had introduced (and which has disappeared for twenty-five years). Several more or less loyal satellites of Venice kept to this style for a time: in Vicenza Buonconsiglio did his best along these lines, following Montagna; this produced some of the most powerful mineral compositions in Italian painting. In Venice itself Carpaccio provided, for his two astonishing *Meditations on the Dead Christ*, a space made of bones and stones. This hardening might be interpreted as a kind of rejection, by anticipation, of the course soon taken by the young Giorgione, with his master Bellini as starting-point.

In Lombardy the situation was almost the same. Here Foppa, starting from the Paduan style, had carried

313 - GIOVANNI BUONCONSIGLIO. PIETÀ — VICENZA, MUSEO CIVICO.

314 - V. FOPPA. VIRGIN AND CHILD WITH SS. JOHN THE BAPTIST AND JOHN THE EVANGELIST — BRERA.

out the necessary reassessments. Grouped about him there were painters who favoured stocky, rounded forms, yet were also interested in light and in the subtle volumes from which Il Borgognone extracted a whole manner —the manner that makes itself felt in the remains of his *St Benedict Polyptych* at Pavia (1490). To this group belongs Martino Spanzotti in whom interest has recently been revived; it was he who painted the large-scale compartmented decoration of the church of Santa Maria Maddalena at Ivrea (a little before 1500). The coming of Leonardo to Milan had marked, of course, a change towards an accentuated, brilliant style of painting with grave rhythms. Sforza was busy trying to find Peruginos. Yet in Milan the relaxation was inevitably partial: not everyone was convinced of its urgency, since Butinone and Zenale were completing their enormous Treviglio altarpiece (commissioned in 1485) with an unshakeable fidelity to gold surfaces, to silhouetted forms, to figures like statues and to that glorification of figures within the grandiose anti-reality of the setting, which had been one of the major concerns of the Quattrocento.

One other group of revealing facts is worth stressing, in order to bring out the power of invention and the diversity that were characteristic of Italy. Recourse to architecture and its forms—real or imaginary—had been the great means of organizing a composition: it was still so for the Ferrara painters, for example, and even became so again for some artists such as Botticelli. The history of the altarpiece from 1460 to 1510 is, with all its wealth, largely that of the *ediculi* and *tempietti*: they give the picture a spatial existence and ennoble the imagined locality—which is often entirely paved. The care with which the young Raphael retained the method of Perugino's *Sposalizio* (Caen Museum) in his own painting

315 - G.M. SPANZOTTI. CHRIST BEFORE CAIAPHAS — IVREA, SAN BERNARDINO.

316 - VITTORE CARPACCIO. SACRA CONVERSAZIONE — CAEN, MUSÉE.
Shaded for demonstration. See list of illustrations.

of the same subject—retained even that frontal view of the central-planned temple which enables us to see light piercing through it—is evidence of the value of this inspired device, about which the imposing space of the platform gravitates. But already for twenty years (chiefly, it is true, in the North of Italy) there had been attempts to break up the architectonic setting, to place the sacred groups in a radiant natural scene, divided up so as to serve as a sublime setting for the event depicted. Since the feeling for architecture persisted in the midst of this 'naturalism', the result was the creation of an exceptional vocabulary of caves, cliffs and giant arches; these were transpositions of the niche, the stately wall and the triumphal arch, disguised now as natural phenomena, as accidents of landscape. In this way the picture was endowed

317 - ANDREA MANTEGNA. MADONNA OF THE QUARRIES — FLORENCE, UFFIZI.
Shaded for demonstration. See list of illustrations.

with a series of planes, making possible the regulation of the light and the free insertion of secondary motifs. In Carpaccio's *Sacra Conversazione* (*c.* 1502, Caen Museum), there is a curving bridge of rocks in the second plane, and this frames a meticulously detailed landscape. Carpaccio had already reflected on how ochre earth and rocks could be made to provide the tragic themes of the Christian faith with an original sounding-board. A few years earlier his *Meditation on the Passion* (New York) had drawn from a dry, mineral landscape an effect that harmonizes admirably with the theme of ruin and death. Mantegna had been before him in the use of red mountains and of precipices heaved up as though by some gigantic force: already in 1484 his small *Virgin and Child* (Uffizi) had as its only setting a kind of geological halo, a formation of volcanic rocks whose value is stressed by a small quarry complete with quarrymen. In his paintings for Isabella d'Este Mantegna stressed the secret vitality of mineral forms still more by giving them expressive colours and outlines. Giovanni Bellini, too, had for some time understood very well what use he could make of a horizon brought up short by striking contours, of planes laid out beneath an amber light and of foliage massed with grace, to invest his backgrounds with a power quite different from that of the traditional rose hedges or walls covered with flowers. And this was at the same time the most convincing support possible for a 'tonal' handling that was more completely unified than ever.

In the years around 1460 the invention of architectural settings had quickly brought painting to its full potentiality. In about 1500 the abandonment of the strict architectonic framework became a condition of the evolution of style. The treatment of the scene in an interior, of which Piero's *Montefeltro Altarpiece* was the forerunner, had been a first stage towards this. But the concern with an enveloping light and a continuity of forms called for a more thoroughgoing decision; in this respect the success of Perugino, with his cleverness at creating an open and tempered space, revealed a need. At the end of the century a new conception of style was seeping in with the work of Leonardo, starting from these premises: in opposition to the dry, architectonic natural world of Mantegna which the Vicenza painters maintained. Leonardo exhibited—and justified by extraordinary cosmological speculations—his cold, blue world, which tended to be as fluid as water. His horizon was really a distance: to the solar light of Bellini he opposed the blue-green glimmer of his moon-

318 - FRANCESCO DEL COSSA. GRIFFONI ALTARPIECE (DETAIL) — MILAN, BRERA.

319 - BERNARDINO ZENALE. THE VIRGIN AND CHILD BETWEEN SAINTS — DENVER, ART MUSEUM.

tinged atmosphere. For the imposing mountain cliffs that had framed the sacred scenes of other painters he substituted caves—the sweating, greenish interior of the cave in the *Virgin of the Rocks*, whose importance is sufficiently attested by the existence of the two versions. Architecture, which he had still contemplated using for the background of his *Adoration of the Magi* (*c.* 1475), had no longer a *raison d'être;* the static world had had its day. Not only were the problems of composition bypassed by so singular an initiative but the style conformed to a principle that rendered useless the hesitation between tonality and contour: *sfumato* absorbed both colour and

320 - LEONARDO DA VINCI. THE VIRGIN AND CHILD WITH ST ANNE (DETAIL) — PARIS, LOUVRE.

design into a new unity, which gave the unfolding of space a more flexible and a more disconcerting quality. Zenale's *Holy Family with St Ambrose and St Jerome* (Denver, U.S.A.), a somewhat exceptional painting, is a strange and complex echo of this style, with a two-fold greenish arcade cut into the rock. In the *St Anne*, which caused something like stupefaction in Florence when it was shown in 1502, nothing of the old conceptions remained: everything that had been the glory of Quattrocento painting, in Padua, Urbino, Ferrara and even Venice, seemed to have melted away. It was soon, as though by enchantment, forgotten or repudiated in the new enthusiasm.

CONCLUSION

THE POWER OF STYLE

THE first historian who was able to describe the development of the arts in Italy—Vasari—sensed so complete a contrast between late fifteenth-century work and that of the sixteenth-century masters that he assigned to 1500 and to the years immediately before and after the decisive link with the 'modern' fulfilment. The Renaissance could only have happened in Italy: the miraculous return to the *buon maniera* had been achieved with the great generation of 1300—the generation of Giotto, Giovanni Pisano, Arnolfo—who had turned away both from the Greek model and from the Gothic aberration; their acquisitions needed to be confirmed after 1400, and they were so, thanks to a fruitful interrogation of both nature and Antiquity, carried through by Brunelleschi, Masaccio and Donatello. But an essential something had still to be attained, and this occurred only after 1500. The key passage, in which the Florentine historian describes this final achievement, is worth quoting for two reasons: it is one of the very earliest documents in which the development of styles is presented as a specific branch of history; and, on the other hand, the lasting and deepseated success obtained for various reasons by Vasari's thesis is apt to prove misleading,—and to supply the corrective to that thesis has been, indeed, one of the aims of this study.

'The dry, hard, trenchant manner' wrote Vasari, had been established by Piero della Francesca (...), Alesso Baldovinetti, Andrea del Castagno (...), Ercole of Ferrara (...), Domenico del Ghirlandaio (...), Sandro Botticelli, Andrea Mantegna, Filippo Filippino Lippi, and Luca Signorelli ... Although their works were for the most part well drawn and without errors, they lacked a certain vivacity, unknown at that time, and a sweetness in the union of colours, which Francia of Bologna and Pietro Perugino were the first to exhibit in their works; and seeing it, men fell, as it were, madly in love with this new and more living beauty. But their error was made plain by the works of Leonardo da Vinci; inaugurating the third manner, which we shall call modern, by virtue of the strength and robustness of his drawing and his ability to render meticulously all the details of the model exactly as it was, with

I - PIERO DI COSIMO. ALLEGORY — WASHINGTON, NATIONAL GALLERY.

correctness, improved order, right measure, perfect drawing and a godlike grace, together with abundance of inventions and a profound knowledge of the craft, he truly gave to his figures the movement and breath of life'.

Along the way thus opened all those masters are to be found, who, from Giorgione to Raphael and from him to Andrea del Sarto, lead on, like some glorious procession, to Michelangelo, in whom a long history is fulfilled and concluded.

Already in 1568, in the second edition of his book, Vasari had to modify this striking thesis, by assigning a less exclusive role to the Florentines and by admitting that 'geniuses' cannot be reduced to one another—that, therefore, there may be more than one final value. But in the rhythm of development described by him the second half of the Quattrocento was still, so to speak, crushed between two periods. Vasari had clearly not paid attention to the fact that Leonardo, the initiator of the third period, was born in 1452 and Giorgione, his Venetian counterpart, in 1477, so that between them there was the gap of a generation—the generation, precisely, of Botticelli, Perugino and Signorelli (to confine ourselves to painters). This gap corresponds to the passage from the 'rigid' style to the 'fluid' style: it is measured, in Umbria, by the opposition of Perugino to Signorelli and at Ferrara by the contrast between the 'terrible' manner of F. del Cossa (born *c.* 1437) and the vague sweetness of Lorenzo Costa (born 1460). The movements represented to us as successive did, in fact, overlap and intermingle. Bramante was born in 1444, and Peruzzi, his pupil and Roman collaborator, in 1481; but Peruzzi was to attach himself directly to the final conclusions of his master. Bramante's career, made up as it was of bold experiments and of reform after reform, and entirely directed towards the conquest of the grand style, still showed him as belonging to the last part of the Quattrocento: in it we have a living example of that deployment of energies, those complementary movements, which subtlety and classical order were to simplify.

It is therefore not surprising that it became necessary to supersede what is arbitrary in Vasari's exposition and to rescue, one by one, over the last century or so, the figures who fascinate us today—for instance, the Ferrarese painters, whom the Tuscan historian presents as a scarcely intelligible eccentricity or accident. To confine ourselves once more to painting: nothing in the traditional scheme of the schools gives us the least hint of the part played by Piero della Francesca,—and yet his influence, rather like that of Giotto at the beginning of the Trecento, broke down, during the third quarter of the Quattrocento, the compartments into which the Provinces were naturally divided. His role may, in the last analysis, have been more decisive than that of Masaccio; for Piero's art was, from the first, more favourable to a modern 'synthesis' than was Masaccio's 'plastic' reform. His career brought out something of essential moment: a transverse line of influence stretching between Urbino and Venice—to be severed afresh, in the crucial years of 1470-1475, by the journey of Antonello da Messina from South to North. In these interactions Florence was, of course, somewhat less important: Botticelli was unknown outside Florence, and was destined to be forgotten even before he died. Vasari and, after him, the 'academic' historians were driven to a sweeping simplification: that what Florence represented in the fifteenth-century, Rome fulfilled in the sixteenth. But that is asking us to forget that already in 1500 Leonardo was beginning to give rise to a whole school in Lombardy, and that Umbria was to play a part as a link—all this before the great Roman initiatives. Above all, a new balance was establishing itself as that other centre of art on the Lagoon grew in authority. To think of the Carmine frescoes in 1425 (rather than of Arezzo in 1450) as its first historically important expression, and of Leonardo's return in 1501 as the second, leads to disregarding the influence of the 'Donatellism' of Padua, as well as of the 'Albertism' of Urbino. The History of the Renaissance has for long been written by the admirers, not to say sectarians, of the grand styles which triumphed by eliminating the most original tendencies of the period here reviewed. If, therefore, one wishes to look at the phenomena more closely, the traditional schemes of explanation must be put in parentheses, as dangerous fictions.

In the sixteenth century Piero, Francesco di Giorgio and Botticelli were no longer mentioned, except in the local chronicles; and this oblivion extended to include those centres which had not continued in the front rank. A kind of disqualification weighed on the numerous painters and sculptors of the Quattrocento whose taste did not foreshadow Raphael, Michelangelo or Correggio. The rescue of Botticelli, Tura, Crivelli, Foppa and others from this oblivion had to wait for the general change which brought back to favour those painters that preceded Raphael —but at the cost of a misunderstanding that for a long time lumped them together with the so-called 'primitives.' The escape from the academic schemes dates back to hardly more than half a century ago. At the beginning of the present century the Vasarian thesis had still not been completely set aside by Berenson. It even enjoyed a king of revival in the doctrine of Wölfflin, who, considering the full classical order as Italy's special vocation, relegated the artists of the fifteenth century to the rank of mere precursors and described them in negative terms, setting their taste for anecdote against the classical simplification, their dispersed compositions against the concentration of the masters, and so on. But this view also has lost nearly all its force. One capital point Wölfflin did recognize: that is was only possible for the Italian masters to assimilate the vast fund of Antiquity when the 'vision' of both the artists and their public had reached a certain point of formal articulation; the reappearance of the Roman and Greek plastic repertory was the first consequence of the Renaissance, not its cause. But this insight is only partial unless realized in history —that is, in a series of initiatives and inventions that are sometimes contradictory. Every fresh kind of form calls forth a selection from the vocabulary of Antiquity to confirm it. The effect obtained might be a new version of 'Gothic'. It is this that gives sharpness to certain 'pre-classical' manifestations, in which the ancient forms, though adapted to enterprises that have nothing of Antiquity about them, suddenly possess an unusual strictness and dignity. In the present book this tension has been emphasized and its repercussions described by stressing, in particular, the contrast between Padua and Urbino, which might quite easily be taken as the typical polarity of the Quattrocento—a variant of that between 'Dionysian' and 'Apollonian'.

By setting aside systematic categories that are either too sweeping or too narrow, one tends to substitute a problem for a definition. The Renaissance, seen as a problem—its own problem—becomes full of fascination; one finds in it the currents and accidents of history, instead of a facile story that gives a poor reconstruction of the real movement of the arts. From the details of historical analysis there emerges finally an essential characteristic of the period, which may be called *the power of style*. That last phase of the Quattrocento abounded in signs that people were beginning to recognize the authority of the artist—but not in the sense of any quasi-mystical prestige of genius. What the fifteenth-century Italian public, of every level and class, liked to feel and was eager to admire, was creative aptitude, the ability to produce complete and powerful works—that is to say, masterpieces. In the light of this concept it is possible to bring out more clearly two somewhat elusive aspects of the spiritual life of the period: the relations of artist to craftsman; and those between art and culture.

In the general enterprise of what Nietzsche described as the 're-Mediterraneanizing' of art and culture, the most modest craftsman, obliged as he constantly was to adapt his stock of forms and ornamental devices, found himself with a part to play. One is struck by the quality of the detail—even when it shows no particular research or pretention—that occurs on the buildings and decoration of the years around 1470 or 1480: not only quality that speaks of the workman's care, but quality that includes inspirations. The distinction that has to be made between the studios that went in for large output and the original studios has already been stressed; but the original studios did not restrict the scope of the craftsmen—quite the contrary. The mason had to learn to execute deep-cut fluting of a kind that had gone out of fashion; the stone-cutter to assimilate new cornice outlines; the painter, new folds of drapery and a whole gamut of details that to him were strange and unprecedented. High-level problems were resolved on the lower level, in terms of forms to be worked out. Everything became significant and precious, as soon as men were bent on recovering whatever was Mediterranean which they found even in the singularities of the Ottoman world or Hebraic epigraphy.

The Italian craftsmen held their own keenly against their Northern colleagues, letting none of the exceptional resources manifested by the sculpture and graphic art north of the Alps escape them. The circulation of motifs was extremely rapid and lively. It was probably at Nuremberg that Jacopo de' Barbari learned the astonishing skill in engraving which enabled him to produce in 1500 his wonderful panorama of Venice. The ceaseless vigilance and activity of its studios, finding a solution to every new problem, gave Italy the exceptional position as intermediary which it had won by 1500. In this context the artist, as we now call him, appears only as the superior—sometimes widespread—version of the craftsman. The Quattrocento artist, whatever his temperament, did not begin by being an intellectual: he was there to demonstrate by his actual output that culture is fulfilled in art.

This concept required time to ripen, and its rise was slow. True, for the first time in centuries the outlook of the sciences—in particular, the attitude to philosophic problems that found expression in an aestheticizing Platonism—was far from excluding such a concept, as it had formerly done. But this applied chiefly to certain advanced circles, and it would be wrong to believe that the men of letters, humanists, rhetoricians and poets were in general concerned to exalt the world of the arts. Most often they reacted as craftsmen of letters: what they sought from the arts—to which their period was becoming attentive—was a support for their own line of activity, an occasion for demonstrating its validity and interest. And there persisted, among the intellectuals, a distrust of those whose *ingenium* found its exercise in manual skill. This comes out clearly in a passage from a recently rediscovered treatise, written between 1450 and 1460, by a humanist of the court of Ferrara. Its author, Decembrio, puts into the mouth of Leonello d'Este arguments for the view that painting is inferior to poetry: *poetarum ingenia quae ad mentem plurimum spectant longe pictorum opera superare quae sola manus ope declarantur.* What is most surprising is that the man of letters reproaches painting for being unable to render nature: the painters, he says, try in vain to evoke what the poet succeeds in describing—storms, the winds, birds, twilight, the night sky. These assertions went against the facts of contemporary development in the arts, and they are not free from a sense of professional rivalry (which has, of course, to be reckoned with, in a world of courts, clans and independent cities). During the half-century that followed, they were to be given the lie. Decembrio, as a good humanist, had taken his impressive list of phenomena not representable in painting from the very passage in which Pliny praises Apelles for having been able to represent them (such inconsistencies were common in the fifteenth century). It was now up to the painters to revive the aims and successes of Apelles, so as to deserve the praise given to him and turn the tables on the poets. And this Leonardo and the Venetians did. By the end of the fifteenth century painting had triumphed over the taunts of the men of letters. It was equipped to evoke *storie* of every kind and to represent nature. It had acquired a dominant position, though this was not yet recognized by all. Leonardo, refusing any compromise, maintained that a poet's description of a battle, a storm or a beautiful person was nothing in comparison with the painter's ability to represent such things: intelligible reality—that reality which was the domain of true culture and the goal of modern activity—was of the order of the visible. And by a bold, decisive stroke (which of course not everyone, even at the court of Lodovico il Moro, was prepared to go along with) Leonardo put forward the painter, suddenly, as a new intellectual hero—before the poet, or the musician, or the philosopher. This exaggeration must be taken as polemical, but it did reflect an order of values closely bound up with the development of the Quattrocento in Italy.

Italy was about to establish itself throughout the West not only as the privileged intermediary between the world of the present and Antiquity, but also as having mastered certain principles of renewal which would come through culture: the Italian artists seemed to possess the secret of style. Foreigners, astonished and sometimes fascinated by the works now revealed to them, were no less beguiled and astonished by the comments and discussions in the circles of the cultivated. The clear articulation of forms had brought out a power of precise statement, a spiritual capacity, which irradiated the style. Growing awareness of the novelty of contemporary aims in art led to the discovery of a necessary reform of culture. And as political events became more confused and disquieting, as the religious situation grew darker, as problems of science or technique began to appear insoluble, people were more inclined to believe that the best reply to these difficulties was, in a sense, to multiply artistic experiments and to begin the reform of the present time by the renovation of style. The French, in particular, clung to this idea—from the time of Louis XII onwards, but especially with Francis I, who had in mind a real programme of intellectual and artistic reform. In the years about 1500 there emerged the conviction that culture was one of the means of saving humanity; and the culture in question was Mediterranean and Graeco-Roman in form. The West looked to Italy for the system of forms, the panoply of concepts, which was to enable men to take possession of a new world full of difficulties and surprises.

PART TWO

Illustrated Documentation

It sometimes happened that painters had occasion to paint portraits of their fellow artists; one of the most remarkable of these for its direct observation is that of Giuliano da Sangallo by Piero di Cosimo (mentioned by Vasari as being among the list of works by Piero di Cosimo in the collection of Francesco da Sangello). See R. Langton Douglas, *Piero di Cosimo*, Chicago, 1946.

The portrait in the Uffizi is traditionally identified as that of Verrocchio painted by Lorenzo di Credi (whose gifts as a portraitist are stressed by Vasari); this identification is, however, uncertain.

But the most interesting phenomenon of the period is the fashion for self-portraits, recognizable by the artist's oblique gaze (due to the image having been studied in a mirror) and his marginal position, a fact often noted by early writers. Thus in *The Adoration of the Magi* by Botticelli, painted in glorification of the Medici, the fair-haired painter appears on the right among the various portraits.

A portrait of the artist frequently appears in the great fresco cycles. Melozzo da Forlì painted his own likeness among the figures of the Palm Sunday fresco (1486) at Loretto, as Perugino did in *The Remission of the Keys* for the Sistine Chapel (1481-1483) and Domenico Ghirlandaio in the scene of Joachim being expelled from the Temple at Santa Maria Novella. Benozzo Gozzoli appears with his name inscribed on his cap among the retinue in the *Procession of the Magi* in the Chapel of the Medici Palace. This self-portrait is equivalent to a signature; Mantegna and Bellini seem to have preferred to use the *cartellino* device.

A very typical example is that of the self-portrait of Pinturicchio at Spello treated in *trompe l'œil* as part of the decoration of the interior in an *Annunciation* (chap. III, ill. 189). It follows on from that by Perugino in the Cambio (1500), as well as Signorelli in the fresco of the Antichrist at Orvieto (1501). There is hardly a painter in the whole of Central Italy who did not think of introducing his own likeness into his frescoes.

2 - GIULIANO DA SANGALLO.

323 - SANDRO BOTTICELLI.

324 - ANDREA VERROCCHIO (?).

325 - MELOZZO DA FORLI.

326 - PERUGINO.

327 - DOMENICO GHIRLANDAIO.

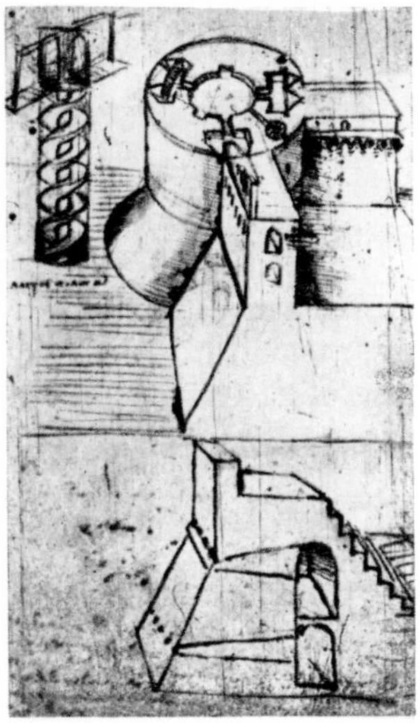

328 - LEONARDO DA VINCI.

329 - LEONARDO DA VINCI.

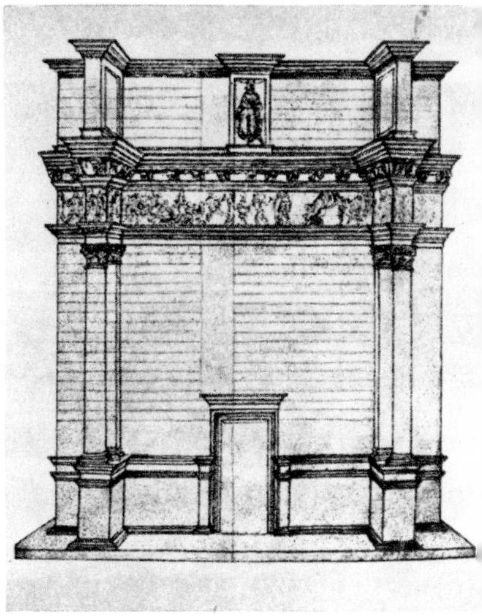

330 - FRANCESCO DI GIORGIO.

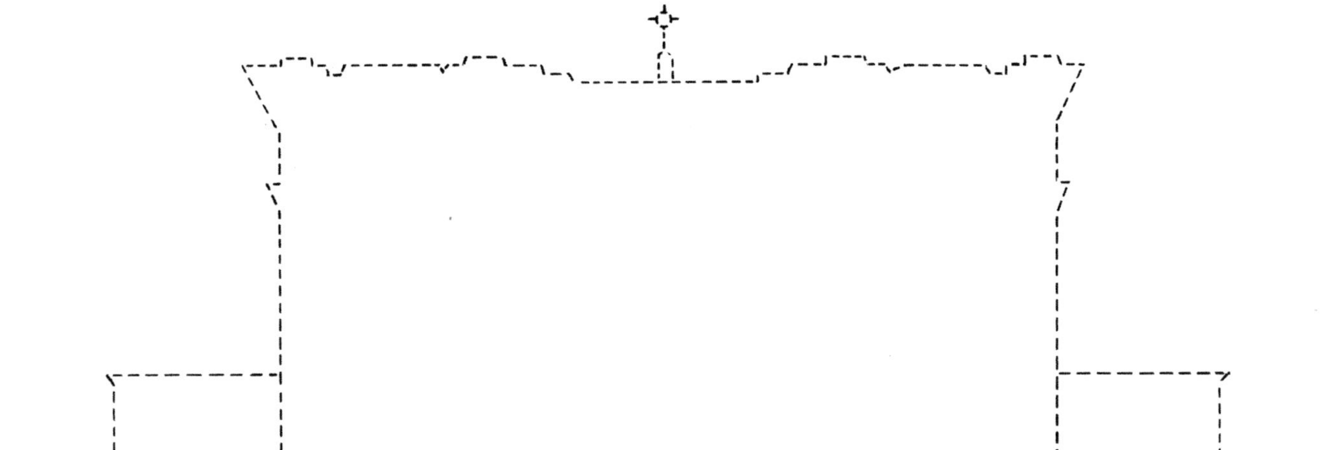

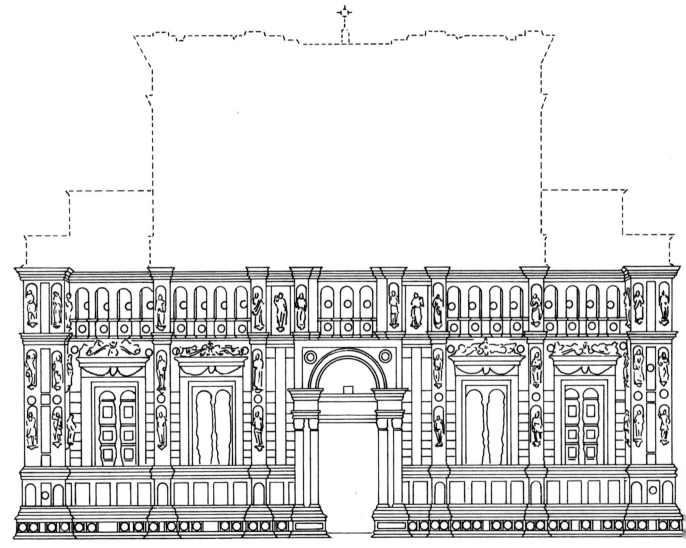

331 - CERTOSA DI PAVIA. RECONSTRUCTION OF THE FAÇADE AT THE END OF THE QUATTROCENTO.

Judging from the facts recently gathered by C. Predetti (bibliog. 269), it appears that in the last years of the fifteenth century Leonardo was entrusted with fairly precise responsibilities in matters of building. Folio 69 r° in Ms B demonstrates his interest in technical fixtures: galleries and wall-walks in a fortress, a staircase with two helicoidal flights of stairs, a variation on the spiral staircase, probably intended as a way of facilitating communication between the different parts of a massive building, and perhaps especially designed for a fortress. The other aspect of Leonardo's architectonic inventiveness, the significance of which was emphasized by L.H. Heydenreich (bibliog. 166), is displayed in his churches, noble edifices for which a decoration of considerable style is needed. Leonardo's study for a monumental façade is usually dated 1490. It takes up again the Albertian design of superimposed tiered storeys with volutes (in the guise of flying buttresses) framing the topmost bay which is surmounted by a pediment. The arrangement is so clear-cut, the disposition of the niches and the bays between the pilasters so precise, the whole effect so spirited, that this façade has been considered as an example of proto-Baroque inspiration (T. Arkin, *Le idee di un grande architetto* in 'Rassegna sovietica', Rome, III, 1952). The anticipation of the forms which were to be in use around 1515-20 has even led to the suggestion that it might in fact have been a project for the façade of San Lorenzo or for the Convent of San Marco, drawn about 1513-16 (bibliog. 269).

At the end of the fifteenth century the screen façade, with a broad wall surface surmounted by a frieze or an attic storey, is a rival design. It is to a certain degree justifiably used in the restoration of ancient edifices, as for example in the design which Francesco di Giorgio evolved based on elements taken from the forum of Nerva (Ms., Biblioteca del Re, Turin). The projection of the columns, treated as buttresses, the spacing of the openings and of the decoration, are opposed to the school of thought that lay behind the harmonious façades of Alberti and Leonardo.

The Certosa di Pavia, founded in 1396 by Giovanni Galeazzo Visconti, was constructed gradually throughout the course of the fifteenth century. The cloisters were built by R. de Stauris, Mantegazza, Amadeo and Briosco in 1473; Amadeo worked there in particular between 1490 and 1499. Giampietro Borlini's recent article, *The Façade of the Certosa in Pavia*, in 'The Art Bulletin', XLV (1963), p. 323 ff., has determined the point the work had reached at the end of the Quattrocento. Only the ground floor and first storey were completed with their abundance of sculpture, decorative motifs, medallions and marble incrustation. The evidence shows that between 1492 and 1494 the façade stopped at the level of the gallery.

In the type of Florentine palazzo built in the form of a block, the open decorated part is the interior courtyard onto which the galleries and communicating passages open out; the exterior façade is treated with greater severity. Here the ground floor is composed of only an entrance archway, and the bays in plain semi-circular arches or in the form of a *bifora* with an oculus, are little decorated. These apertures do not correspond to the interior levels. The storeys, of which the upper levels are progressively reduced in height, are surmounted by a strongly projecting cornice with richly outlined proportions. The rustication is composed of blocks that vary in size from storey to storey. The Palazzo Gondi, built by G. da Sangallo, is one of the most simplified and most austere versions of the Tuscan model. The contrast with the so-called Palazzo dei Diamanti (Diamond Palace) by the Ferrarese Biagio Rossetti is revealing: a more spectacular distribution of the storeys, classical window surrounds, decorated pilasters, and above all the treatment of the regular rustication in small pyramidal blocks, following a picturesque technique probably derived from the South and destined to have a great success in Eastern and Central Europe (bibliog. 425).

Men's imaginations were drawn towards formulae that were freer, more inventive and more representative; these remained, however, both utopian and idealistic and were expressed particularly in plans and in painted architecture. In the view of an *Ideal City* (attributed to F. di Giorgio), the revised conception of the noble house is planned firstly through the application of orders which form bays on the respective storeys, according to the formula established by Alberti; but it is here carried to a new stage of development by opening out the ground floor into a gallery and adding a loggia on the floor above, i.e., by resorting to a *cortile* design in the treatment of the exterior. The interior levels are expressed by the use of stylobates; the window surrounds include decorative elements and triangular pediments are even used in place of a heavy cornice. In the development of the country villa, innovations remain unadventurous except in the cases of Poggio a Caiano or Poggio Reale. An architectural fantasy by Gozzoli in the Campo Santo in Pisa (1478) indicates the type of 'all'antica' models from which villa design could draw inspiration: U-shaped buildings with two projecting wings, traversed by rows of arcades and surmounted by a recessed upper storey. J. Ackerman (bibliog. 2) has compared this arrangement in loggias to part of Innocent VIII's Villa Belvedere.

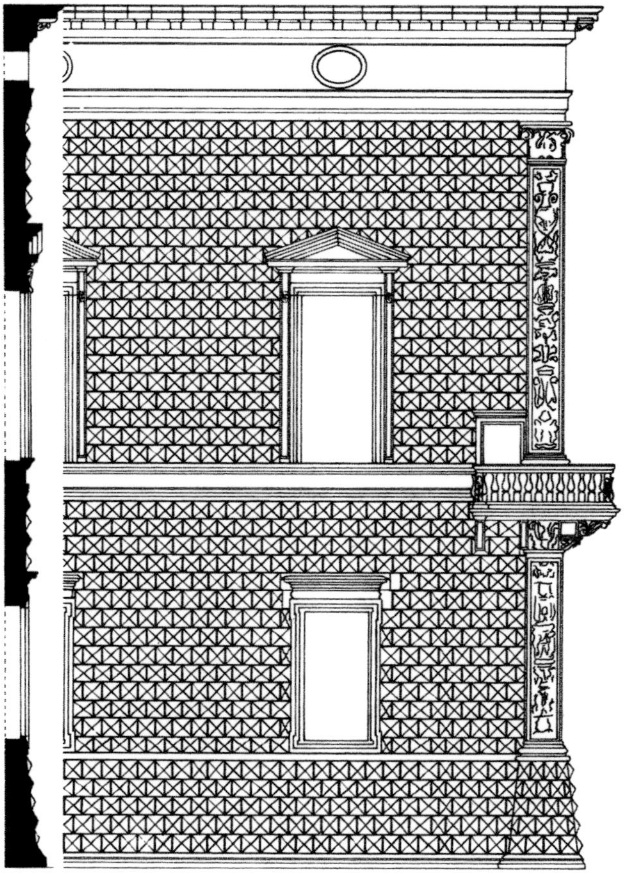

332 - FERRARA, PALAZZO DEI DIAMANTI.

333 - FLORENCE, PALAZZO GONDI.

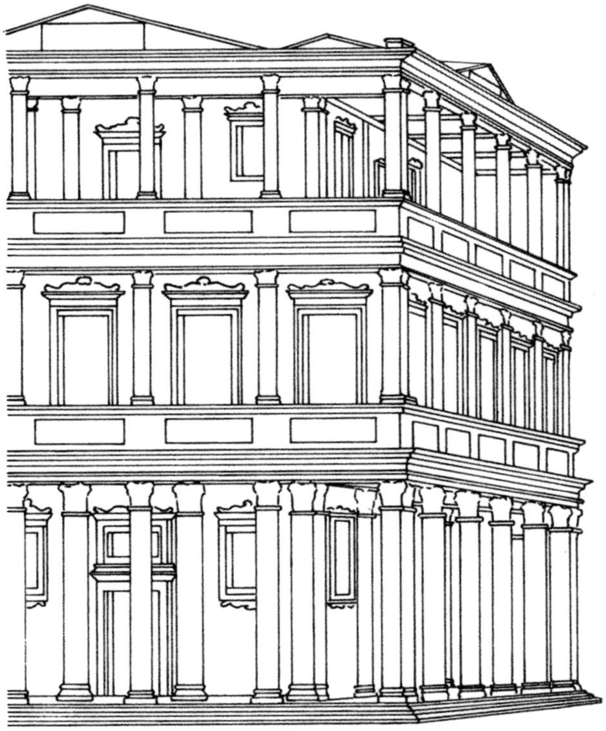

334 - AFTER FRANCESCO DI GIORGIO. BUILDING.

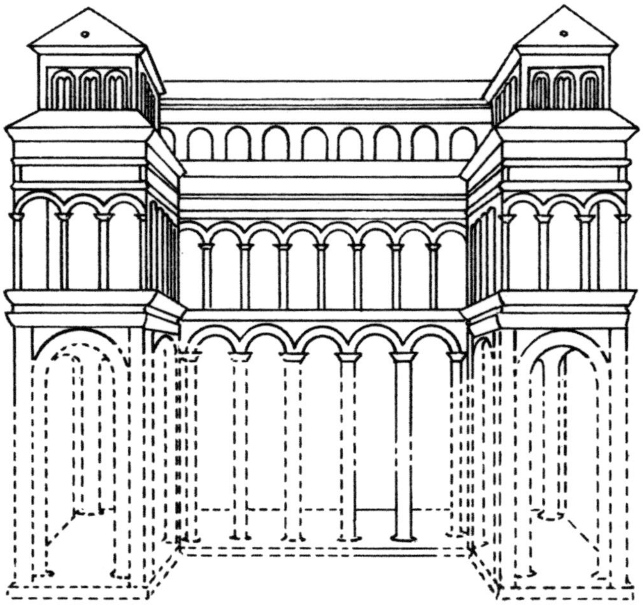

335 - AFTER BENOZZO GOZZOLI. VILLA.

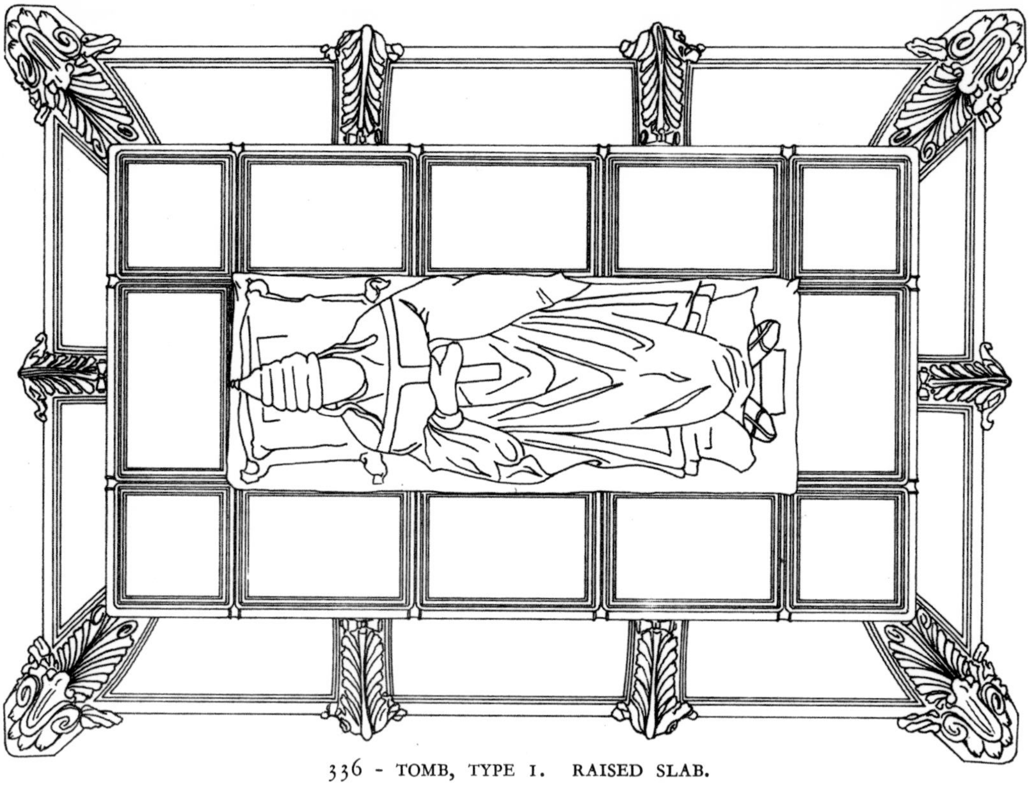

336 - TOMB, TYPE I. RAISED SLAB.

337 - TOMB, TYPE 2. WALL-TOMB IN A NICHE.

338 - TOMB, TYPE 3. AEDICULAR TOMB.

TOMBS

Funerary art is one of the great themes of the Renaissance; its monumental development is easily interpreted within the setting of a civilization which exalted individual activity, associating with the symbols of the afterlife a progressively more and more explicit celebration of the merits of the deceased. The latter is represented as an effigy placed at the threshold of eternal life, whether it be a young prelate, such as the Cardinal of Portugal (died 1459), a Pontiff such as Sixtus IV (died 1484), or a prince such as Giovanni Galeazzo Visconti (died 1402). But this traditional evocation is complemented by an accompaniment of supporting allegorical figures: the Virtues and the Liberal Arts (mourning the death of their patron), scenes depicting the great actions of the personage, often associated with a new allegory, that of Fame. In this way antique motifs find their way into the Christian repertory (bibliog. 106).

But the most outstanding innovation is the transformation of the tomb: the medieval slab is no longer accepted without grandiose additions that transform it into an ornate sarcophagus; Antonio Pollaiuolo's design (completed in 1496) remains an exception (type 1).

The wall tomb was to evolve rapidly from this type revived by Bernardo Rossellino for the tomb of Leonardo Bruni (1445); the monument of Cardinal Jacopo da Portogallo (type 2), which occupies the niche of a funerary chapel owes its charm to the quality and subtlely of the sculpted forms. The Lombardo-Venetian series of tombs are much more strongly characterized by triumphal architecture types 'all'antica,' of which the most emphatic example is found in the Vendramin tomb.

The tomb has yet to be treated as an isolated monument, i.e., as an aedicule composing a funerary chamber with sculpture included in the upper section to form a crown. The type invented by G.C. Romano in Pavia (type 3) was destined to be most successful in France where the Giusti took it as their model for their work in Saint-Denis. (For general literature on tombs see: P. Schubring, *Die italianische Grabmale der Frührenaissance*, Berlin, 1904; F. Burger, *Geschichte des florentinischen Grabmals von den ältesten Zeiten bis Michelangelo*, Strasbourg, 1904; E. Panofsky, *Tomb Sculpture*, London and New York, 1964.

Mural painting developed in a fixed setting incapable of undergoing a similar evolution. It sometimes happened, as in the Ovetari chapel, that there were only two side walls available; some rooms were covered by a ceiling and others by ribbed vaulting. In every case the *storie* unfold above a dado that is usually painted (zoccolo).

The Ovetari Chapel in the Eremitani (1449-54), begun by Pizzolo and continued by Mantegna, shows how determined an effort was made at its organization. The scenes are divided up as follows:

Vault: Perspectival view (A, B, C, D): The Evangelists (Vivarini and Giovanni d'Alemagna).

Choir: The Fathers of the Church (Pizzolo). Panoramic view: (1, 2, 3, 4, 5). Assumption of the Virgin: Mantegna (6).

Left lateral wall: The Story of SS. James and John. (A) The Calling of SS. James and John, (B) St. James expels from the Temple the demons sent by Hermogenes, (C) St. James baptizing Hermogenes, (D) St. James before Herod Agrippa, (E) St. James led to Martyrdom, (F) The Martyrdom of St. James.

Right lateral wall: The Story of St. Christopher. (G and H) St. Christopher crossing the Waters with the Infant Jesus, (J) St. Christopher preaching, (K) St. Christopher struck down, (L) The Removal of the Body of St. Christopher. (G. Fiocco, *La Chapelle Ovetari dans l'église des Érémitiques*, Milan, n.d.).

In Ferrara, the Cycle of the Allegory of the Months in the Palazzo Schifanoia is one of the most noteworthy ensembles in non-religious decoration. The Salone dei Mesi was painted by a group of Ferrarese painters: Ercole de' Roberti, Francesco del Cossa and Cosimo Tura. This room presented a series of walls that were easily divided up into sections corresponding to the months of the year. Each of the twelve sections is further divided up into three pictorial zones. *Upper zone:* (A) The triumph of the mythological divinities who govern human life; *Middle zone:* (B) Zodiacal signs and corresponding decades; *Lower zone:* (C) Evocation of the Life at Court of the Princes of Ferrara. Thus there was displayed in this cycle an astrological tableau of every form of human activity, as A. Warburg has demonstrated in a famous essay (1902). The cycle was also intended to celebrate the fame of the House of Este. It consequently became a manifesto for the Ferrarese school. Following R. Longhi (bibliog. 192) and P. D'Ancona (bibliog. 10) experts are agreed in recognizing the North Wall as being by the hand of Ercole de' Roberti, assisted by Francesco del Cossa (except for the upper register) and the East Wall as being the work of Cossa with the help of assistants on the Month of May.

The Borgia Apartments in the Vatican, decorated by Pinturicchio for Alexander VI, give a good definition of the 'camera picta,' a room that is entirely decorated with paintings. In the Sala dei Santi, the story of the bull Apis and the legend of Isis and Osiris—an allusion to the emblematic bull of the Borgias—figure on the vaults and intermingle with the sumptuous evocation of the Church; the cycle of the Lives of the Saints is divided into six lunettes: (1) The Dispute of St. Catherine, (2) St. Barbara, (3) Susanna and the Elders, (4) The Martyrdom of St. Catherine, (5) The Visitation, (6) St. Anthony and St. Paul the Hermit (F. Ehrle and E. Stevenson, *Gli affreschi del Pinturicchio nell'appartamento Borgia del Palazzo Apostolico Vaticano*, Rome, 1897).

342 - ALTARPIECE, TYPE A. PALA.

343 - TYPE A[1]. PALA.

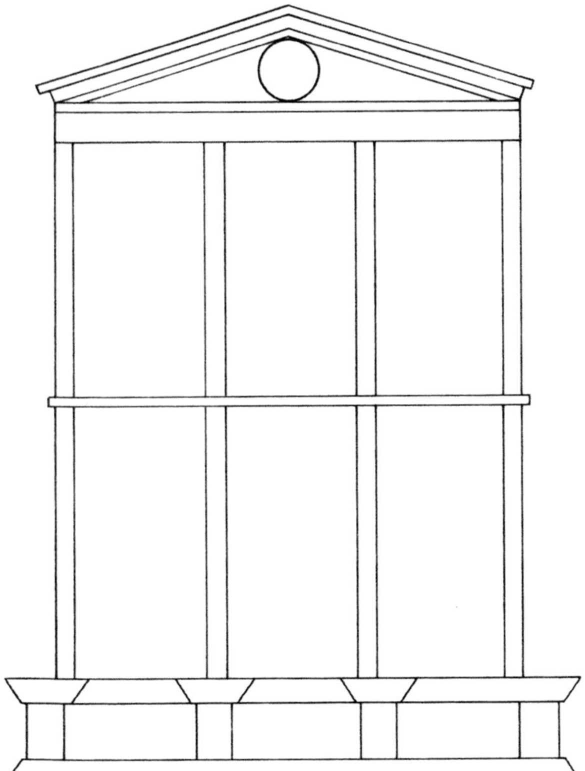

345 - TYPE B[1]. DOUBLE TRIPTYCH.

346 - TYPE C. SINGLE-TIER POLYPTYCH.

344 - TYPE B. TRIPTYCH.

347 - TYPE C[1]. POLYPTYCH IN SEVERAL TIERS.

348 - TYPE D. POLYPTYCH, MIXED (SCULPTURE AND PAINTING).

THE ALTARPIECE

The altarpiece or retable consists of the main part of the painted decoration of the church. It is prominently placed either on the high altar, or on the altars of the side chapels. It always represents a sacred scene, usually of the enthroned Mother and Child, accompanied by saints grouped around the Virgin in 'sacra conversazione,' or ranked in rows according to their specific stations. The central group always includes an architectural element: an apse, for example, or baldacchino or at the very least a monumental throne. The structure of such a throne tends to be defined according to the painting's perspective and may be extended to include all sections of the altarpiece, sometimes being combined with the uprights of the frame itself, which then appears as a section of an imaginary building.

The simplest type (or *pala*) consists of a panel in one unit (A), but usually combining an additional component part, a pediment (or lunette), or small panels in either horizontal or vertical alignment (A^1). Such an arrangement creates a small iconographic organism within the overall structure. The type composed of three sections, or *triptych* (B) (without folding shutters, unlike Flemish examples), may similarly allow for a straightforward juxtaposition of three panels arranged around a single viewpoint, or for a complex system of mounting spread across three levels. A large number of Ferrarese works follow this pattern, which by reason of the increased number of the small panels creates a somewhat distracting disparity between the compositions; but Francesco del Cossa and Ercole de' Roberti must have been aware of this, for they attempted to create a certain unity of vision between the dispersed compositional elements (see following note). The type with five compartments may also be straightforwardly organized (C) or may be given a large-scale arrangement (C^1), prone sometimes to develop into a veritable scaffolding. In such cases the arrangement approaches an architectural device closely allied to the organization of the church façade or triumphal arch (D).

The importance of the sculpted wooden structures is considerable in these arrangements. Often the frame was commissioned before the painted panels which then had to adapt themselves to it.

The evolution of the shape of the niches, of the arches, and of the decorative cusping permits one to follow closely the elimination of the Gothic repertory, varying in its speed and thoroughness from region to region.

This work was originally commissioned c. 1473 for the altar of the Griffoni Chapel in San Petronio, Bologna. In the mid-eighteenth century it passed into the Aldovrandi collection; it was dispersed in 1838, under Pope Gregory XVI. A large work, it stood three metres high. The original composition consisted of three panels, a pediment in three sections, *lateralie* and a predella.

I. In 1888 Frizzoni proposed a first possible reconstruction placing in the centre: St Vincent Ferrer (London, National Gallery) surrounded on the left by St. Peter (Milan, Brera) and on the right by St. John the Baptist (Milan, Brera); the predella at the base contains the story of St. Vincent (Vatican).

II. In 1934 R. Longhi completed Frizzoni's reconstruction by adding the pediment composed of a *tondo* of the Crucifixion (Washington, National Gallery); of the St. Lucy (Washington, National Gallery) with the flower of San Liberale. St. Florian was the donor's patron saint.

The whole group is enclosed by *lateralie:* St. Michael, St. Anthony (Paris, Louvre), St. Apollinaris, St. Petronius, St. Catherine, St. Jerome (London, Duveen Coll.). A diagram of the reconstruction is set out opposite.

III. In 1940 R. Longhi suggested a possible completion of this reconstruction by adding a St. George (formerly in the Rosbury Coll., London) in the topmost panel of the right *lateralia* and two *tondi* of the Annunciation (Milan, Cagnola Coll.) as crowning panels to the *lateralie*.

This *pala* is attributed by R. Longhi to Francesco del Cossa working with the collaboration of Ercole de' Roberti on the predella. The altarpiece belongs to the type of large polyptychs in tiers, following an architectural pattern. It would have occupied the rear of a chapel in the fashion of a triumphal arch.

Bibliography: Frizzoni in *Zeitschrift für bildende Kunst*, 1888, p. 229; R. Longhi, Officina ferrarese, 1934, and *Ampliamenti all'Officina ferrarese*, 1940, re-edited, Florence, 1958.

349 - F. DEL COSSA AND E. DE' ROBERTI. GRIFFONI ALTARPIECE. RECONSTRUCTION.

350 - CARLO CRIVELLI. DEMIDOFF ALTARPIECE. RECONSTRUCTION.

THE DEMIDOFF ALTARPIECE BY CRIVELLI

The altars in the Church of San Domenico at Ascoli Piceno were dismantled in the eighteenth century and the fragments dispersed; in the following century thirteen of them passed into the collection of Prince Demidoff before being acquired by the National Gallery, London, in 1868.

M. Davies, National Gallery, London; The Earlier Italian Schools, London, 1951, no. 788, p. 124 ff., has proposed a regrouping of the panels which has finally been proved incorrect, the facts having been established by F. Zeri in a study in *Arte antica e moderna*, nos. 13-16 (1961), pp. 162-168.

The key to Zeri's criticism is an observation of an iconographic order: it is to be expected that in an altarpiece intended for the Church of San Domenico the patron saints of the order should be represented. St. Dominic's place is at the right of the Madonna; St. John the Baptist must correspondingly stand on Her left. A balance is thus created between the representatives of the medieval Church Militant (on the right) and the Primitive Christian Church (on the left): with the Madonna in the centre, St. Dominic and St. Catherine on the right, St. John the Baptist and St. Peter on the left.

In the upper tier is a row of half-length figures: St. Thomas Aquinas (above St. Dominic), St. Francis (above St. John the Baptist), St. Stephen (above St. Catherine), St. Andrew (above St. Peter). The subject originally represented in the centre of this register remains uncertain.

In general the Madonna and Child are surmounted by a *Pietà*. This is Crivelli's constant practise in his polyptychs at Montefiore dell'Aso (1473) which precedes that at Ascoli Piceno (1476). The same structural system and balance of the iconographic arrangement are found in both these works.

In order to complete the reconstruction one must imagine a decorative sculpted upper tier with half-rosettes and pinnacles, also a predella depicting Christ between the Apostles. Such a reconstruction results in a predictable type. If the work has not been accurately reconstructed outright, the intention has been to insert all the rediscovered sections into a single ensemble. Several of these do not fit into the scheme; it had to be supposed therefore, that fragments of two altarpieces rather than one were under consideration. The documents indicate in fact that in the Church of San Domenico d'Ascoli there was not only a principal altarpiece but also a secondary one. Both of these are described by Tullio Lazzari in *Ascoli in prospettiva*, 1724, p. 76: one of them situated *in fondo al coro*, the other on the secondary altar to the right. It consisted of a polyptych in five compartments with a Madonna and Child in the centre accompanied by saints. It may be compared to the polyptych by B. Vivarini (1464, Accademia, Venice) which is composed of a Madonna (Budapest) and of the four panels from the third level of the Demidoff pseudo-polyptych, St. Peter Martyr and St. Lucy on the right, St. Jerome and St. Michael on the left. Its style is close to that of the main polyptych in the choir; their execution must have been simultaneous. It is also conceivable that it would have had a frame comparable to that by Pietro Alamanno for the Church of the Carità at Ascoli Piceno (today the Pinacoteca, see Catalogue of the Mostra d'Ancona, 1950, ill. 31). Alamanno did not restrict himself to copying the figures but also the frame. The Crivellesque formula thus demonstrated its success and popularity.

THE SAN PIETRO POLYPTYCH BY PERUGINO

Vasari gives this work to Perugino and it is confirmed by early documents (Crispolti, Perugia Augusta, 1648, Lancellotti, *Scorta Sacra*, a seventeenth-century source [Ms. in the Biblioteca Augusta, Perugia]), that the San Pietro Polyptych was commissioned by the 'Black Monks' of Perugia. The contract for the wooden frame was signed in August 1483 by Giovanni di Domenico (who did not deliver it until 1495). The consecration took place in 1500. The work was composed of a large central panel framed by two columns, a lunette, a predella panel in three compartments and two *tondi* on either side of the central panel. The group was dispersed in the eighteenth century. The central section and the lunette were acquired by the Musée de Lyon. A first reconstruction was put forward in 1912 by Bombe, a second in 1913 by Gnoli and a third in 1926 by Canuti and Van Marle.

Accepted reconstruction:

(1) Centre: Ascension (2.80×2.16 m), Lyon, Musée des Beaux-Arts.

(2) Lunette: The Eternal Father in Glory (1.14×2.30 m), Lyon, Musée des Beaux-Arts.

(3) Predella: Epiphany, (4) Baptism of Christ, (5) Resurrection, Rouen, Musée des Beaux-Arts.

Framing each of theses scenes :

(A) St. Herculan (0.32×0.375 m) and St. Costanzo (0.33×0.375 m), Perugia, San Pietro.

(B) St. Maurus (0.32×0.28 m) and St. Benedict (0.335×0.26 m), Perugia, San Pietro; Pinacoteca Vaticana.

(C) St. Scholastica (0.32×0.28 m) and St. Peter bound (0.335×0.26 m), lost since 1916; Perugia, San Pietro.

(D) St. Flavia (0.35×0.26 m) and St. Placida (0.335×0.30 m), Pinacoteca Vaticana.

(6, 7) On the side wings two tondi: Jeremiah and Isaiah (diameter: 1.27 m each), Nantes, Musée des Beaux-Arts.

This system of constructing an altarpiece is, as it were, a simplification of the 'screen' altarpiece with two sides, of which Piero was to make use in Sant' Agostino, Perugia and on which he worked from 1502 onwards.

(See for recent information E. Camesasca, *Tutta la Pittura del Perugino*, Milan, 1959, and R. Jullian in 'Bulletin des Musées lyonnais,' 1961.)

THE BICHI POLYPTYCH BY LUCA SIGNORELLI

The earliest mention of this work is that of a Sienese writer, S. Tizio, who wrote in 1513 that Signorelli had been commissioned in 1498 to paint a picture for the Bichi chapel in the Church of Sant' Agostino in Siena. According to Vasari this chapel was dedicated to St. Christopher and the high altar was composed of a group of saints with a statue of St. Christopher in the centre. Seventeenth-century sources agree with this description, as does Waagen in 1850. In this way a precise relationship was established between the sculpture and the painted panels.

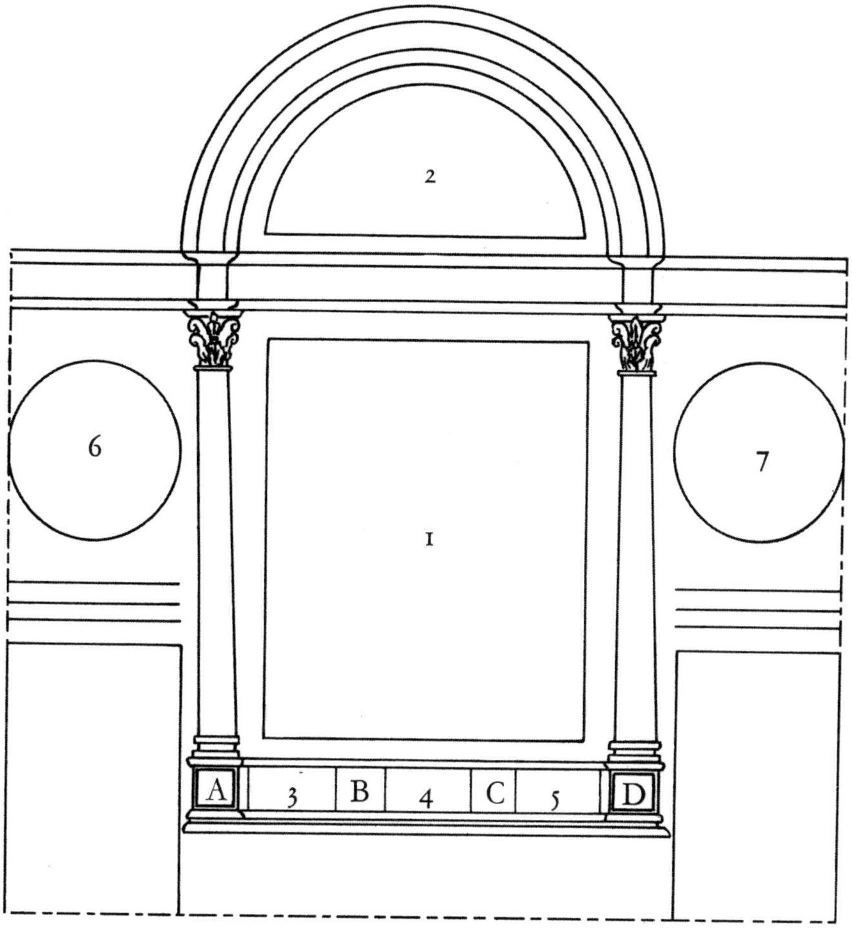

351 - PERUGINO. SAN PIETRO ALTARPIECE. RECONSTRUCTION.

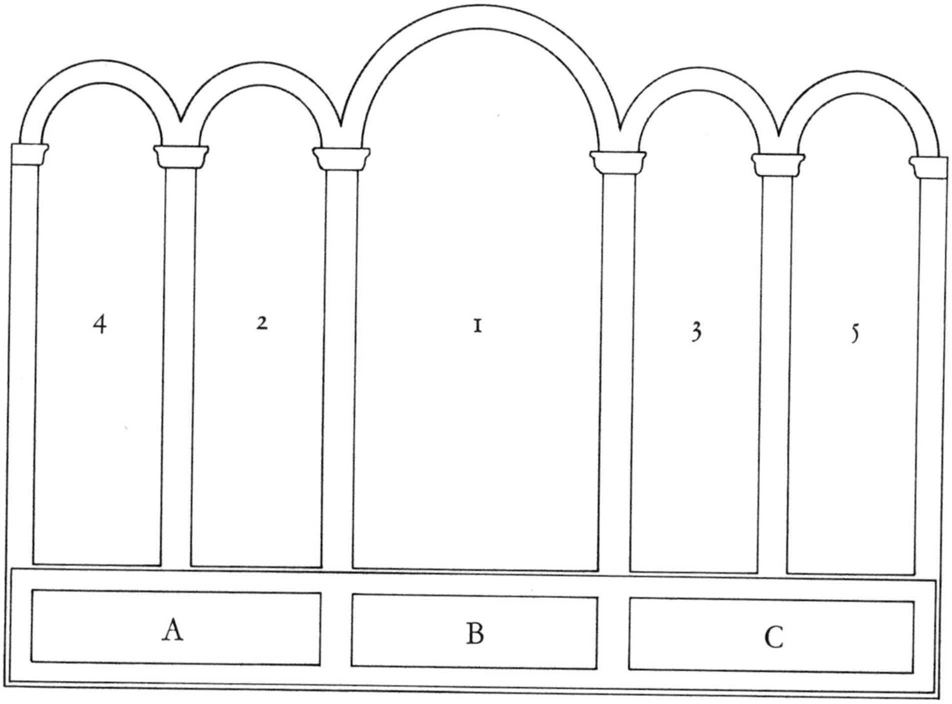

352 - LUCA SIGNORELLI. BICHI ALTARPIECE. RECONSTRUCTION.

T. Borenius ('The Burlington Magazine', 1913) thought he had found a means of reconstructing the group by assuming that two small panels would have been placed behind this statue; but a more accurate hypothesis has recently been put forward in an article, *Signorelli Masterpiece*, in 'Art News,' March 1961, with the following reconstruction:

Polyptych in five compartments + a predella composed of three panels.

(1) Centre: St. Christopher, sculpture by Jacopo della Quercia (Louvre).

(2) Left: St. Catherine of Siena, St. Mary Madgalen and St. Jerome (State Museums, Berlin).

(3) Right: St. Augustine, St. Catherine of Alexandria, St. Anthony of Padua (State Museums, Berlin).

(4, 5) Two panels of nude figures (Toledo, Museum).

Predella: (A) Christ in the house of Simon (Dublin, National Gallery).

(B) *Pietà* (Glasgow, Private Coll.).

(C) The Martyrdom of St. Catherine (Williamstown, Mass., Clark Institute).

NOTES

1 The text occurs in Muratori, *Rerum Italicarum scriptores* Book III, p. 11, col. 949, quoted by U. Boncompagni-Ludovisi, *Roma nel Rinascimento*, Rome, 1928, vol. I, p. 179: *Illa vulgaris opinio doctorum hominum relationibus fundata, magnis aedificiis perpetuis quodammodo monumentis, ac testimoniis paene sempiternis quasi a Deo fabricatis, in dies usque adeo corroboratur et confirmatur, ut in vivos posterosque illarum admirabilium constructionum conspectores continue traducatur.*

('This common opinion, based on the sayings of scholars, is always borne out by great buildings, monuments which are, as it were, eternal and almost indestructible witnesses—as if raised by God Himself, provided that they are handed down to living men and to future generations who will admire these magnificent constructions.')

2 Leonardo's architectural studies often took the form of variations on geometrical schemes, of compositions on a theme,—especially the central ground plan with dome. But at the same time Leonardo liked, in his studies of architecture, to put himself forward as an engineer-theorist. From 1487 to 1490 he was occupied with the *tiburio*—the roofing-in of the crossing—of the cathedral of Milan, and in the draft of a letter to the *Operarii*, he speaks of a *modello da me fatto*, which he considers very suitable for that building. He justifies his intervention by saying that the sick cathedral requires an architect-doctor who knows what a building is and understands the rules of sound construction. In the group of notes for a *Trattato di architettura*, which date from this period, Leonardo attributes an unusual importance to studies of balance and of the resisting power of materials: architecture is a problem of forces. See the edition by J.P. Richter, *op. cit.*, Book II, ch. XIII, nos 770-795; and in A.M. Brizio, *Scritti scelti di Leonardo da Vinci*, Turin, 1954, ch. V (Milanese period) and ch. XVII. Recent researches by C. Pedretti suggest that Leonardo was more actively concerned in actual building than has been thought.

3 The following passage from Filarete shows how freely the theorists used the epithet 'antique': *lodo ben quegli che seguitano la pratica e maniera antica et benedico l'anima di Filippo di ser Brunelleschо, cittadino fiorentino, famoso et degnisimo architetto e sottilissimo imitatore di Dedalo. Il quale risucito nella città nostra di Firenze questo modo antico dello hedificare, per modo che oggi di in altra maniera non s'usa, se non è all' antica, tanto in edifici di chiese, quanto ne publici e privati casamenti* (*Trattato di architettura*, VIII, ed. W. von Oettingen, Vienna, 1896, p. 272).

('I praise those who follow the antique style and method and give my blessing to the spirit of Brunelleschi, citizen of Florence, a worthy and famous architect, a most ingenious disciple of Daedalus: in our town of Florence he has revived the antique manner of building, in such a way that today no style other than 'the antique' is used, as frequently for churches as for public and private buildings.')

4 On the villa of Poggio Reale, see A. Colombo, *Il palazzo e il giardino di Poggio Reale*, in 'Napoli bellissima', I (1892), pp. 81-83; R. Pane, *Architettura del Rinascimento a Napoli*, Naples, 1937, p. 15.

A valuable letter by Summonte gives us information about the architects of this villa: *Questo infelice signore* (Alfonso of Aragon) *prima che arrivasse al sceptro regale, essendo duca di Calabria, cominció ad exequir sue magnanime imprese nella fabrica; e, per fabricare lo Poggio Regale, conduxe in questa terra alcun di quelli architecti che più allora erano stimati; Julian da Majano fiorentino, Francesco da Siena, maestro Antonio Fiorentino, benchè costu fusse più per cose belliche e machinamenti di fortezze; e sopra tutti ebbe qua il bono e singulare Fra Jucundo da Verona.*

('This ill-fated lord before ascending the throne, while he was still Duke of Calabria, began to execute his noble building enterprises and, to construct the villa of Poggio Reale, he brought on to the scene some of the most esteemed architects of the time: the Florentine Giuliano da Maiano, Francesco da Siena, master Antonio Fiorentino, although the latter was more particularly a specialist in the building of fortresses, and surpassing all others, he brought there the excellent and unrivalled Fra Giacondo da Verona.') Letter from P. Summonte to M.A. Michiel (1524), ed. F. Nicolini (1925).

The villa, which lay to the east of the Porta Capuana, was the scene of spectacular festivities during the few months of the French occupation (1495) and again under the Spaniards. In the sixteenth century it belonged to the Spanish crown, then fell into neglect and was used as a charnel-house in the eighteenth century, before vanishing altogether.

5 The procedure used in bronze sculpture at that time is fairly well known: starting sometimes from a drawing, a full-size model was made in wax, then came the casting and after this the refining and finishing (*rinettatura*) in detail—an operation which might take nearly half the total time. This emerges from the evidence relating to major works formed of several panels, for which detailed accounts had to be kept, such as Ghiberti's *Doors of Paradise* (finished in 1452) and Donatello's altar for the Santo in Padua (finished in 1450). This evidence is confirmed by the technical notes given by P. Gauricus in his *De sculptura* (Florence,

1504, edited by H. Brockhaus, Leipzig, 1886; new edition in preparation); by Vasari in the Introduction to chapter XI of his *Vitae* (preferably in the edition of G. Baldwin Brown, London, 1957, republished New York, 1961); and lastly by Benvenuto Cellini, *Due trattati...*, (Florence, 1568, new edition, C. Milanesi, Florence, 1857).

Usually the casting was not done by the master himself. Cellini explained the imperfections of Donatello's *David* as due to the faulty technique of the casting, which the artist could not control. But if the casting was entrusted to a specialist, the sculptor came into his own in the laborious process of finishing. A famous statuette by Bertoldo, the *Bellerophon*, bears the inscription: *expressit me Bertoldus, conflavit Hadrianus* ('Bertoldo modelled me, Hadrian cast me'). Leopardi, to whom Verrocchio left the casting of his *Colleoni* statue, signed it, and this was less impudent than it might at first seem.

6 The existence of polychrome wax portraits, of which there is evidence in Florence, is traditionally associated with the memory of *Orsino Ceraiuolo*. A digression of Vasari's, in his *Life of Verrocchio* (Milanesi edition, III, 373-375), is our source for information on the Benintendi family: they were specialists in wax effigies and were active from the fourteenth to the sixteenth century; their principal representative was Orsino (who married in 1462, was widowed in 1493 and died after 1498); his son Girolamo was also a *ceroplasta*, and his brother Jacopo had a son, Giuliano, whose name also appears in accounts at the end of the century. Vasari used as evidence the account-book of the Annunziata, where Orsino worked from 1474 onwards. To him Vasari attributes three portraits from the life—one of Lorenzo de' Medici, one of the Duke of Burgundy, and a third which has been supposed to be identical with the mask in the Lille Museum (L. Gonse, *Le musée Wicar: la tête de cire*, in 'Gazette des Beaux-Arts', XVII [1878], pp. 193-205; De Fabriczy, *Andrea del Verrocchio al servizio dei Medici*, in 'Archivio storico dell' arte', Series II, I [1895], pp. 163-76), but which is of a later date. These were not death masks, but *ex votos*, and this explains the connection of Benintendi with the Annunziata: see G. Masi, *La Ceroplastica in Firenze*, in 'Rivista d'arte', IX (1916), pp. 124-142. (On the cloister containing the Voti or *Boti*—in the seventeenth century it had more than 600 wax effigies and 22,000 in *papier mâché*—see G. Mazzoni, *I Boti della SS. Annunziata in Firenze*, Florence, 1923; W. Paatz, *Kirchen*, I, p. 121 and note 485).

J. von Schlosser, *Geschichte der Porträtbildnerei in Wachs*, in 'Jahrbuch Kunsth. Samml.' (Vienna), XXIX, (1911) has traced, in Vasari's account of the making of death masks, an adaptation of a passage from Pliny (Natural History, XXXV, 44), concerning Lysistratus, the brother of Lysippus.

The literature about the wax *Flora* is vast: there are summaries by G. Pauli in 'Belvedere', X (1931), pp. 1-11, and O. Kurz, *Fakes*, London 1948, p. 24, and Italian edition, Venice 1961, p. 3. On the fakes by Bastianini (1830-1848) who was responsible for these three famous terracotta fakes, the *Florentine Singing-girl* (Musée Jacquemart-André), the *Marsilio Ficino* (Victoria and Albert Museum) and the *Girolamo Benivieni* (Louvre)—see O. Kurz, *op. cit.*, English edition, p. 148 *ff*, and Italian edition, p. 170 *ff*.
All that is known of Leonardo's sculptures is that they were inspired by Verrocchio's style. There is no reasonable certainty about any of the terracotta *bozzetti* that have been attributed to him. (For an account of the problem, see M.V. Brugnoli, *Documenti notizie e ipotesi sulle sculture di Leonardo*, in the Symposium, 'Leonardo, Studi e Ricerche', Rome, 1954, pp. 363-389).

Even the *Rearing Horse* belonging to the Budapest Museum and the recently considered *Youthful Christ* in the Gallaudt Collection, Rome (see C. Pedretti, *Studi Vinciani*, 1957, pp. 66-67), are no exceptions.

7 On the *cartellino*, M. Meiss, *Toward a more Comprehensive Renaissance Palaeography*, in 'The Art Bulletin' XLII (June 1960), pp. 97-112) has stressed the precocious appearance of 'self-consciousness' in Mantegna, who as early as 1448, in the pride of his seventeen years, signed a lost altarpiece as follows: *Andrea Mantinea pat. an. septem et decem natus sua manu pinxit* ('Painted in his own hand by Andrea Mantegna of Padua aged seventeen years'); again, in 1454, he placed an explicit *cartellino* at the foot of the niche of his Santa Euphemia (Mus. Naz. di Capodimonte, Naples).

The use of the *Cartellino*—a panel or label usually painted in *trompe l'œil* for the purpose of bearing the artist's name and signature—did not begin to spread till the middle of the Quattrocento. The earliest known example seems to be that of Fra Filippo's *Madonna* in the Palazzo Barberini in Rome (c. 1440). Besides Mantegna, a fair number of Paduan painters belonging to the Squarcionesque group used the device. It seems reasonable, therefore, to consider Padua as the centre from which it spread. By 1470-80 it was becoming quite common. In its actual origin it was probably another borrowing from the Flemish painters.

8 '*Un frate Filippo da Firenze, un Piero dal Borgho, uno Andrea da Padova detto Squarcione, uno Cusme da Ferrara, uno altro Vincentio Bresciano.*' *Trattato dell'architettura* by Filarete, *op. cit.*, p. 302.

9 On the technique of fresco painting, the following observations by E. Borsook (*The Mural Painters of Tuscany*, *op. cit.*, pp. 13-14) are particularly valuable: '*Most of Giotto's work at Padua and Masaccio's in the Brancacci chapel was done in true fresco. Only the finishing touches and certain colours (blue and some reds and greens) were added when the surface was already dry. During the fifteenth century more and more was done on dry plaster. But around 1500, true fresco painting was taken up as an academic point of honour. By the middle of the century, Vasari was recalling what he imagined were the good old days of*

true fresco painting as practised by the ancients and the first of the modern masters. For Vasari, and many others, fresco painting was the test of an artist's virtuosity in speed and power of improvisation.'

10 Pictures on canvas by Mantegna:
The *Presentation in the Temple* (Berlin) has given rise to much discussion, both about its authenticity, which is now admitted (there is a closely similar version on wood in the Querini-Stampaglia Collection, Venice) and about its date: Kristeller and Tietze assign it to Padua in about 1454, Fiocco and Gamba to Mantua in about 1466, and Berenson places it at the end of the century. The Mantuan period may be considered probable: see E. Tietze-Conrat, *Mantegna, Paintings, Drawings, Engravings*, London, 1955; *Cat. Expos. Andrea Mantegna*, Mantua, 1961, no 17.

The *Santa Euphemia* has recently been restored: it is painted on extremely fine canvas, which at some unknown date was slightly scorched: see *IV*ª *Mostra di restauri*, Naples 1960, p. 115.

The *Madonna della Vittoria* was carried in procession as a standard in July 1496 (E. Tietze-Conrat, *op. cit.*, pp. 194-5: *Cat. Expos. Mantegna*, 1961, no. 40). It has the devotional interest of being accompanied by an auxiliary cartoon or *spolvero*, which is an exceptionally valuable piece of evidence on the technique: see L. Ozzola, in 'Civiltà' I (1942), p. 67; his interpretation has been rejected, though wrongly, by G. Fiocco in the 'Burlington Magazine', (August, 1949).

11 In an article entitled '*Highlands' in the Lowlands* (Gazette des Beaux-Arts, May-June 1961, pp. 273-314), M. Meiss has developed points outlined by him in *Venezia e l'Europa* (Congress, 1955), Venice, 1956. He describes the platform composition to be found in the *Madonna with the Chancellor Rolin* as a *'juxtaposition of large figures in the foreground, half or more as high as the painting itself, with minute forms in the distance,'* and he then demonstrates how it was adopted at Padua and Urbino in the work of Mantegna, G. Boccati and Piero della Francesca just when the Flemish painters seem to have turned away from it; finally, he shows the return to the Eyckian model in the case of Antonello (in his Antwerp and London *Crucifixions*).

12 One of the most delicate problems in unravelling the relationships between Tuscany and Ferrara is raised by the 1487 *cassone* with the *History of the Argonauts* (Robinson Collection, Capetown: no. 24 in the 1958 London Exhibition). In this the architectural motifs, the figures, certain features of the landscape, etc., suggest the hand of Filippino or of Piero di Cosimo, but under Ferrarese influence. Berenson saw in the landscape the hand of his 'Alunno di Domenico'—i.e. Bartolomeo di Giovanni. To the same painter belong a *Madonna* in Berlin (no. 90a) and a *Crucifixion* (Florence, Casa Horne), see C. Gamba, *Filippino Lippi, l'Amico di Sandro*, in 'Miscellanea in onore di J.B. Supino', Florence 1933.

13 The importance of the new medium had been perceived in various quarters: Alberti mentions: *La nuova invenzione d'impastare coll'olio di livio tutti i colori occorenti, i quali riescono eterni contro ogni ingiuria d'aria e di cielo. purchè la muraglia sia asciuttissima.* (*De re aedif.*, VI, 9). ('A new method of binding all the colours together with olive oil, ensuring their permanent resistance to any possible damage from air or sky, provided that the wall is very dry.') It will be noticed that Alberti has in mind here the use of oil in mural painting. See: G. Mancini, *Vita di L.B. Alberti*, 2nd edition, Florence, 1911, p. 129.

14 The importance of Verrocchio seems to us, therefore, to go beyond his actual work in painting. According to G. Passavant (1959), only a small number of pictures can be considered certainly by him: 1470, *Madonna* (Berlin); 1471-1472 *Crucifixion* (Argiano); 1473 *Tobias* (London); 1474-1475 *Baptism of Christ* (Uffizi), revised by Leonardo; 1478-1479 the Pistoia Altarpiece, completed by Lorenzo di Credi in about 1484-1485.

GLOSSARY-INDEX

GLOSSARY-INDEX

ABBIATEGRASSO, centre near Milan, where Bramante worked in 1497: Santa Maria Nuova, *p.* 74.

ABBOZZO *(bozza, bozze)*: sketch for a painting or sculpture: in the case of a painting, an advanced sketch has been made; in that of a sculpture, the block has been reduced more or less to the intended form, but remains rough. Sometimes the work is abandoned at this point - hence arose the concept of the *non finito.*

ABIRON, *see* KORAH.

ADAM, *ills* 134, 171, 174, 192.

AGAPITO (St), *see* BOLOGNA.

AGOSTINO DI DUCCIO, Florence 1418-Perugia after 1481. Florentine architect and sculptor. Assistant to Alberti at Rimini. Marble *Madonna* for Florence Cathedral (Bargello); façade of the Oratory of San Bernardino, Perugia (1462); altar of the Pietà, Perugia Cathedral (1474). *pp.* 151, 157; *ills* 165, 172. *see bibliog.* 293.

AGRIGENTE (Sicily) after 1086 the town became the wealthiest bishopric in Sicily, rivalling Palermo. *see map* 357.

AJACCIO, city in Corsica, belonged to the Pisans then to the Genoese who founded the new town in 1492. *see map* 357.

ALAMANNO (Pietro), mentioned between 1463 and 1498. Austrian painter born at Göttweih, pupil of Carlo Crivelli, influenced by Antoniazzo Romano and Vittorio Crivelli. Active in the Marches and painted numerous polyptychs (Ascoli Piceno, 1463-1489). *p.* 347. *see bibliog.* 414.

ALBERTI (Leon Battista), Genoa 1404-Rome 1472. Humanist, painter, sculptor and architect; born in exile, educated in Venice and Padua, abbreviator to the Papal court. Author of treatises on painting, sculpture and architecture. Active as an architect after 1446 in Rimini, Florence and Mantua. *pp.* 6, 27, 28, 31, 39, 42, 48, 56, 63, 74, 79, 81, 347, 353; *ill.* 65. *see bibliog.* 234.

ALFONSO OF ARAGON, *see* ARAGON.

AMADEO (Giovanni Antonio), Pavia 1447-Milan 1522. Lombard architect and sculptor, followed Filarete. Active in Bergomo (Colleoni Chapel, 1470-1475) and Pavia (façade of the Certosa and - with Giacomo della Porta - tomb of Giovanni Galeazzo Visconti). *pp.* 67, 82, 154, 163, 333; *ills* 10, 71, 72, 73, 138, 169, 177. *see bibliog.* 6, 15.

AMBROGIO DA MILANO or DA URBINO or BAROCCI, Milan *c.* 1460-*c.* 1530. Lombard sculptor, active in Urbino (Ducal Palace), in Venice (1470-1473, San Michele de Murano), in Ferrara (1473-1475, tomb of Lorenzo Roverella in San Giorgio), in Viterbo (1481, campanile of Santa Maria della Quercia), in Perugia (1487, new altar for the cathedral). *p.* 157.

AMBROSE OF MILAN (St, Italian: AMBROGIO), Treviso *c.* 339-Milan 397, a Doctor of the Church and Bishop of Milan (374-397) of which he became the patron saint. *p.* 319.
Emblems: mitre, crozier.

ANCONA, republic, sea-port of the Marches; later attached to the Papal States. *see maps* 355, 358.

ANDREW (St, Italian: ANDREA), apostle, brother of St Peter, patron saint of Mantua, *p.* 177; *ill.* 227 g.
Emblems: saltire (x-shaped cross), fish.

ANDREA DEL CASTAGNO, *see* CASTAGNO.

ANDREA DELL'AQUILA, *see* AQUILA.

ANDREA DEL SARTO, *see* SARTO.

ANTICO (Pier Jacopo ALARI BONACOLSI, called), Mantua 1460-Gazzuolo 1528. Goldsmith, sculptor and medallist; the creator of sculptures and statues inspired by the antique. *p.* 114; *ill.* 119.

ANTONELLO DA MESSINA, Messina *c.* 1430-1479. Painter trained in Naples under Colantonio. Active in Messina (1456-1473, San Gregorio altarpiece) and in Venice (San Casciano altarpiece, 1476, dispersed; fragments in Kunsthistorisches Museum, Vienna). *pp.* IX, 247, 272, 277, 278, 285, 311, 323; *ills* 272, 273, 274, 275, 276, 277. *see bibliog.* 46, 118, 183, 402, 403, 409.

ANTONIAZZO ROMANO (pseudonym of Antonio AQUILI), Rome *c.* 1435 *c.* 1508. Painter from the Romagna, active in Rome and Latium. Rieti triptych (1464); frescoes for Tor de' Specchi monastery, Rome. *pp.* 186, 187; *ill.* 194. *see bibliog.* 242.

ANTONIO DA FABRIANO (Antonio Agostino di Ser Giovanni da Fabriano), mentioned between 1451 and 1489; painter of altarpieces and polyptychs: *St Jerome* (1451, Walters Art Gallery, Baltimore), *Crucifix* (1452, Piersanti Museum, Matelica), Polyptych (1474, church of San Clemente de Genga). *ill.* 344.

ANTONIO DA MONZA, *see* BIRAGO.

ANTONY OF PADUA (St, Italian : ANTONIO), Lisbon *c.* 1195-Arcella 1231, a Doctor of the Church. Franciscan monk, patron saint of Padua and Spoleto.
Emblems: book, flame, Greek letter tau, heart, lily.

AOSTA, Alpine town at junction of Great St Bernard and Little St Bernard valleys. *see map* 358.

APELLES, the most famous of the ancient Greek painters (4th century BC). The subjects of his works know by Pliny are often taken up again in the XVth century; e. g., *Calumny* by Botticelli. 'The New Apelles' was a term of praises pread by the humanists. *pp.* 326, 327.

APOLLO, Greek God of the Arts, of light and of divination. This god of Antiquity is constantly evoked during the 15th century both as a solar power and as a symbol of poetry. The antique copy of the statue of the God (4th century, Attic) at Grottaferreta, was given a place of honour among the collections in the Belvedere at the end of the 15th century. *ill.* 296.

AQUILA (Andrea dell') Aquila - end of the 15th century. Sculptor and painter from the Abruzzi. Pupil of Donatello. Spent several years in Florence in the entourage of Cosimo de' Medici and above all in Naples. *p.* 89. *see bibliog.* 395.

AQUILA DEGLI ABRUZZI, city in the Abruzzi, founded by Federico II. *see map* 358.

ARAGON, dynasty. Princes of Aragon who ruled the kingdom of Naples, as follows: ALFONSO V (1442-1458), FERDINAND OR FERRANTE I (1458-1494), cousin of Ferdinand the Catholic; his son ALFONSO II (1494-1495), duke of Calabria succeeded him in 1494. After the French invasion the crown passed to FERDINAND II or FERRANDINO (1495-1496), then to FREDERICK, his uncle (1496-1501), and finally to Spain in the person of FERDINAND THE CATHOLIC himself (1504-1516). *pp.* 47, 54, 57, 58, 156, 157, 351; *ill.* 170.

ARCA (Niccolò D'Antonio dell' or da BARI), 1440-Bologna 1494. Apulian sculptor who passed through Naples *c.* 1480. Sculpted canopy to the tomb of St Dominic (1469-1473, Bologna). Entombment, terracotta (1485, Santa Maria della Vita, Bologna). *pp.* 145, 146; *ills* 161, 162. *see bibliog.* 149.

ARCA: (etym. 'ark', a coffer, or chest. The term is used for the monumental receptacle forming part of many tombs. One of the most famous is the Arca of St Dominic at Bologna: thence the name Niccolò dell' Arca.

ARCEVIA, city in the province of Ancona, was one of the important fortresses of the Popes and of the Sforzas. *see map* 358.

ARCH (triumphal): edifice inspired by the triumphal monuments of Antiquity (of which the best-known examples, apart from those in Rome, were at Rimini and Ancona). It was also applied to the design of tombs, altarpieces, façades, etc. *pp.* 46, 76; *ill.* 79.

AREZZO, Tuscan city: under Florence from 1384 onwards. *pp.* 184, 187, 215, 323.
Patron saint: Donato of Arezzo.
Secular buildings: Palazzo della Fraternità dei Laici (1375-1460): porch with Virgin by Rosselino.
Churches: Sant'Annunziata (1491).
Badia (13th century), enlarged by Vasari: tabernacle by B. da Maiano.
Santa Maria delle Grazie: portico by B. da Maiano.
San Francesco (1322): The Story of the True Cross frescoes (1452-1459) by Piero della Francesca. *p.* 181; *ills* 129, 193.

ARGUS, according to Ovid, a prince of Argos endowed with a hundred eyes of which fifty were always open. *p.* 189; *ill.* 201.

ARIADNE, the daughter of Minos and Pasiphae. Infatuated with Theseus, she helped him escape from the Labyrinth, fled with him and was abandoned on Naxos. The theme belonging to the 'Sayings of famous women' may be seen on *cassoni* panels. *ills* 15, 186.

ARION, Methymna in Lesbos 7th century B.C., Greek lyric poet, said to have invented the Greek dithyramb. *ill.* 118.

ARISTOTLE, Stageira 384-Chalcis 322 B.C. Greek scholar and philosopher. *ill.* 281.

ARNOLFO DI CAMBIO, Colle di Val d'Elsa *c.* 1240 - Florence *c.* 1302. Florentine sculptor and architect.

ARRICCIO *(arricciato,* Ital.: bristly, rough-cast), rough coating upon which the mortar for a fresco was laid.

ARTE/ARTI *(arte,* Ital.; *ars,* Lat.), designates the great intellectual or technical disciplines: music, medicine, law ...; is also applicable to the guilds, in particular: *arte della lana, arte della seta* ... The concept of intellectual activity dominating technique was formed slowly during the 15th century, linked to the concept of inspiration; it will lead to the idea of the community of the plastic arts with the foundation of drawing, hence the *Accademia delle arti del disegno* (1563).

ASCOLI PICENO, city in the Marches subject to the Papal States in 1502 (after diverse vicissitudes. *pp.* 3, 246.)
Patron saints: Emidius of Ascoli, James of the Marches, Helen.
Churches: Cathedral, enlarged *c.* 1482 (restored in 19th century); polyptych by Carlo Crivelli (1473) *pp.* 242, 258, 347; *ill.* 260. Sant'Agostino, altered (1485) by Giuliano di Zanobi de San Miniato. — (1485) by Giuliano du Zanobi de San Miniato. *Pinacoteca.*

ASOLA, city in the province of Mantua, from which it depended from 1440 and which in 1487 definitively became a Venetian possession. *see map* 356.

ASSISI, Umbrian city, birthplace of St Francis: in 14th and 15th centuries a possession of the Visconti, of the Montefeltre, then, under Pius II, of the Papal States. *see map* 358.

ASTI, Piedmontese city: a republic in the Middle Ages, and then a Duchy, which, from 1494-1551 came under Milanese rule. *p.* 82.
Patron saint: San Secondo d'Asti.
Church: San Pietro in Conzavia.

ATRI, small town in the Abruzzi (Teramo), from 1393 onwards a possession of the counts of Acquaviva. *p.* 179.

AUGUSTINE (St), Tagaste 354-Hippo 430. Bishop of Hippo, writer of *The City of God*. One of the four great Doctors of the Church. Very popular in Tuscany. *p.* 246; *ill.* 264.
Emblems: Bishop's vestments, dead bird. E.g., S. Botticelli, Ognissanti (Florence).

BACCHUS, Greek god of wine and of drunkenness, taken by the Florentine humanists (Ficino...) as a symbol of inspiration and mystical delirium. E.g., Michelangelo, *The (Drunken) Bacchus*, Bargello (Florence). *ills* 15, 186.

BACCIO DA MONTELUPO (Bartolomeo SINIBALDI, called), Montelupo 1469-Lucca 1535. Florentine architect and sculptor. *p.* 151.

BADIA (abbreviation of the word *abbazia)*, abbey inhabited by monks, governed by an abbot (Pomposa, Nonantola, etc.). It comprises an abbey church, a cloister and monastic buildings arranged according to a plan imposed by the rule of the order.

BALDOVINETTI (Alessio), Florence 1425-1499. Florentine painter and mosaicist, follower of Domenico Veneziano and Andrea del Castagno; *Madonna* in the Louvre (1450); frescoes in the Chapel of the Cardinal of Portugal (1466-1474, San Miniato al Monte). *pp.* 184, 209, 321; *ills* 219, 245. *see bibliog.* 89, 176.

BARBARI (Jacopo de'), Venice *c.* 1440-Brussels 1516. Venetian painter. Pupil of Alvise Vivarini; painted polyptychs and altarpieces and in 1500 drew up a plan of Venice. *p.* 326; *ill.* 60. *see bibliog.* 159, 364.

BARBARIGO, Venetian noble family which produced the two Doges: MARCO (1485-1486) and AGOSTINO (1486-1501). *ill.* 178.

BARI, city in southern Italy (Apulia), passed from the Normans to the Aragonese and in 1464 came under the governorship of Maria Sforza. *see map* 357.

BARTOLOMEO DELLA GATTA (Fra), pseudonym of Piero d'Antonio DEI, Florence 1448-Arezzo 1502. Tuscan painter and architect, a monk at the Monastery of Santa Maria in Gradi (1470), Prior of the Monastery of San Clemente d'Arezzo (1487). Painted a picture of *San Rocco* (1475). *p.* 184; *ill.* 196. *see bibliog.* 42, 223.

BARTOLOMEO DI GIOVANNI, mentioned between 1483 and 1511. Pupil and collaborator of D. Ghirlandaio. Painted seven panels for the predella of the *Adoration of the Kings* by D. Ghirlandaio. *p.* 353. *see bibliog.* 132.

BATTAGIO (Giovanni), late 15th century. Lombard sculptor and architect. Church of the *Incoronata* at Lodi (1488-1494), Church of Santa Maria della Croce near Crema (*c.* 1500), Como cathedral (1491-1519). *pp.* 84, 164; *ill.* 89. *see bibliog.* 387.

BELFORTE SUL CHIENTE or DEL CHIENTE, town in the province of Macerata, whose evolution the town followed. *see map* 356.

BELLANO (Bartolommeo), Padua *c.* 1434-*c.* 1497. Architect and sculptor, pupil of Donatello, active in Rome, Perugia and Padua where he sculpted the reliefs in the Santo (1485-1488). *pp.* 89, 95, 151; *ill.* 105. *see bibliog.* 37, 274.

BELLINI (Gentile), Venice *c.* 1429-1507; Venetian painter, son of Jacopo Bellini, brother of Giovanni. Official portrait painter to the Republic of Venice; portraits of *Lorenzo Giustiniani* (1465, Accademia), *Mahomet II* (1480, London, National Gallery). As a painter-chronicler, he gave a picturesque vision of Venetian life: *Procession in the Piazza San Marco* (1496, Accademia). *pp.* x, 18, 119, 234, 257; *ills* 239, 240.

BELLINI (Giovanni) or GIAMBELLINO, Venice *c.* 1430-1516. Venetian painter, brother of Gentile and brother-in-law of Mantegna. Painted historical panels in the Sala del Gran Consiglio (1480, destroyed in 1577), and numerous altarpieces: the four triptychs for the Carità (1464, Accademia, Venice), polyptych of St Vincent Ferrer (*c.* 1465, SS. Giovanni e Paolo), Pesaro altarpiece (c. 1475), the San Giobbe altarpiece (1486-1487), the San Zaccaria altarpiece (1505). He also created a type of Madonna: e. g., *Virgin and Sleeping Child* (*c.* 1470, Accademia), and those (c. 1490) at Bergamo and in the Louvre. *pp.* x, 178, 229, 248, 154, 257, 272, 277, 278, 311, 317, 330; *ills* 278, 342. *see bibliog.* 105, 141, 160, 256.

BELLINI (Jacopo), Venice *c.* 1400-1470. Venetian painter, father of Giovanni and Gentile. Collections of drawings and perspective studies. *pp.* 192, 229, 234, 235, 257. *see bibliog.* 317.

BELLUNO, city in the Veneto, subject to Venice from 1404. *see map* 358.

BENEDETTO DA MAIANO, Maiano 1442-Florence 1497. Architect, sculptor and craftsman in marble. Active in Florence, collaborated with Cronaca in building the Palazzo Strozzi (Santa Maria Novella), bust of Fillipo Strozzi, altar of Santa Fina (San Gimignano). Collaborated with his brother Giuliano on the church at Loretto. *pp.* 116, 137, 156; *ills* 34, 152. *see bibliog.* 103.

BENEDETTO DA ROVEZZANO (Canapale, Pistoia 1474-Vallambrosa 1552). Sculptor and architect. *p.* 151.

BENINTENDI, family of Florentine artists who specialized in wax-modelling, active at the end of the 15th century; one of the family, ORSINI, was a pupil of Verrocchio. *pp.* 140, 352.

BENVENUTO DI GIOVANNI, Siena 1436-*c.* 1518. Sienese painter who produced the paintings in the Baptistry at Siena and also numerous altarpieces. *pp.* x, 201.

BERENSON (Bernard), Vilna 1865-Florence 1959. Art historian and writer. *pp.* 189, 305, 324, 353.

BERGAMO, city in Lombardy: a domain of the Lombard kings, a free commune, and then (1427) under Venice. pp. x, 181, 189, 278.

Patron saints: Adelaida of Bergamo, Alessandro of Bergamo, Asteria, Grata, Giulia of Corsica, Lupo of Bergamo.
Churches: Cathedral (1457-1487). *pp.* 82.
Colleoni Chapel (1470 - *c.* 1475) by G. Amadeo; tombs of B. Colleoni and his daughter, by G. Amadeo. *pp.* 22, 67, 82, 128, 129, 163; *ills* 10, 71, 138.

BERNADINE OF SIENA (St), Massa Maritima 1380-Aquila 1444. Franciscan preacher, revived the order of the 'Observants'. A patron saint of Siena. *p.* 21; *ills* 21, 157.
Emblems: horsehair robe, monogram of the letters IHS, flame, and three mitres (Siena, Ferrara, Messina). Eg., Pinturicchio, cycle of the Life of St Bernardine in Santa Maria in Aracoeli (Rome, 1485).

BERNINI (Gian Lorenzo), Naples 1598-Rome 1680. Architect, painter and sculptor of international fame, a master of decorative and monumental baroque style. *p.* 116.

BERRUGUETE (Pedro, known as Pietro SPAGNUOLO), Paredes de Nava, *c.* 1450-Avila 1504. Spanish painter. Worked at Urbino for the Duke of Montefeltro, between 1477 and 1482. *pp.* 189, 281; *ills* 281, 282, 283, 285. *see bibliog.* 140.

BERTOLDO DI GIOVANNI, Florence *c.* 1420-Poggio a Caiano 1491. Florentine sculptor and medallist, pupil of Donatello; taught Michelangelo; keeper of the Medici collections. Worked with Bellano on the pulpits in San Lorenzo, Florence. Produced plaquettes and Madonnas. *pp.* 89, 95, 102, 113, 352; *ill.* 116. *see bibliog.* 38.

BIELLA, town in Piedmont in the province of Vercelli, from 1379 became a possession of the Duchy of Savoy.
Churches: Baptistry (10th and 11th centuries); paintings (13th century); campanile (13th century). *p.* 82.
San Sebastiano (1504).

BIFORA: Italian term for . window divided into twin bays under a single round arch. *pp.* 53, 334.

BIRAGO (Giampetrino), mentioned at the end of the 15th century. Miniaturist to the Sforzas. Designated as the Master of the Book of Hours of Bonne de Savoie or the 'Pseudo-Antonio da Monza'. *ill.* 195. *see bibliog.* 338.

BISSONE, North Italian village on lake Lugano. *p.* 157.

BISTICCI (Vespasiano da), Bisticci 1421-Antella 1498. Humanist and librarian to the Medici and to Federico da Montefeltro. Author of the *Vite d'uomini illustri del secolo XV* (1482). *pp.* 280, 281.

BOCCATI (Giovanni di PIERMATTEO, called Il), Camerino *c.* 1420-1490. Painter from the Marches. Produced numerous polyptychs: 1468, altarpiece at Belforte sul Chiente; 1474, *Madonna del Pergolato. p.* 353. *see bibliog.* 424.

BOLOGNA, city in Emilia; played important part in the Lombard League between 12th and 13th centuries, governed in 14th and 15th centuries by the Viscontis and the Bentivoglios. *pp.* 36, 49, 53, 151, 230, 257, 278, 310, 344.
Patron saints: Agapito, Agricola, Barbatiano of Ravenna, Florian, Nicolo, Petronio, Procule.
Secular buildings: Palazzo Bevilacqua (1481), *pp.* 50, 54, *ill.* 51, Palazzo dei Drappieri (1486-1496), Palazzo Fava (1484-1491), p. 50, Palazzo Pallavicini-Fibbia (1497), Palazzo del Podestà (13th century, rebuilt in 1472), Palazzo Poggi (1472), Zamboni colonnade (1477), columns of Tommaso Filippi, Torre dei Asinelli, Loggia (1488).
Churches: San Domenico (1221), containing tomb of St Dominic (1267). Completed by Niccolò dell'Arca (1468-1473) and Michelangelo (1494). Corpus Domini (1478-1480), *p.* 132. Madonna di Galliera (façade, 1491), *pp.* 36, 66, *ill.* 37. San Giovanni in Monte (major alterations in the 15th century), façade (1474), stained glass by F. Del Cossa, *Virgin and Saints* (1497) and *Coronation of the Virgin* (1501) by L. Costa, pp. 245, 295. San Michele in Bosco (rebuilt 1494-1510). San Petronio (rebuilt 1445-1525), stalls (1468-1477) by A. De Marchi, p. 245. Santo Spirito (1481-1497), terracotta decoration (1497) by Sperandio, *p.* 67, *ill.* 70.

BOLSENA, city forming part of the County of the Monaldeschi from 1377 to 1451, the date at which it was definitively restored to the Papal States.
Patron saint: Santa Cristina da Bolsena.
Church: Santa Cristina (11th century), façade (1494), terracotta decorations by the Della Robbia, p. 148.

BONA OF PISA (St), 1150-1207. Patron saint of Siena, famous for the pilgrimage she is said to have made to Santiago de Compostela where she is recorded as having had a vision of Christ.

BONASCIA (Bartolomeo), Modena *c.* 1450-1527. Architect, painter and marquetrist, influenced by Piero della Francesca and Mantegna. Active in Modena where he worked from 1468 to 1470, for the hospital of the confraternity of San Giovanni della Morte. Only one dated work: *Pietà* (1485, Galleria d'Este, Modena). *p.* 189; *ill.* 188. *see bibliog.* 323.

BONFIGLI (Benedetto), Perugia *c.* 1420-1496. Painter of the School of Perugia, mentioned for the first time in Rome in 1445. Working in the Vatican, 1450. Commissioned to decorate new chapel of the Priors, Perugia, 1454. *Adoration of the Magi* and *Annunciation* (Pinacoteca, Perugia). *p.* 188. *see bibliog.* 41.

BONIFACIO, town in Corsica, at the southern tip of the island, under Pisan rule then governed by Genoa from 1195 to 1768. *see map* 357.

BORENIUS (Carl Tancred), Viipuri 1885-1948. Finnish art historian. *p.* 350.

BORGOGNONE (Ambrogio da FOSSANO, called Il) or BERGOGNONE, Fossano *c.* 1450-1523. Lombard painter, active in Milan, Lodi and at the Certosa di Pavia (1488-1494). A pupil of Foppa, painted numerous altarpieces and the frescoes at San Simpliciano in Milan (1522). *pp.* 245, 313. *see bibliog.* 10, 179.

BORGO SAN SEPOLCRO, small city in the province of Arezzo. Its destiny was dependent upon this town and, in 1440, it permanently became a Papal possession. *see maps* 353, 358.

BOTTEGA: studio or workshop, in which the master worked with the help of assistants and apprentices whom he trained in their craft and provided with food and lodging. *pp.* IX-XI, 257.

BOTTICELLI (Alessandro di Mariano Filipepi, known as Sandro Botticelli), Florence, 1445-1510. Florentine painter, pupil of Filippo Lippi; many altarpieces in Florence; *Adoration of the Magi*, *Altarpiece of San Barnaba* (1485-1486, Uffizi), *Coronation of the Virgin* (1488, Uffizi). Also secular paintings: *Primavera*, *Birth of Venus*. One of the painters of the frescoes in the Sistine Chapel (1481-1482). Towards the end of the century, illustrations for Dante's *Divina Commedia*. *pp.* IX, X, 15, 177, 197, 216, 223, 230, 239, 248, 260, 289, 307, 309, 314, 321, 322, 323, 324, 330; *ills* 14, 25, 208, 227 b, d, f, 228, 229, 261, 262, 263, 264, 265, 294, 308, 309, 310, 323. *see bibliog.* 75, 101, 232, 341.

BOTTICINI, family of Florentine artists: among them: Francesco, Florence 1446-1497, pupil of Neri di Bicci, active in Empoli and Florence. Altarpieces: *Assumption* (London), *Madonna and Saints* (1482, Louvre), predella for the altarpiece of St Sebastian and the Holy Sacrament (1484-1491, the parish church, Empoli). *p.* 18.

BRACCESCO (Carlo), *c.* 1460-1510. Painter of Milanese origin, active in Genoa and Liguria. Only signed and dated work: polyptych in the parish church of Montegrazie (1478). Painter of the *Annunciation* triptych in the Louvre. Attributed to him: an altarpiece of St Andrew (dispersed) and the fresco of the *Coronation of the Virgin* in Santa Maria di Castello, Genoa. *pp.* X, 177. *see bibliog.* 72, 194.

BRAMANTE (Donato di Angelo), Monte Adrualdo (Fermignano) 1444-Rome 1514. Painter and architect trained at Urbino. Active in Lombardy 1477-1499: façade of the Palazzo del Podestà, Bergamo; and then in the service of Lodovico il Moro in Milan; sculptural decoration to Casa Panigarola (Men at Arms). Worked on Santa Maria presso San Satiro, on apse of Santa Maria delle Grazie and on Pavia Cathedral. After 1500, Roman period: cloister of Santa Maria della Pace (completed 1504). *Tempietto* of San Pietro in Montorio, 1502, and after 1505 reconstruction of the Vatican; initial work on the new St Peter's (after 1506), of which the central plan design was his, and on the courtyard of the Belvedere. *pp.* *X*, *XI*, 6, 41, 75, 76, 79, 84, 189, 297, 322; *ills* 49, 50, 77, 90, 150, 200. *see bibliog.* 112, 128, 129, 146, 209, 318, 320.

BRAMANTINO (Bartolomeo Suardi, called Il), Milan 1450-1536. Architect and painter. *p.* 189; *ill.* 201. *see bibliog.* 137.

BREA (Lodovico), Nice *c.* 1450-*c.* 1523. Painter from Nice, active in the County of Nizza and in Liguria; collaborated with Foppa in 1490 on the polyptych for Santa Maria di Castello, Savona. Painted numerous polyptychs at Nice, Savona, Taggia, Montalto and Genoa. *p.* X; *ill.* 348. *see bibliog.* 178.

BREGNO (Andrea), Osteno 1418-Rome 1506. Lombard sculptor, active in Rome: tomb in Santa Maria sopra Minerva. (Cardinal De Coca, 1477). Collaborated with Pontelli on the façade of Santa Maria del Popolo. In Tuscany, he worked on Siena Cathedral and on Monte Oliveto Maggiore. In Venice he worked on the Foscari tomb. *pp.* 120, 157; *ills* 49, 50.

BRESCIA, Lombard city, ruled by various overlords; then under Venice from 1426 onwards. *pp.* 53, 181, 246.
Patron saints: Apollonius of Brescia, Faustino, Giovita, Gaudenzio, Paterio, Afra of Brescia, Angela Merici, Giulia of Corsica.
Secular buildings: Palazzo Communale, Loggia (1492-1574).
Monte di Pietà (Monte Vecchio, 1484).
Churches: Sant'Agostino (façade with terracotta decoration 15th century). Madonna del Carmine. Santa Maria dei Miracoli (1488-1523), *pp.* 36, 84, 165; *ills* 36, 91.
San Giovanni Evangelista (15th century).

BRESSANONE, city in the Veneto, an ecclesiastical principality from 1027 to 1803. *see map* 358.

BRIOSCO, Milanese sculptors; Bartolomeo, mentioned at Milan Cathedral between 1475 and 1499; Benedetto, mentioned at Milan Cathedral in 1483. Collaborated with Amadeo on the façade of the Certosa di Pavia; Cristoforo, mentioned at the end of the 15th century and at the beginning of the 16th century; Pietro, active in Milan (1473) and at Bologna. *pp.* 67, 163, 333; *ills* 72, 73.

BRUNELLESCHI (Filippo), Florence 1377-1446. Goldsmith, sculptor and architect, active in Florence in the service of Cosimo de' Medici. Revived architecture. Dome of Santa Maria del Fiore (1420). *pp.* 12, 30, 31, 39, 79, 148, 321, 351; *ill.* 66. *see bibliog.* 153.

BRUNI (Leonardo), Arezzo 1370-1444. Humanist and politician, wrote a Latin history of Florence, eulogist of Dante. *p.* 337.

BUONCONSIGLIO (Giovanni, called Il Marescalco), Vicenza 1470-Venice 1535-1537. Painter from Vicenza, pupil of Montagna. Painted the *Pietà* (Museo Civico, Vicenza). *p.* 311; *ill.* 313. *see bibliog.* 126.

BURCKHARDT (Jacob), Basle 1818-1897. Swiss historian. *pp.* 29, 33, 246.

BUSSETO, commune in Emilia-Romagna; came under the Pallavicinis and then, after 1588, the Farneses. *p.* 146.

BUTINONE (Bernardino), Treviglio *c.* 1450-*c.* 1507. Lombard painter trained in the School of Foppa. Produced altarpieces, worked in 1485 with Bernardino Zenale on the San Martino altarpiece, Treviglio. *pp.* 251, 314; *ills* 253, 254, 345. *see bibliog.* 330.

CAFAGGIOLO, locality near Barberino di Mugello, famous for its Medici villa built (1451) by Michelozzo for Cosimo the Elder. *ill.* 46.

CAGLI, small town in the province of Urbino, followed the destiny of this duchy from the mid-14th century until 1631. *see map* 353.

CAGLIARI, town and seaport in southern Sardinia, under Pisan rule until 1284, then governed by Genoa until 1326, then by the Catalans. *see map* 357.

CAMERA PICTA: term used for rooms whose walls are entirely covered with painting, like the Sala degli Sposi, by Mantegna, in the Ducal Palace at Mantua. *pp.* 229, 338; *ill.* 234.

CAMERINO, ancient city of the Marches, centre of the domain of the Varanos from the 13th to the 16th century. *p.* 246.
Patron saint: San Venanzio da Camerino.
Churches: San Venanzio (15th century), Annunziata (15th century).

CANTIANO, village in the Duchy of Urbino whose political fluctuations it followed. *see map* 353.

CAPORALI, family of Umbrian artists. JACOPO, ?-1478. Miniaturist, responsible for the illustration of an antiphonary belonging to San Pietro, Perugia. BARTOLOMEO, Perugia *c.* 1420-1508. Painter; worked with Bonfigli, and painted a *Madonna* (Uffizi). GIOVANNI PAOLO, ?-1533. Goldsmith in Perugia, son of Bartolomeo: admitted in 1482 to the Guild of Goldsmiths of Porta Santa Susanna. Worked with Rodolfo Compagni for the Cathedral of San Biagio. *p.* 188. *see bibliog.* 332.

CAPUA a fortified city in Campagna, situated on the left bank of the Volturno, built in the 9th century and rebuilt at various times throughout the centuries. *see map* 357.

CAPRAROLA, town in the province of Viterbo, twelve mile from this city. Famous for its grandiose Farnese palace built for Cardinal Alessandro Farnese by Vignola (1549-1559). *see map* 353.

CARADOSSO Cristoforo FOPPA, called Il), Mondonico *c.* 1452-1527. Goldsmith, enameller and medallist. *pp.* 76, 164; *ill.* 78.

CARAFFA (Diomede), Naples *c.* 1406-1487. Writer politician, and Neapolitan patron of the Arts. *p.* 45

CAREGGI, *see* FLORENCE.

CARIANI (Giovanni), Venice *c.* 1480-1547. Painter from Bergamo, active in Bergamo and in Venice. *p.* 278.

CARPACCIO (Vittore), Venice *c.* 1455-1526. Venetian painter, a pupil of Gentile Bellini and, like him, with a gift for large-scale narrative schemes. The San Giorgio degli Schiavoni cycle (1502-1508) and the St Ursula cycle (1490-1498, Academia, Venice). *pp.* 18, 115, 179, 235, 278, 311, 317; *ills* 94, 108, 191, 241, 242, 312, 316. *see bibliog.* 71, 185, 257, 271, 277.

CARTA TINTA: paper prepared so as to give a coloured ground (grey, dark blue, salmon pink, etc.) for a drawing, usually gouache, much favoured by the Florentines in the 15th century, from Gozzoli to Lorenzo di Credi and Leonardo. *see* A. Chastel, 'Carta tinta', in 'L'Œil', december 1955.

CARTOON: a full-scale drawing used as a model for the execution of a fresco, being either copied, if the squaring-out procedure is used, or employed directly by the so-called 'spolvero' method.

CASSONE: a chest, usually of wood; in a more specialized sense, a marriage chest decorated either with the coat of arms of husband and wife or with secular, historical or mythological themes alluding to 'marriage'. In the second half of the 15th century *cassoni* were more and more frequently decorated in marquetry (views of cities, etc.) and sometimes they were of gigantic proportions. *pp.* 9, 12, 22, 184, 206, 305, 309, 353; *ills* 212, 216.

CASTAGNO (Andrea del), San Martino a Corella 1423-Florence 1457. Florentine painter specializing in large-scale compositions. *pp.* 209, 245, 321.

CASTELFIORENTINO, agricultural centre in the district of Florence governed by this city from the 12th century.
Church: Madonna della Torre. *p.* 244; *ill.* 247.

CASTIGLIONE (Baldassare), Casanatico (Mantua) 1478-Toledo 1529. Author of *The Courtier*, a breviary of a man of the world, which had an immense success both in Italy and throughout Europe. *p.* 91.

CASTIGLIONE D'OLONA, small city in Lombardy, whose importance was increased by Cardinal Branda da Castiglione (1350-1443). *p.* 184.
Church: Church of Villa (15th century).

CATANE, a town and seaport in eastern Sicily, on the Ionian Sea. In 1409 came under Aragonese rule. Famous for its earthquake in 1169 and for its epidemic of the plague in 1423. *see map* 357.

CATENA (Vicenzo), Venice *c.* 1470-*c.* 1531. Venetian painter, a pupil of Giovanni Bellini. *p.* 278.

CATHERINE OF ALEXANDRIA (St), martyred under Maxentius, revered for her learning and for her resistance to heresy. E.g., *Sala dei Santi* in the Borgia Apartments (1493-1494).
Emblem: a broken wheel (referring to the method of her torture).

CATHERINE OF SIENA (St), 1347-1380. Sienese virgin saint, of the 'third order' of Dominican nuns. Canonized in 1461 by Pius II. Created the patron saint of Italy by Pius XII in 1939.
Emblems: lily, crucifix, Dominican habit.

CAVALLO: Italian for horse, often used to designate an equestrian statue. Used, in particular, with reference to Leonardo's huge terracotta model in the Castello Sforzesco, for an equestrian statue of Francesco Sforza. *pp.* 102, 109; *ills* 106, 109, 110, 111.

CECROPS, mythical founder of Athens represented in the *Florentine Picture-Chronicle* by Maso Finiguerra. *ill.* 11.

CELSO (St), born in the 1st century. His cult was linked to that of St Nazarius and spread to Milan, Verona and Brescia.

CESENA, city in Emilia, subject to Bologna in the Middle Ages, then in the 15th century to the Malatestas.
Secular buildings: Castle of the Malatesta (1466-1476), Biblioteca Malatestiana (1452), by M. Nuti.
Church: Cathedral; altar by Pietro Lombardo, *ill.* 144.

CESPEDES (Pablo de), Cordova 1538-1608. Scholar, art theoretician, painter and sculptor. Active in Rome (1559-1566), in Italy (1566-1576), in Cordova and in Seville (1577-1608). *p.* 281.

CHARLES VIII, 1470-1498, King of France 1483-1498, son of Louis XI. Began the Italian Wars in September 1494, with an expedition which took him as far as Florence, Rome and Naples but ended in a precipitate retreat: (battle of Fornova, 6th July 1495). He brought back from Italy Neapolitan craftsmen and technicians. *p.* 6.

CHELLINI (Giovanni), died in 1461. Tomb in San Miniato. *p.* 137; *ill.* 153

CHELLINO (Antonio da), mentioned as active in the mid-15th century. One of Donatello's four assistants in work on the high altar of the Santo, Padua (1446-1448). Sculptor of one of the reliefs representing the symbols of the Evangelists. *p.* 89. *see bibliog.* 172.

CHIAROSCURO: contrasting use of light and shadow in a painting (as in paintings by Caravaggio). *pp.* 229, 230.

CHIGI (Agostino), called the Magnificent, Siena 1465-Rome 1520. Banker and art patron. *p.* 58.

CHIGI (Villa), near Siena. *p.* 58; *ill.* 59.

CHIOS, Greek island in the Aegean, governed by Genoa between 1304 and 1566. *p.* 40.

CHOISY (Auguste), Vitry-le-François 1841-1909. French engineer and archaeologist. *p.* 29.

CIMA DA CONEGLIANO (Giambattista), Conegliano *c.* 1459-1517. Venetian painter, pupil of Montagna, came under the influence of the Bellini. Painted altarpieces; *San Vicenza altarpiece* (1489), *Baptism of Christ*, in San Giovanni in Bragora (1494); *Virgin* in Santa Maria del Carmine (1509-1510). *pp.* 254, 278; *ill.* 256. *see bibliog.* 80, 87.

CINGOLI, village 17 miles from Macerata which belonged to the Papal States from 1293. *see map* 358.

CITTÀ DI CASTELLO, Umbrian city, governed by the Vitelli family from 1450. *see map* 358.

CIVITA CASTELLANA, small town situated 23 miles from Viterbo which belonged to the Papal States from the 8th century. *see map* 353.

CIVITALI, family of Tuscan sculptors. MATTEO, Lucca 1436-1501. Sculpted statues for the Chapel of the Volto Santo, and the Chapel of St John in Genoa Cathedral (1491-1492); MASSEO DI BARTOLOMEO, his nephew, worked on the doors of the cathedral. *pp.* 151, 156. *see bibliog.* 299.

CIVITAVECCHIA, town in Latium 45 miles from Rome. From the 9th century onwards belonged to the Papal States. Famous for its fortress built in 1508, destroyed in 1944. *see map* 353.

CLAUDIUS (Tiberius Drusus), Lyons 10 B.C.-Rome A.D. 54. Roman emperor. *ill.* 169.

CODUCCI (Mauro), Val Brembana *c.* 1440-Venice 1504. Bergamese architect, active in Venice; San Michele in Isola (1479); façade of the Scuola San Marco (1485-1495); completed the campanile of San Pietro di Castello (1488). *pp.* 50, 84, 124, 134; *ills* 52, 53, 75, 147.

COLLEONI (Bartolommeo), Solza (Bergamo) 1400-Malparga 1475. Condottiere who enjoyed great authority in Bergamo, Colleoni Chapel. In 1456, he became Generalissimo of the Venetian Republic. (Statue by Verrocchio, Piazza San Zanipoli, Venice). *p.* 109; *ills* 109, 111.

COLLEONI (Medea), daughter of Bartolommeo, ?-1470. *pp.* 128, 129; *ill.* 138.

COLONNA (Fra Francesco), Treviso? 1433-Venice 1527. A monk at the Dominican monastery in Treviso. Author of the *Hypnerotomachia* (1467, published in Venice in 1499 by Aldus Manutius). *p.* 79.

COMMYNES (Philippe de), Renescure 1447-Argenton 1511. French chronicler, diplomat and royal counsellor. *p.* 54.

COMO, a city in Lombardy, integrated with the Duchy of Milan in 1335. *p.* 157.
Patron saints: Abundius, Campophorus, the Quattro Incoronati, Liberata, Faustina.
Churches: Cathedral, work resumed in 1396, completed in 1519. Façade and side doors (1498-1507-1509) by the Rodaris. *p.* 132; *ills* 146, 175.

CONDOTTIERE: adventurer who led a band of soldiers of fortune and placed himself in the pay of different princes. A condottiere often became lord of a fief, of a city or even of a state - as, for instance, Federico da Montefeltro at Urbino, Sigismondo Malatesta at Rimini, Francesco Sforza at Milan.

CONFRATERNITIES (Italian *confraternita*, Latin *sodalitates*). Association of laymen devoted to pious and charitable works. These institutions were greatly developed during the 15th century. They took part in processions and the endowment of altars and chapels.

CONVERSAZIONE (SACRA): group consisting of the Madonna and Saints, on a terrace or under an aedicule, intended for the contemplation of the faithful. The theme appears with Fra Angelico and Domenico Veneziano, and was to become immensely successful in Venice, in Florence and in Umbria. *pp.* 16, 178, 254, 317, 343; *ills* 273, 316.

CORRADO TEUTONICO, German 15th century sculptor, active in Cingola and in Arcevia, *p.* 142.

CORREGIO (Antonio ALLEGRI, called), Corregio *c.* 1489-1534. The great master who worked in Mantua and in Parma. *p.* 324.

CORSIGNANO, *see* PIENZA.

CORTEMAGGIORE, ancient city of Emilia, which was replanned in the time of the Marchese Gian Lodovico Pallavicino. *p.* 1.
Town-planning: the town was rebuilt between 1470 and 1481.

CORTONA, Tuscan city, subject to Florence from 1411 onwards. *p.* 306.
Patron saint: Santa Margherita da Cortona.
Churches: Santa Maria delle Grazie del Calcinaio (1485) by F. di Giorgio Martini. *p.* 33.
Church of the Gesu (1498-1505). Now the diocesan museum.

COSIMO I, *see* MEDICI.

COSSA (Francesco del), Ferrara *c.* 1436-Bologne 1477. Painter and sculptor, one of the three masters of the Ferrarese School; took part in the decoration of the Palazzo Schifanoia. Painted altarpieces in Ferrara and Bologna (Griffoni altarpiece in San Petronio, 1473; Dresden *Annunciation). pp.* 217, 230, 245, 257, 259, 322, 338, 343; *ills* 209, 258, 318, 340, 349. *see bibliog.* 249.

COSTA (Lorenzo), Ferrara *c.* 1450-Mantua 1535. Ferrarese painter, active in Bologna : Bentivoglio Madonna (San Giacomo Madonna 1483). Painted pictures in the studiolo of Isabella d Este (Mantua). *pp.* 245, 278, 295, 322.

CREDI (Lorenzo di), Florence *c.* 1459-1537. Florentine painter, Verrocchio's principal pupil along with Leonardo. *Madonnas* (London, Berlin, etc.) close in style to Leonardo and to the Pistoia altarpiece. *pp.* IX, 116, 285, 301, 306, 307, 330, 353; *ill.* 324. *see bibliog.* 27, 77, 95, 96.

CREMA, city in Lombardy, one of the Lombard communes destroyed by Frederick Barbarossa (1159); became subject to Venice in 1449.
Church: Santa Maria della Croce (*c.* 1500) by Battagio and Montanari. *p.* 84, *ills* 88, 89.

CREMONA, city in Lombardy, became a free commune in 1098, then in the 14th century came under the Visconti and in the 15th century under the Sforzas. *p.* 82.
Patron saints: Homobonus (Omobuono), Himerius, (Gismonde), Marius of Persia, Hilary of Padua, Agatha of Catania, Margherita, Eusebius.
Secular buildings: Palazzo Fodri (late 15th century). *p.* 164.
Palazzo Trucchi-Raimondi (1496), *pp.* 54, 164.
Palazzo Stagna (*c.* 1550), *pp.* 132, 164; *ills* 30, 33, 145.
Portico of A. Carrara (1491-1525).
Churches: Cathedral (1190-1273), restoration begun in 1491 by P. da Rho. Bishops' thrones (1482) by Amadeo and Piatti, stalls (1490) by G.M. Platina, *ill.* 169.
Sant' Agostino (1339), campanile (1461).
Baptistry, *ill.* 86.
San Imerio, *p.* 163.

CRESCENZI (Pietro de'), Bologna 1230-1320, judge and humanist. Writer of the *Liber ruralium commodorum,* written in 1305, 1st Latin edition 1471, Italian 1478, *p.* 56.

CRIVELLI (Carlo), Venice *c.* 1430-*c.* 1493. Venetian painter, who left Venice in 1470 for Dalmatia, active in the Marches where he painted numerous polyptychs heightened with gilding at Ascoli Piceno (1475), *Annunciation with St Emidius* (1486, London), *Coronation of the Virgin* (1482, Brera). *p.* IX, 190, 194, 242, 246, 257, 258, 259, 278, 324, 347; *ills* 205, 206, 207, 260, 347, 350. *see bibliog.* 177, 415, 416, 423.

CRONACA (Simone del POLLAIOLO, called Il), Florence 1457-1508. Florentine architect and sculptor, worked on the Palazzo Strozzi (1489). *pp.* 33, 86; *ill.* 34. *see bibliog.* 211.

CROTONE (until December 1928: COTRONE), town in the province of Catanzaro, on the east coast of Calabria, incorporated into the royal domain in 1444 by Alfonso of Aragon. *see map* 357.

DATHAN, *see* KORAH.

DAVID, king of Israel, about 1010-970 B.C. Founded Jerusalem, represented in two ways, as the young shepherd who defeated Goliath and as a king. The first was a favourite subject for sculpture in the Quattrocento. *ills* 117, 181, 182.

DECEMBRIO (Angelo), *c.* 1415-after 1466. Italian humanist, accredited to the court of Ferrara, went on to Spain in 1458. Wrote the *Politia litteraria. p.* 326.

DEIANEIRA, legendary wife of Hercules. Having been abandoned by him, she re-dressed him in the poisoned tunic of the centaur Nessus: several popular themes have grown out of this tragic story. *ills* 288, 289.

DELITIO (Andrea), end of the 15th century. Venetian painter identified with Andrea da Lecce. Painted the frescoes in the cathedral of Sulmona and in the cathedral of Guardiagrele (1473). *p.* 179.

DEMIDOFF (Anatole), prince of San Donato, Moscow 1812-Paris 1870. Diplomat and Russian art patron. *p.* 347; *ill.* 350

DESIDERIO DA SETTIGNANO, Settignagno *c.* 1428-Florence 1464. Florentine sculptor specializing in *schiacciato* relief; a pupil of Donatello he worked in Florence and in Orvieto. Designed the tomb of Carlo Marsuppini (Santa Croce). *pp.* 151, 156, 167; *ill.* 167. *see bibliog.* 89, 289.

DISTEMPER: method of painting with water, particularly for frescoes; the colours are thinned out in water, to which a gelatinous substance has been added.

DOMENICO VENEZIANO, *see* VENEZIANO.

DONATO OF AREZZO (St), martyred ? 361. Bishop of Arezzo.
Emblems: Mitre, chalice (the chalice fell from the hands of the deacon during the Mass and he miraculously mended it).

DONATELLO (Donato di Betto BARDI, called), Florence 1386-1466. Florentine sculptor, whose force and originality exercised an influence all over Italy. After his work for Or San Michele (the *St George*, 1416) and for Florence Cathedral (*Prophets* for the West front), *c.* 1410; *Prophets* for the campanile, 1433-1439, the Cantoria, 1433-1440) he went to Rome (1432-1433) and then spent a long time (1443-1453) at Padua, where he produced the Gattamelata statue and the altar of the Santo. Returned to Florence and worked on the bronze pulpits in San Lorenzo. *pp.* IX, 89, 91, 94, 95, 102, 116, 137, 151, 156, 167, 170, 182, 321, 351, 352; *ills* 95, 96, 97, 98, 99, 100, 101, 102, 103, 107, 110, 166, 182. *see bibliog.* 89, 171, 172, 290.

ELOI (St, Italian: ELIGIO), *c.* 590-660. French saint whose cult spread to Germany and to Italy. The patron saint of a great number of guilds, goldsmiths and tool-makers.
Emblems: tongs, hammer, horseshoe.

EMIDIUS OF ASCOLI (St), martyred in 390. First bishop of Ascoli, he was a protector against earthquakes. Frequently represented as a Martyr holding his head in his hands. Carlo Crivelli: *Annunciation* (St Emidius kneeling behind the angel holding a model of the town of Ascoli, London, National Gallery).

EMPOLI, Tuscan city, on the left bank of the Arno; under Florence from 1182 onwards. *see map* 358.

ERRI (Agnolo and Bartolomeo degli), second half of 15th century. Painters in Modena, who produced altarpieces. Triptych in the Pinacoteca, Moderna. *p.* 247.

ESTE, Italian princely house which ruled over Este, Ferrara and Modena. After Lionello who reigned from 1441 to 1450, Borso (1413-1471) who ruled from 1450 to 1471, inaugurated the decisive phase of the Renaissance. Ercole (1435-1505) ruled from 1471 to 1505. Isabella (1471-1539) daughter of Ercole 1st, married Francesco Gonzaga, duke of Mantua. Beatrice (1475-1505), daughter of Ercole 1st, married Lodovico Il Moro. *pp.* 1, 109, 113, 230, 317, 326, 338.

EUPHEMIA (St, Italian: EUFEMIA), Maiden saint from Chalcedon, martyred in 304. *p.* 230; *ill.* 235.

EUTORGIO OF MILAN (St), 315-331. Bishop of Milan, patron saint of Milan.
Emblems: Bishop's robes, crozier and mitre.

EVE, *ills* 135, 136, 171, 174.

FABRIANO, city in the Marches: absorbed by the Papal States in the middle of the 15th century. *see map* 358.

FAENZA, city in the Romagna, a domain of the Manfredis, attached to the Papal States in 1501. Centre of the majolica industry. *pp.* 3, 194.
Patron saints: San Venanzio, San Giacomo della Marca.
Churches: Cathedral (1474-1486), by G. da Maiano.
Shrine of San Savino (1476) by B. da Maiano.

FANCELLI (Luca), Florence 1430-1495. Architect, sculptor and engineer, active in Florence and in Mantua where he worked at the court of Lodovico Gonzaga. *ill.* 76.

FANO, city in the Marches. Came under the Malatestas in the 15th century, from 1463 attached to the Papal States. *p.* 76; *ill.* 79.
Patron saint: San Paterniano of Fano.
Secular buildings: Arco Bramantesco (1491).
Palazzo Malatesta (15th century) [now the Malatesta Museum].
Loggia San Michele (15th century).
Churches: Santa Maria Nuova (redesigned in 1500).
Madonna dei Piattellenti, doorway (1480).

FAUSTINO (St) and GIOVITA (St) OF BRESCIA, beheaded under Hadrian. Patron saints of Brescia.
Emblem: palm.

FELTRE, a city in the Veneto, at the foot of the Venetian Alps; a Venetian domain from 1404. *see map* 358.

FEO (Jacopo) ?-Forlì 1495. The lover (or possibly husband) of Caterina Sforza Riario. *Ill.* 198.

FERNINAND II, OF ARAGON, *see* ARAGON.

FERRARA, city in Emilia, from 1208 to 1597 a possession of the house of Este. In the 15th century the reigning princes were: Lionello d'Este (1441-1450), Borso d'Este (1450-1471) and Ercole d'Este (1471-1505). *pp.* 1,2 , 41, 49, 57, 91, 102, 146, 189, 190, 192, 194, 197, 242, 258, 278, 295, 309, 316, 319, 322, 326, 353; *ill.* 2.
Patron saints: Barbara, Maurelio.
Town planning: new quarter designed by Biagio Rossetti (1471-1505).
Secular buildings: Palazzo dei Diamanti (1492) by B. Rossetti, *pp.* 54, 334; *ills* 56, 332.
Palazzo Constabilis (1494). Palazzo Scrofa, *p.* 50.
Palazzo Communale, redesigned (1475-1481) by Benvenuti and (1493) by B. Rossetti.
Palazzo Pareschi (1475-1487).
Palazzo Schifanoia (begun in 1391 and enlarged 1458-1478) by B. Rossetti, with frescoes (Sala dei Mesi by F. del Cossa, Ercole dei Roberti, Cosimo Tura), *pp.* 181, 215, 216, 217, 229, 338; *ills* 209, 340.
Palazzo Sacrati (1493-1500).
Palazzo Trucchi-Raimondi (1496), *p.* 54.
Churches: San Benedetto (1496-1554).
Cathedral (12th century) with campanile (1425-1594), *p.* 230.
San Francesco (1494-1530) by Biagio Rossetti, *p.* 66; *ill.* 68.
Santa Maria degli Angeli (1471-1494).
Santa Maria in Vado (1495-1508).
San Giorgio (1485) by Biagio Rossetti, with the

Roverella tomb (1475) by Ambrogio da Milano and Antonio Rossellino, *pp.* 242, 257; *ills* 243, 244. The Certosa (1461).
Pinacoteca.

FERRUCCI, family of sculptors who originated from Fiesole; FRANCESCO DI SIMONE, Fiesole 1437-1492. A pupil of Simone Nanni, his father who collaborated with Ghiberti and Desiderio. Worked in Rimini and Urbino. Author of the Tartagni tomb in San Somenico, Bologna (1477); ANDREA called DA FIESOLE, Fiesole 1465-1526. Son of Peiro di Marco, active in Florence and Pistoia, worked on the cathedral at Fiesole (1492-1493), baptismal font for Pistoia Cathedral (1497-1499). *p.* 128, 151; *ills* 32, 51, 137.

FIESOLE, Tuscan town just outside Florence. Its fortunes echo those of Florence from 1125 onwards. *see maps* 355, 358.

FILARETE (Antonio AVERLINO, called), Florence 1400-Rome *c.* 1465. Florentine architect and sculptor, who worked on the Castello at Milan (1451-1454) and on the Ospedale Maggiore (1456-1465). Major influence on Lombard architecture. Author of a treatise on architecture. *pp.* 4, 6, 30, 31, 36, 40, 41, 82, 181, 351, 352; *ills* 6, 29, 39. *see bibliog.* 120, 325, 333, 390.

FILIPPINO, *see* LIPPI.

FILIPPO, *see* LIPPI.

FINA (St), born at San Gimignano, died at the age of 15 in 1254. Patron saint of San Gimignano, performed many miracles, died of paralysis on a straw pallet swarming with rats which after her death became transformed into a bed of flowers.
Emblems: rats, flowers.
Domenico Ghirlandaio: fresco cycle in the Cathedral depicting her death and burial (1475).

FINIGUERRA (Maso), Florence 1426-1464. Florentine draughtsman, goldsmith and niellist. Worked at Santa Maria del Fiore. Author of the *Florentine Picture-Chronicle*, *c.* 1460. *ills* 11, 81.

FIORENZO DI LORENZO, Perugia *c.* 1445-1525. Florentine painter taught by Benozzo Gozzoli and close to the Umbrian school. *Madonna della Misericordia* (1476, Perugia), polyptych for Santa Maria Nuova (1487-1493, Perugia). *pp.* 21, 188. *see bibliog.* 148.

FLORENCE, ancient republican city in Tuscany, subject to the Medici after 1434. COSIMO I (1389-1464), PIERO I (1416-1469), LORENZO THE MAGNIFICENT (1449-1492), PIERO II (1471-1503), expelled by a revolution in 1494. Savonarola's Christian Republic lasted only until 1498. It was followed by a provisional regime under the gonfalonier Soderini, which prepared the way for the return of the Medici. This became inevitable when Cardinal Giovanni (1475-1521) was raised to the pontificate under the name of Leo X (in 1513). *pp.* 6, 10, 33, 46, 48, 77, 89, 94, 95, 109, 110, 113, 114, 120, 121, 137, 140, 142, 148, 151, 154, 184, 209, 224, 247, 260, 272, 279, 285, 288, 289, 292, 295, 297, 305, 307, 309, 319, 322, 351, 352.
Patron saints: John the Baptist, Eugenius of Florence, Frediano of Lucca, Reparta of Florence, Zenobius of Florence, Miniato, Barnabus, all of whom were frequently represented in Tuscan art.
Secular buildings: Loggia Rucellai (1460) by Alberti, *pp.* 30, 39, 54.
Palazzo dei Antinori (*c.* 1465) attributed to G. da Maiano.
Palazzo Gondi (1490-1494) by Giuliano da Sangallo, *pp.* 39, 334; *ill.* 333.
Palazzo Medici (later Riccardi [1444-1460], by Michelozzo, chapel with frescoes by Benozzo Gozzoli (1459), *p.* 39; *ill.* 38.
Palazzo Pazzi (1430), continued (1462-1472) by G. da Maiano.
Palazzo della Signoria: containing audience chamber and Sala dei Gigli, doorways and ceilings sculpted by G. and B. da Maiano.
Palazzo Strozzi (1489-1536), by B. da Maiano and Cronaca, *p.* 36; *ill.* 34.
Palazzo Serristori (1474) by Baccio d'Agnolo.
Villa of Careggi, *p.* 56; *ill.* 57.
Villa of Poggia a Caiano, rebuilt for Lorenzo de' Medici by G. da Sangallo, *pp.* 56, 57, 58, 60, 148, 334; *ills* 45, 58.
Villa of Poggio Imperiale, fortified in 1488 by G. da Sangallo, *p.* 1.
Churches: Santa Maria del Fiore, the Cathedral (1296), dome (1426-1461).
SS. Annunziata (1250); tribune rebuilt *c.* 1450 by Michelozzo after Alberti's advice had been sought, *p.* 79.
Badia (10th century), enlarged in 1285 and rebuilt in 1627; doorway (1495) by B. da Rovezzano, tomb of Count Ugo (1469-1481) by Mino da Fiesole, *p.* 116; *ills* 123, 124.
Santa Croce (13th century); tombs of Leonardo Bruni by B. Rossellino, of Marsuppini by Desiderio da Settignano, *p.* 156.
Capella dei Pazzi, built by Brunelleschi (1430-1444) in the cloister next to Santa Croce. Second cloister by Brunelleschi, *p.* 148.
Sant' Egidio (1420), frescoes (now lost) by Domenico Veneziano, Piero della Francesca and Andrea del Castagno, *p.* 286.
San Lorenzo by Brunelleschi, finished by A. Manetti (1460); tabernacle in marble by Desiderio, bronze pulpits by Donatello and assistants; in the Old Sacristy which was decorated by Donatello (*c.* 1440) is the tomb of Giovanni and Piero de' Medici (1472) by Verrocchio, *pp.* 63, 75, 79; *ills* 66, 96-103, 107, 109, 167.
Santa Maria Novella (1278-1360): façade (1456-1470) designed by Alberti; choir frescoes (1485-1490) by Ghirlandaio; frescoes of Strozzi chapel by Filippino Lippi, *pp.* 27, 66, 211, 215, 218; *ills* 65, 222, 223, 224, 225, 268, 327.
Santa Maria Maddalena de' Pazzi (13th century) rebuilt between 1480-1492 by G. da Sangallo, *p.* 298.
San Miniato al Monte (1018): containing Chapel of the Cardinal of Portugal (1460), *p.* 243; *ills* 245, 337.
Ognissanti (1239), with frescoes by Botticelli and

Ghirlandaio; cloister by Michelozzo; refectory with *Last Supper* by Ghirlandaio (1480). *p.* 223, 260; *ills* 230, 264.
Or San Michele (1336); with statues by Donatello, Verrocchio and Luca della Robbia; *ill.* 183.
Santo Spirito (1434-1481), vestibule and sacristy (1489-1494), by Cronaca and G. da Sangallo, *pp.* 16, 86.
Santa Trinità (1258-1280) Sassetti Chapel, frescoes by Ghirlandaio, *p.* 211; *ill.* 221.
San Martino della Scala, *p.* 223; *ills* 228, 229.
Convent of Sant'Apollonia, refectory (1445-1450), frescoes by Andrea del Castagno.
Baptistry, *pp.* 77, 110; *ill.* 113.

FOGGIA, town in Apulia, the favourite residence of Federigo II, it came under Aragonese rule in 1447. *see map* 357.

FOLIGNO, Umbrian city, attached to the Papal States from 1439 onwards.
Patron saint: Beata Angela da Foligno.
Secular building: Palazzo Deli (15th century).
Churches: Oratory of the Annunciation (1494).
Santa Maria Infraportas (12th century), 15th century frescoes.

FONDULI (Agostino), mentioned at the end of the 15th century and the beginning of the 16th. Sculptor and architect from Crema, mentioned at Pienza *c.* 1483. Worked on the decoration of churches and palaces, *p.* 164. *see bibliog.* 15.

FOPPA (Vincenzo), Brecia *c.* 1427-*c.* 1515. Lombard painter, whose activity extended to Genoa and Pavia; he dominated the second half of the 15th century in Lombardy. Capella Portinari (*c.* 1468, in the church of Sant'Eustorgio, Milan). Painted polyptychs including one for Santa Maria delle Grazie (Brera, Milan). He worked with L. Brea on the Cardinal della Rovere altarpiece (1490, Santa Maria di Castello, Savona). *pp.* 181, 192, 245, 311, 313, 324; *ills* 314, 348. *see bibliog.* 348.

FORLÌ, city in the Romagna, subject to the Ordelaffi family from 1315-1480, then to Girolamo Riario till 1500, when it became part of the Papal States. *pp.* 128, 151, 187; *ills* 137, 198.
Patron saints: Mercuriale, Valerian, Beato Giacomo Salamone of Forlì, Peregrinus.
Secular building: Palazzo del Municipio (1459-1460).

FORTEGUERRI (Niccolò), Pistoia 1419-Viterbo 1473. A relation of Pius II, cardinal and papal legate. *p.* 116; *ills* 125, 126.

FOSCARI (Francesco), Venice 1373-1457. Doge of Venice 1423-1457. *p.* 120.

FOSSOMBRONE, city in the Marches, a possession of the Malatestas and then of the Montefeltros during the 14th and 15th centuries. *see map* 358.

FRANCESCA (Piero della), Borgo San Sepolcro *c.* 1410-1492. Tuscan painter, pupil of Domenico Veneziano in Florence: did not return there after 1445. His work was mainly in the courts of Urbino and Ferrara (at Ferrara he executed frescoes now destroyed) and in towns in the Apennines, such as Arezzo, where the church of San Francesco has his *Story of the True Cross* frescoes (1452-1459), and Borgo San Sepolcro. Of his altarpieces, the Montefeltro (*c.* 1490) is in the Brera, Milan; the Sant' Agostino polyptych (1454-1459) is dispersed (in Lisbon, London, and in the Frick Collection, New York); the Senigallia Madonna is in Urbino. He wrote a treatise on perspective and a study of pure geometric forms which were used by his friend Luca Pacioli. *pp.* x, XI, 18, 42, 89, 91, 181, 184, 186, 187, 188, 189, 190, 197, 206, 209, 217, 224, 246, 247, 257, 269, 272, 277, 278, 279, 280, 283, 284, 285, 288, 317, 321, 323, 324, 353; *ills* 192, 193, 269, 270, 286. *see bibliog.* 81, 82, 123, 196, 230, 334, 335, 426.

FRANCESCO DEL PUGLIESE, A follower of Savonarola, *p.* 295.

FRANCESCO DI GIORGIO MARTINI, Siena 1439-1502. Architect, engineer, sculptor in wood and bronze, painter and decorative designer, — a man whose wide-ranging individuality spread its influence from Siena to Urbino, where he took part in the building of the Ducal Palace. Author of a treatise on architecture. *pp.* 4, 6, 8, 22, 28, 41, 42, 44, 45, 46, 77, 79, 102, 113, 142, 201, 324, 333, 334; *ills* 5, 9, 22, 23, 26, 27, 31, 43, 48, 63, 64, 82, 115, 156, 212, 213, 330, 334. *see bibliog.* 262, 408.

FRANCESCO DI SIMONE, *see* FERRUCCI.

FRANCIA (Francesco RAIBOLINI, called Il), Bologna *c.* 1450-1517. Goldsmith and painter from Emilia. Spread the Umbrian manner in Northern Italy: oratory of Santa Cecilia, Bologna (1506). Collaborated with Lorenzo Costa on work for Giovanni Il Bentivoglio. *pp.* 295, 322; *ill.* 311. *see bibliog.* 273.

FRANCIS OF ASSISI (St, Italian: FRANCESCO), Assisi 1182-1226. Founded the order of the Friars Minor. One of the most popular of Christian saints. Ecstatic vision of St Francis (Christ among the Seraphim) and the Stigmata. *ills* 221, 257, 278.

Emblems: Habit of rough cloth, thrice knotted girdle (three vows: chastity, poverty, obedience), crucifix, stigmata on the hands and feet.

FRANCIS I, Cognac 1494-Rambouillet 1547; king of France, 1515-1547. *p.* 327.

FRESCO: mural painting, applied direct to wet plaster on the wall, the colours being mixed with water and some adhesive ingredient; this method requires that the painting be done during the time it takes to dry, that is to say, prepared very carefully and then carried out very quickly. *pp.* 209-229, 235, 286, 305, 338, 352; e.g., *ill.* 227.

FRIZZONI (Gustavo), Bergamo 1840-Milan 1919. Italian art critic. *p.* 344.

GAGGINI, family of Genoese sculptors and architects active in Sicily; GIOVANNI D'ANDREA DA CAMPIONE, active between 1460 and 1491. Worked on the Palazzo of Marco and Lazzaro Doria (1468); GIOVANNI III 1470-?, sculptor at Palermo, worked in 1492 with A. Mancino; STEFANO, mentioned between 1473 and 1487, sculptor at Palermo; PACE, mentioned between 1483 and 1522. Worked at the Certosa di Pavia and at Genoa; DOMENICO, died in 1492, head of the Sicilian branch of the family. *pp.* IX, 157; *ill.* 170. *see bibliog.* 1, 74.

GALGANO OF SIENA (St), 1150-1181. Hermit, allied to the Cistercian order, patron saint of Siena and of San Galgano in Tuscany.
Emblem: represented with the Archangel Michael and his sword driven into a rock.

GAMBELLO (Antonio), ?-1479. Architect and sculptor active in Venice, San Zaccaria (1458), San Giobbe (1471), Santa Chiara da Murano. Designed military architecture in Istria and at the Lido. *ill.* 75.

GATTAMELATA (Erasmo da NARNI, called), *c.* 1370-Padua 1443, Paduan condottiere. *p.* 102; *ill.* 110.

GAURICO (Pomponio), Gauro (Salerno), 1481-1530. Professor and teacher, established himself at Padua in 1501. There he came in contact with literary, artistic and scientific circles. Wrote a treatise *De Sculptura*, Florence, 1504, which deals with the canon of proportions, physiognomy and perspective at the end of which he mentions the most noteworthy sculptors. *pp.* 115, 116, 137, 151, 351.

GENOA, important maritime city in Liguria; at times during the 15th century was subject to the Dorias. *p.* 157.
Patron saints: Alessandro, Sauli of Genoa, Apelles, Catherine, George, John the Baptist, Siro of Genoa.
Secular building: Palazzo Serra (15th century).
Churches: San Stefano: tribune (1499). San Lorenzo: chapel of St John the Baptist, *p.* 134. *Gallery of the Palazzo Bianco.*

GENTILE DA FABRIANO, Fabriano *c.* 1370-Rome 1427. Painter from the Marches, worked in Orvieto, Pisa, Venice and Rome; painted altarpieces and decorations in San Giovanni in Laterano, Rome. *p.* 229.

GEORGE (St), according to legend martyred in 303. Young legionary in the Guard of the Emperor Diocletian. *p.* 242; *ills* 237, 243.
Emblems: the saint himself in knight's armour, Dragon, broken lance, banner, sword (as in Mantegna's *St George*, Accademia, Venice and his *Madonna della Vittoria* in the Louvre).

GEROLAMA DA VICENZA, Vicenza? *c.* 1510. Painter from Vicenza, active between 1480 and 1510, a pupil of Montagna. Painted the *Assumption* (1488, National Gallery, London). *p.* 12; *ill.* 13.

GHIBERTI (Lorenzo), Florence 1378-1455. His son VITTORIO I, Florence 1416-1496, was a goldsmith, bronze founder and sculptor, who collaborated with him on the third bronze door of the Baptistry in Florence; BUONACORSO, Florence 1451-1516, was an architect, engineer and metal caster, active from 1487 to 1495; he cast cannons during wars fought by Florence against Sarzana and Pisa. *pp.* 16, 91, 245, 247, 351.

GHIRLANDAIO, family of Florentine painters; DOMENICO, Florence 1449-1494. He was a pupil of Baldovinetti, was influenced by Verrocchio and the Flemish school, worked in the Sistine Chapel (1481) and painted the frescoes in the choir of Santa Maria Novella (1485-1490), his masterpiece. He also produced altarpieces: *Adoration of the Magi* (1488, Ospedale dei *Innocenti*), *Visitation* (1491, Louvre); DAVIDE, Florence 1452-1525, carried on the studio of his brother Domenico after 1490; specialized in mosaic; BENEDETTO, Florence 1458-1497, the younger brother of Domenico and Davide, was a Florentine painter who also worked in France. *pp.* X, 211, 215, 223, 235, 245, 254, 286, 322, 330; *ills* 221, 222, 223, 227g, 230, 327, 343. *see bibliog.* 78, 184, 392.

GIACOMO DA PIETRASANTA, ?-died 1495, architect and sculptor, active in Rome from 1452. *p.* 58.

GIMIGNANO (St), died 396. Bishop of Modena, patron saint of Modena and of San Gimignano, where he is said to have performed miracles.
Emblems: Model of the town of Modena, mirror with the image of the Virgin.

GIOCONDO (Giovanni da VERONA, called Fra), Verona *c.* 1433-Rome 1515. Architect, theoretician, Veronese epigraphist, drew up the plans for the Loggia del Consiglio; called to Naples for consultation and accompanied Charles VIII back to France, where he made his mark in Paris as an engineer and commentator on Euclid. Took part in Rome in discussions on the new St Peter's. *p.* 351. *see bibliog.* 200.

GIORGIO D'ALLEMAGNA, Modena ?-*c.* 1479. Painter and miniaturist from Ferrara, mentioned in the service of the Marchese Lionello of Ferrara (1441-1462) for whom he illustrated breviaries and manuscripts. *p.* 338.

GIORGIONE (Giorgio da CASTELFRANCO, called), Castelfranco Veneto 1477-1510. Venetian painter, celebrated pupil of Giovanni Bellini, painted both religious and secular compositions. *pp.* 172, 254, 311, 322; *ills* 188, 257.

GIOTTO, Colle di Vespignano 1266-Florence 1337. Florentine painter, mosaicist and a master-builder; pupil of Cimabue and Cavallini. Active in Padua (Arena Chapel frescoes) and in Florence. From the 15th century has been generally regarded as the founder of the 'modern manner' in painting. *pp.* 218, 321, 322, 352.

GIOVANNI D'ALEMAGNA or ZUAN TEDESCO, painter from the North, worked with Antonio Vivarini; died in Padua in 1450. *pp.* 247, 338.

GIOVANNI DA CAMERINO, late 15th century. Painter from the Marches. Trained in Perugia, stayed in Florence from 1447 to 1450. Collaborated with Giovanni Boccati on the decoration of the Ducal Palace in Urbino and was also often identified with this painter, as he was with the Master of the Barberini panels. *p.* 21. *see bibliog.* 424.

GIOVANNI DA VERONA (Fra), Verona *c.* 1457-1525. A Dominican monk, and the most highly esteemed of the intarsia designers of the late 15th and early 16th centuries. Designed the church furnishings of Santa Maria in Organo, Verona (1500) and of Monte Oliveto Maggiore. He was also responsible for the marquetry in the Sala della Segnatura (now disappeared). *frontispiece.*

GIOVANNI DI PAOLO. Siena *c.* 1399-1482. Sienese painter, influenced by Taddeo di Bartolo and Sassetta. Painted a *pala* for the University of the Pizzicaioli (1449) and an altarpiece for Pienza Cathedral (1463). *p.* 201; *ill.* 211. *see bibliog.* 51.

GIOVANNINO (Italian for 'Little St John'). Patron saint of Florence, to whom the Baptistry was dedicated. St John the Baptist is an extremely popular saint in Italy, revered as the 'little St John', the precursor and later companion of Jesus.

GIROLAMO DA CREMONA. Painter and miniaturist. Recorded as having worked between 1467 and 1473 with Liberale da Verona on the illustration of manuscripts and antiphonaries for the cathedral library at Siena. *p.* 206; *ill.* 217.

GIULIANO DA MAIANO, Maiano 1432-Naples 1490. Florentine architect and sculptor. Worked at Faenza Cathedral (1476), and at Arezzo, Siena and Naples where he built the Porta Capuana (1485). Worked at Loretto with his brother Benedetto, and with Cronaca on the Palazzo Strozzi (after 1489). *pp.* 58, 151, 243, 351; *ill.* 246.

GIUSTI (les JUSTE) family of Italian sculptors who worked in France and in the 15th and 16th centuries. ANTOINE (1479-1519) established himself in France in 1504, worked mainly at Gaillon. JEAN I (1485-1549), his brother worked at Tours and Saint-Denis.

GIUSTINIANI, *see* LORENZO GIUSTINIANI.

GNOLI (Domenico), Rome 1838-1915. Italian writer and librarian. *p.* 348.

GONZAGA, ruling family of Mantua, which became a marquisate in 1433 and a duchy in 1530. GIANFRANCESCO (1407-1444) summoned Pisanello and the humanist Vittorino da Feltre to Mantua. LUIGI III (1444-1478) turned his attention to L.B. Alberti and to Mantegna. Under FRANCESCO II, who married Isabella d'Este in 1490, there was a period of brilliant cultural development, culminating in the building and decoration of the Palazzo del Tè by Giulio Romano; FRANCESCO, Mantua 1444-Porretta 1483, cardinal and humanist, *p.* 81; *ill.* 234.

GOTHIC: in the 15th century from the time of Filarete onwards, the term 'Gothic' designated, in architecture, the style prevailing beyond the Alps; in the 16th century it meant all the outworn manifestations of the Middle Ages. The term 'International Gothic' has been created by modern writers to cover the court art of the years round about 1400, together with its romantic and precious continuations in Burgundy, Bohemia, Tuscany and Venice. *pp.* 9, 12, 21, 30, 53, 63, 76, 142, 179, 189, 197, 260, 265, 321 324, 343.

GOZZOLI, Florentine painters. BENOZZO, Florence 1420-Pistoia 1497. Florentine painter, apprenticed to Ghiberti as a goldsmith, pupil of Fra Angelico whom he helped in the decoration of the chapel of Nicholas V in Rome. After 1449 he became a decorative painter on his own; church of San Fortunato de Montefalco (1450-1452). Worked at Viterbo and Rome: Medici Chapel, Florence (1459); frescoes at San Gimignano and the Campo Santo, Pisa (after 1468); BERNARDO, Florence c. 1429-? Brother and collaborator of Benozzo. *pp.* 12, 211, 244, 330, 334; *ills* 24, 220, 247, 335. *see bibliog.* 36.

GRIFFONI (Matteo), Bologna 1351-1426. Notary, poet and chronicler. *p.* 257; *ills* 1, 258, 267, 318, 349.

GROTESQUE: in the years 1490-1495 and thereabouts, the explorations by painters in the 'grottoes' of the Esquiline—that is to say, the ruins of Nero's Golden House—became more and more intensive; the decorative motifs found there began to be exploited by Pinturicchio, Signorelli, Morto da Feltre, until they were fully assimilated in the classical decoration by Giovanni da Udine in the Loggias of the Vatican.

GROTTAFERRATA, small town 14 miles from Rome. Famous for its Abbey of the Basilian monks founded in 1004 by St Nilus. *see map* 353.

GUBBIO, Umbrian city and domain of the Montefeltros until 1508. *p.* 43.
Patron saint: Ubaldo of Gubbio.
Secular building: Palazzo Ducale (*c.* 1470) based on plans by L. Laurana.
Churches: Madonna fra San Pietro e San Paolo (1473) by Bernardino di Narni. Chapel of Santa Maria dei Laici (1313): crypt decorated with a fresco cycle of the Passion (frescoes *c.* 1460).

HUMANISM (in Italian *umanesimo*): the taste for and practice of *litterae humanitatis*,—that is, of a culture based on the study, spread and use of the ancient Greek and Roman authors. The movement stemmed from Petrarch: its first real effect was on moral philosophy, but after 1450-1460 it spread to each cultural discipline in turn, until it became the characteristic flavour of the cultural phase of the Renaissance. *pp.* 28, 79.

IGNUDO, Italian for nude figure. As distinct from *putto*, the secular version of a cherub, the *ignudo* is a representation of an adolescent whose pose and gestures form part of the setting and contribute to great figure compositions, as for example, in the ceiling of the Sistine Chapel.

IMOLA, city in Emilia, annexed by the Viscontis of Milan (1424) and then incorporated in the Papal States from 1447. *pp.* 3, 5, 49; *ill.* 7.
Patron saints: Cassiano of Imola, Maurelio of Ferrara.
Secular buildings: Palazzo della Volpe (1482).
Palazzo Paterlini (1482), by Giorgio Fiorentino.
Palazzo Sersanti (1482).
The castle (1332), fortified (1473).
Porta Appia (1482).
Churches: The Osservanza (*c.* 1473).
Cathedral campanile (1473).
Santa Maria dei Servi (*c.* 1490).

IMPERIA, town in western Liguria, the result of the union which took place in 1923 of Porto Maurizio and Oneglia. From 1276 became the capital of the Genoese vicariate of western Liguria. *see map* 356.

INNOCENT VIII, *see* POPES.

INNOCENTS (the Holy), the children of Israel massacred by Herod in his abortive attempt to kill the Child Jesus. The sudden importance which this theme assumed in Siena from 1480 onwards may be related to the horrors of Otranto.

INTARSIA or TARSIA: Italian term for marquetry, a technique which enjoyed a remarkable development between 1460 and 1510. *pp.* 22, 91, 189; *frontispiece.*

IVREA, city in Piedmont. From 1313 belonged to the Duchy of Savoy, with only brief interruptions. *p.* 313; *ill.* 315.

JACOMO DA PIETRASANTA, *see* PIETRASANTA.

JACOPO DA MONTAGNANA, *see* MONTAGNANA.

JACOPO DELLA QUERCIA, Quercia Grossa, Siena *c.* 1367-Siena 1438. Sienese sculptor with a robust and lively style, created several tombs in Lucca.

JAMES THE GREATER (St, Italian: GIACOMO), the son of Zebedee and brother of St John, martyred in AD 44 and the first apostle to be called. Patron saint of pilgrims, also of many cities in Italy: Pesaro, Pistoia, Rome, Bologna. *p.* 338; *ill.* 266.
Emblems: pilgrim, apostle, scallop-shell.

JANUARIUS (St, Italian: GENNARO), martyred in 305, patron saint of Naples and of Benevento. Bishop of Benevento.
Emblems: bishop's vestments, book, phial of precious blood (the saint was beheaded and had the index finger of his right hand cut off).

JEROME (St, Italian : GIROLAMO), Strido 347-Bethlehem 420. One of the four great doctors of the Church. Wrote the life of St Paul the Hermit and translated the Bible into Latin. Led the life of an anchorite in the desert. *p.* 319; *ills* 176, 196, 251, 291, 316.
Emblems: lion, cardinal's biretta.

JERUSALEM, holy city for the Jews, Christians and Moslems. The Temple built by Solomon is mentioned with admiration in the Bible. The city is frequently represented as an antique or oriental city in the background of landscapes and architectural views, this is found particularly in Crucifixion scenes. E.g., A. Mantegna, *The Agony in the Garden* (National Gallery, London). *pp.* 23, 79.

JESI, a town in the Marches belonging to the Papal States from 1447. *see map* 358.

JOHN THE BAPTIST (St, Italian: GIOVANNI BATTISTA), called the Precursor of Christ, beheaded in 28 AD. Patron saint of Florence. *pp.* 110, 246, 344, 347; *ills* 113, 251, 293, 314, 316.
Emblems: goat-skin, cross.

JULIUS II, *see* ROVERE *and* POPES.

JUSTUS OF GHENT (Joos Van WASSENHOVE, called), Ghent *c.* 1435-Urbino? 1480. Flemish painter active in Urbino between 1472-1475 where he worked for the Duke of Montefeltro. *pp.* 189, 280, 281; *ill.* 280. *see bibliog.* 174.

KREMLIN, the complex of imperial palaces in Moscow, where Italian artists were commissioned to work in the 15th century. *pp.* 41, 54.

LAURANA (Francesco), mentioned between 1458 and 1502. Dalmatian architect, medallist and sculptor, born in Vrana, active in Naples (Arch of Alfonso of Aragon) and Urbino. Entered the service of King René in Provence. Produced busts of great refinement. *p.* 138; *ill.* 151. *see bibliog.* 49, 272.

LAURANA (Luciano), Zara *c.* 1420-Pesaro 1479. Dalmatian architect, responsible for the rebuilding of the palace at Urbino after 1465. *pp.* 42, 91, 138; *ill.* 42. *see bibliog.* 84, 272.

LENDINARA (Cristoforo and Lorenzo CANOZZI da, called). Two brothers, marquetrists and painters, born in Lendinara: LORENZO, 1425-1477, worked with his brother at Ferrara; designed choir-stalls for the Cathedrals at Modena, Ferrara and Padua, the stalls for the Santo (partly lost, the remains being preserved in the Museo dell'Arca). CRISTOFORO, 1420-*c.* 1491, after working with his brother settled in Parma, worked on the stalls for the Cathedral there, produced panels adorned with Evangelists for Modena Cathedral and pews and vestment cupboards for Lucca Cathedral (now in the museum there). *p.* 189.

LEONARDO DA VINCI, Vinci 1452-Amboise 1519. Painter, sculptor, architect, engineer, who also left notebooks covering a wide range of scientific observations, reflections on the technique and nature of art, etc. Pupil of Verrocchio (1469-1475),—and to this period belongs the unfinished *Adoration of the Magi.* Left Florence in 1481 or 1482 and served Lodovico Il Moro in various capacities till 1499; there he produced the *Virgin of the Rocks*, the *Last Supper* and the full-size model for a great equestrian statue. Back in Florence again 1500-1506; *Virgin and St Anne*, *Mona Lisa*, *Battle of Anghiari* (lost). Milan 1507-1513. Rome 1513-1515, in the service of Giulio de' Medici. Amboise 1515-1519, in the service of Francis I. His output as a painter was relatively small, but his influence was immense, particularly his exploration of *chiaroscuro* and the many subtle effects related to it. Leonardo brought to a conclusion the theoretical researches of the 15th century and elaborated, though in fragmentary form, a scientific encyclopaedia of surprising variety and precision. *pp.* 5, 6, 12, 27, 28, 41, 77, 81, 86, 91, 109, 110, 129, 140, 170, 209, 223, 224, 225, 246, 230, 285, 292, 297, 301, 313, 317, 318, 322, 327, 333, 351, 352, 353; *ills* 7, 28, 93, 141, 142, 231, 269, 292, 293, 320, 328, 329. *see bibliog.* 68, 140.

LEOPARDI (Alessandro de), Venice *c.* 1465-1523. Venetian architect, sculptor and bronze founder; cast the equestrian statue of Colleoni, collaborated with Antonio Lombardo on the tomb of Cardinal Zen in the Church of San Marco. *pp.* 109, 170, 352.

LIBERALE OF TREVISO (St), died at Treviso *c.* 400. Patron saint of Treviso and of Venice. Young knight. *ills* 257, 273.
Emblems: armour, standard.

LIBERALE DA VERONA, Verona *c.* 1445-1529. Veronese painter and miniaturist. Frescoes in churches of San Fermo Maggiore and Sant' Anastasia, Verona; choir-books at Chiusi (1467-1469) and Siena (1470-1476). *pp.* x, 206; *ills* 216, 218. *see bibliog.* 52, 66, 197, 405, 418.

LIBERATA (St) and FAUSTINA (St), two virgin martyrs at Como, died 580; patron saints of Como.
Emblem: palm.

LIPPI (Fra Filippo), Florence 1406-Spoleto 1469. Florentine painter, Carmelite monk, the pupil of Lorenzo Monaco and influenced by Masaccio. Frescoes in Prato Cathedral (1452-1464) and the apse of Spoleto Cathedral (1467-1469). *pp.* 181, 260, 285, 352. *see bibliog.* 89, 278, 292, 407.

LIPPI (Filippino), Prato 1457-Florence 1504. Florentine painter, son of Fra Filippo Lippi and of a Prato nun; worked in conjunction with Botticelli. *The Virgin appearing to St Bernard* (1480, Badia), finished the Brancacci Chapel of the Carmine, Florence *c.* 1485. In Rome he worked on the Caraffa Chapel in the Minerva (1489). Again in Florence: Strozzi Chapel in Santa Maria Novella (1495-1502). Also many altarpieces, panel paintings and *cassoni*. *pp.* x, 16, 211, 215, 218, 228, 235, 265, 297, 305, 322, 353; *ills* 17, 224, 225, 249, 268, 305. *see bibliog.* 353.

LODI, city in Lombardy, subject to the Viscontis of Milan from 1336 to 1447. Peace signed at (1454).
Patron saints: Bassiano, Felice, Nabore.
Churches: Santa Maria Incoronata (1487) by G. Battagio and G. Dolcebuono. *ill.* 87.

LODOVICO IL MORO, *see* SFORZA *and* MILAN.

LOMBARDI (Pietro, Antonio and Tullio). Venetian architects and sculptors; PIETRO, Carona *c.* 1435-Venice 1515. Worked at Venice and at Faenza; tombs in SS. Giovanni e Paolo, Venice; reliefs at Faenza. ANTONIO, Ferrara 1458-1516. Pietro's son and assistant. TULLIO, *c.* 1465-Venice 1532. Sculptor: recumbent figure of G. Guidarelli at Ravenna. *pp.* 36, 109, 116, 120, 121, 134, 154, 165, 170, 172; *ills* 35, 53, 74, 127, 129, 130, 132, 144, 149, 178, 184, 185, 186. *see bibliog.* 216.

LONGHI (Roberto). Italian art critic and historian; born in Alba in 1890. *pp.* 184, 188, 190, 191, 192, 242, 278, 338, 344.

LORENZO DI CREDI, *see* CREDI.

LORENZO GIUSTINIANI (St), Venice 1381-1456. First patriarch of Venice, reformed the Order of the canons regular at San Giorgio. *p.* 257; *ill.* 240.

LORETTO, small town 15 miles from Ancona. Famous for its Basilica of Santa Croce, built from 1468 onwards. *p.* 330; *ill.* 325. *see maps* 353, 358.

LOUIS XII, Blois 1462-Paris 1515; King of France, 1498-1515. *p.* 327.

LUCA DA CORTONA, *see* SIGNORELLI.

LUCCA, city in Tuscany, flourished as a self-governing community, 1370-1799. *pp.* 53, 151.
Patron saints: Anselmo of Luca, Frediano, Peregrino, Regula, Paulina, Zita, Reparta.
Secular buildings: Palazzo Pretorio (1492-1501-1588) after plans by M. Civitali.
Palazzo Orsetti (15th century).
Churches: Cathedral (13th century), with *Sacra Conversazione* by D. Ghirlandaio in the sacristy; in the transept, tombs (1480) by M. Civitali, altar of St Regulus (1484), choir and stained-glass windows (1485), stalls, (1452). 'Tempietto de Volto Santo' (1480), *p.* 156.

LUCY (St, Italian: LUCIA), martyred at Syracuse in A.D. 304. Popular in Sicily (Syracuse Cathedral is dedicated to her), Naples, Rome, Milan and Venice. Protectress against disorders of the eye. *p.* 344.
Emblem: eyes on a platter.

LUGANO, city in the Tessino, in the province of Como, southern Switzerland.
Churches: Santa Maria degli Angeli (1499-1515).
Cathedral. *p.* 67.
San Lorenzo. *ill.* 69.

LUNETTE (in Italian *mezzaluna*); the term is used in painting to designate the upper, arch-shaped part of an altarpiece. *pp.* 36, 148, 228, 229, 343, 348.

LYSIPPUS, Sicyon *c.* 390-*c.* 310 B.C. One of the greatest Greek sculptors.

LYSISTRATUS, Greek sculptor of the 4th century BC, the brother of Lysippus. *p.* 352.

MACERATA, town in the Marches, belonged to the Papal States from 1455 onwards. *see maps* 356, 358.

MAGDALEN (St Mary), Mary of Magdala, the sinner saved by Jesus whom she followed throughout his ministry. Her cult spread from Provence (where her relics now are) to Italy, especially Senigallia. *ills* 166, 167, 273, 274, 298.

MAIANO (Benedetto da), *see* BENEDETTO.

MAIANO (Giuliano da), *see* GIULIANO.

MALE (Émile), Commentry 1862-Chaalis 1954. French art historian. *p.* 10.

MALIPIERO (Pasquale), Venice?-1462. Doge from 1457-1462. *ill.* 132.

MANET (Édouard), Paris 1832-1883. French painter and engraver. *p.* 277.

MANETTI (Giannozzo), Florence 1396-Naples 1459, politician and humanist, writer of a treatise *De dignitate et excellentia hominis* (*c.* 1450, published in 1532). *p.* 23.

MANFREDI, notable family from Forlì, a member of which, BARBARA, married Pino Ordelaffi. *p.* 128; *ill.* 137.

MANFREDONIA, small town 22 1/2 miles from Foggia, founded in 1258 by King Manfred of Sicily. Its most famous monuments are the castle and the church of San Domenico. *see map* 357.

MANSUETI (Giovanni di NICCOLO), mentioned *c.* 1485-1527. Venetian painter, pupil of Gentile Bellini. *p.* 18.

MANTEGAZZA (Cristoforo and Antonio), two Lombard sculptors and brothers; CRISTOFORO, ?-1482; ANTONIO, ?-1495. They worked together at the Certosa di Pavia. Painted: *St John the Baptist*, *Virgin and Kneeling St John*, *Faith, Hope and Charity* (Louvre). *pp.* 154, 163, 333; *ills* 72, 73, 173, 174. *see bibliog.* 6, 14, 15.

MANTEGNA (Andrea), Padua 1431-Mantua 1506. Mantuan painter and engraver, pupil of Squarcione. Work at Padua included frescoes in the Eremitani (1449-1454), at Verona, the San Zeno altarpiece (1457-1458), at Mantua in the service of the Gonzagas, he produced the frescoes of the Sala degli Sposi (Ducal Palace) and paintings for the Studiolo of Isabella d'Este (the *Parnassus* in the Louvre). Major influence on the artists of Padua, Venice and Ferrara and on Dürer. *pp.* 181, 189, 192, 194, 197, 228, 229, 230, 234, 236, 257, 258, 259, 272, 278, 284, 297, 310, 317, 322, 330, 338, 352, 353; *ills* 234, 235, 236, 255, 271, 317, 339. *see bibliog.* 43, 54, 100, 119, 254, 255, 308.

MANTUA, city in Lombardy, enjoyed a period of brilliance under the Gonzagas - Francesco II (1484-1519), husband of Isabella d'Este, and Federigo II (1519-1540). *pp.* 41, 91, 114, 192, 297, 310, 353. *Patron saints:* Andrew, Anselmo of Lucca, Longinus, Filippo Neri, Barbara Osanna of Mantua.
Secular building: Palazzo Ducale (13th and 14th centuries) containing Camera degli Sposi (1474, frescoes by Mantegna). Studiolo of Isabella d'Este by Mantegna and Perugino. *pp.* 228, 229, 258; *ill.* 234. *Churches:* Sant' Andrea (begun in 1470) by J. Fancelli from designs by Alberti. *p.* 74; *ill.* 76. San Sebastiano (1466) by Fancelli from plans by Alberti. *p.* 81.

MARCANOVA (Giovanni), Venice 1418-Bologna 1467. Doctor, archæologist and humanist, friend of Felice Feliciano. Author of *De antiquitatibus* (1465), a somewhat romantic compilation of archæology and epigraphy. *ill.* 12.

MARCELLO (Niccolò), Venice *c.* 1398-1474. Doge. *p.* 120.

MARCUS AURELIUS, Rome 121-180. Roman Emperor. His equestrian statue in Rome became the type of equestrian statue that was taken up by Donatello for the *Gattemalata Monument*. *ill.* 106.

MARIA OF ARAGON, the natural daughter of Ferrante, king of Naples, married in 1461 to Ferdinando Piccolomini, made Duchess of Amalfi, died in 1470.

MARK (St, Italian: MARCO), one of the four Evangelists. Patron saint of Venice. *ills* 184, 185.

MARQUETRY, *see* INTARSIA.

MARSYAS, in Greek legend a Phrygian musician and inventor of the flute; he defied Apollo. Having been beaten, he was flayed alive by the God. *ill.* 296.

MARTINI (Francesco di Giorgio), *see* FRANCESCO DI GIORGIO.

MASACCIO (Tommaso), Castel San Giovanni di Val d'Arno 1401-Rome 1428. Florentine painter, pupil of Masolino and Ghiberti. Worked with Masolino on the Brancacci Chapel in the Carmine, Florence. Exercised great influence on Tuscan art of the Quattrocento. *pp.* 9, 209, 211, 224, 310, 321, 322, 352.

MASEGNA, local name used in the Veneto to describe the trachyte rock of the Euganean Mountains. *p.* 36.

MASO DI BARTOLOMEO, Val d'Ambra 1406-*c.* 1456. Tuscan sculptor and bronze founder. *p.* x.

MASTER OF THE BARBERINI PANELS, 15th century painter identified by F. Zeri with Giovanni da Camerino. *pp.* 21, 178; *ills* 20, 190.

MATTEO DE' PASTI, Verona ?-Rimini 1467. Veronese architect and medallist. *p.* 27.

MATTEO DI GIOVANNI, Borgo San Sepolcro 1430-Siena 1495. Sienese painter, pupil of Vecchietta. Dominated the Sienese school in the second half of the century. Active in Pienza and in Siena. *Crucifixion* (1460, Asciano); *Assumption* (*c.* 1475, London), *Massacre of the Innocents* (1482, Sant' Agostino, Siena). *see bibliog.* 68.

MAURELIO (St), Bishop of Ferrara and patron of this town. *p.* 242; *ill.* 243. *Emblems:* mitre, crozier.

MAZZONE or MASSONE (Giovanni), Genoa *c.* 1430-1512. Painter from Liguria, active in Genoa and Savona. Painted numerous altarpieces: *Annunciation* (1463, Santa Maria di Castello, Genoa), triptych of the *Nativity* (1480, Louvre), *Annunciation* (1483, Savona). *p.* x.

MAZZONI (Guido), Modena *c.* 1450-1518. Sculptor who introduced woodcarving and terracotta work to Naples. Polychrome groups (San Sepolcro de Monte Oliveto, Naples). Was taken to France by Charles VIII in 1495. *pp.* 144, 146; *ills* 158, 159, 160. *see bibliog.* 34.

MEDICI, family of bankers, who dominated political life in Florence after 1431. *see* FLORENCE. Through their interest in the arts and the favours they bestowed on certain masters, its leading members are closely bound up with the development of the arts in the Quattrocento. *pp.* 39, 40, 56, 57, 58, 94, 109, 132, 167, 177, 260, 330; *ills* 38, 45, 46, 57, 58, 143, 263.

MELOZZO DA FORLÌ, Forlì 1438-1494. Painter from the Romagna, pupil of Piero della Francesca. Worked at Urbino from 1465-1475 (the Urbino *Christ*); from 1475-1480 he divided his time between Rome and Urbino (*Madonna of Montefalco*, Urbino Studiolo). In Rome he decorated the Vatican Library and the apse of Santi Apostoli. Worked at Loretto (1484) and at Forlì until his death. *pp.* 186, 187, 189, 228, 284, 309, 330; *ills* 197, 198, 325. *see bibliog.* 60, 242, 260.

MEMLING (Hans), Seligenstadt *c.* 1433-Bruges 1494. Flemish painter who headed a very active studio. *p.* 296.

MESSINA, city in north-west Sicily, famous for its antique ruins and its churches: the Cathedral, San Francesco and the Annunziata dei Catalini. *see map* 357.

MICHAEL (Archangel, Italian: MICHELE), according to the Bible captain of the Heavenly Hosts. The protector of Israel and later of the Christian Church. *p.* 246; *ills* 163, 251, 267.

MICHELANGELO BUONARROTI, Caprese (Casentino) 1475-Rome 1564. Florentine sculptor, painter and architect. The work of his youth classes him with the second phase of the Quattrocento. Trained in the studios of Ghirlandaio and Bertoldo, he became a protégé of Lorenzo de' Medici. In 1494 he visited Venice and Bologna, and in 1496 went to Rome. Back in Florence in 1502: the *David* and frescoes for the Palazzo Vecchio. Called to Rome in 1506 by Julius II to work on the Pope's tomb and to decorate the Sistine Chapel ceiling (1509-1512); work on the tomb was resumed later, but it was left unfinished; the completed section is in San Pietro in Vincoli. Back in Florence from 1520-1534: tombs of the Medici in new sacristy of San Lorenzo. Settled in Rome after 1534: frescoes of *Last Judgement*, *Conversion of St Peter*, *Conversion of St Paul;* work on architecture and town planning; St Peter's, the Capitol. *pp.* 76, 89, 116, 151, 172, 235, 278, 296, 324; *ill.* 187. *see bibliog.* 2, 391.

MICHELOZZO DI BARTOLOMMEO, Florence 1396-1472. Florentine architect, sculptor and ornamentalist, pupil of Ghiberti and Donatello. Active at Florence: Monasteries of San Francesco in Bigallo (Bosco ai Frati), San Marco (1437-1452). Master builder at the Cathedral, 1446-1451, built Palazzo Medici (1444-1459). In Milan he built the Palazzo del Banco and the Chapel of Sant' Eustorgio (1462). *pp.* 39, 40, 79, 132; *ills* 38, 40, 46, 57, 66, 143. *see bibliog.* 153, 239.

MICHIEL (Marcantonio), Venice 1484-1552. Humanist and historian. Writer of the *Diarî*, interesting documents which remain to a large extent unedited, and of the *Notizie di opere di disegno.* *p.* 60.

MILAN, principal city of Lombardy, ruled by the Sforzas from 1450-1535; Francesco (1450), Galeazzo Maria (1466), Gian Galeazzo Maria (1476), Lodovico Il Moro (1494-1499). *pp.* XI, 5, 10, 12, 31, 45, 86, 129, 132, 135, 156, 157, 189, 192, 229, 249, 301, 313, *ills* 40, 143.
Patron saints: Ambrogio, Barnabas, Carlo Borromeo, Eustorgio of Milan, Celso, Gervasius, Protasius, Peter, Satiro, Theodelinda of Marza.
Secular buildings: Castello Sforzesco by Filarete and Bramante.
Cenacolo Vinciano in former Dominican monastery, *Last Supper* (1499) by Leonardo da Vinci.
Ospedale, begun by Filarete (1456-1465) and C. Solari in charge of decoration.
Casa della Fontana (façade 1475).
Churches: Sant' Eustorgio (12th and 13th centuries): Portinari Chapel (1462) by Michelozzo, frescoes (1468) by V. Foppa. *pp.* 81, 82, 181; *ill.* 83.
Santa Maria della Grazie (1465-1490) by G. Solari, enlarged by Bramante (1492-1498). *p.* 84; *ill.* 90.
Santa Maria presso San Celso (1491) by Dolcebuono, Solari and C. Lombardo.
Santa Maria della Passione (1485-1530), enlarged 1591); octogonal dome by C. Solari.
Santa Maria presso San Satiro (1476) by Bramante with Baptistry by Bramante. *pp.* 75, 84, 135, 164; *ills* 77, 84, 150.
Church at 'La Conca del Naviglio' (1469).
Santa Maria della Pace (1466-1497) by G. Solari.
San Lorenzo, *pp.* 77, 82; *ill.* 80.
San Miniato al Monte, *p.* 81.
Lazzaretto (1488).
Pinacoteca Ambrosiana.
Pinacoteca di Brera.

MINIATURE: the illumination of books still, in the 15th century, kept many specialized studios busy, at Ferrara, Florence, Venice and elsewhere; some of the masterpieces of the period are to be found in choir-books (e.g., at Siena) and illustrated manuscripts of the works of poets (especially Dante). *p.* 22. *see bibliog.* 188, 338.

MINO DA FIESOLE, Poppi 1429-Florence 1484. Florentine sculptor, who produced many busts and tombs. Panels for Prato Cathedral, tomb of Paul II in Rome. *pp.* 116, 128, 138, 151, 156, 157; *ills* 123, 124, 154; *see bibliog.* 11, 89.

MIRANDOLA, city in Emilia, ruled by the Mirandola family from 1311 to 1510 its most famous prince being Giovanni II (1463-1494). *p.* 181.
Patron saint: San Felice de Cantalice.
Churches: Collegiata (1440-1470).
San Francesco (rebuilt in 15th century): tomb of Prendiparte Pico (1499) by P. delle Masegne.

MOCENIGO (Pietro), Venice 1406-1476. Doge from 1474 to 1476. *p.* 120; *ills* 129, 184, 185.

MOCETTO (Girolamo), Murano 1458-1531. Painter and sculptor active in Venice. *p.* 245; *ill.* 248.

MODENA, city of Emilia, raised to a duchy by the princes of the house of Este in 1452. *pp.* 146, 189, 247.
Patron saints: Gimignano of Modena, Pellegrino.
Churches: Cathedral (11th to 13th centuries); marquetry in the choir (1461-1465) by the Lendinara brothers.
San Pietro (rebuilt in 1476), *p.* 66; *ill.* 67.

MONDAVIO, free commune in the Marches, famous for its *rocca* ('rock' or fortress). *ill.* 44.

MONTAGNA (Bartolomeo), Orzinovi, Brescia *c.* 1450-Vicenza 1523. Painter, founder of the school of Vicenza, pupil of Domenico Morone. Produced altarpieces. *pp.* 272, 278, 311. *see bibliog.* 127, 304, 337.

MONTAGNANA (Jacopo da), Montagnana *c.* 1443-Padua *c.* 1499. Paduan painter also active in Belluno. *p.* 16; *ill.* 16.

MONTEFALCO, Umbrian city, taken over in 1400 by Ugolino Trinci, but soon afterwards by the Papal States. *see map* 358.

MONTEFELTRO (Federico and Guidobaldo da), *see* URBINO.

MONTEFIASCONE, village 8 1/2 miles from Viterbo, to the south of the lake of Bolsena. Church of San Flaviano. *see map* 353.

MONTEFIORE DELL'ASO, free commune in the Marches, near Ascoli Piceno. *p.* 347.

MONTE OLIVETO MAGGIORE, Abbey near Buonconvento, to the south-east of Siena, founded in 1319 by Giovanni Tolomei and observing the Benedictine rule. Cloister decorated with scenes of the life of St Benedict by Signorelli, then by Sodoma. *p.* 206. *see map* 358.

MONTEPULCIANO, small town 43 1/2 miles from Siena, under Florentine rule from 1390 to 1495. *see map* 353.

MONTERUBBIANO, small city 37 1/2 miles from Ascoli Piceno, was an important Ghibelline centre. Famous monuments : San Giovanni with its frescoes. Sant' Angelo; frescoes and ogival portal. *see map* 356.

MONTE SAN MARTINO, small town 46 kilometres from Macerata. *see map* 356.

MORONE, Veronese painters. DOMENICO, Verona *c.* 1422-after 1517. Painter formed by Mantegna, mentioned in the Verona archives as one of the best artists of that city (1491-1493): religious pictures. FRANCESCO, Verona 1471-*c.* 1529: son, pupil and collaborator of Domenico; one of his earliest works was a *Descent from the Cross* (1498) in the Chapel of San Bernardino. *p.* 311. *see bibliog.* 53, 55.

MOSAIC (Italian: *opera mosaica*): the technique of making pictures (mostly mural) out of small cubes of vitreous and coloured matter *(tesserae)*. The technique was revived in Florence for the Baptistry and in Venice for St Mark's. In the second half of the Quattrocento it was sufficiently popular to be extended to portable panels and to the decoration of the reredos as well as to that of doors and archivolts: it was much practised by the studio of D. Ghirlandaio. *pp.* 33, 178, 229.

NAPLES, in 1435 the Kingdom of Naples passed to the Princes of Aragon (for names and dates see ARAGON). *pp.* 10, 146, 151, 156, 157, 272, 352; *ill.* 47.
Patron saints: Asprenas, Athanasius, Biagio, Eligio, Francesco di Paolo, Gennaro, Louis of Anjou, Lucia, Restituta, Rosalia of Palermo.
Secular buildings: Porta Capuana (1485) by G. da Maiano.
Castelnuovo (1283): entrance arch (1452-1466) by F. Laurana and P. da Milano, *p.* 46.
Palazzo Carafa (1466), *pp.* 45, 46.
Palazzo Colobrano (1466), *p.* 46.
Palazzo Cuomo (1464-1490).
Palazzo dell' Ospedale (*c.* 1500).
Palazzo Orsini (1471).
Palazzo Sanseverino, *pp.* 46, 54; *ill.* 55.
Palazzo Santangelo (1467).
Villa of Poggio Reale (1487) by G. da Maiano, *pp.* 47, 57, 58, 60, 334, 351; *ills* 61, 62.
Churches: Sant' Anna dei Lombardi (1414), tomb of Maria of Aragon, by A. Rossellino (1470), Pietà (1490), by Guido Mazzoni. With marquetry (1505), by Fra Giovanni da Verona. *p.* 144.
San Gennaro (1294-1323) rebuilt in 15th century.
SS. Severino and Sosio (1494-1537).
Capella Pontano (1492), by a pupil of Brunelleschi.
San Lorenzo Maggiore (exterior, 1487-1507).
Capella Carafa (1497-1507).
San Giuseppe Maggiore (founded in 1500).
San Pietro a Maiella (1403-1508).
Monte Oliveto: Mastroianni chapel, *p.* 243; *ill.* 246.

NARNI, small town 8 miles from Terni, a possession of the Orsini family in 1373, of Ladislas, king of Naples, in 1403, then of the Papal States about 1420. *see map* 353.

NEPI, small town 23 miles from Viterbo, famous for its Etruscan and Roman ruins. Palazzo Municipale from designs by Vignola. *see map* 353.

NERI DI BICCI, 1415-1491. Florentine painter who ran a large-scale artisanal studio: *cassoni*, altarpieces. Left a journal. *p.* x. *see bibliog.* 250.

NEROCCIO DI BARTOLOMEO DE' LANDI, Siena 1447-1500. Painter and sculptor, a pupil of Vecchietta. Worked in Siena and Lucca. Produced statue of *Santa Caterina* and the tomb of T. Piccolomini and numerous altarpieces: triptych (1476, Pinacoteca, Siena), Montespicini altarpiece (1492). *pp.* x, 201; *ills* 157, 214, 215.

NETTUNO, small city 38 miles from Rome, a possession of the Grottaferrata, then of the Frangipane, the Colonna family and in 1594 of the Papal States. Fortress erected by G. da Sangallo for Alexander VI. *see map* 353.

NICCOLÒ DELL'ARCA, *see* ARCA.

NICHE (Italian: *nicchia)*: a recess in which statues were often framed. The transformation of the Gothic niche into an aedicule with pediment took place in Florence from 1420 onwards, but did not spread to the rest of Italy until after 1450-1500. *pp.* 86, 109, 124, 177, 178, 247, 248, 315, 333, 343.

NICHOLAS V, *see* POPES.

NON FINITO, term applied to works left in a state of *abbozzo*. The concept was at first a negative one, but shortly after 1500 began to be associated with inspiration *(furor)* and to be given a positive value, largely as a result of the work of Leonardo and Michelangelo. Already in 1450 an academic dispute on the 'unfinished' in art began; it was summed up by Vasari in his *Life of Luca della Robbia* (edition of 1568). *pp.* 94, 102.

NOVARA, city in Lombardy under the protection of Milan from 12th century onwards. *see map* 358.

NOVELLO DA SAN LUCANO, Neapolitan architect active between 1470-1487, planned the Palazzo Sanseverino (*c.* 1470), and the church of Gesù Nuovo. *p.* 54, *ill.* 55.

NUREMBERG, town in Bavaria, imperial city from 1256, an important commercial and artistic centre in the 15th century.

OCULUS: Latin word used in term for round window. Used as an architectural motif in a wall, tynpanum or in a roof. *pp.* 243, 334.

OFFIDA, small town 14 1/2 miles from Ascoli Piceno. Came under Florentine rule in the 13th century. Famous for its church of Santa Maria della Rocca. *see map* 353.

ORDER: term for a type of column complete with base and capital and all the characteristics appropriate to each type. The concept was propagated by Vitruvius, but applied only spasmodically before the 16th century. *pp.* 31, 334.

ORPHEUS, the legendary musician and magician who became the object of numerous philosophical speculations (Marsilio Ficino, Pico della Mirandola) as well as inspiring poetic interpretations (Politian). Such works are echoed in the art of the 15th century. *p.* 113; *ill.* 116.

ORSINI (Virginio) I, duke of Bracciano and count of Tagliacozzo. *p.* 109.

ORVIETO, Umbrian city, definitively became a possession of the Church in 1450. *p.* 306.
Patron saints: Dominic, Daniel, the Blessed Giovanna of Orvieto.
Secular building: Palazzo Simoncelli (15th century).
Churches: Cathedral (1290-1319), holy-water stoup (1455) by A. Federighi; Capella San Brizio; frescoes (1499-1504) by Signorelli, *p.* 225; *ills* 232, 233.
San Lorenzo de' Arari: 15th century frescoes.

OSIMO, town 9 miles from Ancona which at the beginning of the 15th century fell into the hands of the Malatestas, then in 1433 of Francesco Sforza. From 1487 onwards its destiny followed that of the Marches and it remained a dependency of the Papal States until 1860. *see map* 356.

OSTIA, small town belonging to the Papal States 15 miles from Rome. *p.* 1. *see bibliog.* 98.
Patron saints: Monica, Peter, Damian.
Secular building: the 'Rock' (1488), by Sangallo and B. Pontelli.

OTRANTO: seaport in the south-east of Italy at the confines of the Adriatic and the Ionian Sea. *see map* 357.

OVETARI (Antonio), died in 1448, founded a chapel in the Eremitani, consecated to St James and St Christopher. *p.* 338; *ill.* 339.

PACIOLI (Luca), Borgo San Sepolcro 1445-Rome *c.* 1510. A Franciscan monk and mathematician, friend of Piero della Francesca and of Leonardo da Vinci, close to the court of Urbino, teacher of the young duke Guidabaldo. Author of *Summa de arithmetica* (1494) and of the *De divina proportione* (1496 and 1509). *p.* 33.

PADUA, city in the Veneto, from 1405 a possession of Venice, *pp.* IX, 53, 89, 91, 94, 95, 102, 113, 120, 154, 167, 190, 194, 265, 319, 353.
Patron saints: Anthony, Giustina.
Secular buildings: Loggia del Consiglio (1498-1523).
Villa Olzignani (1467) by P. Lombardo.
Palazzo del Capitano (15th century).
Università (12th century), façade 15th century.
Churches: Cathedral, Sant'Antonio, known as il Santo (1223-1307): altar of the Santo (1447-1450), by Donatello (restored in 1895), *ill.* 127.
SS. Filippo e Giacomo (Eremitani), Roselli tombs (1467) by Bellano, Ovetari chapel with frescoes (1449-1454), by Mantegna, *pp.* 120, 228, 338, *ills* 127, 339.
Scuola del Santo: frescoes of the *Life of St Anthony* by B. Montagna. Monastery of Praglia (near Padua): church of the Assunta (1490-1548), by T. Lombardo.
Santa Giustina: Chapel of St Luke with St Luke polyptych (1454) by Mantegna.

PALA: Italian for an altar painting. *pp.* 243, 246, 247, 248, 249, 257, 269, 272, 278, 279, 280, 343, 344, 347; *ills* 243, 250, 256, 267, 269, 270, 273, 274, 279, 349, 350, 351, 352.

PALERMO, important city Sicily, suject to the Princes of Aragon from 1282 onwards. *p.* 157.
Patron saints: Agatha, Ninfa of Palermo, Rosalia, Oliva, Sylvia.
Secular buildings: Palazzo Abbatelli (1495), by M. Carnevelivari.
Palazzo Aiutamicristo (1490) by M. Carnelivari.
Palazzo del Municipio (1463).

Palazzo Petragliata (15th century), by M. Carnelivari. Palazzo Sclafani (1330) turned into a hospital in the 15th century.
Churches: Santa Maria della Catena (15th century), by M. Carnelivari.
Cathedral (1185), alterations made in 15th century: stalls (15th century), statues by Gagini, the *Virgin and Child* (1469) by F. Laurana.
Sant' Agostino (14th century): doorway (1463) by G. Gagini.
Pinacoteca.

PALLADIO (Andrea di PIETRO, called), Padua 1508-Vicenza 1580. Venetian architect, created a type of villa after the classical style. Built several palaces in Vicenza. *p.* 47.

PALLAVICINI (Gian Lodovico), 1425-1481, from the Cortemaggiore branch of this noble family. *p.* 1.

PALMA (Jacopo NIGRETTI, called), Il Vecchio, Serina, *c.* 1480-Venice 1528. Venetian painter, a pupil of Giovanni Bellini. *p.* 278.

PALMEZZANO (Marco), Forlì *c.* 1456-1539. Painter, pupil of Melozzo, active in Forlì. *p.* 187.

PAOLO UCCELLO, *see* UCCELLO.

PARENTINO or PARENZANO (Bernardo), Parenzo *c.* 1437-Vicenza 1531. Painter from the Romagna. Painted picture of *Christ carrying the Cross, St Jerome before a crucifix, and a bishop* (Galleria, Modena). Also unfinished fresco *(Life of St Benedict)* in the Convent of Santa Giustina, Padua. *p.* 194. *see bibliog.* 35.

PARMA, city in Emilia, subject to the Sforzas, rulers of Milan, from 1449-1500. *p.* 82.
Patron saints: Bernardo degli Uberti, Ilario, Tommaso.
Churches: Cathedral, San Giovanni Evangelista (1494-1510).
San Francesco del Prato (1298) finished in 1445-1462.

PASTEL, a coloured paste or chalk, used already in the 15th century for the heightening of drawings, especially on *carta tinta.*

PAUL (St, Italian: PAOLO), martyred *c.* AD 64. Assimilated into the number of the twelve apostles. A universally revered saint. *ill.* 243.

PAUL II, *see* POPES.

PAVIA, city in Lombardy, subject to the Viscontis and Sforzas from 1364 onwards. *pp.* 86, 154, 156, 164, 245, 313, 337.
Patron saints: Augustine, Siro.
Churches: Cathedral (1488) by C. Rocchi, Bramante and Amadeo. *p.* 84.
Santa Maria del Carmine (1494-1513).
Certosa (1396): the monastery was finished in 1452, cloister (1465 onwards), by R. de Stauris, Mantegazza, Amadeo and Briosco (1473-1499). Interior: frescoes and paintings by Borgognone, funerary monuments of Lodovico Il Moro and Beatrice d'Este by C. Solari; tomb of Gian Galeazzo Visconti (1493-1497) by G.C. Romano, *pp.* 67, 129, 163, 333; *ills* 72, 73, 139, 140, 156, 173, 174, 177, 331, 338.

PENSIERO: Italian term for the initial idea of a composition, for its rough sketch.

PERETOLA, 3 miles from Florence, church of Santa Maria (15th century) especially famous for its *ciborio* by Luca della Robbia. *p.* 148.

PERSPECTIVE (in Italian *prospettiva):* term for any major ordering of spatial depth, especially in accordance with the system of projection of Alberti and Brunelleschi. Marquetry became a favoured interpreter of perspective, owing to its sharply defined network of lines; hence the close association between *intarsia* and the art of the perspectivists, especially in Florence. *pp.* 9, 10, 12, 76, 223, 228, 242, 272, 309; *ills* 22, 23, 28.

PERUGIA, Umbrian city, subject in 1392 to Boniface IX: captured in 1416 by the condottiere Braccio Fortebracci; bacame subject in the 15th century to Pope Eugenius IV but still was disputed by the Oddi and Baglioni families until 1520, when Leo X made it a Papal city. *pp.* x, 21, 95, 151, 187, 188, 225, 242, 246, 247, 272, 295, 311, 348.
Patron saints: Constantine, Herculanus of Perugia, Colomba of Rieti.
Secular buildings: Porta San Pietro (1475-1477) by A. di Duccio and Polidore di Stefano.
Collegio del Cambio (1451-1457); audience chamber (1508) by Perugino and Raphael.
Palazzo della Vecchia Università (1483-1515).
Palazzo del Capitano del Popolo (1472-1481).
Churches: San Domenico (1305, rebuilt in 1632), altar (1459) by A. di Duccio, stalls (1489).
Santa Maria di Monte Luce (13th-15th centuries), façade by A. di Duccio.
San Pietro (10th century), campanile (1468).
Oratorio di San Bernardino (1457-1461) by A. di Duccio. *p.* 22.

PERUGINO (Pietro VANUCCI, called), Città della Pieve *c.* 1450-Fontignano 1523. Umbrian painter, pupil of Verrocchio: worked mainly at Perugia. Decorated Collegio del Cambio, Perugia, with the young Raphael. At Rome contributed to the Sistine Chapel frescoes. Worked also at Mantua in the service of Isabell d'Este. *pp.* x, 21, 79, 184, 187, 188, 216, 230, 242, 244, 250, 251, 286, 289, 292, 295, 296, 297, 305, 310, 316, 317, 322, 330, 348; *ills* 21, 251, 252, 196, 297, 298, 299, 326, 351. *see bibliog.* 65, 355.

PERUZZI (Baldassare), Siena 1481-Rome 1536. Sienese architect and painter who came to Rome in 1503 where he worked with Bramante and Raphael. Worked on the Farnesina and the Villa Chigi (1508-1511) and the Palazzo Massimo alle Colonne. Worked as a decorator and scenagrapher in Rome and in Siena. *pp.* 33, 58, 60, 322; *ills* 59, 61, 62.

PESARO, city in the Marches, subject to the Malatestas (1285), then to the Sforzas (1445) and to the Della Rovere family (1512). *see maps* 356, 358.

PETER (St), martyred in A.D. 57. The First Apostle. Founder of the Church. The first Pope. *p.* 344; *ill.* 227g.

PETRONIO (St), Bishop of Bologna from 433 to 450 and the town's patron saint, often celebrated in the 15th century.

PHILIP (St), one of the twelve apostles, born at Bethesda, who preached the Gospel to the Gentiles. Also called the Deacon Philip. *ills* 225, 268.

PIACENZA, city in Lombardy, 41 miles from Milan. *Secular building:* Palazzo Landi or dei Tribunali (1493). *p.* 164.

PIENZA, city formerly called Corsignano: it belonged to the Piccolominis and its transformation by Pius II began in 1459. *p.* 1.
Patron saints: Pius, Vito, Crescenzio.
Secular buildings: Palazzo Piccolomini (1459-1463) by B. Rossellino. Bishop's Palace by B. Rossellino.
Churches: Cathedral (1459-1462), by B. Rossellino, stalls (1462), triptych (1461) by Vecchietta, *ills* 3, 210.

PIERO DELLA FRANCESCA, *see* FRANCESCA.

PIERO DI COSIMO, Florence *c.* 1462-*c.* 1521. Florentine painter, a pupil of Cosimo Rosselli and influenced by Leonardo and Signorelli. A specialist in works with fantastic or legendary themes. *pp.* 301, 302, 303, 304, 321, 322. *see bibliog.* 182, 190.

PIETÀ: Italian term for a representation of the Virgin lamenting the dead Christ. *pp.* 142, 307, 347; *ills* 206, 207, 306, 308, 313.

PIETRACUTA, town in the province of Urbino, 6 1/2 miles from San Leo, a possession of the Montefeltros, famous for its castle. *see map* 353.

PIETRA FORTE: name used in Tuscany for a type of fine-grained stone rich in arenaceous limestone.

PIETRA SERENA: grey stone of Florence, often used, from Brunelleschi onwards to pick out the structural features of a building. *p.* 86.

PIETRO ALAMANNO, *see* ALAMANNO.

PIETRO DA RHO (Giovanni), born *c.* 1464-d.?. Sculptor of Milanese origin, active in Cremona. *ills* 30, 33, 145, 176.

PIETRO SPAGNUOLO, *see* BERRUGUETE.

PIGNA, village in the province of Imperia, in the mountain valley of Nervia, known for its medieval appearance. *see map* 356.

PINTURICCHIO (Bernardino di BETTO, called Il), Perugia 1454-Siena 1513. Umbrian painter, a pupil of Perugino. Worked at Rome; Borgia Apartments (1493-1494), at Spello (1500-1501) and at Siena (1503-1508). *pp.* 177, 187, 229, 330, 338; *ills* 189, 227e, 341. *see bibliog.* 62, 69, 225.

PIOMBINO, Tuscan city, from 1400-1634 a possession of the house of Appiano. *see map* 353.

PISANELLO (Antonio PISANI, called Il), 1395-after 1450, painter and medallist of Veronese origin. *pp.* 9, 229.

PISANO (Giovanni), Pisa *c.* 1245-after 1314. Sculptor. *p.* 321.

PISA, Tuscan city, subject to the Viscontis until 1405, then ceded to Florence. *p.* 246.
Patron saints: Bona of Pisa, Efeso of Cagliari, Rainier of Pisa, Torpeo.
Secular buildings: Archbishop's palace (courtyard, end of 15th century). Fortress and new citadel (1468) rebuilt in 1512.
Religious building: Campo Santo (1278) finished in 15th century; frescoes by Benozzo Gozzoli (1408-1484). *ills* 220, 335.

PISTOIA, Tuscan city, a free commune from 1329 onwards. *see map* 310.
Patron saints: Atho, James the Greater, Zeno
Churches: Cathedral (12th century): Forteguerri monument (1476) by Verrocchio; altarpiece (1485) by Leonardo and Verrocchio; bust of Donato de' Medici (1475) by A. Rossellino. *pp.* 116, 353; *ills* 125, 126. Santa Maria delle Grazie (1452-1469) by Michelozzo. San Giovanni Battista (1487-1516).
Madonna dell'Umilità (1495), *p.* 86.

PIUS II PICCOLOMINI, *see* POPES.

PIZZOLO (Niccolo), Vicenza 1421-Padua 1453. Paduan painter and sculptor, pupil and assistant of Squarcione. Preceded A. Mantegna in the decoration of the Ovetari chapel int the Eremitani, Padua. *p.* 338.

PLINY THE ELDER (Gaius Plinius Secundus, called), Como 23-Stabies 79. Roman naturalist and writer. *pp.* 326, 352; *ill.* 175.

POGGIBONSI, town in the province of Siena, subject to Florence in the 14th century. *p.* 1.

POGGIO A CAIANO, *see* FLORENCE.

POGGIO IMPERIALE, *see* FLORENCE.

POGGIO REALE, *see* NAPLES.

POLICASTRO, small town in the province of Salerno and on the gulf of the same name. Belonged to the Grimaldi and then to the Caraffa families, destroyed by the Turks in 1542. *see map* 357.

POLLAIUOLI, family of Florentine artists. JACOPO D'ANTONIO DEL POLLAIUOLO, 1399-1480. Goldsmith, father of Antonio and Piero. ANTONIO BENCI, Florence 1432-Rome 1498. Painter, sculptor and medallist, collaborated with Ghiberti, and follower of Donatello and Uccello (collaborated on *Labours of Hercules* series *c.* 1465-1470): called to Rome in 1490 for tombs of Pope Sixtus IV and Innocent VIII (1493-1499); also an outstanding engraver. PIERO, Florence 1443-Rome 1496. Painter and sculptor, brother and collaborator of Antonio, painted the *Virtues* (Uffizi) and the *Coronation of the Virgin* (Sant' Agostino at San Gimignano, 1483). *pp.* 58, 91, 94, 109, 116, 151, 184, 243, 260, 286, 288, 337; *ills* 112, 117, 245, 288, 289, 291, 336. *see bibliog.* 83, 106.

PONTELLI (Baccio), Florence *c.* 1450-Urbino 1492. Florentine architect and sculptor. Pupil of Francesco di Giorgio. Worked at Urbino, and at Rome for Sixtus IV (Ospedale di Santo Spirito, façades of churches of San Pietro in Vincoli and Santi Apostoli). Also built the 'Rocca' at Ostia and made choir stalls for Pisa Cathedral. *pp.* 66, 75. *see bibliog.* 83, 106.

POPES, during the Quattrocento, as follows:
NICHOLAS V (Pope 1447-1455), promoter of the Peace of the Church and of the 1450 Jubilee. *p.* 23.
CALIXTUS III (Pope 1455-1458).
PIUS II (Aeneas Sylvius Piccolomini) (Pope 1458-1464): famous humanist before he became Pope, steered the Church in the direction of modern culture, transformed the town of Pienza to suit his own taste. *pp.* 1, 186.
PAUL II (1464-1471).
SIXTUS IV (Pope 1471-1484), a member of the Della Rovere family, uncle of Cardinal Giuliano, took major initiative in the replanning of Rome. *pp.* 2, 109, 186, 216, 337.
INNOCENT VIII (Pope 1484-1492); showed greater reserve with regard to modern culture. *pp.* IX, 57, 229, 334.
ALEXANDER VI BORGIA (Pope 1492-1503); chiefly concerned for the political expansion of the Roman State, *p.* 338.
JULIUS II (Cardinal Giuliano Della Rovere, Pope 1503-1513); gathered up and brought to fruition the ambitions of previous Popes, in politics, town planning and cultural affairs. *pp.* 129, 186.

PORCELLO (Giovan Antonio PANDONI, called Il), Naples *c.* 1405-1485. Humanist. Spent time in Ferrara, Naples, Rimini, Milan and Rome. Writer of the *Trionfi* for Alfonso of Naples, of the poem *De amore Jovis in Isottam* for Malatesta, and of the *Feltria* for F. da Montefeltro, *p.* 94.

PORTINARI, family of Florentine bankers; in about 1480 TOMMASO presented the *Nativity* triptych of Hugo Van der Goes (now in the Uffizi) to the church of Sant' Egidio, Florence. *p.* 286; *ill.* 83.

PORTUGAL (Jacopo da Portugallo, Cardinal of) ?-Florence 1459, Archbishop of Lisbon, died prematurely in Italy. Funerary chapel in San Miniato. *pp.* 116, 156, 209, 243, 337; *ills* 245, 337.

POTENZA, town in Basilicata (Lucania). In the 14th century a possession of the Sanseverino family and then of the Guevaras. *see map* 357.

PRATO, Tuscan city, subject to Florence from 1351 onwards.
Patron saints: Caterina dei Ricci of Florence, Stephen.
Churches: Cathedral (13th century), façade 1365-1457, throne (1473) by Mino da Fiesole; frescoes (1456-1466) by Filippo Lippi. *p.* 305.
San Francesco (13th century), Renaissance façade; Inghiarini tomb (1460) by B. Rossellino.
Santa Maria delle Carceri (1485-1492) by G. da Sangallo, *p.* 86; *ill.* 85.

PREDELLA: lower part of an altarpiece, divided into several compartments (either painted or sculpted). A *predella* usually shows scenes related to the lives of the saints, of Christ or of the Virgin, according to the altar's dedication. *pp.* 9, 239, 242, 344.

PREPARATION: treatment of the panel or canvas of a picture, before the colours are laid on.

PREVITALI (Andrea), Bergamo 1470-1528. Venetian painter, pupil of Giovanni Bellini, after 1502 was influenced by Palma and Lotto. *p.* 278.

PROCRIS, according to the legend, the daughter of Cecrops and wife of Cephalus, who accidentally killed her while out hunting and then grief-stricken killed himself; the subject of profane decorative schemes and of *cassoni* panels. *ill.* 302.

PROCULUS (St), martyred in 303. Patron saint of Bologna, often associated with St Petronius.
Emblems: sword, axe, his head in his hands.

PROMETHEUS, in Greek mythology a Titan who is supposed to have created mankind and to have stolen fire from heaven. He was punished by Zeus who sent a vulture every day to devour his liver, he was rescued by Hercules; a mythological subject frequently found on *cassoni* panels.

PUTTO (Italian: small child): the motif of the child angel without wings became, during the Renaissance, a frequent decorative motif, especially in sculpture; Donatello, Desiderio and others made of it a kind of lyrical accompaniment to their scenes with figures. *pp.* 113, 156, 157; *ill.* 177.

RAFFAELLINO DEL GARBO, Florence *c.* 1466-*c.* 1526. Florentine painter, pupil of Filippino Lippi, a specialist in embroidery designs for ecclesiastical vestments. *p.* 301; *ill.* 306.

RAGUSA, town in the south-east of Sicily, famous for its asphalt deposits.
Secular building: Palazzo dei Rettori, restored by Michelozzo in 1464. *p.* 40.

RAPHAEL (Raffaelo SANZIO, called), Urbino 1483-Rome 1520. Painter and architect, pupil of Perugino, worked at Perugia and Florence, and at Rome in the service of Popes Julius II and Leo X. *pp.* 79, 187, 297, 307, 316, 322, 323; *ill.* 300.

RAPPRESENTAZIONE (SACRA): Italian term for a 'mystery play' commenting in the form of *tableaux vivants* on the liturgy, the Bible or the lives of saints.

RAVENNA, city in the Romagna, subject to Venice from 1441 to 1509 then part of the Papal States. *see map* 358.

RECANTI, city in the Marches, possession of the Papal States from 13th century. *see map* 358.

REGGIO DI CALABRIA, principal town in Calabria, underwent numerous changes in government and finally bacame subject to Aragonese rule in 1443. *see map* 357.

REGGIO NELL'EMILIA, city in Emilia, one of the Lombard republics, it then came under the house of Este in 1409. *see map* 358.

REGULUS OF LUCCA (St), martyred in 542. Patron saint of Lucca where his relics are kept and of Massa Marittima. *p.* 156.
Emblem: The saint holding his head in his hands.
Tomb of St Regulus (1484, Lucca), by M. Civtali.

REPARTA (St), martyred at the age of twelve under Decius. Patron saint of Florence.
Emblems: palm, cooking pot, windlass.

RIARIO, ruling family of Imola and of Forlì; RAFFAELE (*c.* 1455-1521), cardinal, nephew of Sixtus IV, and PIETRO (d. 1474), nephew of Sixtus IV, a noteworthy patron of the arts. *pp.* 121, 157; *ills* 49, 50.

RICCIO (Andrea BRIOSCO, called Il), Padua 1470-1532. Paduan sculptor in bronze of Della Torre tomb in San Fermo Maggiore, Verona (fragment in the Louvre) and of numerous statuettes. A specialist in small decorative bronzes. *pp.* 95, 113, 114, 170; *ills* 118, 121, 122. *see bibliog.* 276, 281.

RIDOLFI (Carlo), Lonigo 1594-Venice 1658. Painter, sculptor and writer. *p.* 234.

RIMINI, capital of the Pentapola and domain of the Malatestas, the most remarkable of whom was Sigismondo Pandolfo (1417-1468). Included in the Papal States from 1509 onwards. *pp.* 27, 74, 151; *ill.* 172.
Patron saints: Cordulus of Cologne, Gaudenzio of Rimini.
Churches: San Francesco (13th century) rebuilt from plans by Alberti, it became the 'Tempio Malatestiano'; reliefs by A. di Duccio, tomb of Sigismondo Malatesta atrributed to F. Ferruci, tomb of Isotta degli Atti (third wife of Sigismondo) by A. di Duccio, frescoes by Piero della Francesca.

RIZZO (Antonio), mentioned 1465-1498. Veronese sculptor and architect. Worked at the Certosa di Pavia (1465) and later at Venice (the Tron monument, 1473), *pp.* X, 116, 120, 121, 124, 151, 154; *ills* 128, 131, 133, 134, 135, 136, 168. *see bibliog.* 13.

ROBBIA (Della), family of Florentine sculptors and ceramic artists. LUCA, Florence 1399-1482, originated the art of sculpture in terracotta with polychrome glazes; *cantoria* in stone for Florence Cathedral (1431-1437); medallions for campanile (1437-1439); bronze door for Cathedral (1446). ANDREA, Florence 1435-1528: nephew and pupil of Luca; continued the making of glazed faïence, assisted by his sons, GIOVANNI (1469-*c.* 1529) and GIROLAMO (1488-1566). *pp.* 36, 148; *ills* 163, 164. *see bibliog.* 39, 89, 220, 221, 222, 286.

ROBERTI (Ercole de'), Ferrara *c.* 1450-1496. Ferrarese painter, pupil of Cosimo Tura with whom he collaborated in the Palazzo Schifanoia. Official painter (1477), active in Bologna where he worked with Cossa on the Griffoni Altarpiece (1480-1486). San Lazzaro Altarpiece (Berlin, destroyed). Accompanied Alfonso d'Este to Rome in 1492. *pp.* 217, 249, 257, 278, 295, 321, 338, 343; *ills* 1, 250, 267, 279, 340, 349. *see bibliog.* 352.

ROCCA: the central and most heavily protected part of a fortress; by extension: fortress or fort. *ills* 43, 44.

RODARI, family of architects and sculptors active during the 15th and 16th centuries originating from Maroggia on Lake Lugano; GABRIELE, worked at Milan Cathedral (1486); GIACOMO, worked at Como Cathedral (1487); TOMMASO, worked at Como Cathedral for forty years (1487-1526). *pp.* 132, 153; *ills* 146, 175. *see bibliog.* 270.

ROMANO (Antoniazzo), *see* ANTONIAZZO.

ROMANO (Gian Cristoforo), Rome *c.* 1465-Loretto 1512. Architect, sculptor and medallist, active in Mantua, Urbino and Naples. Portraits of Beatrice d'Este and of Isabella d'Este (1490); collaborated on tomb of Galeazzo Visconti (1493-1497). *pp.* 129, 164, 337; *ills* 139, 140, 338. *see bibliog.* 130.

ROME, enjoyed a great political and cultural revival from 1450 onwards. *pp.* IX, XI, 2, 3, 10, 33, 89, 102, 109, 121, 128, 137, 157, 181, 186, 215, 244, 250, 272, 305, 322, 338; *ill.* 106.
Emblems: broken column barred by initials S.P.Q.R. in gold, preceded by a cross in gold.
Patron saints: Bibiana, Francesca Romana, Paul, Peter, Prassede, Pudentiana, Sabina of Rome, Sebastian, Susanna of Rome.
Secular buildings: Palazzo Capranica (1457).
Palazzo della Cancelleria (1483-1511) by A. Bregno and Bramante. *p.* 48; *ills* 49, 50.
Palazzo Corsini (15th century) rebuilt in 1732.
Palazzo Corneto (later Torlonia) built from 1496 onwards.
Palazzo dei Penitenti (1480).
Palazzo Venezia (*c.* 1455) attributed to Alberti.
Palazzo Santa Croce, *p.* 54.
House of the Knights of Rhodes (restored between 1467-1479).
Ospedale del Spirito Santo (*c.* 1471) by Baccio Pontelli, entrance arch by A. Bregno.
Churches: Sant'Agostino (1479-1483) by G. da Pietrasanta.
San Cosimato: 15th century cloister, church rebuilt in 1475, *p.* 66.
San Giovanni Battista dei Genovesi (1481), cloister by Baccio Pontelli.
Santa Maria della Consolazione.
Santa Maria di Monserrato (*c.* 1495) by A. da Sangallo.
San Marco, rebuilt in 1468.
Santa Maria del Popolo (rebuilt 1472-1477) by Baccio Pontelli and A. Bregno, *pp.* 66, 229.
San Pietro in Vincoli, rebuit in 1475.
Sans Pietro in Montori, rebuilt in 1505 by Bacio Pontelli.
Cappella dell'Aracoeli (1409).
Santa Maria sopra Minerva (1280, façade 1453); the Carafa Chapel with frescoes by Filippino Lippi (1489-1490).
Santa Saba (restored in 1458).
San Vitale (1475).

Santa Croce in Gerusalemme, *ill.* 194.
Santa Maria dell'Anima, *p.* 67.
The Vatican: first Basilica of St Peter (324-344); in 1452 Nicholas V decided on rebuilding which was begun by B. Rossellino; this was later entrusted by Julius II to G. da Sangallo, and then to Bramante. *pp.* 76, 77, 86, 129; *ills* 78, 186, 244, 338, 341.
Grotte Vaticane; tomb of Paul II (1475) by Mino da Fiesole; tomb of Sixtus IV (1483-1494) by A. Pollaiuolo, *p.* 109; *ill.* 336.
Vatican Palace; first building 1272-1280 constantly enlarged throughout the Renaissance.
Chapel of Nicholas V (1447-1449).
Sistine Chapel (1473-1484), *pp.* 79, 184, 186, 216, 218, 228, 330; *ills* 226, 227, 326.
Borgia Apartments for Alexander VI (1492-1495), by Pinturricchio.
Stanze by Raphael and his pupils (1510-1520).
Belvedere (1489-1492) built under Innocent VIII, *pp.* 57, 58, 60, 334.
Vatican Museums.
Quirinal Museums.

RONDINELLI (Niccolo), *c.* 1450-*c.* 1510. Painter of the Romagna School, a native of Lugo and pupil of Giovanni Bellini (1490-1495), also came under the influence of Cima da Conegliano and of Carpaccio. Worked in Venice, Ravenna (1496-1500) and Forlì. Painted altarpieces: triptychs (Accademia, Ravenna) [1490, Walters Art Gallery, Baltimore]. *p.* 177. *see bibliog.* 242.

ROSSELLI (Antonio), Arezzo 1380-Padua 1466. Juriconsult. *p.* 120. *ill.* 127.

ROSSELLI (Cosimo), Florence 1439-1507. Florentine painter, pupil of Neri di Bicci and of Benozzo Gozzoli. Active in Florence (1476, fresco in the Annunziata), in Rome (to which he was called by Sixtus IV to work with Signorelli, Ghirlandaio and Perugino on the Sistine Chapel. He also worked in Lucca. *ills* 227c, h.

ROSSELLI (Domenico di Giovanni di Bartolomeo), Pistoia 1439-Fossombrone *c.* 1498. Florentine sculptor, the brother of Francesco di Giorgio, mentioned in Florence in 1464 as a member of the Guild of Sculptors. Also worked in Bologna and in Pisa. *pp.* 157, 163; *ill.* 171.

ROSSELLINI, family of Tuscan architects and sculptors. BERNARDO ROSSELINO, Settignano 1409-Florence 1464. Architect and sculptor trained by Alberti. Rossellino worked on the Palazzo Venezia, Rome (1455); Palazzo Rucellai (1446-1450), town plan and Bishop's Palace, Pienza; tomb of Leonardo Bruni (1444-1451 Santa Croce, Florence); ANTONIO, Settignano 1427-Florence 1479. Brother of Bernardo, worked at Empoli, Faenza, Pistoia, Ferrara, Naples and Prato. Tomb of the Cardinal of Portugal (1461), many busts and reliefs of Madonnas. *pp.* 1, 116, 137, 156, 337; *ills* 3, 153, 337. *see bibliog.* 288

ROSSETTI (Biagio) Ferrara *c.* 1447-1516. Bolognese architect; made town plan of Ferrara for Ercole I; built Palazzo dei Diamanti (begun 1492); Palazzo Constabilio, church of San Francesco (1494). *p.* 334; *ills* 56, 68. *see bibliog.* 425.

ROVERE (Cardinal Della), *see* POPES.

ROVERELLA, Ferrarese family, art patrons. LORENZO, a bishop of the 15th century presented an altarpiece to the church of San Giorgio, Ferrara. *pp.* 242, 257; *ills* 243, 244.

ROVEZZANO (Benedetto da), *see* BENEDETTO.

RUSTICATION: term used when parts of the walls of a building, most often at the base, are built of stone blocks deliberately left in a rough state.

RUSTICI (Giovan Francesco), Florence 1474-Tours 1554. Florentine painter and sculptor, a pupil of Ghirlandaio and fellow-student with Michelangelo. Also worked in the studio of Verrocchio. Left for France in 1528. *pp.* 110, 172; *ill.* 113. *see bibliog.* 235.

SALERNO, town situated on the gulf of the same name, from 1076 was governed by various families. Famous for its school of medicine, the most famous in Europe at the time. *see map* 357.

SAMSON, a judge and hero of the Israelite people of undoubtedly legendary origin. Endowed with herculean strength by virtue of his long hair, he allowed himself to be duped by the courtesan Delilah who caused him to lose his strength by cutting off his hair. He was taken prisoner by the Philistines and blinded. He brought down the temple of Dagon upon both himself and his enemies; this subject is reperesented in series of scenes from the Old Testament both in sculpture and in painting. *ill.* 105.

SANGALLO, family of architects-Florence, then Rome. GIULIANO GIAMBERTI known as Giuliano da SANGALLO. Florence *c.* 1445-1516. Sculptor and architect, oldest of a line of architects; began as woodcarver (stalls of Medici Chapel), then as architect responsible for Santa Maria delle Carceri, Prato (1485-1491), Villa of Poggio a Caiano (1480-1485) and sacristy of Santo Spirito in collaboration with Cronaca (1489-1492). Worked at Loretto, Naples, Savona and Rome in the service of Julius II; author of a collection of studies and designs. ANTONIO GIAMBERTI DA SANGALLO called the ELDER), Florence *c.* 1455-1534; architect, pupil of his brother, Giuliano; built the Annunziata at Arezzo, and San Biagio, Montepulciano (1519-1526). *pp.* IX, X, 1, 3, 6, 22, 29, 39, 46, 47, 48, 58, 76, 77, 79, 86, 116, 309, 330, 334; *ills* 4, 8, 47, 58, 79, 92, 330, 334. *see bibliog.* 169, 212.

SAN GIMIGNANO, Tuscan city, a free commune which came under Florence from 1353.
Patron saints: Bartolo Buompedoni, Gimignano, Fina.
Churches: Cappella di Santa Fina (1468) by G. da Maiano, frescoes by Ghirlandaio, altar (1475) by B. da Maiano.
Sant'Agostino (1280-1298); in the choir, *Life of St Augustine* (1463-1465) by Benozzo Gozzoli. *p.* 156.

SANGUINE: drawing done with red or brown stone. In 15th century was used mostly together with charcoal and chalk, but sometimes alone.

SAN LEO, small town in the province of Pesaro, came under the rule of the Montefeltro family. *see map.* 353.

SAN MARINO, a tiny republic and enclave of the Papal States. *see map* 358.

SANMICHELI (Bartolommeo), Porlezza 1426-Casale 1512. Architect active between 1486-1493 on the Palazzo del Consiglio in Verona. *pp.* 6, 44.

SANO DI PIETRO, Siena 1406-1481. Sienese painter, master of a very active studio which produced a large number of Madonnas and village altarpieces. In about 1445-1450 he painted scenes from the *Life of St Bernardino* for the Osservanza, Siena; also an *Assumption. pp.* x, 201.

SANSOVINO (Andrea CONTUCCI, called Il), Monte Savino *c.* 1460-1529. Florentine sculptor and architect, pupil of Bramante. Worked at Rome and Loretto, in Tuscany (Siena), in Central Italy and in Portugal. *Baptism of Christ* (1500-1502) in Florence Baptistry; tombs in Santa Maria del Popolo, Rome. *pp.* 116, 148, 151, 172, 234. *see bibliog.* 170.

SANTI (Giovanni), Colbordolo ?-Urbino 1494. Painter from the Marches, the father of Raphael, and assistant to Melozzo and Berruguete in the Studiolo at Urbino. Painted altarpieces including those at Berlin and Fano (1484), at Montefiorentino (1489), and the *Apostles* (Urbino). Shortly before his death he was called to Mantua to paint the portrait of Lodovico. Wrote a *Rhymed Chronicle* dedicated to the duke Guidobaldo. *p.* 284. *see bibliog.* 219.

SARONNO, town in the province of Varese, 25 miles to the south-west. Sanctuary of the Madonna dei Miracoli founded in 1498. *see map.* 354.

SARTO (Andrea del), Florence 1486-1531. Florentine painter, a pupil of Piero di Cosimo, formed by Leonardo. *p.* 322.

SASSETTI (Francesco), Florence ?-1488. Humanist and agent of the Medicis; with his wife Nera CORSI he founded a chapel in Santa Trinità, Florence.

SASSOCORVARO, commune in the Marches, famous for its *rocca* in the form of a ship. *p.* 43; *ill.* 43.

SASSOFERRATO, village in the province of Ancona, passed to the Malatestas (1349), to the Feltre (1391) and then to the Papal States in 1488. Church of Santa Croce in Triporzo, San Francesco. *see map* 353.

SATIRO (St), died 392. Brother of St Ambrose, patron saint of Milan.
Emblems: mitre, crozier.

SAVONAROLA (Girolamo), Ferrara 1452-Florence 1498. Florentine Dominican monk, who distinguished himself by his piety, his preaching and his writings; raised a party against the Medici, preached reform of the Church and declaimed against the clergy. Excommunicated by Alexander VI, he was hanged and burned as a heretic, *pp.* 137, 295.

SAVONA, city and port in Liguria, centre of a Marquisate of the Alerami, a free commune subject to Genoa in 1528. *see maps* 356, 358.

SCALETTI, painters of the Romagnola school; LEONARDO, Faenza ?-after 1486. Works attributed to him: *Madonna enthroned with St John the Evangelist and the Blessed Bertoni* (*c.* 1483, Pinacoteca, Faenza), *Pietà* (Pinecoteca, Faenza), *Madonna and Child between St Francis and St Jerome* (National Gallery, Edinburgh); GASPARE, mentioned between 1477 and 1529, the son of Leonardo, specialized in painting *cassoni* or marriage chests. *p.* 194; *ill.* 202. *see bibliog.* 242.

SCHIAVONE (Giorgio or Gregorio di Tomaso CHIULINOVITCH, called), Scurdone (Dalmatia) 1436 - Sebenico 1504. Pupil of Squarcione (1456-1459) then active in Sebenico. *pp.* IX, 194; *ill.* 203. *see bibliog.* 298.

SCIPIO (Publius Cornelius Scipio Africanus), 235-183 B.C. Roman general and politician; a frequent subject in series of portraits of famous men. *ill.* 179.

SEBASTIAN (St), according to his legendary *Acts*, martyred in 288; a centurion, he was martyred when archers used his body as a target. Hence he became the patron saint of the Guild of Archers and his name was invoked especially as a protection against the plague. *ills* 271, 272, 273.
Emblem: arrows.

SECCO: Italian term (*a secco*) for mural painting or fresco in which paint is applied after the surface has dried; used particularly of retouching with distemper. *p.* 209.

SENIGALLIA, small town, 17 miles from Ancona, alternately a possession of the Malatestas and of the Papal States. Its *rocca* was built by B. Pontelli (1480-1491) who also built Santa Maria delle Grazie. *see map* 358.

SERLIO (Sebastiano), Bologna 1475-Fontainebleau 1554. Architect and theoretician of classical architecture, pupil of B. Peruzzi; his *Trattato di architettura* had a great influence. *pp.* 33, 60; *ill.* 61. *see bibliog.* 99.

SERRAPETRONA, commune in the Marches, near Macerata, on the right bank of the Cesolene. *see map* 356.

SEVERO DA RAVENNA, mentioned during the last quarter of the 15th century and the beginning of the 16th. Sculptor and bronze founder active in Padua: *St John the Baptist* (the 'Santo'). *p.* 115. *see bibliog.* 284.

SFORZA, Ducal family, Milan. Reigning dukes in 15th century: FRANCESCO, 1401-1466; he became ruler of Milan, brought many artists there and so began to make the court of Milan a rival to Florence; GALEAZZO MARIA, 1466-1476. GIAN GALEAZZO, 1476-1494; dethroned by his uncle Lodovico Il Moro; LODOVICO IL MORO (who reigned 1494-1508) brought the French into Italy and died at Loches; like Francesco he imported great brilliance to the court of Milan, to which he brought Leonardo da Vinci. *pp.* x, 3, 6, 31, 36, 40, 41, 84, 109, 272, 297, 316, 327; *ills* 39, 112.

SFUMATO: Italian term for the veiled, smoky, atmospheric tone introduced into painting by Leonardo and simultaneously, by Giorgione.

SIENA, Tuscan city, a powerful republic at enmity with Florence; subjected to Gian Galeazzo Visconti in 1399, but recovered its liberty in 1487. *pp.* x, 58, 89, 94, 142, 201, 206.
Patron saints: Bernadino of Siena, Catherine of Siena, Cresenzio, Galgano, Vittorio, Alberto.
Secular buildings: Palazzo Pubblico (1325-1340); stalls of chapel (1423-1433) by D. de' Cori.
Palazzo del Magnifico (1453-1505) by G. Cozzarelli.
Piccolimini Library (1495), *pp.* 177, 246; *ill.* 217.
Palazzo Spannocchi (1473).
Churches: Cathedral, San Domenico (1226) enlarged *c.* 1465. Chapel of St Catherine.
Church of Fontegiusta (1426-1475); façade (1484), doorway (1489) by Urbano da Cortona. Osservanza (1476) by F. di Giorgio and Cozzarelli.
Sant'Agostino (1258), San Sacramento Chapel (*Massacre of the Innocents* by M. di Giovanni, 1482), *pp.* 201, 348, 351.
Loggia del Papa (1462) by A. Federighi.
Pinecoteca, ills 213, 215.

SIGNORELLI (Luca), Cortona 1450-1523. Umbrian painter, pupil and collaborator of Piero della Francesca. Worked in the Marches, in Rome (1482, in the Sistine Chapel), in Monte Oliveto, in Florence (*c.* 1490, *The Education of Pan*, for Lorenzo de' Medici, destroyed, Berlin), at Orvieto (1499-1503, in the San Brizio Chapel in the Cathedral). Painted many altarpieces, which include the *Madonna* (1484) at Perugia; San Merdardo polyptych (1508) at Arcevia; and the Bichi polyptych (1498) now dispersed. *pp.* 184, 216, 225, 269, 305, 306, 322, 330, 348, 350, 351; *ills* 227a, 232, 233, 307, 352. *see bibliog.* 104, 336, 367.

SILOÉ (Diego de), Burgos *c.* 1495-Grenada 1563. Spanish architect, active in Salamanca, Burgos and Grenada. *p.* 79.

SILVESTRO DELL'AQUILA (properly Silvestro da Sulmona), ? *c.* 1450-Aquila 1504. Architect, sculptor and painter from Sulmona (in the Abruzzi), formed in the Florentine school, active in Aquila: tombs, statues, bas-reliefs. In 1480 he signed the tomb of Cardinal Aquifili which had been begun in 1476. *p.* 156. *see bibliog.* 202.

SINOPIA: preparatory drawing for a fresco, full-size sketch on the wall outlined in red ochre on the 'arriccio'. The term is derived from the city of Sinope in Asia Minor, which was famous for its red pigments. *p.* 209. *see bibliog.* 300.

SIXTUS IV, *see* POPES.

SOLARI (Guiniforte or Boniforte), Milan 1429-1481. Architect and sculptor, worked at the Certosa di Pavia, at Milan (Cathedral, Cloister of the Oratory of Santa Maria delle Grazie, 1477). *p.* 116. *see bibliog.* 229.

SOLARIO or SOLARI (Cristoforo), Angora?-Milan 1527. Architect and sculptor, brother of Andrea, active in Venice: Chapel of St George (1489, Santa Maria della Carità), and especially in Milan, tomb of Lodovico Il Moro (1497), sculptures for the cathedral (1501). *p.* 164; *ills* 72, 73, 90. *see bibliog.* 207.

SOLON, Athens 640-*c.* 558 B.C. Athenian statesman and legislator, often represented in the galleries of famous men. *ill.* 282.

SPANZOTTI, Piedmontese painters. FRANCESCO, ?-Casale 1531. Active at Casale from 1483 onwards, father of Pietro. GIAN MARTINO, Casale *c.* 1456-Chivasso 1528. Worked at Casale. Vercellio and Ivrae (cycle of frescoes of the *Life of Christ* at San Bernardino); painted altarpieces including triptych (1480-1490) in the Turin Gallery; in 1507 became painter to the court of Savoy. *p.* 313; *ill.* 315. *see bibliog.* 155, 389.

SPELLO, small town in the province of Perugia, on the slopes of Mount Subasio, from 1449 was attached to the Papal States. *p.* 177.
Church: Santa Maria Maggiore, frescoes by Pinturicchio (1501), *p.* 177; *ill.* 189.

SPERANDIO (Savelli), Mantua *c.* 1425-Venice 1504. Architect, sculptor, goldsmith and medallist. Active in Ferrara, Mantua, Faenza, Bologna and Venice. Produced marble medallions, portrait of Giovanni II Bentivoglio (Louvre), bas-reliefs and bust of Ercole d'Este I (Louvre). *p.* 132; *ill.* 70.

SPOLETO, Umbrian city, included in the Papal States from 1354 onwards. *see maps* 353, 355, 358.

SPOLVERO: Italian term used in fresco technique to designate the dotted outlines produced by pouncing coloured powder through the pricked holes in the cartoon or preparatory sketch. *p.* 209, 353.

SQUARCIONE (Franceso), Padua 1397-1468. Paduan collector and painter, teacher of Mantegna. *pp.* 181, 192, 197, 257, 259; *ill.* 204. *see bibliog.* 246.

STAURIS (Rinaldo de), Cremona?-. Lombard sculptor in the service of the Duke of Milan (1461), worked on the Certosa di Pavia, 1464-1490. Produced terracottas, medallions and *putti*. *p.* 333.

STIACCIATO (now SCHIACCIATO), Italian: flattened. Used to describe a bas-relief in which the forms are very lightly modelled and appear as if inscribed in the depth of the panel. Also used to describe the manner of Donatello.

STROZZI, wealthy Florentine family. FILIPPO STROZZI began the building of the imposing palace in Florence, whose architects were Cronaca and B. da Maiano. *ills* 34, 154, 224, 225.

STUDIO: Italian for workroom or study; this was often decorated with allegorical paintings and woodcarvings, as at Urbino and at Gubbio.

SUBIACO, small town 48 miles from Rome, particularly famous for its typically medieval appearance and for its Abbey,. founded by St Benedict and in which he applied his rule, also for the Convent of Nuns founded by St Scholastica, the sister of St Benedict. *see map* 353.

SUMMONTE (Pietro), Naples 1453-1526, humanist, grammarian and writer of epigrams. *p.* 351.

SYLVIUS (Aeneas), *see* PICCOLOMINI and POPES.

SYRACUSE, Sicilian city, under Spanish rule after 1282. *see map* 357.

TACCUINO, Italian for a sketchbook.

TAGGIA, small provincial town 19 miles from Imperia, subjected to Genoese rule from 1228 onwards. Its Dominican monastery was important during the 15th and 16th centuries. *see map* 356.

TARENTO, town in Apulia, on the Gulf of the same name. In 1301 became the domain of Philip, son of Charles II, King of Sicily, in 1463 passed to Ferdinand the Catholic. *see map* 357.

TARSIA, *see* INTARSIA.

TEMPERA: Italian term for paints mixed with white of egg and glue, used in particular cases for certain frescoes. *pp.* 230, 286, 288.

TEMPIETTO (Italian for 'small temple'): term applied to models or miniatures of buildings, or sometimes actually to a small building such as Bramante's San Pietro in Montorio. *pp.* 4, 14, 79, 129, 170, 242, 248.

TERNI, town in Umbria, on the Nera. At the end of the 14th century became attached to the Papal States. *see map* 353.

TERRA VERDE (Italian for 'green earth'): a shade of earth used for preparatory paintings.

THOMAS (St), apostle, very popular in Tuscany. Patron saint of Parma and Urbino. *pp.* 109, 167; *ill.* 183.
Emblems: Apostle's robe, set-square, girdle of the Virgin, lance.

TITIAN (Tiziano VECELLI or VECELLIO, called), Pieve di Cadore *c.* 1490-Venice 1576. Venetian painter, had a profound influence upon European painting. *p.* 278.

TIVOLI, town in Latium, 25 miles from Rome. Pius II was responsible for building the 'rocca' and Sixtus IV for its university. *see map* 353.

TOBIAS (the younger), a Jew of the 7th century B.C. who went to Nineveh in Media to look for his father's estates and brought back his wife from there. He was accompanied by the Archangel Raphael. *ill.* 290.

TODI, Umbrian city, became part of the Papal States at the end of the 15th century. *see map* 358.

TOLFA (La), commune near Rome, well-known for its mines of iron, alum, lead and zinc. *see map* 358.

TOMASO DI MALVITO, painter from Como mentioned at the end of the 15th century. Tomb *p.* 337.

TONDO: a type of round picture, much in fashion in the years round about 1470-1490. *pp.* IX, 18, 344, 348; *ill.* 19.

TOSCANELLA, *see* TUSCANIA.

TRAVERTINE: a king of calcareous stone from the neighbourhood of Tivoli, of which many buildings in Rome, both secular and religious are built. *p.* 33.

TREVI, Umbrian city, subject to the Trinci family from 1392, became part of the Papal States after undergoing many vicissitudes in the 15th century. *see map* 358.

TREVIGLIO, small town in Lombardy; self-governing between 1311 and 1454 when it was attached to the republic of Venice. *pp.* 246, 251, 316.
Patron saint: Martin.
Church: San Martino: polyptych (1485-1500) by B. Butinone and B. Zenale. *p.* 251; *ills* 253, 254.

TREVISO, city of the Veneto, came under Venetian rule in 1388. *see map* 358.

TRIVULCIO (Giangiacomo), Milan 1441-Arpajon 1518. Marshall of France of Milanese origin, covered himself with glory in the Italian Wars. *p.* 129, *ill.* 141.

TRON (Niccolò), Venice ?-1473. Doge of Venice between 1471 and 1473. *p.* 120; *ills* 128, 131.

TURA (Cosimo), Ferrara 1430-1495. Ferrarese painter, trained under Squarcione at Padua. Met Piero della Francesca at Ferrara in 1450. One of the three masters of the Palazzo Schifanoia paintings (1470); organ doors for Ferrara Cathedral. Altarpiece (Roverella polyptych, 1470-1475, dispersed); many portraits, *pp.* x, 181, 190, 192, 230, 242, 249, 257, 259, 324, 338, 352; *ills* 237, 238, 243, 244, 266. *see bibliog.* 163. 248, 324, 339.

TUSCANIA (called TOSCANELLA from the 14th century until 1911), town in the province of Viterbo, from 1337 became part of the Papal States. *p.* 134; *ill.* 148.

UCCELLO (Paolo di DONO, called), Pratovecchio 1397-Florence 1475. Florentine painter, decorator and mosaicist, pupil of Ghiberti. Mosaics for St Mark's, Venice (1425). Designs for stained glass windows for Florence Cathedral (1445) Hawkswood monument, a mural painting of an equestrian statue (1436), in Florence Cathedral. *Battle of San Romano* series (1456-1460, Louvre, Uffizi, London, National Gallery). Old Testament frescoes in cloister of Santa Maria Novella (*c.* 1445). His works were distinguished by their pioneering of perspective. *p.* 10, 180. *see bibliog.* 67, 89, 369.

UDINE, capital of the Friuli; came under Venice in 1420.
Patron saints: Ermagora, Fortunato.
Church building: Cathedral campanile (1450).
Town planning: Piazza Contarena (1448-1533), now Piazza della Libertà. *p.* 3.

UGO (Count), Marquis of Tuscany (*c.* 953-Pistoia 1001). *p.* 116; *ills* 123, 124.

URBINO, city of the Marches, centre of the domain of the Montefeltro family from the 13th century. Raised to extraordinary brilliancy under Federico (1421-1482) and Guidobaldo (1472-1508). *pp.* x, 6, 45, 132, 142, 157, 187, 188, 189, 278, 279, 281, 283, 284, 319, 323, 353; *ills* 41, 269, 285, 287.
Patron saints: Michelina of Pesario, Thomas.
Secular building: Palazzo Ducale (begun in 1444), resumed in 1465 by Laurana and in 1475 by F. di Giorgio Martini. *pp.* 42, 43; *ills* 31, 32, 42, 158, 171.
Churches: San Domenico (doorway 1449-1451) by M. di Bartolomeo known as Maraccio.
San Bernardino dei Zoccolanti (1472-1491).
National Gallery of the Marches.

UTENS (Giusto), ?-died 1609, Italian painter. *ills* 45, 46.

VALERIAN (St) martyred in 229. Militant saint, the husband of Santa Cecilia.
Patron saint of Forlì and also venerated in Bologna.
Emblem: suit of armour.

VAN EYCK (Jan), Maastrich? *c.* 1390-Bruges 1441. Flemish painter. *p.* 283.

VAN MARLE (Raymond), The Hague 1887-Perugia 1936. Art critic. *p.* 348.

VARAZZE, city in the province of Savona, on the Riviera di Ponente. *see map* 356.

VASARI (Giorgio), Arezzo 1512-Florence 1574. Painter, architect and historian; famous for his *Vite* (1st ed., 1550). *pp.* x, 58, 110, 186, 229, 234, 235, 259, 278, 288, 297, 321, 322, 323, 324, 330, 348, 352.

VECCHIETTA (Lorenzo di PIETRO, called Il), Castiglione d'Orcia *c.* 1412-Siena 1480. Sienese painter and sculptor. Frescoes in the Siena Baptistry (1450); triptych of the *Assumption* for Pienza Cathedral (1461-1462), His sculptures include both bronzes (*Resurrection* 1472, New York, Frick Collection); the *Risen Christ* (1476, Ospedale, Siena) and wood carvings (*St Antony Abbot*, Narni; *St Bernardino*, Bargello, Florence). *pp.* 89, 109, 113, 142, 201, 206; *ills* 114, 210. *see bibliog.* 404.

VENDRAMIN (Andrea), Venice ?-1478. Doge between 1476 and 1478. *pp.* 120, 337; *ills* 53, 130.

VENEZIANO (Domenico), Venice *c.* 1400-Florence 1461; Venetian painter, active in Florence where he worked on the choir frescoes (destroyed) of Sant' Egidio (1439-1445). Collaborated with Piero and Baldovinetti. *pp.* 18, 209, 247.

VENICE: powerful republic, governed by a Doge and Council. *pp.* x, 3, 18, 33, 48, 56, 57, 58, 102, 115, 116, 121, 134, 137, 151, 170, 189, 190, 192, 234, 235, 236, 247, 258, 265, 272, 285, 309, 310, 311, 319, 322, 326; *ills* 109, 111, 147.
Patron saints: Mark, Bassus of Venice, Christina, Justina of Padua, Liberale of Treviso, Magnus, Rocco, George, Trifone (Tryphonius) of Dalmatia, Jerome.
Secular buildings: Palazzo Ducale (8th century) partly rebuilt in 14th century, east wing end of 15th century. Courtyard by A. Rizzo, then P. Lombardo; Foscari arch (1457) by the Boni; Scala dei Giganti (1484-1501). *pp.* 54, 124, 154, 229; *ills* 133, 134, 135, 136, 168, 234.
Fondaco de' Turchi, built about 1250 by Palmieri.
Palazzo Corner-Spinelli by M. Coducci. *p.* 50; *ill.* 52.
Palazzo Dario (1487) by P. Lombardo. *p.* 36; *ill.* 35.
Palazzo Vendramin-Calergi (1481), begun by M. Coducci, *p.* 50, 53, 54; *ill.* 53.
Vecchie Procurati (1480-1514) attributed to Coducci.
Clock-tower (1496) attributed to Coducci.
Campo di SS. Giovanni e Paolo; with equestrian statue (1481-1486) of B. Colleoni by Verrocchio.
Churches: San Giovanni Crisostomo (after 1497) by Coducci, *p.* 84. SS. Giovanni e Paolo (or Zanipolo), 13th century; tombs of the Doges by P. Mocenigo (*c.* 1485) and P. Malipiero (1462) by P. Lombardo. In one of the chapels, altarpiece by Giovanni Bellini; altarpiece by Girolamo Mocetto, *pp.* 120, 245; *ills* 129, 130, 132, 184, 185, 248.
San Giovanni in Bragora (1475): paintings by Cima da Conegliano and B. and A. Vivarini, *ill.* 259.
Santa Maria del Carmelo (14th century); paintings by Cima da Conegliano, *Deposition* (bas-relief) by Francesco di Giorgio.
Santa Maria Formosa (1492), by Coducci.
Santa Maria Gloriosa dei Frari (1340-1443); many tombs; including those of the Doge Fr. Foscari by A. Bregno, of N. Tron (1473) by A. Rizzo; in sacristy, *Madonna with four saints* (1488) by Giovanni Bellini, *p.* 120; *ills* 128, 131.
Santa Maria dei Miracoli (*c.* 1489) by P. Lombardo, *pp.* 67, 135, 154; *ills* 74, 149.
Santa Maria dell'Orto (15th century).
San Michele in Isola (1469-1479) by Coducci.
San Rocco (1495) by Bartolomeo Bon.
San Trovaso, rebuilt after 1583; *St Chrysogonus* fresco (1462) by M. Gambono (or Jacobello del Fiore).
San Zaccaria (9th century), rebuilt from 1458 to 1515. *pp.* 67, 229; *ill.* 75.
Scuola di San Giorgio degli Schiavoni: paintings by V. Carpaccio (1502-1511).
St Mark's: Zen Chapel (1485-1495) by the Lombardis, *pp.* 109, 229.
Mascoli Chapel (mosaic *c.* 1450), *p.* 229.
Accademia.
Ca d'Oro, *ill.* 178.
Museo Corner.

VENUS, Roman goddess of love: the Greek Aphrodite. Raised by the Humanists to the highest symbolic level in the new culture. E.g., *Venus Rising from the Waves* and the *Primavera* by Botticelli, *ills* 119, 172, 208.

VERONA, North Italian city, an ancient commune, the city of the Scaliger family; a Venetian possession from 1405 onwards. *pp.* 54, 142, 154, 206.
Patron saints: Celso, Nazario, Peter martyr of Verona, Zeno of Verona.
Secular buildings: North-east door of Piazza delle Erbe (1480), rebuilt in 1532-1537.
Loggia del Consiglio (1476), *p.* 53; *ill.* 54.
Casa Camozzini (15th century).

Churches: S. Anastasia (beginning of 14th century), completed from 1423-1481: in the Grini Chapel, *St George* (1463), by Pisanello, *p.* 9.
San Bernardino (1451-1466).
San Fermo Maggiore (11th-12th centuries); *Annunciation (fresco)* by Pisanello.
Santa Maria in Organo (15th century).
SS. Nazario e Celso (rebuilt from 1464-1483).
San Tommaso Cantuariense (rebuilt in 15th century).
San Giorgio in Braida (1477-1536).
San Zeno (1120-1138): triptych (1457-1459) by Mantegna.

VERROCCHIO (Andrea di CIONE, called), Florence 1435-Venice 1488. Sculptor, goldsmith and painter. In his studio in Florence, one of the most important in the city (1465-1480) many works were executed, including busts, breast-plates, the tombs of Giovanni and Piero de' Medici (San Lorenzo, 1472); bronze group of *Christ and St Thomas* for Or San Michele (*c.* 1460-1482). In 1482 Verrocchio left for Venice, where he made the Colleoni statue. Verrocchio's paintings include the *Baptism of Christ* (*c.* 1470-1475), on which Leonardo da Vinci collaborated, and the Pistoia altarpiece (1478-1482), on which Lorenzo di Credi collaborated. His pupils included Leonardo, L. di Credi and Perugino). *pp.* IX, X, 91, 94, 109, 110, 113, 116, 124, 128, 138, 140, 151, 156, 165, 167, 170, 172, 184, 285, 286, 288, 289, 301, 307, 330, 352, 353; *ills* 109, 111, 125, 126, 155, 180, 181, 183, 290, 292, 293, 324. *see bibliog.* 27, 77, 95, 107, 264, 287.

VESPASIANO DA BISTICCI, *see* BISTICCI.

VICENZA, city in the Veneto, subjected to Venice in 1404. *pp.* 278, 311, 317.
Patron saints: Leonzio da Vicenza, Vincenzo, Giovanni Schio of Vicenza.
Secular buildings: Casa Arnaldi (15th century).
Palazzo Brunello (15th century).
Palazzo della Banca Populare: façade (1483) by Lorenzo da Bologna.
Palazzo Colleoni Porto-Breganze (1481) by Lorenzo da Bologna.
Palazzo Clementi (1477).
Monte di Pietà (1499-1553).
Palazzo Negri (end of 15th century).
Palazzo della Ragione (1449-1477).
Palazzo Da Schio (15th century).
Palazzo Thiene (15th century).
Bishop's Palace: courtyard (1494).
Churches: Cathedral: façade (1467), apse (1482-1508).
San Rocco (1485), with the exception of the façade.
Santa Corona (chancel raised in 1482).

VICOVARO, small town 21 miles from Rome. In 1191 given by Coelestinus III to Orsini, count of Tagliacozzo. Church of San Giacomo built by Domenico di Capodistria, 1454-1465. *see map* 353.

VIESTE, small town in the province of Foggia on the eastern side of the Gargano peninsula. *see map* 357.

VIGEVANO, Lombard city, Milanese possession in the 15th century, *p.* 3.
Secular buildings: Piazza Ducale (1492), built after plans by Bramante. The castle (1340) restored in the 15th century by Bramante.

VILLA: the word meant, in the Quattrocento, a country house, usually the centre of a country estate; Alberti wrote a treatise on its proper design and function. At the end of the 15th century the villa developed into either a country retreat or a country mansion. *pp.* 47, 56, 57, 58, 60, 334; *ills* 45, 46, 57, 58, 59, 60, 61, 335.

VINCENT FERRER (St, Italian: VINCENZO FERRERI), Valencia *c.* 1355-Vannes 1419. Spanish monk. *pp.* 257, 344; *ill.* 258.

VIRGINIA, died in Rome, *c.* 441 B.C. Pursued by the decemvir Appius Claudius, she was killed by her father, a centurion, to save her from dishonour; this act caused the fall of the decemvirs. *ill.* 310.

VISCONTI, Lombard family who ruled Milan from 1277 to 1447. *pp.* 31, 129, 333, 337; *ills* 139, 140, 338.

VITERBO, town in Latium, at the foot of the Cimini mountains belonging to the Papal States. *p.* 206; *ill.* 218.

VITRUVIUS (Marcus Vitruvius Pollio), 1st century B.C. Roman architect, author of the *De architectura*. The manuscript was rediscovered—but without the illustrations—at the beginning of the 15th century and was made the subject of an important edition by G. Sulpicio and Pomponio, in 1486, which was followed by those of Fra Giocondo (Venice, 1511) and C. Cesariano dedicated to Francis I (Milan, 1521). *p.* 23.

VIVARINI, family of Venetian painters. ANTONIO, Murano *c.* 1415-Venice *c.* 1476 or 1484; Venetian painter, brother of Bartolommeo and father of Alvise; collaborated with Giovanni d'Alemagna until 1450; many altarpieces and polyptychs. BARTOLOMMEO, Murano? (active 1450-1499); brother and collaborator of Antonio; worked with his brother on many altarpieces; *Madonna and child* (1478), etc. ALVISE, Venice *c.* 1445-1503-5; son of Antonio and nephew of Bartolommeo; *Virgin and Child with Saints* (Franciscan Monastery of Monte Fiorentino), *Virgin and Child* (1483) at church of Sant'Andrea, Barletta; *Virgin and Child* (1485) in Vienna Gallery. *pp.* 257, 272, 278, 338, 347; *ills* 259, 346. *see bibliog.* 258.

VOLTERRA, Tuscan city, a self-governing community which came under Florentine rule in 1366. *p.* 172.
Church: Baptistry (1283), baptismal font (1502) by A. Sansovino.

WARBURG (Abry), Hamburg 1866-1929. German art historian. *p.* 338.

WEYDEN (Rogier Van der, known as ROGER DE LA PATURE), Tournai 1399-Brussels 1464. Flemish painter. *pp.* 230, 283.

ZANOBI DEL LAMA (Gaspare di), 15th century Florentine merchant who endowed a chapel in Santa Maria Novella. *p.* 260.

ZENALE (Bernardino), Treviglio *c.* 1436-Milan 1526. Lombard painter, trained in the same studio as Butinone, with whom he collaborated on the frescoes in the church of San Pietro in Gessate, Milan, and on the Treviglio polyptych (1485). Painted other altarpieces. *pp.* 251, 316, 319; *ills* 253, 254, 319, 345. *see bibliog.* 381.

ZENOBIUS (St, Italian: ZANOBI), 344-417. Bishop of Florence, exorciser of devils. *pp.* 15, 309; *ill.* 14. *Emblems:* mitre, Florence lily, dead tree (on the day of his death a dried up tree is said to have flowered again).

ZENO (St), Bishop of Verona from 362 to 372. Patron saint of Verona and other Italian cities (including Pistoia).
Emblems: mitre, crozier (*see* Montagna's San Zeno Altarpiece).

ZOPPO (Marco), Cento 1433-Venice 1478. Bolognese painter, author of a collection of designs at one time attributed to Mantegna. Active in the Marches (Pesaro Altarpiece), in Bologna (Triptych of the Collegio di Spagna) and in Venice, *p.* 194.

ZOTTO (Agnolo), mentioned at the end of the 15th century. Paduan painter and pupil of Montagna. Painted the frescoes of the *Crucifixion* (1489, Old Refectory of Santa Giustina, Padua). *p.* 194. *see bibliog.* 303.

BIBLIOGRAPHY

Only a small number of the references already given in *The Golden Age of the Renaissance* will be repeated in the following list. The selection has been specially designed to document the personalities of the artists, specific problems or those concerning individual works. Compilations or histories covering several centuries or several countries have been omitted but on the other hand references to journals, the irreplaceable organs of research, have been considerably increased.

ABBREVIATIONS USED IN THE BIBLIOGRAPHY

A.	Arte, *Rome.*
A.B.	The Art Bulletin, *New York.*
A. in A.	Art in America, *New York.*
A.L.	Arte Lombarda, *Milan.*
A. St.	Archivio storico dell'Arte, *Rome.*
A.V.	Arte Veneta, *Venice.*
B.A.	Bollettino d'Arte, *Rome and Milan.*
B.M.	The Burlington Magazine, *London.*
B.S.H.A.F.	Bulletin de la Société d'histoire de l'art français, *Paris.*
Com.	Commentari, *Rome.*
G.B.A.	Gazette des Beaux-Arts, *Paris, New York* (1940-1954), *Paris.*
H.R.	Bibliothèque d'Humanisme et Renaissance, *Paris* then *Geneva.*
J.B.	Jahrbuch der preussischen Kunstsammlungen, *Berlin.*
J.W.	Jahrbuch der kunsthistorischen Sammlungen in Wien, *Vienna.*
J.W.C.I.	Journal of the Warburg and Courtauld Institutes, *London.*
M.F.K.	Monatshefte für Kunstwissenschaft, *Leipzig.*
O.M.D.	Old Master Drawings, *London.*
Pa.	Paragone, *Florence.*
R.A.	Rassegna d'Arte, *Milan.*
R.F.K.	Repertorium für Kunstwissenschaft, *Munich.*
Riv. A.	Rivista d'Arte, *Florence.*
R.J.	Römisches Jahrbuch für Kunstgeschichte, *Rome.*
W.J.K.G.	Wiener Jahrbuch für Kunstgeschichte, *Vienna.*
Z.B.K.	Zeitschrift für bildende Kunst, *Leipzig.*
Z.K.G.	Zeitschrft für Kunstgeschichte, *Munich and Berlin.*

BIBLIOGRAPHY

1. ACCASCINA (M.), *Aggiunte a Domenico Gaggini*, in 'B.A.', XLIV (1959).

2. ACKERMAN (James), *The Architecture of Michelangelo*, 2 vols, London, 1961.

3. ACKERMAN (James), *The Cortile del Belvedere*, in *Studi e Documenti per la Storia del Palazzo Apostolico Vaticano*, vol III, Città del Vaticano, 1954.

4. ACKERMAN (James), *Report on* no. 136, in 'A.B.', Sept. 1962.

5. ACKERMAN (James), *Sources of the Renaissance Villa*, See no. 376.

6. ACQUA (G. Dell'), *Problemi di scultura lombarda Mantegazza e Amadeo*, in 'Proporzioni', II (1948).

7. ACQUA (G. Dell'), *Il polittico di San Martino e Treviglio*, Bergamo, 1956.

8. AGNELLI (G.), *I monumenti di Niccolo III e Borso d'Este in Ferrara*, in 'Atti e memorie della deputazione ferrarese di storia patria', XXIII (1919).

9. ALISIO (G.), *La Cappella Pontano*, in 'Napoli Nobilissima', III (1963).

10. ANCONA (Paolo d'), *Les Mois de Schifanoia à Ferrare*, French trans., Milan, 1954.

11. ANGELI (D'), *Mino da Fiesole*, Florence, 1905.

12. APRA (N.), *Ambrogio da Fossano detto il Borgognone*. Milan, 1945.

13. ARSLAN (A.), *L'Œuvre de jeunesse d'Antonio Rizzo*, in 'G.B.A.', XLII, series 6 (1953).

14. ARSLAN (E.), *Sui Mantegazza*, in 'B.A.', XXXV (1950).

15. ARSLAN (Wart), *I Mantegazza il de Fonduti, l'Amadeo*, in *Storia di Milano*, vol. VII (1956).

16. ARSLAN (Wart), *Studi belliniani*, in 'B.A.', XLVII (1962).

17. *Arte lombarda dai Visconti agli Sforza*, Exhibition catalogue by G. BELLONI, R. CIPRIANI, F. MAZZINI and F. RUSSOLI, Preface by R. LONGHI Milan 1958.

18. BACCI (P.), *Bernardino Fungai*, Siena, 1947.

19. BARDT (K.), *Andrea Solario*, Leipzig, 1914.

20. BARONI (Costantino), *Elementi stilistici fiorentini negli studi vinciani di architettura a cupola*, in *Atti del III° congresso di storia dell architettura*, Florence, 1938.

21. BARONI (Costantino), *Il problema di Michelozzo a Milano*, in *Atti del IV° congresso nazionale di storia dell' architettura*, Milan, 1939.

22. BARONI (Costantino), *La pittura lombarda del Quattrocento*, Messina, 1952.

23. BECHERUCCI (L.) and GNUDI (C.), *Mostra di Melozzo e del Quattrocento romagolo*, Forlì, 1938.

24. BELTRAMI (L.), *La sala dei maestri d'arme nella casa dei Panigarola in San Bernardino (ora via Lanzone) dipinta da Bramante*, in 'R.A.', II (1902).

25. BERENSON (Bernard), *Alunno di Domenico*, in 'B.M.', I (1903).

26. BERENSON (Bernard), *Tre disegni di Giovanni Battista Utili da Faenza*, in 'Riv. A.', XV (1933).

27. BERENSON (Bernard), *Verrocchio e Leonardo, Leonardo e Credi*, in 'B.A.', XXVII (1933).

28. BERENSON (Bernard), *Italian Pictures of the Renaissance*, Oxford, 1932.

29. BERENSON (Bernard), *The Drawings of the Florentine Painters*, 2nd ed., 3 vols, Chicago, 1938.

30. BERENSON (Bernard), *Italian Painters of the Renaissance*, 4 vols, 1894-1907; re-edited, London, 1952.

31. BERENSON (Bernard), *Venetian Painters*, 2 vols, London, 1957.

32. BERGSTRÖM (Ingvar), *Revival of Antique Illusionistic Wallpainting in Renaissance Art* (Acta Universitatis, XIII), Gothenburg, 1957.

33. BERNARDINI (Giorgio), *Le pitture dell'appartamento di Innocenzo VIII in Vaticano*, in 'R.A.', V n.s. (1918).

34. BERTONI (G.) and VICINI (P.), *Della giovinezza del Paganino (G. Mazzoni), nuovi documenti*, in 'R.A.', VI n.s. (1919).

35. BOATO (M.), *Un frammento di Bernardino Parentino*, in 'B.A.', XXVIII (1934).

36. BOCCABIANCA (G.M.), *Benozzo Gozzoli*, Milan, 1957.

37. BODE (W. von), *Bartolommeo Bellano da Padova*, in 'A. St.', IV (1891).

38. BODE (W. von), *Florentiner Bildhauer der Renaissance*, Berlin, 1910.

39. BODE (W. von), *Der Familie della Robbia*, Berlin, 1914.

40. BOLOGNA (F.), *Una madonna lombarda del Quattrocentro*, in 'Pa.', no. 93 (1957).

41. BOMBE (W.), *Benedetto Bonfigli*, Berlin, 1904.

42. BONICATTI (M.), *Nuovo contributo a Bartolommeo della Gatta ed a Guglielmo Giraldi*, in 'Com.', IX (1958).

43. BONICATTI (M.), *Nota mantegnesca*, in 'Com.', XII (1961).

44. BORLINI, *Giovanni, Giacomo Dolcebuono*, in 'Rendiconte dell'Istituto lombardo di Scienze e Lettere', LXXXVII (1954).

45. BORSOOK (E.), *The Mural Painters of Tuscany, from Cimabue to Andrea del Sarto*, London, 1960.

46. BOTTARI (Stefano), *Antonello da Messina*, Milan, 1953.

47. BOTTARI (Stefano), *La Pittura del Quattrocento in Sicilia*, Messina, 1954.

48. BOTTARI (Stefano), *Riccardo Quartararo*, in 'Arte Antica e Moderna', VI (1959).

49. BOTTARI (Stefano), *Un'opera di Francesco Laurana*, in 'B.A.', XLVI (1961).

50. BRAGHIROLLI (W.), *Luca Fancelli, scultore, architetto e idraulico del secolo XV°*, in 'Archivio Storico Lombardo', III (1876).

51. BRANDI (C.), *Giovanni di Paolo*, Florence, 1947.

52. BRAVO (C. Del), *Liberale a Siena*, in 'Pa', no. 129 (Sept. 1960).

53. BRAVO (C. Del), *Sul seguito veronese di A. Mantegna* in 'Pa.', no. 147 (March 1962).

54. BRAVO (C. Del), *F. Morone*, in 'Pa.', no. 151 (July 1962).

55. BRENZONI (R.), *Domenico Morone*, Florence, 1956.

56. BRENZONI (R.), *Fra Giovanni da Verona*, Verona, 1960.

57. *Bronzetti italiani del Rinascimento*, Exhibition at the Palazzo Strozzi, Florence, 1962.

58. BURCKHARDT (L.), *Geschichte der nueren Baukunst* (edited by W. Lübke), I, *Italien*, Stuttgart, 1867; 3rd ed., 1891.

59. BURGER (Fritz), *Geschichte des florentinischen Grabmals von den ältesten Zeiten bis Michelangelo*, Strasbourg, 1904.

60. BUSCAROLI (Rezio), *Melozzo e il melozzisimo*, Bologna, 1955.

61. CAGNOLA (C.), *Intorno a Francesco Napoletano*, in 'R.A.', V n.s. (1905).

62. CALOSSO (A.B.), *Gli affreschi del Pinturicchio del Duomo di Spoleto*, in 'Riv. Ist. Nap. Archeologia e Storia dell'Arte', II (1953).

63. CALVESI (Maurizio), *Nuovi affreschi ferraresi dell'Oratorio della Concezione*, in 'B.A.', XLIII (1958).

64. CAMESASCA (E.), *Tutta la Pittura del Perugino*, Milan, 1959.

65. CANUTI (F.), *Il Perugino*, 2 vols, Siena, 1931.

66. CARLI (Enzo), *Liberale da Verona*, Milan, 1953.

67. CARLI (Enzo), *Tutta la pittura di Paolo Uccello*, Milan, 1954.

68. CARLI (Enzo), *Sienese Painting*, London, 1956.

69. CARLI (Enzo), *Il Pinturicchio*, Milan, 1960.

70. CARLI (Enzo), *La scultura lignea italiana*, Milan, 1960.

71. *Carpaccio*, Exhibition in Venice, catalogue by P. Zampetti, Venice, 1963.

72. CASTELNUOVI (G. V.), *Un affresco del Braccesco*, in 'Emporium', April 1951.

73. CASTELNUOVI (G.V.), *Giovanni Barbagelata*, in 'B.A.', XXXVI (1951).

74. CERVETO (A.), *I Gaggini da Bissone*, Milan, 1903.

75. CHASTEL (André), *Botticelli*, Milan, 1958.

76. CHASTEL (André), *Renaissance méridionale, 1460-1500*, Paris, 1965.

77. CHIAPPELLI (A.), *Il Verrocchio e Lorenzo di Credi a Pistoia*, in 'B.A.', V n.s. (1925).

78. CHIARINI (M.), *Ghirlandajo alla Cappella Sassetti in Santa Trinità*, Milan, 1961.

79. CIARDI DUPRE (M.G.), *Brevi Note sui 'Bronzetti italiani del Rinascimento'*, in 'Pa.' no. 151 (July 1962).

80. *Cima da Conegliano*, Exhibition, catalogue by L. Menegazzi, Treviso, 1962.

81. CLARK (Kenneth), *Piero della Francesca's St Augustine Altarpiece*, in 'B.M.', LXXXIX (1947).

82. CLARK (Kenneth), *Piero della Francesca*, London, 1954.

83. COLACICCHI (G.), *A. del Pollaiuolo*, Florence, 1945.

84. COLASANTI (A.), *Luciano Laurana*, Rome, 1922.

85. COLETTI (G.L.), *Intorno a Francesco Bissolo*, in 'B.A.', VIII n.s. (1928).

86. COLETTI (G.L.), *Su Antonio da Cadore e i pittori serravallesi*, in 'Venezia e l'Europa', (Venice Congress, 1955).

87. COLETTI (G.L.), *Cima da Conegliano*, Venice, 1959.

88. CONSTABLE (W.G.), *Painting in the Marlay Collection at Cambridge*, in 'B.M', XLVII (1925).

89. CORTI (G.) and HARTT (F.), *New Documents concerning Donatello, Luca and Andrea della Robbia, Desiderio, Mino, Uccello, Pollaiuolo, Filippo Lippi, Baldovinetti and Others*, in 'A.B.', XLIV (1962).

90. CORWEGH (R.), *Farbige Wandgräber der Renaissance*, in 'Mitteilungen des kunsthistorischen Instituts in Florenz', I (1911).

91. CRISTOFARI (G.), *Appunti critici sulla scuola folignate*, in 'B.A.', V (1911).

92. DAVIES (G.), *Renaissance: The Sculptural Tombs of the Fifteenth Century in Rome*, London, 1910.

93. DAVIES (Martin), *The Earlier Italian Schools*, National Gallery Catalogue, London, 1951.

94. *De artibus opuscula* XL, Essays presented to E. Panofsky, 2 vols, Princeton, 1960.

95. DEGENHART (B.), *Di alcuni problemi di sviluppo della pittura nella bottega del Verrocchio, di Leonardo e di Lorenzo di Credi*, in 'Riv. A.', XIV n.s. (1932).

96. DEGENHART (B.), *Die Schüler des Lorenzo di Credi*, in 'Münchner Jahrbuch für bildende Kunst', IX (1932).

97. *De Giotto à Bellini, les Primitifs italiens dans les musées de France*, Exhibition, catalogue by M. Laclotte; Introduction: Le goût des 'préraphaelites' en France, by A. Chastel, Paris, 1956.

98. DESPY (G.), *La Rocca di Ostia, problema di data e forme architettoniche*, in 'B.A.', XXXVI (1951).

99. DINSMOOR (W.B.), *The Literary Remains of Sebastiano Serlio*, in 'A.B.', XXIV (1924).

100. DODGSON (C.), *A Book of Drawings Attributed to Mantegna*, London, 1923.

101. DONATI (L.), *Il Botticelli, le prime illustrazioni della Divina Commedia*, Florence, 1962.

102. DURM (J.), *Die Baukunst der Renaissance in Italien*, 2nd ed., Leipzig, 1914.

103. DUSSLER (L.), *Benedetto da Majano*, Munich, 1924.

104. DUSSLER (L.), *Signorelli*, Berlin, 1927.

105. DUSSLER (L.), *Giovanni Bellini*, Frankfurt-on-Main, 1935.

106. ETTLINGER (L.D.), *Pollaiuolo's Tomb of Sixtus IV*, in 'J.W.C.I.', XVI (1953).

107. FABRICZY (C. de), *Andrea del Verrocchio al servizio de' Medici*, in 'A. St.', I (1895).

108. FAUSTI (C.), *Mostra delle opere di Giovanni di Pietro*, catalogue, Spoleto, 1928.

109. FERRARI (Giulio), *La tomba nell'arte italiana*, Milan, n.d. (1909).

110. FERRARI (Giulio), *La terracotta e i pavimenti in laterizio nell'arte italiana*, Milan, 1928.

111. FERRARI (M.L.), *Giovanni Pietro da Cemmo*, Milan, 1956.

112. FERRARI (M.L.), *L'ampio raggio degli affreschi di Bramante in Bergamo*, in 'Pa.', no. 171 (March 1964).-

113. FILIPPINI (F.), *Le opere architettoniche di A. Fiora vanti in Bologna e in Russia*, in 'Cronache', 1925.

114. FIOCCO (Giuseppe), *Piccoli Maestri*, in 'B.A.', II n.s. (1923).

115. FIOCCO (Giuseppe), *La data di nascita di Francesco Granacci e un'ipotesi michelangiolesca*, in 'Riv. A.', XII (1930).

116. FIOCCO (Giuseppe), *Antonio da Firenze*, in 'Riv. A.', XXII (1940).

117. FIOCCO (Giuseppe), *Postilla a Pietro Torrigiano*, in 'Riv.A.', XXVI (1950).

118. FIOCCO (Giuseppe), *Colantonio e Antonello*, in 'Emporium', CXI (1950).

119. FIOCCO (Giuseppe), *L'arte di Andrea Mantegna*, re-edited, Venice 1959.

120. FIRPO (L.), *La Città ideale del Filarete*, in *Studi in memoria di Gioele Solari*, Turin, 1954.

121. FIRPO (L.), *Leonardo architetto e urbanista*, Turin, 1963.

122. FLORES D'ARCAIS (F.), *Il ciclo di affreschi degli Eremitani di Padova*, in 'Arte Antica e Moderna', no. 17 (1962).

123. FOCILLON (Henri), *Piero della Francesca*, Paris, 1952.

124. FOGOLARI (G.), *Cristoforo Scacco da Verona pittore*, in 'Le Gallerie nazionali italiane', V (1902).

125. FOGOLARI (G.), *Ancora di Bartolomeo Bon*, in 'A.', XXXV (1932).

126. FORATTI (A.), *Giovanni Buonconsiglio*, pittore vicentino, Padua, 1907.

127. FORATTI (A.), *Bartolomeo Montagna*, Padua, 1908.

128. FORSTER (O.M.), *Bramantes erste Jahre in Rom*, in 'Wallraf-Richartz Jahrbuch', XV (1953).

129. FORSTER (O.M.), *Bramante*, Vienna, 1956.

130. FOVILLE (J. de), *Le Médailleur à l'amour captif (Cristoforo Romano)*, in 'G.B.A.', XXXIX (1908).

131. FRANCASTEL (Pierre), *Imagination et réalité dans l'architecture civile du Quattrocento*, in *Hommage à Lucien Febvre*, Paris, 1954; taken up again in *La Réalité figurative*, Paris, 1965.

132. FRANCOVITCH (G. de), *Nuovi aspetti della personalità di Bartolommeo di Giovanni*, in 'B.A.', VI n.s. (1926).

133. FRANKL (P.), *Die Renaissance Architektur in Italien*, Leipzig, 1912.

134. FREEMANN (L.J.), *Italian Sculpture of the Renaissance*, New York, 1927.

135. FRIEDLAENDER (W.), *Venetian Paintings of the XVth and XVIth Centuries*, in 'A. in A.', XXVI (1938).

136. FROMMEL (C.L.), *Die Farnesina und Peruzzis architektonisches Frühwerk*, in the Collection 'Neue Münchner Beiträge zur Kunstgeschichte', I, Berlin, 1961.

137. GABRIELLI (Mariarosa), *Aggiunte a Bramantino*, in 'B.A.', XXVII (1933-1934).

138. GAILLARD (E.), *Un peintre siennois au XVe siècle: Sano di Pietro*, Chambéry, 1923.

139. GALASSI (Giuseppe), *La scultura fiorentina del Quattrocento*, Milan, 1949.

140. GAMBA (Carlo), *Pietro Berruguete*, in 'Dedalo', VII (1926-1927).

141. GIBBONS (F.), *G. Bellini e Rocco Marconi*, in 'A.B.', XLIV (1962).

142. GIGLIOLI (O.), *Nota su Marcantonio Raimondi e Jacopo Francia*, in 'Riv.A.', XVI (1934).

143. GIOVANNONI (Gustavo), *Disegni sangalleschi per il Palazzo Medici in Roma*, in *Architettura ed arti decorative*, 1925.

144. GIOVANNONI (Gustavo), *Saggi sull' architettura del Rinascimento*, Milan, 1931.

145. GNOLI (D.), *Luigi Capponi*, in 'A. St.', VI (1893).

146. GNOLI (U.), *La cancelleria e altri palazzi attribuit. a Bramante*, in 'A.St.', V (1892).

147. GNOLI (U.), *Giannicola di Paolo*, in 'B.A.', XII (1918).

148. GNOLI (U.), *Madonne di F. di L.* in 'Dedalo', Nov. 1920.

149. GNUDI (C.), *Niccolò dell'Arca*, Turin, 1942.

150. GODFREY (F.M.), *Early Venetian Painters*, London, 1954.

151. GOLDBLAIT (M.H.), *Leonardo da Vinci and Andrea Salai*, in 'The Connoisseur', 1950.

152. GOMBRICH (E.H.), *A Panel by Apollonio di Giovanni*, in 'J.W.C.I.', XVII (1954).

153. GORI (L.), *Montanelli, Brunelleschi e Michelozzo*, Florence, 1956.

154. GOULD (Cecil), *An introduction to Italian Renaissance Painting*, London, 1957.

155. GREGORI (Mina), *Due opere dello Spanzotti*, in 'Pa.', no. 49 (1954).

156. GRIGIONI (C.), *Lorenzo da Viterbo*, in 'A.', XXXI (1928).

157. GUBERNATIS (A. De), *Dizionario degli artisti d'Italia*, Florence, 1906.

158. GUERRIERI (R.), *Il Polittico di Niccolo Alunno*, dans 'B.A.', X n.s. (1930).

159. HEINEMANN (F.), *Das Bildnis des Johannes Corvinus in der alter Pinakothek und die Jugendentwicklung des Jacopo de' Barbari*, in 'A.V.', XV (1961).

160. HEINEMANN (F.), *G. Bellini e i Belliniani*, in 'Saggi e studi di storia dell' arte', I, Venice, 1962.

161. HELLMANN (G.), *Die Zeichnung Leonardos zu Vitruv*, in *Festschrift Förster*, Cologne, 1960.

162. HENDY (P.), *Antonio Cicognara*, dans 'A. in A.', XIX (1930).

163. HERMANN (H.J.), *Die Gemälde des Cosimo Tura in der Bibliothek des Pico von Mirandola*, in 'J.W.', XIX (1898).

164. HERMANN (H.J.), *Pier Jacopo Ilari Bonaccolsi gen. Antico*, in 'J.W.', XXVIII (1910).

165. HEYDENREICH (L.H.), *Pius II als Bauherr von Pienza*, 'Z.K.G.', VI (1937).

166. HEYDENREICH (L.H.), *Leonardo da Vinci*, 2 vols, Basle, 1953.

167. HEYDENREICH (L.H.), *Eine italienische Bildbüste des frühen 16. Jh.*, in 'Die Kunst', 1958.

168. HILDERBRAND (A. von), *Italienische Porträtskulpturen des XV. Jh.*, Berlin, 1883.

169. HÜLSEN (C.), *Il libro di Giovanni da Sangallo* (Cod. Barb. 4424), Leipzig, 1910.

170. HUNTLEY (G.H.), *Andrea Sansovino*, Cambridge, 1935.

171. JANSON (H.W.), *The Sculpture of Donatello*, 2 vols, Princeton, 1957.

172. JANSON (H.W.), *Giovanni Chellini's 'Libro' and Donatello; See* no. 375.

173. JULLIAN (R.), *Le Retable de l'Ascension par Pérugin...*, in 'Bulletin des Musées lyonnais', 1961.

174. *Juste de Gand, Berruguete et la Cour d'Urbin*, Ghent, 1957, Exhibition, catalogue by P. Eeckhout.

175. KALLAB (W.), *Die toskanische Landschaftsmalerei im XIV. und XV Jh.*, in 'J.W.', XXI (1900).

176. KENNEDY (R.W.), *Alessio Baldovinetti*, New Haven, 1938.

177. KÜNSTLER (G.), *Gestaltungsanregungen auf die Londoner Verkündigung des Crivelli*, in 'Miscell. Bibl. Hertziana', 1962.

178. LABANDE (A.), *Les Brea*, Nice, 1937.

179. LACLOTTE (Michel), *Une prédelle de Bergognone*, in 'La Revue des Arts', 1954.

180. LA CROIX (H. de), *Military Architecture and the Radial City Plan in XVIth. Cent. Italy*, in 'A.B.', XLII (1960).

181. LANDAIS (H.), *Les Bronzes italiens de la Renaissance*, Paris, 1958.

182. LANGTON DOUGLAS (R.), *Piero di Cosimo*, Chicago, 1946.

183. LAUTS (Jan), *Antonello da Messina*, Vienna, 1940.

184. LAUTS (Jan), *Domenico Ghirlandajo*, Vienna, 1943.

185. LAUTS (Jan), *Carpaccio*, London, 1962.

186. LAVAGNINO (E.), *Andrea Bregno e la sua bottega*, in 'A', XXVII (1924).

187. LAZZARINI (Andrea), *Documenti relativi alla pittura padovana del secolo XV°*, in 'Archivio Veneto', 1908.

188. LEVI D'ANCONA (Mirella), *Miniatura e miniatori a Firenze dal XIV° al XVI° secolo*, Florence, 1962.

189. LIPMAN (J.), *The Florentine Profile Portrait*, in 'A.B.', XVIII (1936).

190. LIPMAN (J.), *Piero di Cosimo*, in 'A. in A.', XXVII (1939).

191. LOESER (C.), *Un'opera di Ambrogio da Predis* in 'R.A.', I (1901).

192. LONGHI (Roberto), *Officina ferrarese*, Rome, 1934; new enlarged edition, Florence, 1958.

193. LONGHI (Roberto), *Monumenti della pittura bolognese*, in 'L'Archiginnasio', Bologna, 1935.

194. LONGHI (Roberto), *Carlo Braccesco*, Florence, 1942.

195. LONGHI (Roberto), *Viatico per cinque secoli di pittura veneziana*, Florence, 1946.

196. LONGHI (Roberto), *Piero della Francesca*, 2nd, ed., Milan, 1946.

197. LONGHI (Roberto), *Un apice espressionistico* di Liberale da Verona, in 'Pa.', no. 65 (May 1955).

198. LORENZETTI (G.), *Lorenzo da Bologna*, Venice 1963.

199. LOTZ (W.), *Notizen zum kirchlichen Zentralbau der Renaissance; See* no. 375.

200. LUGANO (F.), *Fra da Verona*, Siena, 1905.

201. McCANN (G.L.), *Sienese Altarpeice*, in 'The Museum Collection, Cincinnati', 1933.

202. MACK BONGIORNO (L.), *Notes sur l'art de Silvestro dell'Aquila*, in 'A.B.', XXIV (1942).

203. MACLAGAN (E.R.D.), *Italian Sculpture of the Renaissance*, Cambridge, 1935.

204. MAGNUSON (Torgil), *Studies in Roman Quattrocento Architecture* (coll. Figura 9), Stockholm, 1958.

205. MALGUZZI-VALERI (F.), *L'Architettura a Bologna nel Rinasamento*, Rocca San Casciano, 1899.

206. MALAGUZZI-VALERI (F.), *Maestri minori lombardi*, in 'R.A.', V (1905).

207. MALAGUZZI-VALERI (F.), *I Solari, architetti e scultori lombardi del XV° secolo* in 'Italienische Forschungen des kunsthistorischen Instituts in Florenz', I (1906).

208. MALAGUZZI-VALERI (F.), *Sul miniatore frate Antonio da Monza*, in 'R.A.', III n.s. (1916).

209. MALAGUZZI-VALERI (F.), *Donato Bramante*, Rome, 1924.

210. MARBOTTINI (A.), *Giovanni da Milano*, Florence, 1950.

211. MARCHINI (Giuseppe), *Il Cronaca*, in 'Riv. A.', XXIII (1941).

212. MARCHINI (Giuseppe), *Giuliano da Sangallo*, Florence, 1942.

213. MARCHINI (Giuseppe), *Le Vertrate italiane*, Milan, 1955.

214. MARCHINI (Giuseppe), *Aggiunte al Palazzo Ducale di Urbino*, in 'B.A.', XLV (1960).

215. MARETTE (Jacqueline), *Connaissance des primitifs par l'étude du bois, du XIIe au XVIe siècle*, Paris, 1961.

216. MARIACHER (Giovanni), *Tullio Lombardi Studies*, in 'B.M', XCVI (1954).

217. MARINI (Remigio), *Arte veneta e arte nordica in Gianfrancesco da Tolmezzo*, in 'Emporium', 1955.

218. MARLE (R. Van), *The Development of the Italian Schools of Painting*, 19 vols, The Hague, 1923-1939.

219. MARLE (R. Van), *Giovanni Santi e Evangelista di Pian di Meleto*, in 'B.A.', XXVI (1932-1933).

220. MARQUAND (Allan), *Luca della Robbia*, Princeton, 1914.

221. MARQUAND (Allan), *Andrea della Robbia and his Atelier*, 2 vols, London, 1922.

222. MARQUAND (Allan), *The Brothers of Giovanni della Robbia*, Princeton, 1928.

223. MARTINI (A.), *The Early Work of Bartolomeo della Gatta*, in 'A.B.', XLII (1960).

224. MASI (O.), *La ceroplastica in Firenze*, in 'R.A.', IX (1916).

225. MASON-PERKINS (F.), *Dipinti inediti del Pinturicchio e di Bernardino di Mariotte*, in 'R.A.' (1910).

226. MASSARA (A.), *I primordi dell'arte novarese*, in 'R.A.', VI (1906).

227. MATALON (S.) and MAZZINI (F.), *Affreschi del Tre e Quattrocento in Lombardia*, Milan, 1958.

228. MAUCERI (E.), *Una nuova di Antonello de Saliba* in 'B.A.', V n.s. (1925).

229. MEAZZA (G.), *L'architetto Guniforte Solari e l'umanesimo lombardo*, in 'Acme', I (1951).

230. MEISS (Millard), *A Documented Altarpiece by Piero della Francesca*, in 'A.B.', XXIII (1941).

231. MENDES (Manuel), *A capela do Cardenal de Portugal em Florenza a luz de novos documentos*, I, in *Studi in onore di Amintore Fanfani*, Milan, 1961.

232. MESNIL (Jacques), *Botticelli*, Paris, 1938.

233. MEYER (A.G.), *Oberitalienische Frührenaissance, Bauten und Bildwerke der Lombarden*, 2 vols, Berlin, 1897-1900.

234. MICHEL (P.H.), *La Pensée de L.B. Alberti*, Paris, 1933.

235. MIDDLEDORF (U.), *New Attributions to Giovanni Francesco Rustici*, in 'B.M.' I (1935).

236. MÖLLER (Emil), *Leonardo da Vinci, Entwurf eines Madonnenbildes für S. Francesco in Brescia (1947)*, in 'R.F.K.', XXXV (1912).

237. MONOD-HERZEN (E.), *Léonard de Vinci, le problème de la Sala delle asse à Milan*, in 'Revue d'Esthétique', XV (1962).

238. MONTANARI (L.), *Un quadro di Baldassare Carrari*, in 'Studi romagnoli', VII (1956).

239. MORISANI (O.), *Michelozzo*, Turin, 1951.

240. MORRISON (Jane), *The Central Building in Italian Painting*, unedited thesis at the University of Chicago, August 1937.

241. MORRISON (R.C.), *Some Painting by Girolamo di Benvenuto*, in 'A. in A.', XVIII (1930-1931).

242. *Mostra di Melozzo e del Quattrocento romagnolo*, Forlì, 1938.

243. MÜNTZ (Eugène), *Il Belvedere d'Innocenzo VIII*, in 'A. St.', II (1889).

244. MÜNTZ (Eugène), *L'architettura a Roma durante il Pontificato di Innocenzo VIII*, in 'A.St.', IV (1891).

245. MURARO (Michelangelo), *La Scala senza giganti; See* no. 95.

246. MURARO (Michelangelo), *A Cycle of Frescoes by Squarcione in Padua*, in 'B.M.', CI (1959).

247. NEBBIA (Ugo), *La scultura del Duomo di Milano*, Milan, 1908.

248. NEPPI (A.), *Cosmè Tura*, Milan, 1953.

249. NEPPI (A.), *Francesco del Cossa*, Florence, 1959.

250. NERI DI BICCI, *Le Ricordanze (1453-1485)*, Edited by Poggi, in 'Il Vasari', 1927, 1929, 1930.

251. NICOLINI (F.), *L'Arte napoletana del Rinascimento*, Naples, 1925.

252. NICOLSON (Benedict), *The Painters of Ferrara*, London, 1950.

253. PAATZ (W. and E.), *Die Kirchen von Florenz*, 6 vols, Frankfurt-on-Main, 1940-1954.

254. PACCAGNINI (G.), *Il Mantegna e la plastica settentrionale*, in 'B.A.', XLVI (1961).

255. PACCAGNINI (G.), *Mantegna*, Exhibition catalogue, Mantua, 1961.

256. PALLUCHINI (R.), *Giovanni Bellini*, Exhibition catalogue, Venice, 1949.

257. PALLUCHINI (R.), *I teleri del Carpaccio in San Giorgio degli Schiavoni* with an Appendix by G. Perocco, Milan, 1961.

258. PALLUCHINI (R.), *I Vivarni*, Venice, 1962.

259. PANE (Roberto), *L'architettura del Rinascimento a Napoli*, Naples, 1935.

260. PANTUCCI (M.), *Melozzo da Forlì*, Milan, 1943.

261. PAOLETTI (Pietro), *L'architettura e la scultura del Rinascimento in Venezia*, 2 vols, Venice, 1893-1897.

262. PAPINI (R.), *Francesco di Giorgio architetto*, Florence, 1946.

263. PARKER (K.T.), *A. di Donino*, in 'O.M.D.', III (1929).

264. PASSAVANT (Gunt), *Andrea del Verrocchio*, Munich 1959.

265. PASSAVANT (Gunt), *Beobachtungen am Verkündigungsbild von Monte Oliveto*, in 'Mitteilungen des kunsthistorischen Instituts in Florenz', IX (1959-1960).

266. PATZAK (Bernhard), *Palast und Villa in Toskana*, 2 vols, Leipzig, 1912-1913.

267. PATZAK (Bernhard), *Die Renaissance und Barockvillen in Italien*, 2 vols, Leipzig, 1913.

268. PEASE (M.) and STOUT (G.), *Oil on Canvas*, in 'Art News', XLII (May 1948).

269. PEDRETTI (Carlo), *A Chronology of Leonardo da Vinci's Architectural Studies after 1500*, Geneva, 1962.

270. PERER (M.L.), *Aspetti della scultura lombarda: Tommaso Rodari (1484-1526)*, in 'Acme', VI (1953).

271. PEROCCO (G.), *Carpaccio*, Milan, 1960.

272. PETROVITCH (P.), *Questi Schiavoni, il Luciano e Francesco Laurana*, in 'G.B.A.', XXXI (1947).

273. PHILIPP (F.), *Bartolommeo Bellano*, in 'Bibl. Nat. Gall. Victoria', VIII (1954).

274. PIAZZI (G.), *Le opere di F. Ribolini detto Il Francia, orificiere e pittore*, Bologna, 1925.

275. PICCIRILLI (Pietro), *Monumenti abruzzesi e l'arte teutonica a Caramanico*, in 'A', XVIII (1915).

276. PIGNATTI (T.), *Andrea Riccio* in 'A.V.', VII (1953).

277. PIGNATTI (T.), *Carpaccio*, Geneva, 1958.

278. PITTALUGA (M.), *Filippo Lippi*, Florence, 1949.

279. *Pittura ferrarese del Rinascimento*, catalogue by N. Barbantini, Ferrara, 1933.

280. PLANISCIG (Leo), *Venezianische Bildauer der Renaissance*. Vienna, 1921.

281. PLANISCIG (Leo), *Andrea Riccio*, Vienna, 1927.

282. PLANISCIG (Leo), *Piccoli bronzi italiani del Rinascimento*, Milan, 1930.

283. PLANISCIG (Leo), *Del Giorgionismo nella scultura veneziana all'inizio del Cinquecento*, in 'B.A.', XXVIII (1934-1935).

284. PLANISCIG (Leo), *Severo da Ravenna*, in 'J.W.', IX (1935).

285. PLANISCIG (Leo), *Pietro Tullio und Antonio Lombardi*, in 'J.W.', XI (1937).

286. PLANISCIG (Leo), *Luca della Robbia*, Florence, 1940.

287. PLANISCIG (Leo), *Verrocchio*, Vienna, 1941.

288. PLANISCIG (Leo), *Bernardo und Antonio Rossellino*, Vienna, 1942.

289. PLANISCIG (Leo), *Desiderio da Settignano*, Vienna, 1942.

290. PLANISCIG (Leo), *Donatello*, Florence, 1947.

291. POHL (J.), *Die Verwendung des Naturabgusses in der italienischen Porträtplastik*, Würzburg, 1938.

292. POMPILLI (L.), *L'ultima opera di fra Filippo Lippi*, Spoleto, 1957.

293. POPE-HENNESSY (J.), *An Introduction to Italian Sculpture*, II, *Italian Renaissance Sculpture*, London, 1958.

294. POPE-HENNESSY (J.), *Bronzetti italiani del Rinascimento*, Exhibition London-Amsterdam-Florence, 1961-1962, Catalogue by J. Pope-Hennessy.

295. POPE-HENNESSY (J.), *Catalogue of Italian Sculpture in the Victoria and Albert Museum*, 3 vols, London, 1964.

296. PRETELLI (L.), *Felice Feliciano alla luce dei suoi codici*, in 'Atti dell' Istituto Veneto', CXIX (1939-40).

297. PREVITALI (G.), *Una data per il problema dei pulpiti di San Lorenzo* in 'Pa', no. 133 (January 1961).

298. PRIJATELI (K.), *Profilo di Giorgio Schiavone*, in 'A', IX (1960).

299. PROCACCI (Ugo), *Il tempietto sepolcrale dei S.S. Pellegrino e B. di M. Civitali*, in 'R.A.', XIII (1931).

300. PROCACCI (Ugo), *Sinopie e affreschi*, Milan, 1961.

301. PUERARI (A.), *Gli affreschi cremonesi di Giovanni Pietro da Cemmo*, in 'B.A.', XXXVII (1952).

302. PUERARI (A.), *Boccaccino Boccaccio*, Milan, 1957.

303. PUPPI (L.), *Angelo Zotto et quelques fresques padouanes du XVe siècle* in 'Bulletin du musée hongrois des Beaux-Arts', no. 21 (1962).

304. PUPPI (L.), *Bartolomeo Montagna*, Venice, 1962.

305. RAULE (A.), *L'Architettura bolognese*, Bologna, 1952.

306. REDIG DE CAMPOS (D.), *Il Belvedere di Innocenzo VIII in Vaticano*, in *Omaggio a Pio XII*, Vatican, 1958, II.

307. REYMOND (Marcel), *La Sculpture florentine*, 4 vols, Florence, 1897-1900.

308. RIBONI (E.), *Nuovi documenti sul Mantegna*, in 'Atti dell' Istituto Veneto', LXXXVII (1927-1928).

309. RICCI (S. de), *New Pictures by Francesco Napoli*, in 'B.M.', XVIII (1910).

310. RICCI (S. de), *Renaissance Bronzes: the Gustave Dreyfus Collection*, Oxford, 1931.

311. RICHTER (G.), *Rehabilitation of Fra Carnevale*, in 'The Art Quarterly', 1940.

312. RODOLICO (Francesco), *Le Pietre delle città d'Italia*, Florence, 1953.

313. ROLFS (Wilhelm), *Geschichte der Malerei Neapels*, Leipzig, 1910.

314. ROSENTHAL (E.), *The House of Andrea Mantegna in Mantua*, in 'G.B.A.', LX (1962).

315. ROSENTHAL (E.), *The Antecedents of Bramante's Tempietto*, in 'Journal of the Society of Architectural Historians', XXIII (1964).

316. RÖTHLISBERGER (M.), *Un libro inedito del Rinascimento lombardo con disegni architettonici*, in 'Palladio', (1957).

317. RÖTHLISBERGER (M.), *Studi su Jacopo Bellini*, in *Saggi e memorie di Storia dell' arte*, II, 1959.

318. ROTONDI (Pasquale), *Bramante pittore*, in 'Emporium', March 1950.

319. ROTONDI (Pasquale), *Il palazzo ducale di Urbino*, 2 vols, Urbino, 1953.

320. ROTONDI (Pasquale), *Nuovi contributi al Bramante pittore*, in 'A.L.', IV (1959).

321. RUDEL (Jean), *Le Problème du support dans l'histoire de la peinture*, in 'L'Information d'histoire de l'art', 1962, no. 5.

322. RUHEMAN (H.), *Leonardo's Use of Sfumato*, in 'The British Journal of Aesthetics', I (1960-1961).

323. RUHMER (E.), *Bartolomeo Bonascia*, in 'Münchner Jahrbuch für bildende Kunst', IV (1954).

324. RUHMER (E.), *Tura*, London, 1958.

325. SAALMAN (H.), *Early Renaissance Architectural Theory and Practice in Antonio Filarete's Trattato di Architettura*, in 'A.B.', XLI (1959).

326. SALMI (M.), *Cristoforo Scacco da Verona pittore*, in 'Le Gallerie nazionali italiane', V (1902).

327. SALMI (M.), *Nuova opera di Filippo Mazzola*, in 'R.A.', IV (1917).

328. SALMI (M.), *Luca Bauda de Novara*, in 'B.A.', VI n.s. (1925-1926).

329. SALMI (M.), *Intorno al Cicognara*, in 'B.A.', VI n.s. (1926-27).

330. SALMI (M.), *Bernardo Butinone*, in 'Dedalo', X (1929-1930).

331. SALMI (M.), *Un affresco di Lorentino d'Arezzo*, in 'Riv. A.', XII (1930).

332. SALMI (M.), *G. Caporali a Firenze*, in 'Riv. A', XV (1933).

333. SALMI (M.), *Antonio Filarete e l'architettura lombardo del primo Rinascimento* in *Atti del 1° Congresso nazionale di Storia dell'architettura*, Florence, 1936.

334. SALMI (M.), *La Bibbia di Borso d'Este e Piero della Francesca*, in 'Rinascita', 1943, nos. 32-33.

335. SALMI (M.), *Piero della Francesca e il Palazzo Ducale di Urbino*, Florence, 1945.

336. SALMI (M.), *Signorelli*, Rome, 1953.

337. SALMI (M.), *Nota su Bonifacio Bembo*, in 'Com.', IV (1953).

338. SALMI (M.), *La miniatura italiana*, Milan, 1954.

339. SALMI (M.), *Cosmè Tura*, Milan, 1957.

340. SALMI (M.), *Schifanoia e le miniature ferraresi*, in 'Com', XII (1961).

341. SALVINI (R.), *Tutta la pittura del Botticelli*, Milan, 1958.

342. SALVINI (R.) and TRAVERSO (L.), *Predelle dal 200 al 500*, Florence 1959.

343. SAMBON (A.), *Donato Bernardo di Giovanni Bragadin*, in 'A', XXXII (1929).

344. SANDBERG VAVALA (E.), *Lazzaro Bastiani's Madonnas*, in 'B.M.', LIX (1931).

345. SANDBERG VAVALA (E.), *Attributions to Cristoforo Caselli* in 'A. in A.', XXI (1932).

346. SANDBERG VAVALA (E.), *Francesco Benaglio*, in 'A. in A.', XXI (1932).

347. SANDSTRÖM (Sven), *The Program of the Decoration of the Belvedere of Innocent VIII*, in 'Kunsthistorisk Tidskrift', I, II (1960).

348. SANDSTRÖM (Sven), *Levels of Unreality, Studies in Structure and Construction in Italian Mural Painting during the Renaissance*, Uppsala, 1963.

349. SANPAOLESI (P.), *Venturi Vetoni, architetto di Pistoia*, in 'Palladio' (1934).

350. SAPORI (F.), *Due Quadri di Guidoccio Cozzarelli*, in 'R.A.', April-May 1916.

351. SAS-ZALOZIECKY, *Kuppellösungen Brunelleschis und die römische Architektur*, in *Mélanges Suida*, New York, 1959.

352. SAVONUZZI (Claudio), *Una scultura di Ercole de' Roberti*, in *Studi in onore de Matteo Marangoni*, Florence, 1959.

353. SCHARF (A.), *Filippino Lippi*, Vienna, 1935; 2nd ed. 1950.

354. SCHMARSOW (Auguste), *Antonio Federighi*, in 'R.F.K.', XII (1889).

355. SCHMARSOW (Auguste), *Peruginos erste Schaffensperiode*, in '*Abhandl. d. philos.-histor. Kl. der kgl. sächs Ges. d. Wiss*', XXXI, no 11.

356. SCHMIDT (L.), *Leonardo Zum Städtebau*, in *Festschrift für Hubert Schrade*, Stuttgart, 1960.

357. SCHREIBER (F.), *Die französische Renaissance - Architektur und die Poggio Reale Variationen des Sebastiano Serlio*, Berlin, 1939.

358. SCHUBRING (Paul), *Das italienische Grabmal der Frührenaissance*, Berlin, 1904.

359. SCHUBRING (Paul), *Die italienische Plastik des Quattrocento*, Berlin, 1919.

360. SCOTT (L.), *Fra Bartolomeo*, New York, n.d.

361. SERRA (B.), *Giovanni Dalmata nel tempietto di Vicovara*, in 'A.', XXV (1922).

362. SERRA (L.), *Antonio da Fabriano*, in 'B.A.', XXVI (1933).

363. SERRA (L.), *L'Arte nelle Marche*, Rome, 1934.

364. SERVOLINI (L.), *Jacopo da Barbari*, Padua, 1944.

365. SHAW (J.B.), *Timoteo Viti*, in 'O.M.D.', XIII (1938).

366. SHEARMAN (J.), *Leonardo's Colour and Chiaroscuro*, in 'Z.K.G.', XXV (1962).

367. SIGNORELLI, Exhibition, Catalogue by M. Moriondo, Florence-Cortona, 1953.

368. SIMSON (O. von), *Leonardo et Attavante*, in 'G.B.A.', XXIV (1943).

369. SINDONA (E.), *Paolo Uccello*, Milan, 1957.

370. SPENCER (J.R.), *The Dome of Sforzinda Cathedral*, in 'A.B.', XLI (1959).

371. STEGMANN (C.) and GEYMÜLLER (H. von), *Die Architektur der Renaissance in Toskana*, 10 vols, Munich, 1885-1908.

372. STEIMANN (E.), *Antonio da Viterbo*, Munich, 1901.

373. STRACK (Heinrich), *Central und Kuppelkirchen des Renaissances in Italien*, Berlin, 1882.

374. STRACK (Heinrich), *Ziegelbauwerke des Mittelalters und der Renaissance in Italien*, Berlin, 1889.

375. *Studien zur toskanischen Kunst* (Festschrift für L.H. Heydenreich), Munich, 1964.

376. *Studies in Western Art*, Records of the New York Congress (1961), vol II, New York, 1963.

377. SUAREZ (R. de), *Bartolomeo Montagna*, Florence, 1921.

378. SUIDA (W.), *Leonardo und sein Kreis*, Munich, 1929.

379. SUIDA (W.), *Antonio Maria da Carpi* in 'Belvedere', XVI (1930).

380. SUIDA (W.), *Ein Bildnis von B. Mainardi*, in 'Pantheon', II (1930).

381. SUIDA (W.), *Bernardino Zenale*, in 'A. in A.' (1943).

382. SUIDA (W.), *Pittura lombarda del Rinascimento*, in 'R.A.', XXXII (1957).

383. SUPINO (I.B.), *La scultura in Bologna nel secolo XV° Ricerche e studi*, Bologna, 1910.

384. TERNI DE GREGORY (W.) *I Fonduli, dinastia* in, A. St', VIII (1948).

385. TERRASSE (C.), *L'Architecture lombarde de la Renaissance 1450-1525*, Paris, 1926.

386. TERVARENT (G. de), *Sur deux frises d'inspiration antique (Poggio a Cajano)*, in 'G.B.A.', LV (1960).

387. TERZAGHI (A.), *L'Incoronata di Lodi*, in 'Palladio', III (1953).

388. TESTI (L.), *Storia della pittura veneziana*, 2 vols, Bergamo, 1909-1915.

389. TESTORI (G.), *G. Martino Spanzotti: gli affreschi di Ivrea*, Ivrea (1958).

390. TIGLER (Peter), *Die Architekturtheorie des Filarete*, Berlin, 1963.

391. TOLNAY (C. de), *The Youth of Michelangelo*, I, Princeton, 1947.

392. TOLNAY (C. de), *Two Frescoes by Domenico and David Ghirlandajo in S. Trinità in Florence*, in 'Wallraf-Richartz Jahrbuch', XXIII (1961).

393. TOMEI (Piero). *L'Architettura di Roma nel Quattrocento*, Rome 1942.

394. TRUBNER (E.), *Die stilistiche Entwicklung der Tabelbilder des Sano di Pietro*, Strasbourg, 1925.

395. VALENTINER (R.), *Andrea and Silvesto dell' Aquila*, in 'A. in A.', XIII (1925).

396. VALENTINER (W.R.), *Studies in Italian Renaissance Sculpture*, New York, 1950.

397. VENTURI (A.), *Baldassare d'Este*, in 'L'Art', XXVII (1884).

398. VENTURI (A.), *L'Arte a Ferrare nel periodo di Borso d'Este*, in 'Rivista Storica Italiana', 1885.

399. VENTURI (A.), *Storia dell'arte italiana*, 23 vols, Milan, 1901-1941.
Vol. VI, *La Scultura del Quattrocento*, Milan, 1908.
Vol. VII¹, VII², VII³, *La Pittura del Quattrocento*, Milan 1911-1914.
Vol. VIII¹, VIII², *L'architettura del Quattrocento*, Milan, 1923.

400. VENTURI (A.), *La Pittura del Quattrocento nell' Emilia*, Verona, 1931.

401. VENTURI (A.), *A traverso le Marche*, in 'A', XVIII (1915).

402. VIGNI (G.), *Tutta la pittura di Antonello da Messina*, Milan, 1952.

403. VIGNI (G.) and CARENDENTE (G.), Catalogue to the Antonello da Messina Exhibition, Venice, 1930.

404. VIGONI (P.), *Lorenzo di Pietro*, Florence, 1917.

405. VOLPE (C.), *L'apice espressionistico ferrarese di Liberale da Verona*, in 'Arte Antica e Moderna', nos. 13-16 (1961).

406. VOLTINI (F.), *Antonio della Corna*, in 'Pa', no. 97 (1958).

407. WALKER (J.), *A Note on Cristoforo Robetta and Filippo Lippi*, in 'Fogg Art Museum', II (1933).

408. WELLER (A.S.), *Francesco di Giorgio Martini*, Chicago, 1943.

409. WILDE (J.), *Die Pala di San Casciano von Antonello da Messina*, in 'J.W.', III (1929).

410. WILLICH (H.) and ZUCKER (P.), *Die Baukunst der Renaissance in Italian*, Postdam, 1914.

411. WITTGENS (F.), *Foppa*, Milan, n.d. [1950].

412. WITTKOWER (R.), *Architectural Principles in the Age of Humanism*, London, 2nd ed., 1952.

413. WÖLFFLIN (Heinrich), *Die klassiche Kunst*, Munich, 1899; English ed. *Classic Art*, London, 1952.

414. ZAMPETTI (P.), *Considerazioni su 'Pietro Alamanno'*, in 'A.V.', V (1951).

415. ZAMPETTI (P.), *Carlo Crivelli nelle Marche*, Urbino, 1952.

416. ZAMPETTI (P.), *Carlo Crivelli e i Crivelleschi*, Exhibition Catalogue, Venice, 1961.

417. ZERI (F.), *Per Antonio Aleotti*, in 'Proporzioni', II (1948).

418. ZERI (F.), *The Beginnings of Liberale da Verona*, in 'B.M.', XCIII (1951).

419. ZERI (F.), *Una pala d'altare di Lorenzo da Viterbo*, in 'B.A.', IV n.s. (1953).

420. ZERI (F.), *Il maestro dell'Annunciazione Gardner*, in 'B.A.', IV n.s. (1953).

421. ZERI (F.), *La mostra della pittura viterbese*, in 'B.A.', IV n.s. (1955).

422. ZERI (F.), *Un'aggiunta al problema della 'Madonna' Cagnola*, in 'Pa', no. 93 (1957).

423. ZERI (F.), *Cinque schede per C. Crivelli*, in 'Studi di Storia dell'Arte', Florence, 1961.

424. ZERI (F.), *Due dipinti, la filologia e un nome, il maestro delle tavole Barberini*, Turin, 1961.

425. ZEVI (Bruno), *Biaggio Rossetti, architetto ferrarese, il primo urbanista moderno europeo*, Turin, 1960.

426. ZIPPEL (G.), *Piero della Francesca a Roma*, in 'R.A.', VI n.s. (1919).

427. ZOCCA (E.), *Girolamo da Treviso il Vecchio*, in 'B.A.', XXV (1932).

428. ZOTTI (R.), *Morto da Feltre*, Padua, 1911.

429. ZUCCHINI (G.), *Le Vetrate di San Giovanni in Monte*, in 'B.A.', X (1917).

INDEX TO THE BIBLIOGRAPHY

LIST OF ILLUSTRATIONS

LIST OF ILLUSTRATIONS

painted on two panels. The scenes are: *The healing of the cripple, the freeing of the prisoner, the miracle of the eagle, the healing of a child, the healing of a wounded man with a spade, two miracles of San Berdardino, the raising of the still-born child, the healing of a man gored by a bull. Photograph shaded to emphasize palace architecture and gallery effects. (Photo: U.D.F. - La Photothèque.)*

22 *Sienese art.* Urbino, Ducal Palace. FRANCESCO DI GIORGIO MARTINI (attr.). *Architectural Perspective* (detail). *c. 1470-1480.* Baltimore, Walters Art Gallery. Oils on panel. *Cf. ill. 23. (Photos: Walters Art Gallery.)*

23 *Sienese art.* Urbino, Ducal Palace. FRANCESCO DI GIORGIO MARTINI (attr.). *Architectural perspective. c. 1470-1480.* Baltimore, Walters Art Gallery. Oils on panel; 2.17×0.78 *m.* Atributed by some to Luciano Laurana. *(Photo: Walters Art Gallery.)*

24 *Tuscan art.* Pisa, Campo Santo. BENOZZO GOZZOLI. *The Building of the Tower of Babel* (detail). *1467-1484. In situ, Fresco. (Photo: U.D.F. - La Photothèque.)*

25 *Florentine art.* Vatican, Sistine chapel, left wall. SANDRO BOTTICELLI. *The Punishment of Korah, Dathan and Abiron* (detail). *c. 1481-1482. In situ.* Fresco; 3.50×5.70 m. overall. One of the paintings commissioned by Sixtus IV from Signorelli, Botticelli, Ghirlandaio, Pinturicchio, Rosselli and Perugino between 1481 and 1483. *cf. ill. 227. (Photo: Pasquale de Antonis.)*

26 *Sienese art.* FRANCESCO DI GIORGIO MARTINI. *Study of proportions, relating a basilica to the human body. Second half of 15th century.* Florence, Biblioteca Nazionale. Pen drawing. From the Codex Magliabechiano, C. 42 *verso. (Photo U.D.F. - La Photothèque.)*

27 *Sienese art.* FRANCESCO DI GIORGIO MARTINI. *Schema for a column* (detail). *Second half of 15th century.* Turin, Biblioteca del Re. Pen drawing; 0.266×0.380 m. A study of the relationship between architectural proportions and the human body. From the *Codice architettonico di monumenti antichi di Roma e d'altri luoghi. (Photo: U.D.F. - La Photothèque.)*

28 *Florentine art.* LEONARDO DA VINCI. *Study in perspective* for *The Adoration of the Kings. c. 1481.* Florence, Uffizi. Pen and silverpoint on pink-washed paper; 0.16×0.29 m. *(Photo U.D.F. - La Photothèque.)*

29 *Florentine art.* ANTONIO FILARETE. *Exterior of a Castle. 1460-1464.* Florence, Biblioteca Nazionale. Pen and wash drawing. From Codex Magliabechiano, Book XX. *Cf. ill. 9. (Photo: U.D.F. - La Photothèque.)*

30 *Lombard art.* Cremona, Palazzo Stagna. PIETRO DA RHO. *Doorway* (detail). *End of 15th century.* Paris, Louvre. Marble; 7.10×5.48 m. *(Photo: U.D.F. - La Photothèque.)*

31 Urbino, Ducal Palace, east wall. FRANCESCO DI GIORGIO MARTINI. *Window with twin bays. 1475-1480. In situ.* After a drawing by Francesco di Giorgio. *(Photo: Anderson-Giraudon.)*

32 Urbino, Ducal Palace. FRANCESCO DI SIMONE FERRUCCI. *Doorway leading to the Throne Room. 1475-1480. In situ.* The original design may have been by Francesco di Giorgio. *(Photo: U.D.F. - La Photothèque.)*

33 *Lombard art.* Cremona, Palazzo Stagna. PIETRO DA RHO (attr.). *Courtyard, terracotta decoration. End of 15th century. In situ. (Photo: Alinari-Giraudon.)*

34 *Florentine art.* Florence, Palazzo Strozzi. BENEDETTO DA MAIANO and CRONACA. *Façade. 1489-1507. In situ. (Photo: Alinari.)*

35 *Venetian art.* Venice, Palazzo Dario. PIETRO LOMBARDO. *Façade. c. 1480-1487. In situ.* Faced with marble. *(Photo: U.D.F. - La Photothèque.)*

36 *Lombard art.* Brescia, Santa Maria dei Miracoli. *Façade (central portion). 1488-1508. In situ.* Faced with marble. *(Photo: Anderson-Giraudon.)*

37 *Bolognese art.* Bologna, Santa Maria di Galliera. *Façade. 1491-1510. In situ.* Grey *masegna.* This façade was restored in 1510 by D. di Gaio di Cernobbio. *(Photo: U.D.F. - La Photothèque.)*

38 *Florentine art.* Florence, Palazzo Medici. MICHELOZZO DI BARTOLOMMEO. *1444-1460.* This was the residence of the Medici family until 1540, when it became known as the Palazzo Riccardi. *(Photo: Brogi.)*

39 Milan, Castello Sforzesco. ANTONIO FILARETE. *1452-1453. In situ.* Aerial view. *(Photo Alinari.)*

40 *Tuscan art.* Milan, Medici bank. MICHELOZZO DI BARTOLOMMEO. *Doorway. 1462-1464.* Milan, Archaeological Museum. The palazzo housing the Medici bank was completely rebuilt under the direction of Michelozzo, with the collaboration of Filarete. *(Photo: Brogi.)*

41 Urbino: aerial view. *(Photo: Fotomero.)*

42 Urbino, Ducal Palace. LUCIANO LAURANA. *Courtyard.* c. *1465.* The first castle was begun in 1444 and continued by Laurana in 1465 and Francesco di Giorgio after 1475. *(Photo: U.D.F. - La Photothèque.)*

43 Sassocorvaro, the 'Rock.' FRANCESCO DI GIORGIO MARTINI. c. *1475-1480. In situ. (Photo: Fotomero.)*

44 Mondavio, the 'Rock'. FRANCESCO DI GIORGIO MARTINI. *c. 1475-1482. In situ. (Photo: Ministry of Education, Rome.)*

45 GIUSTO UTENS. *View of the Medici Villa at Poggio a Caiano. 17th Century.* Florence, Topographical Museum. A bird's-eye view of the villa built by Giuliano da Sangallo in 1480-1485 for Lorenzo de' Medici. *(Photo: U.D.F. - La Photothèque.)*

46 GIUSTO UTENS. *View of the Medici Villa at Cafaggiolo. 17th century.* Florence, Topographical Museum. The villa was built by Michelozzo in 1451 for Cosimo de' Medici. *(Photo: Alinari.)*

47 GIULIANO DA SANGALLO. *Project for the castle of Ferdinand of Aragon in Naples.* Plan. *1488.* Vatican Library, Barberini collection. Drawing on parchment; 0.46×0.40 m. Ms 4424, f. 41 *verso* (formerly 39 *verso*). *(Photo: Vatican Library.)*

48 *Sienese art.* FRANCESCO DI GIORGIO MARTINI. *Thermae.* Plan. *c. 1480.* Turin, Biblioteca del Re. Drawing; 0.226×0.380 m. Ms. Saluzzo 148, f. 73 *recto.* From *Codice architettonico* (see 27, above). *(Photo: Biblioteca del Re - Chomont Perino.)*

49 *Roman art.* Rome, Palazzo Riario, otherwise known as the Palazzo della Cancelleria. ANDREA BREGNO. *Façade. 1489-1495. In situ.* The building, begun in 1483, was completed under the direction of Bramante in 1511. *(Photo: Alinari.)*

50 *Roman art.* Rome, Palazzo Riario, otherwise known as the Palazzo della Cancelleria. ANDREA BREGNO and DONATO BRAMANTE. *Courtyard. 1483-1511. In situ. (Photo: Anderson-Giraudon.)*

51 Bologna, Palazzo Bevilacqua. FRANCESCO DI SIMONE FERRUCCI. *Façade. 1481-1494. In situ. (Photo: U.D.F. - La Photothèque.)*

52 *Venetian art.* Venice, Palazzo Corner-Spinelli. MAURO CODUCCI. *Façade. End of 15th century. In situ. (Photo: U.D.F. - La Photothèque.)*

53 *Venetian art.* Venice, Palazzo Vendramin-Calergi. MAURO CODUCCI and PIETRO LOMBARDO. *Façade. 1481-1509. In situ.* Begun by Coducci in 1481, completed by Lombardo in 1509. *(Photo: Ferruzzi).*

54 Verona, Palazzo del Consiglio. *Loggia. 1470-1492. In situ. (Photo: Alinari-Giraudon.)*

55 *Neapolitan art.* Naples, Palazzo Sanseverino. NOVELLO DI SAN LUCANO. *Façade. 1470. In situ. Now forms part of the church of Gesù Nuovo.* 17th century doorway. *(Photo: U.D.F. - La Photothèque.)*

56 *Ferrarese art.* Ferrara, Palazzo de' Diamanti. BIAGIO ROSSETTI. *1492. In situ.* Completed in 1565. *(Photo: Alinari-Giraudon.)*

57 *Tuscan art.* Careggi, the Medici Villa. MICHELOZZO DI BARTOLOMMEO. *1434. In situ.* A feudal villa acquired by the Medici and modernized. *(Photo: Alinari.)*

58 *Tuscan art.* Poggio a Caiano, the Medici Villa. GIULIANO DA SANGALLO. *1480-1485. In situ.* Built for Lorenzo de' Medici. *(Photo: U.D.F. - La Photothèque.)*

59 *Sienese art.* BALDASSARE PERUZZI. *Villa Chigi delle Volte. 1508-1511.* Vatican Library, Chigi Collection, P. VIII, 17 f. 7. *(Photo: Varitan Library.)*

60 *Venetian art.* JACOPO DE' BARBARI. *Plan of Venice* (detail): *villas and gardens on the Giudecca.* Amsterdam, Rijksmuseum. Wood-engraving. Part of the celebrated plan of Venice in perspective. *(Photo: Rijksmuseum.)*

61 *Bolognese art.* SEBASTIANO SERLIO. *Plan and elevation of Poggio Reale. 1537.* From Serlio's treatise on architecture in *Tutte le opere d'architettura et perspettiva di Sebastiano Serlio Bolognese,* Venice, 1619, p. 122.

62 BALDASSARE PERUZZI. *Plan of villa and garden at Poggio Reale. Beginning of 16th century.* Florence, Uffizi. Pen drawing. *(Photo: U.D.F. - La Photothèque.)*

63 *Sienese art.* FRANCESCO DI GIORGIO MARTINI. *Project for a fortified villa and a palace.* Florence, Uffizi. Pen drawing; 0.24×0.197 m. From *Taccuino di Viaggio* (c. 1491-1495), fig. 336. *(Photo: U.D.F. - La Photothèque.)*

64 *Sienese art.* FRANCESCO DI GIORGIO MARTINI. *Project for a large villa.* Florence, Uffizi. Drawing; 0.288×0.202 m. From *Taccuino di Viaggio* (c. 1491-1495). *(Photo: U.D.F. - La Photothèque.)*

65 *Florentine art.* Florence, Santa Maria Novella. LEONE BATTISTA ALBERTI. *Façade. 1456-1470. In situ.* Work on this church, begun in 1278, continued during the 14th century and was completed at the end of the 15th. *(Photo: Anderson.)*

66 *Florentine art.* Florence, San Lorenzo. FILIPPO BRUNELLESCHI and MICHELOZZO DI BARTOLOMMEO. *Façade. 1450-1460. In situ (Photo: Alinari.)*

67 *Emilian art.* Modena, San Pietro. *Façade. End of 15th century. In situ. (Photo: U.D.F. - La Photothèque.)*

68 *Ferrarese art.* Ferrara, San Francesco. BIAGIO ROSSETTI. *Façade. 1495-1515. In situ.* From Julius Baum, *Baukunst und dekorative Plastik der Frührenaissance in Italien,* Stuttgart 1926, p. 28.

69 Lugano, San Lorenzo. *Façade. End of 15th century. In situ. (Photo: Bruno Sulzer.)*

70 Bologna, Santo Spirito. SPERANDIO (attr.). *Façade. End of 15th century. In situ. (Photo: A. Villani e Figli.)*

71 *Lombard art.* Bergamo, Colleoni chapel. GIOVANNI ANTONIO AMADEO. *Façade* (detail). *1470-1475. In situ.* Faced and inlaid with coloured marble. *(Photo: U.D.F. - La Photothèque.)*

72 *Lombard art.* Certosa di Pavia. GIOVANNI ANTONIO AMADEO, ANDREA SOLARIO, ANDREA BRIOSCO and C. and A. MANTEGAZZA. *Façade. End of 15th and beginning of 16th centuries. In situ.* Inlaid with coloured marbles. The façade of the *certosa* (charterhouse) of Pavia was begun between 1473 and 1499 and completed in the 16th century. *(Photo: Scala.)*

73 *Lombard art.* Certosa di Pavia. GIOVANNI ANTONIO AMADEO, ANDREA SOLARIO, ANDREA BRIOSCO and C. and A. MANTEGAZZA. *Façade (detail). 1473-1499.* Inlaid with coloured marbles. *Cf. ill. 72. (Photo: Anderson.)*

74 *Venetian art.* Venice, Santa Maria dei Miracoli. PIETRO LOMBARDO. *c. 1489. In situ.* Faced and inlaid with coloured marbles. *(Photo: Osvaldo Böhm.)*

75 *Venetian art.* Venice, San Zaccaria. ANTONIO GAMBELLO and MAURO CODUCCI. *Façade. 1458-1515. In situ.* Faced and inlaid with

coloured marbles. Founded in the 9th century, rebuilt in the 15th. *(Photo: Alinari.)*

76 *Emilian art.* Mantua, Sant' Andrea. LUCA FANCELLI, after a project by LEONE BATTISTA ALBERTI. *Façade. 1472-1494. In situ.* This church was completed between 1597 and 1600. Cupola added in the 18th century. *(Photo: Anderson-Giraudon.)*

77 DONATO BRAMANTE. *Study for the façade of Santa Maria presso San Satiro, Milan. 1480.* Paris, Louvre. Pen and brush drawing. *(Photo: U.D.F. - La Photothèque.)*

78 CARADOSSO. *Saint Peter's, Rome, as projected by Bramante. c. 1505.* London, British Museum, Dreyfus collection. Bronze medal; diameter 0.057 m. There are other copies of this medal in Berlin, London and Milan. *(Photo: British Museum.)*

79 *Florentine art.* GIULIANO DA SANGALLO. *The Triumphal Arch of Fano* (detail). *1463.* Vatican Library. Pen and wash drawing on parchment; 0.46×0.40 m. From Codex Barberini, 4424, f. 61 *verso.* On the *recto* there is a plan of a circular church. *(Photo: Vatican Library.)*

80 *Lombard art.* ANON. *Banner showing view of San Lorenzo, Milan. 16th century.* Formerly in the sacristy of San Lorenzo, has now disappeared. Canvas. *(Photo: Institut d'art et d'archéologie, Paris.)*

81 *Florentine art.* MASO FINIGUERRA. *Florentine Picture-Chronicle: The Temple of Themis. c. 1460.* London, British Museum. Pen and wash drawing; 0.330×0.228 m. *Cf. ill. 11. (Photo: British Museum.)*

82 *Sienese art.* FRANCESCO DI GIORGIO MARTINI. *Buildings on a central plan.* Florence, Biblioteca, Laurenziana. Drawing (f. 12 *recto*). *(Photo: U.D.F. - La Photothèque.)*

83 *Lombard art.* Milan, Sant' Eustorgio. *Interior of Portinari chapel. 1462. In situ.* Built in the 12th and 13th centuries, Sant' Eustorgio was transformed by the addition of chapels in the 15th and 16th centuries. *(Photo: Alinari.)*

84 *Lombard art.* Milan, Santa Maria presso San Satiro. *1462-1486.* Section from H. Strack, *Central- und Kuppelkirchen der Renaissance in Italien,* Berlin, 1882, pl. 27.

85 *Tuscan art.* Prato, Santa Maria dei Carceri. *1485-1492.* Section from *L'Arte nel Rinascimento,* T. C. I., VI, 1962, p. 28, pl. 14.

86 *Lombard art.* Cremona, Baptistry. *1167. In situ. (Photo: Alinari.)*

87 *Lombard art.* Lodi, Santa Maria l'Incoronata. *1487-1494.* Elevation from H. Strack, *Central- und Kuppelkirchen der Renaissance in Italien,* Berlin, 1882, pl. 1, fig. 3.

88 *Lombard art.* Crema, Santa Maria della Croce. *c. 1493.* Plan from *L'Arte nel Rinascimento,* T. C. I., VI, 1962, p. 56, pl. 44.

89 *Lombard art.* Crema, Santa Maria della Croce. GIOVANNI BATTAGIO. *1493-1500. In situ.* Begun by Battagio, completed by G. A. Montanaro. *(Photo: U.D.F. - La Photothèque.)*

90 *Lombard art.* Milan, Santa Maria delle Grazie. CRISTOFORO SOLARIO and DONATO BRAMANTE. *Cloisters. 1465-1497. In situ.* This church was begun by Solario in 1465 and completed in 1492 by Bramante. *(Photo: U.D.F. - La Photothèque.)*

91 *Lombard art.* Brescia, Santa Maria dei Miracoli. *1488.* Plan from J. Burckhardt, *Geschichte der Renaissance in Italien,* 1912, p. 123, pl. 98-100.

92 *Florentine art.* GIULIANO DA SANGALLO. *Temples on a central plan.* Plan and elevation. *Second half of fourteenth century.* Florence, Uffizi. Pen drawing. *(Photo: Soprintendenza alle Gallerie.)*

93 LEONARDO DA VINCI. *Building on a central plan.* Plan and elevation. *End of fifteenth century.* Paris, Bibliothèque de l'Institut. Pen drawing. Codex Ashburnam 2037, f. 5 *verso. (Photo: Giraudon.)*

94 *Venetian art.* V. CARPACCIO. *The presentation at the temple* (detail). *c. 1500-1506.* Florence, Uffizi. Pen drawing; 0.565×0.245 m. *(Photo: U.D.F. - La Photothèque.)*

95 *Florentine art.* Padua, the 'Santo,' high altar. DONATELLO. *Santa Giustina* (detail). *1448-1450. In situ.* Bronze, in the round; height 1.54 m. This altar suffered dispersal at one stage and was reassembled, with the original Donatello statues and bas-reliefs, in 1895. *(Photo U.D.F. - La Photothèque.)*

96 *Florentine art.* Florence, San Lorenzo, right pulpit. DONATELLO. *The Resurrection* (detail). *c. 1460-1470. In situ.* Bronze, bas-relief (the whole pulpit is 1.23 m. high and 2.92 m. wide. *(Photo: Brogi.)*

97 *Florentine art.* Florence, San Lorenzo, right pulpit. DONATELLO. *Christ in Limbo* (detail). *c. 1460-1470. In situ.* Bronze, bas-relief. *Cf. ill. 96. (Photo: U.D.F. - La Photothèque.)*

98 *Florentine art.* Florence, San Lorenzo, left pulpit. DONATELLO. *The Crucifixion* (detail). *c. 1460-1470. In situ.* Bronze, bas-relief; the whole pulpit is 1.37 m. high and 2.80 m. wide. *(Photo U.D.F. - La Photothèque.)*

99 *Florentine art.* Florence, San Lorenzo, right pulpit. DONATELLO. *Pentecost* (detail). *c. 1460-1470. In situ.* Bronze, bas-relief. *Cf. ill.* 96. *(Photo: Borgi.)*

100 *Florentine art.* Florence, San Lorenzo, left pulpit. DONATELLO. *The Entombment* (detail). *c. 1460-1470. In situ.* Bronze, bas-relief. *Cf. fig.* 98. *(Photo: Brogi.)*

101 *Florentine art.* Florence, San Lorenzo, right pulpit. DONATELLO. *The Martyrdom of Saint Lawrence* (detail). *c. 1460-1470 In situ.* Bronze, bas-relief. *Cf. ill.* 96. *(Photo: Brogi.)*

102 *Florentine art.* Florence, San Lorenzo, right pulpit. DONATELLO. *The Martyrdom of Saint Lawrence. c. 1460-1470. In situ.* Bronze, bas-relief. *Cf. ill. 96. (Photo: Brogi.)*

103 *Florentine art.* Florence, San Lorenzo, right pulpit. DONATELLO. *The Martyrdom of Saint*

Lawrence (detail). *c. 1460-1470. In situ.* Bronze, bas-relief. *Cf. ill. 96. (Photo: Alinari.)*

104 *Art of Northern Italy.* ANON. PADUAN. *Pietà with the Virgin and Saint John. End of 15th century.* Washington, National Gallery of Art, Kress Collection. Bronze, haut-relief. *(Photo: National Gallery of Art.)*

105 Padua, the 'Santo.' BARTOLOMMEO. BELLANO. *Samson destroying the Temple* (detail). *1484-1490. In situ.* Bronze, bas-relief. One of a series of Old Testament scenes. *(Photo: U.D.F. - La Photothèque.)*

106 *Roman art.* Rome, Capitol. *Equestrian statue of Marcus Aurelius. In situ.* Bronze, in the round. *(Photo: Alinari-Giraudon.)*

107 *Florentine art.* Florence, San Lorenzo, right pulpit. DONATELLO. *The Horse Trainer. c. 1460-1470. In situ.* Bronze, bas-relief. *Cf. ill. 96 (Photo: Brogi.)*

108 *Venetian art.* Venice, Scuola di Santo Stefano. VITTORE CARPACCIO. *The Dispute of Saint Stephen* (detail). *c. 1511.* Milan, Brera. Canvas: the whole picture measures 1.47×1.72 m. One of four scenes which adorned the walls of the chapel of the guild of Saint Stephen until its demolition in 1806. The others are *Saint Stephen preaching*, in the Louvre, *The Consecration of the seven deacons*, in Berlin, and *The Stoning*, in Stuttgart. *(Photo: U.D.F. - La Photothèque.)*

109 *Florentine art.* Venice, Campo di SS. Giovanni e Paolo. ANDREA VERROCCHIO. *Colleoni monument.* Detail. *1479-1488. In situ.* Bronze. in the round. Only the model was in existence at the time of Verrocchio's death in 1488. The statue was cast by Leopardi and completed in 1494. *(Photo: Alinari.)*

110 *Florentine art.* Padua, Piazza del Santo. DONATELLO. *The Gattamelata Monument* (detail). *1447-1453. In situ.* Bronze, in the round; the whole monument measures 3.40 m.×7.80 m. *(Photo: Anderson.)*

111 *Florentine art.* Venice, Campo di S. Giovanni e Paolo. ANDREA VERROCCHIO. *The Colleoni monument* (detail). *1479-1488. In situ.* Bronze, in the round. *Cf. ill. 9. (Photo: Anderson-Giraudon.)*

112 *Florentine art.* ANTONIO POLLAIUOLO. *Study for the Sforza monument. 1479.* New York, private collection, pen-and-ink drawing. The blue background was added later. This subject was taken up by Leonardo in his giant *Cavallo* which was never cast in bronze. *(Photo: Private Coll.)*

113 *Florentine art.* Florence, baptistery, north door. GIOVANNI FRANCESCO RUSTICI. *Saint John the Baptist preaching. 1506-1511. In situ.* Bronze, in the round. *(Photo: Alinari.)*

114 *Sienese art.* Siena, Santa Maria della Scala. VECCHIETTA. *The risen Christ. 1476. In situ.* Bronze, in the round; 1.83 m. high. *(Photo: U.D.F. - La Photothèque.)*

115 *Sienese art.* FRANCESCO DI GIORGIO MARTINI. *Flagellation of Christ. Second half of 15th century.* Perugia, National Gallery of Umbria. Bronze, bas-relief; 0.56×0.41 m. *(Photo: U.D.F. - La Photothèque.)*

116 *Florentine art.* BERTOLDO DI GIOVANNI. *Orpheus. Second half of 15th century.* Florence, Bargello. Bronze, in the round: 0.44 m. high. *(Photo: U.D.F. - La Photothèque.)*

117 *Florentine art.* ANTONIO POLLAIUOLO (attr.) *David. Second half of 15th century.* Naples, Museo e Gallerie Nazionali di Capodimonte. Bronze, in the round; 0.33 m. high. This statue was cast only once, using the '*cire perdue*' process. *(Photo: U.D.F. - La Photothèque.)*

118 *Art of Northern Italy.* RICCIO. *Arion. Beginning of 16th century.* Paris, Louvre. Bronze, in the round; 0.25 m. high. *(Photo: Archives Monuments historiques.)*

119 *Art of Northern Italy.* ANTICO. *Venus. Second half of 15th century.* Vienna, Kunsthistorisches Museum. Bronze, partly gilded, in the round; 0.32 m. high. *(Photo: Kunsthistorisches Museum.)*

120 *Art of Northern Italy.* ANON. PADUAN. *Gnome riding a snail. Beginning of 16th century.* Paris, Louvre. Bronze, in the round: 0.37 m. high. H. Landais says: "Proof of the early appearance of baroque subject-matter in sculpture is furnished by the inventory drawn up by Gonzaga, who mentions as early as 1496 an inkwell consisting of a figure mounted on a tortoise. *(Photo: Archives Monuments historiques.)*

121 *Art of northern Italy.* RICCIO. *Satyr. End of 15th - beginning of 16th century.* Florence, Bargello. Bronze statuette. *Cf. ill.* 120. *(Photo: U.D.F. - La Photothèque).*

122. *Art of Northern Italy.* Padua, the 'Santo.' RICCIO. *Paschal Candlestick. 1507-1516. In situ.* Bronze; 3.92 m. high. This candlestick, on its marble base, is made up of fifty separately cast pieces of bronze. *(Photo: Alinari.)*

123 *Florentine art.* Florence, Badia. MINO DA FIESOLE. *Tomb of Count Hugo of Tuscany. c. 1470-1480. In situ.* Marble, in the round. *(Photo: Alinari.)*

124 *Florentine art.* Florence, Badia. MINO DA FIESOLE. *Tomb of Count Hugo of Tuscany* (detail): *Charity. c. 1470-1480. In situ. Marble, in the round. (Photo: Alinari.)*

125 *Tuscan art.* ANDREA VERROCCHIO. *Forteguerri Tomb*, maquette (detail). *c. 1473.* London, Victoria and Albert Museum. Terracotta. The tomb, now in the cathedral at Pistoia, was re-modelled in the 17th century. *(Photo: Victoria and Albert Museum.)*

126 *Tuscan art.* ANDREA VERROCCHIO. *Angel for the Forteguerri tomb:* maquette. *c. 1473.* Paris, Louvre, Terracotta; 0.38×0.35 m. The Louvre possesses another *Angel* which forms a pair with this one. *(Photo: U.D.F. - La Photothèque.)*

127 *Venetian art.* Padua, the 'Santo.' PIETRO LOMBARDO. *Tomb of Antonio Rosselli. 1464-1467. In situ.* Marble. *(Photo: Alinari.)*

128 *Venetian art.* Venice, Santa Maria Gloriosa dei Frari. ANTONIO RIZZO. *Tomb of the Doge Niccolò Tron. c. 1473. In situ.* Marble. *(Photo: Anderson-Giraudon.)*

129 *Venetian art.* Venice, SS. Giovanni e Paolo. PIETRO LOMBARDO. *Tomb of the Doge Pietro Mocenigo. 1485. In situ.* Marble. *(Photo: Alinari.)*

130 *Lombard art.* Venice, SS. Giovanni e Paolo. PIETRO and TULLIO LOMBARDO. *Tomb of Andrea Vendramin. 1493. In situ.* Marble. *(Photo: Osvaldo Böhm.)*

131 *Venetian art.* Venice, Santa Maria Gloriosa dei Frari. ANTONIO RIZZO. *Tomb of the Doge Niccolò Tron* (detail): *Virtue. c. 1473. In situ.* Marble, in the round; the whole tomb is 1.67 m. high. *(Photo: Osvaldo Böhm.)*

132 *Venetian art.* Venice, SS. Giovanni e Paolo. PIETRO LOMBARDO. *Tomb of the Doge Pasquale Malipiero* (detail): *Virtue. c. 1462-1463. In situ.* Marble, in the round. *(Photo: Osvaldo Böhm.)*

133 *Venetian art.* Venice, Doge's Palace, Foscari Arch. ANTONIO RIZZO. *Warrior. c. 1476. In situ.* Marble, in the round. Attributed by some to A. Bregno. *(Photo: Osvaldo Böhm.)*

134 *Venetian art.* Venice, Doge's Palace, Foscari Arch. ANTONIO RIZZO. *Adam. 1484-1490.* Venice, Doge's Palace. Istrian stone; 2.06 m. high. This figure, with the same artist's *Eve*, formerly stood on the Foscari Arch. Both have now been replaced with copies. *(Photo: Ferruzzi.)*

135 *Venetian art.* Venice, Doge's Palace, Foscari Arch. After ANTONIO RIZZO. *Eve. 1484-1490. In situ.* Marble, in the round; 2.04 m. high. Copy of the *Eve* by Antonio Rizzo which has been moved from the Foscari Arch to a hall in the Doge's Palace. *Cf. ill. 136. (Photo: Anderson-Giraudon.)*

136 *Venetian art.* Venice, Doge's Palace, Foscari arch. ANTONIO RIZZO. *Eve* (detail). *1484-1490. Venice, Doge's Palace.* Istrian stone, in the round. *Cf. ill.* 135. *(Photo: Osvaldo Böhm.)*

137 *Florentine art.* Forlì, San Biagio in San Girolamo. FRANCESCO DI SIMONE FERRUCCI. *Tomb of Barbara Manfredi. c. 1467-1480. In situ.* Marble. *(Photo: Alinari.)*

138 *Lombard art.* Bergamo, Colleoni Chapel. GIOVANNI ANTONIO AMADEO. *Tomb of Medea Colleoni. 1475. In situ.* Marble. *(Photo: Alinari.)*

139 *Lombard art.* Certosa di Pavia. GIAN CRISTOFORO ROMANO. *Tomb of Gian Galeazzo Visconti. 1491-1497. In situ.* Marble. *(Photo: U.D.F. - La Photothèque.)*

140 *Lombard art.* Certosa di Pavia. GIAN CRISTOFORO ROMANO. *Tomb of Gian Galeazzo Visconti* (detail). *1491-1497. In situ. Marble. (Photo: U.D.F. - La Photothèque.)*

141 LEONARDO DA VINCI. *Study for the Trivulzio Monument. c. 1511.* Windsor Castle, Royal Library. Pen and bistre on grey paper. During his stay in Milan, the artist made many studies for equestrian monuments to Francesco Sforza and later Marshal Trivulzio. *(Photo: Royal Library.)*

142 *Florentine art.* STUDIO OF LEONARDO DA VINCI. *Horseman. c. 1506-1508.* Budapest, Museum of Fine Arts. Bronze, in the round; 0.235 m. high. *(Photo: Museum of Fine Arts.)*

143 *Tuscan art.* Milan, Medici Bank. MICHELOZZO DI BARTOLOMMEO. *Doorway.* Milan, Archaeological Museum. *Cf. ill.* 40. *(Photo: Alinari.)*

144 *Lombard art.* Cesena, cathedral. PIETRO LOMBARDO. *Altar of Corpus Domini. c. 1481. In situ.* Marble. *(Photo: Alinari.)*

145 *Lombard art.* Cremona, Palazzo Stanga. PIETRO DA RHO. *Doorway* (detail). *Second half of 15th century.* Paris, Louvre. The whole doorway is 7.10×5.48 m. *(Photo: U.D.F. - La Photothèque.)*

146 *Lombart art.* Como, cathedral. TOMMASO RODARI. *Doorway* (detail). *1498. In situ. (Photo: U.D.F. - La Photothèque.)*

147 *Venetian art.* Venice, Scuola di San Giovanni Evangelista. MAURO CODUCCI. *Staircase. 1501. in situ. (photo: Osvaldo Böhm.)*

148 *Tuscan art.* Toscanella (now Tuscania), Seminary Church. *Ludovisi Chapel. 1486. In Situ. (Photo: Brogi.)*

149 *Venetian art.* Venice, Santa Maria dei Miracoli. PIETRO LOMBARDO. *Choir. c. 1489. In situ. (Photo: Anderson.)*

150 *Lombart art.* Milan, Santa Maria presso San Satiro. DONATO BRAMANTE. *Choir. c. 1480-1486. In situ. (Photo: U.D.F. - La Photothèque.)*

151 *Neapolitan art.* FRANCESCO LAURANA. *Bust of a Young Woman* (detail). *End of 15th century.* Paris, Louvre. Marble, in the round; 0.43 m. high. *(Photo: U.D.F. - La Photothèque.)*

152 *Florentine art.* BENEDETTO DA MAIANO. *Bust of Pietro Mellini. 1474.* Florence, Bargello. Marble, in the round; 0.53 m. high. Inscribed with the names of the artist and his model, and the date. *(Photo: Anderson.)*

153 *Florentine art.* ANTONIO ROSSELLINO. *Bust of Giovanni Chellini. c. 1456.* London, Victoria and Albert Museum. Marble, in the round; 0.511 m. high. *(Photo: Victoria and Albert Museum.)*

154 *Florentine art.* MINO DA FIESOLE. *Bust of Niccolò Strozzi. 1454.* Berlin-Dahlem, Staatliche Museen. Marble, in the round; 0.49 m. high. *(Photo: Braun.)*

155 *Florentine art.* ANDREA VERROCCHIO. *Bust of a lady. Second half of 15th century.* Florence, Bargello. Marble, in the round. *(Photo: U.D.F. - La Photothèque.)*

156 *Sienese art.* FRANCESCO DI GIORGIO MARTINI (attr.). *Saint Christopher. c. 1470-1480.* Paris, Louvre. Painted and gilded wood, in the round; 1.63 m. high.

Carli advances good arguments for his attribution of this work to Francesco. *(Photo: U.D.F. - La Photothèque.)*

157 *Sienese art.* NEROCCIO DI BARTOLOMMEO DE' LANDI. *San Bernardino* (detail). *c. 1467.* Borgo a Mozzano, San Jacopo. Painted wood, in the round. *(Photo: U.D.F. - La Photothèque.)*

158 *Emilian art.* Modena, San Giovanni Battista. GUIDO MAZZONI. *The Deposition. 1476. In situ.* Coloured terracotta, in the round. *(Photo U.D.F. - La Photothèque.)*

159 *Emilian art.* Venice, monastery of Sant' Antonio di Castello. GUIDO MAZZONI. *Figure of Mourner: Saint Mary Magdalen. 1489.* Padua, Museo Civico. Coloured terracotta, in the round. Part of a *Deposition* now shared between Venice and Padua. *(Photo: U.D.F. - La Photothèque.)*

160 *Emilian art.* Venice, monastery of Sant' Antonio di Castello. GUIDO MAZZONI. *Figure of Mourner: Holy Woman. 1489.* Padua, Museo Civico. Coloured terracotta, in the round. *Cf. ill. 159. (Photo: U.D.F. - La Photothèque.)*

161 *Apulian art.* Bologna, Santa Maria della Vita. NICCOLÒ DELL' ARCA. *The Deposition. 1485. In situ.* Terracotta, in the round. **(Photo: U.D.F. - La Photothèque.)**

162 *Apulian art.* Bologna, Santa Maria della Vita. NICCOLÒ DELL' ARCA. *The Deposition* (detail): *Saint Mary Magdalen. 1485. In situ.* Terracotta, in the round. *(Photo: U.D.F. - La Photothèque.)*

163 *Florentine art.* Faenza, San Michele. ANDREA DELLA ROBBIA. *The Archangel Michael. c. 1475.* New York, Metropolitan Museum of Art. Enamelled terracotta, haut-relief; 0.80×1.60 m. *(Photo: Metropolitan Museum of Art.)*

164 *Florentine art.* Florence, San Miniato al Monte, chapel of Cardinal of Portugal. LUCA DELLA ROBBIA. *Temperance. 1460-1466. In situ.* Enamelled terracotta, bas-relief; diameter 2 m. *(Photo: U.D.F. - La Photothèque.)*

165 *Florentine art.* Rimini, Tempio Malatestiano, chapel of Sigismondo, left wall. AGOSTINO DI DUCCIO. *Angel drawing a curtain. 1447-1452. In situ.* Marble, bas-relief. *(Photo: U.D.F. - La Photothèque.)*

166 *Florentine art.* Florence, baptistry. DONATELLO. *Saint Mary Magdalen. c. 1455. In situ.* Wood, in the round; 1.88 m. high. *(Photo: Alinari.)*

167 *Florentine art.* Florence, Santa Trinità. DESIDERIO DA SETTIGNANO. *Saint Mary Magdalen. c. 1455. In situ.* Wood with traces of successive layers of paint; 1.83 m. high. *(Photo: Alinari.)*

168 *Venetian art.* Venice, Doge's Palace. ANTONIO RIZZO. *Staircase. 1484-1501. In situ.* Istrian stone. *The photograph has been retouched to show the staircase as it was before the two statues of 'Giganti' were placed in position. (Photo: U.D.F. - La Photothèque.)*

169 *Lombard art.* Cremona, cathedral, pulpit. GIOVANNI ANTONIO AMADEO (attr.) *The Martyrs before the Emperor Claudius. c. 1480. In situ.* Bas-relief. Part of the so-called Pulpit of the Martyrs. *(Photo: U.D.F. - La Photothèque.)*

170 *Genoese art.* Naples. DOMENICO GAGGINI. *Lintel portraying Ferdinand of Aragon. c. 1490.* Los Angeles, County Museum of Art. Marble, haut-relief. *(Photo: County Museum of Art.)*

171 Urbino, Palazzo Ducale, Sala dei Angeli. DOMENICO ROSSELLI? *Capital: Adam and Eve. c. 1476. In situ. (Photo: Alinari.)*

172 *Florentine art.* Rimini, Tempio Malatestiano, Chapel of the Planets. AGOSTINO DI DUCCIO (attr.). *Venus* (detail). *c. 1454-1457. In situ.* Marble, bas-relief. Attributed by some to Matteo de' Pasti. *(Photo: Alinari.)*

173 *Lombard art.* Certosa di Pavia, Chapter House. ANTONIO MANTEGAZZA. *The Lamentation* (detail). *End of 15th century. In situ.* Marble, bas-relief; 1.96×1.10 m. *(Photo: Alinari.)*

174 *Lombard art.* Certosa di Pavia, façade. CRISTOFORO and ANTONIO MANTEGAZZA. *The Expulsion from Paradise* (detail): *Adam and Eve. 1480-1490. In situ.* Bas-relief. From R. Longhi, *Proporzioni*, II, 1948, pl. 121.

175 *Lombard art.* Como, cathedral, façade. TOMMASO RODARI. *Aedicule with a statue of Pliny the Elder. c. 1463. In situ.* Marble, in the round; overall height including aedicule 3.05 m. *(Photo: Alinari.)*

176 *Lombard art.* Cremona, San Girolamo. PIETRO DA RHO. *Saint Jerome. End of 15th - beginning of 16th century.* Cremona, Museo. Marble, haut-relief. *(Photo: U.D.F. - La Photothèque.)*

177 *Lombard art.* Certosa di Pavia, small cloister. GIOVANNI ANTONIO AMADEO. *Tympanum* (detail): *Medallion-bust of a prophet flaked by putti with garlands. c. 1465-1470. In situ.* Terracotta, bas-relief. *(Photo: U.D.F. - La Photothèque.)*

178 *Venetian art.* Venice, La Carità. TULLIO LOMBARDO. *Barbarigo Tomb* (detail): *Assumption of the Virgin. Beginning of 16th century.* Venice, Ca' d'Oro. Bronze, haut-relief. Tomb of the Doges Marco and Agostino Barbarigo. *(Photo: Osvaldo Böhm.)*

179 *Florentine art.* ANON. FLORENTINE. *Idealized Portrait of Scipio. End of 15th - beginning of 16th century.* Paris, Louvre. Marble, bas-relief; 0.68×0.39 m. The artist probably belonged to the studio of Verrocchio. Inscribed 'P. Scipioni.' *(Photo: U.D.F. - La Photothèque.)*

180 *Florentine art.* Florence, San Lorenzo, Old Sacristy. ANDREA VERROCCHIO. *Lavabo* (detail): *Chimaera. c. 1470. In situ.* Marble. *(Photo: Soprintendenza alla Gallerie.)*

181 *Florentine art.* ANDREA VERROCCHIO. *David. c. 1476.* Florence, Bargello. Bronze, in the round. From J. Pope-Hennessy, *Italian Renaissance Sculpture*, London, 1958, pl. 79.

182 *Florentine art.* DONATELLO. *David.* *c. 1430-1432.* Florence, Bargello. Bronze, in the round; 1.58 m. high. From J. Pope-Hennessy, *Italian Renaissance Sculpture*, London, 1958, pl. 30.

183 *Florentine art.* Florence, Or San Michele. ANDREA VERROCCHIO. *Christ and Saint Thomas.* *c. 1467-1483.* *In situ.* Bronze, in the round. *(Photo: U.D.F. - La Photothèque.)*

184 *Venetian art.* Venice, SS. Giovanni e Paolo. TULLIO LOMBARDO. *Tomb of Pietro Mocenigo* (detail): *Saint Mark baptising Ammianus.* *c. 1481.* *In situ.* Marble, haut-relief; 1.07 × 1.54 m. *(Photo: Osvaldo Böhm.)*

185 *Venetian art.* Venice, SS. Giovann e Paolo. TULLIO LOMBARDO. *Saint Mark baptising Ammianus* (detail). *c. 1481.* *In situ.* Marble. *Cf. ill. 184.* *(Photo: Osvaldo Böhm.)*

186 TULLIO LOMBARDO. *Bacchus and Ariadne.* *End of 15th - beginning of 16th century.* Vienna, Kunsthistorisches Museum. Stone, haut-relief. *(Photo: Kunsthistorisches Museum.)*

187 *Florentine art.* Michelangelo. *Tb Battle of the Centaurs.* *c. 1493.* Florence, Casa Buonarroti. Marble haut-relief, *non finito*; 0.79 m × 0.88 m. *(Photo: Alinari.)*

188 *Venetian art.* Padua, Giustiniani Collection. GIORGIONE. *Portrait of a Young Man.* *Beginning of 16th century.* Berlin-Dahlem, Staatliche Museen, Gemäldegalerie. Canvas; 0.58 × 0.46 m. *(Photo: Staatliche Museen - Walter Steinkopf.)*

189 Spello, Santa Maria Maggiore, Baglioni chapel. BERNARDINO PINTURICCHIO. *Self-Portrait.* *1501.* *In situ.* Fresco. This self-portrait accompanies the *cartellino*, giving the artist's name, at the edge of his *Annunciation.* *(Photo: Villani e Figli.)*

190 *Art of the Marches.* MASTER OF THE BARBERINI PANELS. *Presentation of the Virgin* (detail). *c. 1460.* Boston, The Museum of Fine Arts. Painted on panel. According to F. Zeri, this picture and the *Birth of the Virgin* now at the Metropolitan Museum of Arts, New York, come from the walls of a room or alcove rather than an altarpiece. The anonymous artist seems to have been Giovanni da Camerino. *Photograph shaded to emphasize the picture-within-a-picture.* *Cf. ill. 20.* *(Photo: Museum of Fine Arts.)*

191 *Venetian art.* Venice, Scuola di Sant' Orsola. VITTORE CARPACCIO (signed in a *cartellino*). *Legend of Saint Ursula: Arrival of the English Ambassadors* (detail). *1495.* Venice, Accademia. Canvas; overall size 2.75 × 5.89 m. Part of a cycle depicting scenes from the life of Saint Ursula. *Photograph shaded to emphasize the picture-within-a-picture.* *(Photo: U.D.F. - La Photothèque.)*

192 *Art of Central Italy.* Arezzo, San Francesco, choir. PIERO DELLA FRANCESCA. *The Story of the True Cross: The Death of Adam* (detail). *1452-1466.* *In situ.* Fresco; overall size 3.56 × 7.47 m. *(Photo: Scala.)*

193 *Art of Central Italy.* Arezzo, San Francesco, choir. PIERO DELLA FRANCESCA. *The Story of the True Cross: The Discovery of the Cross* (detail). *1452-1466.* *In situ.* Fresco. *Cf. ill. 192.* *(Photo: Scala.)*

194 Rome, Santa Croce in Gerusalemme, apse. ANTONIAZZO ROMANO. *The story of the True Cross: The Discovery of the Cross* (detail). *1480.* *In situ.* Fresco. *(Photo: U.D.F. - La Photothèque.)*

195 GIAMPETRINO BIRAGO. *Nativity of the Virgin.* *End of 15th century.* Modena, Museo e Gallerie Estense. Ms Codex R. 1, 7. Lat. 1022. M. Salmi identifies Birago with the pseudo-Antonio da Monza. *(Photo: U.D.F. - La Photothèque.)*

196 *Florentine art.* Arezzo, cathedral, Gozzari chapel. BARTOLOMMEO DELLA GATTA. *Saint Jerome.* *c. 1480.* Fresco in sacristy. *(Photo: U.D.F. - La Photothèque.)*

197 *Art of the Marches.* Rome, SS. Apostoli, apse. MELOZZO DA FORLÌ. *Christ giving his Blessing.* *c. 1478-1480.* Rome, Palazzo del Quirinale. Fresco. This work, representing Christ surrounded by cherubs, angels with musical instruments, and apostles, was divided between the Quirinal and the Vatican afther the destruction of the apse in 1711. *(Photo: Anderson-Giraudon.)*

198 *Art of the Marches.* Forlì, San Biagio in San Girolamo. MELOZZO DA FORLÌ. *Vault of the Feo Chapel* (detail): *A Prophet.* *1493-1494.* Fresco. Destroyed during the 1939-1945 war. There were eight prophets in all, with the Feo coat of arms encircled by cherubs and a *putto* bearing a standard in each corner. *(Photo: Anderson.)*

199 BARTOLOMEO BONASCIA. *Pietà with the Virgin and Saint John.* *1485.* Modena, Museo e Gallerie Estense. Painting on wood; 1.33 × 1.73 m. *(Photo: U.D.F. - La Photothèque.)*

200 *Lombard art.* Bergamo, Casa di via dell' Arena. DONATO BRAMANTE (attr.). *Faith (?).* *Second half of 15th century.* *In situ.* Fresco. *(Photo: U.D.F. - La Photothèque.)*

201 Milan, Castello Sforzesco, treasure chamber. BRAMANTINO. *Argus.* *c. 1493.* *In situ.* Fresco. *(Photo: U.D.F. - La Photothèque.)*

202 *Art of the Romagna.* Faenza, San Giovanni dei Servi. LEONARDO SCALETTI (attr.). *The Virgin and Child with Saint John the Evangelist and the blessed Bertoni.* *1483-1484.* Faenza, Pinacoteca Civica. Painted on panel; 1.37 × 2 m. *(Photo: U.D.F. - La Photothèque.)*

203 *Venetian art.* GIORGIO SCHIAVONE. *The Virgin and Child.* *End of 15th century.* Amsterdam, Rijksmuseum. Painted on poplar-wood panel: 1.035 × 1.02 m. *(Photo: Rijksmuseum.)*

204 *Art of Northern Italy.* Bergamo, monastero degli Agostini (?). SCHOOL OF SQUARCIONE. *Angels carrying the instruments of the Passion* (detail). *End of 15th - beginning of 16th century.* Bergamo, Accademia Carrara. Tempera on panel; 0.58 × 0.21 m. Fragments, according to Ricci, of a lost polyptych. *(Photo: U.D.F. - La Photothèque.)*

205 *Venetian art.* Venice, monastery of San Lorenzo. CARLO CRIVELLI. *Virgin of the Passion. c. 1493.* Verona, Museo Civico. Painted on panel; 0.71×0.48 m The title of this picture is explained by the inclusion of the symbols of the Passion. *(Photo: U.D.F. - La Photothèque.)*

206 *Venetian art.* CARLO CRIVELLI. *Pietà. 1485* (signed and dated). Boston, Museum of Fine Arts. Painted on panel; 0.87×0.52 m. *(Photo: Museum of Fine Arts.)*

207 *Venetian art.* CARLO CRIVELLI. *Pietà* (detail). *1485* (signed and dated). Boston, The Museum of Fine Arts. Painted on panel. *Cf. ill. 206. (Photograph: Museum of Fine Arts.)*

208 *Florentine art.* Castello, Medici Villa. SANDRO BOTTICELLI. *The Birth of Venus. c. 1485-1486.* Florence, Uffizi. Canvas; 1.725×2.785 m. *(Photo: U.D.F. - La Photothèque.)*

209 *Ferrarese art.* Ferrara, Palazzo Schifanoia, Sala dei Mesi. FRANCESCO DEL COSSA. *The Month of April* (detail): *The Three Graces. 1458-1478. In situ.* Fresco. On the upper part of the east wall. *(Photo: UD.F. - La Photothèque.)*

210 *Sienese art.* Pienza, cathedral VECCHIETTA. Triptych: *Assumtion of the Virgin. 1461-1462. In situ.* Painted on panel. *(Photo: U.D.F. - La Photothèque.)*

211 *Sienese art.* Siena, San Domenico. GIOVANNI DI PAOLO. *The Last Judgement: Paradise* (detail). *c. 1460-1465.* Siena, Pinacoteca. Painted on panel; 2.53×0.41 m. overall. Predella of altarpiece painted for the Guelphs. Panels depicting the Creation and the Deluge have been lost. *(Photo: U.D.F. - La Photothèque.)*

212 *Sienese art.* FRANCESCO DI GIORGIO MARTINI (attr.). *Cassone* panel: *The Rape of Europa* (detail). *c. 1473-1475.* Paris, Louvre. Painted on panel; 0.35×1.17 m. *(Photo: U.D.F. - La Photothèque.)*

213 *Sienese art.* Siena, San Domenico. FRANCESCO DI GIORGIO MARTINI. *Annunciation. 1471.* Siena, Pinacoteca. Painted on panel; 0.74×0.48 m. *(Photo: U.D.F. - La Photothèque.)*

214 *Sienese art.* NEROCCIO DI BARTOLOMMEO DE' LANDI. *Portrait of a Lady. c. 1500.* Washington, National Gallery, Widener Collection. Painted on panel; 0.465×0.305 m. *(Photo: National Gallery.)*

215 *Sienese art.* NEROCCIO DI BARTOLOMMEO DE' LANDI. *The Virgin and Child between Saints* (detail). *c. 1475.* Siena, Pinacoteca. Painted on panel; 0.52×1.01 m. *(Photo: U.D.F. - La Photothèque.)*

216 *Veronese art.* LIBERALE DA VERONA. *Cassone* panel. *The Rape of Helen* (detail). *c. 1475.* Campana Collection. Painted on panel; 0.40×1.10 m. *(Photo: U.D.F. - La Photothèque.)*

217 GIROLAMO DA CREMONA. *Adoration of the Magi. 1467-1475.* Siena, Piccolomini Library. Miniature. Detail from a page of a Gradual, chant 4, f. 7. *(Photo: U.D.F. - La Photothèque.)*

218 *Veronese art.* Viterbo, cathedral. LIBERALE DA VERONA. *Christ between four Saints. End of 15th century. In situ.* Painted on panel. *(Photo: U.D.F. - La Photothèque.)*

219 *Florentine art.* Florence, SS. Annunziata, the Cloister. ALESSIO BALDOVINETTI. *Nativity* (detail): *Landscape. 1460-1462. In situ.* Fresco. *(Photo: U.D.F. - La Photothèque.)*

220 *Florentine art.* Pisa, Campo Santo. BENOZZO GOZZOLI. *The building of the Tower of Babel* (detail). *1468-1484. In situ.* Fresco. Part of the Campo Santo cycle, heavily damaged in 1944, which is now being restored. *(Photo: U.D.F. - La Photothèque.)*

221 *Florentine art.* Florence, Santa Trinità, Sassetti chapel. DOMENICO GHIRLANDAIO. *Saint Francis raising a child (of the Sassetti family) from the dead. 1482-1486. In situ.* Part of the cycle *The story of Saint Francis.* The artist introduces his contemporaries into the events of the saint's life. *(Photo: U.D.F. - La Photothèque.)*

222 *Florentine art.* Florence, Santa Maria Novella, choir. DOMENICO GHIRLANDAIO. *Frescoes. 1486-1490. In situ.* The frescoes, not all of which are seen here, depict scenes from the life of the Virgin and Saint John the Baptist and incorporate portraits of the Tornabuoni family. *(Photo: Brogi.)*

223 *Florentine art.* Florence, Santa Maria Novella, choir. DOMENICO GHIRLANDAIO. *The Visitation* (detail). *1486-1490. In situ.* Fresco. *Cf. ill. 222. (Photo: Scala.)*

224 *Florentine art.* Florence, Santa Maria Novella, Strozzi chapel. FILIPPINO LIPPI. *Frescoes. 1502. In situ.* From E. Borsook, *The Mural Painters of Tuscany*, Phaidon, London, 1960, pl. 86.

225 *Florentine art.* Florence, Santa Maria Novella, Strozzi chapel, right wall. FILIPPINO LIPPI. *Miracle of Saint Philip. 1502. In situ.* Fresco. *(Photo: Alinari.)*

226 UGO TOGNETTI. *The Sistine Chapel between 1488 and 1508. 18th century.* Engraving. The murals were divided into three zones: a series of papal portraits at the top, sacred scenes in the middle and *trompe-l'œil* drapery effects at the bottom. Behind the high altar, frescoes by Perugino occupied the space now taken up by the *Last Judgement. (Photo: Anderson.)*

227 *A Umbrian art.* The Vatican, Sistine chapel, left wall. LUCA SIGNORELLI. *The Last Days of Moses. 1483. In situ.* Fresco. One of the paintings commissioned by Sixtus IV from Signorelli, Botticelli, Ghirlandaio, Pinturicchio, Cosimo Rosselli and Perugino between 1481 and 1483. There were six scenes on each wall: Old Testament scenes and the life of Moses on the left and the life of Christ on the right. *(Photo: Bruno del Priore.)*

227 B *Florentine art.* The Vatican, Sistine chapel, left wall. SANDRO BOTTICELLI. *The Punishment of Korah, Dathan and Abiron. c. 1482-1483. In situ.* Fresco. *Cf. ill. 25, 227 (A). (Photo: Bruno del Priore.)*

227 C *Florentine art.* The Vatican, Sistine Chapel, left wall. COSIMO ROSSELLI. *Moses receiving the tablets of the Law and destroying the Golden Calf. 1482-1483. In situ.* Fresco. *Cf. ill. 227 (A). (Photo: Bruno del Priore.)*

227 D *Florentine art.* The Vatican, Sistine chapel, left wall. SANDRO BOTTICELLI. *Scenes from the life of Moses. 1482-1483. In situ.* Fresco. *Cf. ill. 227 (A). (Photo: Bruno del Priore.)*

227 E *Umbrian art.* The Vatican, Sistine chapel, left wall. PINTURICCHIO. *Circumcision of the sons of Moses. 1482-1483. In situ.* Fresco. Signor Pittaluga says that the cartoon for this was by Perugino. *Cf. ill. 227 (A). (Photo: Bruno del Priore.)*

227 F *Florentine art.* The Vatican, Sistine chapel, right wall. SANDRO BOTTICELLI. *Temptation of Christ and the leper's sacrifice. 1482-1483. In situ.* Fresco. *Cf. ill. 227 (A). (Photo: Bruno del Priore.)*

227 G *Florentine art.* The Vatican, Sistine chapel, right wall. DOMENICO GHIRLANDAIO. *The Calling of Saint Peter and Saint Andrew. 1482-1483. In situ.* Fresco. *Cf. ill. 227 (A). (Photo: Bruno del Priore.)*

227 H *Florentine art.* The Vatican, Sistine chapel, right wall. COSIMO ROSSELLI. *The Last Supper. 1482-1483. In situ.* Fresco. *Cf. ill. 227 (A). (Photo: Bruno del Priore.)*

228 *Florentine art.* Florence, San Martino della Scala. SANDRO BOTTICELLI. *Annunciation* (detail). *c. 1480. In situ.* Fresco; 2.43×5.50 m. *(Photo: U.D.F. - La Photothèque.)*

229 *Florentine art.* Florence, San Martino della Scala. SANDRO BOTTICELLI. *Annunciation. c. 1480. In situ.* Fresco; 2.43×5.50 m. *(Photo: U.D.F. - La Photothèque.)*

230. *Florentine art.* Florence, Ognissanti, Convent. DOMENICO GHIRLANDAIO. *The Last Supper. 1480. In situ.* Fresco; 1.77×8.12 m. *(Photo: U.D.F. - La Photothèque.)*

231 *Florentine art.* Milan, Santa Maria delle Grazie, refectory of the Dominican monastery. LEONARDO DA VINCI. *The Last Supper. 1495-1498. In situ.* Mural in oils; 4.20×9.10 m. *(Photo: Scala.)*

232 *Umbrian art.* Orvieto, cathedral, Capella di San Brizio. LUCA SIGNORELLI. *Frescoes. 1499-1504. In situ.* The cycle of *The Last Judgement:* Antichrist. *(Photo: Scala.)*

233 *Umbrian art.* Orvieto, cathedral, Capella di San Brizio. LUCA SIGNORELLI. *The Last Judgement: The Damned* (detail). *1499-1500. In situ.* Fresco. *Cf. fig. 232. (Photo: Scala.)*

234 *Art of Northern Italy.* Mantua, Palazzo Ducale, La Camera degli Sposi. ANDREA MANTEGNA. *Frescoes* (detail). *1474. In situ.* Classic exemple of the *camera picta.* Scenes of court life incorporating portraits of the Gonzaga family. *(Photo: U.D.F. - La Photothèque.)*

235 *Art of Northern Italy.* ANDREA MANTEGNA. *Saint Euphemia. 1454.* Naples, Museo di Capodimonte. Tempera on canvas; 1.71×0.78 m. Signed and dated on a *cartellino.* This work, badly damaged in a fire, has now been restored. *(Photo: U.D.F. - La Photothèque.)*

236 *Art of Northern Italy.* Mantua, Castello Vecchio. ANDREA MANTEGNA. *The Triumph of Caesar: IV. The Vase Bearers. 1482-1492.* London, Hampton Court Palace, Royal Collection. Painted on paper stuck to canvas; 2.74×2.74 m. Part of the series *The Triumph of Caesar* commissioned for a room in the Castello Vecchio where plays were performed. There are nine panels forming a frieze 27 m.×3 m. *(Photo: A. C. Cooper, London, by gracious permission of Her Majesty the Queen.)*

237 *Ferrarese art.* Ferrara, cathedral. COSIMO TURA. *Saint George and the Princess* (detail). *1469.* Ferrara, Museo del Duomo. Oils on canvas: 4.13×3.38 m. Together with the *Annunciation,* this formed the organ doors of the cathedral. *(Photo: U.D.F. - La Photothèque.)*

238 *Ferrarese art.* Ferrara, cathedral. COSIMO TURA. *Annunciation. 1469.* Ferrara, Museo del Duomo. Oils on canvas: 4.13×3.38 m. *Cf. ill. 237. (Photo: U.D.F. - La Photothèque.)*

239 *Venetian art.* Venice, San Giovanni Evangelista. GENTILE BELLINI. *Miracle of the Holy Cross* (detail). *1496* (signed and dated). Venice, Accademia. Canvas; 3.16×4.22 m. *(Photo : U.D.F. - La Photothèque.)*

240 *Venetian art.* Venice, Madonna dell' Orto, GENTILE BELLINI. *The Blessed Lorenzo Giustiniani. 1465.* Venice, Accademia. Canvas; 2.21×1.55 m. *(Photo: U.D.F. - La Photothèque.)*

241 *Venetian art.* Venice, Scuola di Sant' Orsola. VITTORE CARPACCIO. *The Legend of Saint Ursula: Meeting and departure of the betrothed* (detail). *1495* (signed and dated). Venice, Accademia. Painting on canvas; 2.80×6.11 m. Part of series on the life of Saint Ursula. *(Photo: U.D.F. - La Photothèque.)*

242 *Venetian art.* VITTORE CARPACCIO (attr.). *Design for a Triptych. c. 1515.* Copenhagen, Statens Museum for Kunst. Charcoal on white paper; 0.480×0.326 m. *(Photo: Statens Museum for Kunst.)*

243 *Ferrarese art.* Ferrara, San Giorgio fuori le Mura. COSIMO TURA. *Roverella Altarpiece. 1474.* Oils on wood. Dispersed in 1709. Reconstruction by M. Salmi.
1) lunette: *Pietà.* Paris, Louvre.
2) panel on left: *Bust of Saint George.* San Diego, Calif., The Fine Arts Gallery.
3) central panel: *Madonna.* London, The National Gallery.
4) panel on right: *Olivetano Rove-*

rella, Saint Paul and Saint Maurelius. Rome, Casa Colonna.
Predella: three *tondi.*
5) *The Circumcision.* Boston Gardner Museum.
6) *Adoration of the Magi.* Cambridge, Mass., Fogg Art Museum.
7) *The Flight into Egypt.* New York, The Metropolitan Museum of Art. This reconstruction is still incomplete; four of the *tondi*, the figures on the left-hand panel and two busts of saints which belong above the side panels are still missing. *(Photos: U.D.F. - La Photothèque* [*1, 3*], *M. Salmi,* Cosmè Tura, *Electa ed., Florence, 1957, pl. XVII* [*4*], *the galleries concerned* [*2, 5, 3, 6, 7*].*)*

244 *Ferrarese art.* Ferrara, San Giorgio fuori le Mura. COSIMO TURA. *Madonna surrounded by angels playing musical instruments. 1474.* London, The National Gallery. Painted on panel; 2.39×1.02 m. Central panel of the Roverella Altarpiece, now dispersed. *Cf. ill. 243. (Photo: U.D.F. - La Photothèque.)*

245 *Florentine art.* Florence, San Miniato al Monte. Chapel of the Cardinal of Portugal. ALESSIO BALDOVINETTI and ANTONIO POLLAIUOLO. *Frescoes. 1466-1467. In situ.* 4.80×10.30 m. Baldovinetti painted the frescoes on the walls: eight prophets, four evangelists, four doctors of the church. Pollaiuolo completed the decoration and painted the three figures of saints above the altar. *Photograph shaded to emphasize the decoration surrounding the altarpiece. (Photo; U.D.F. - La Photothèque.)*

246 *Florentine art.* Naples, Monte Oliveto, Mastroianni chapel. GIULIANO DA MAIANO. *Altarpiece. 1489. In situ.* Marble, in the round and bas-relief. *(Photo: U.D.F. - La Photothèque.)*

247 *Florentine art.* Castelfiorentino, Santa Maria della Tosse. BENOZZO GOZZOLI. *Madonna and Child with Saints. 1484* (signed and dated). *In situ.* Fresco: 4.47×3.35 m. *(Photo: U.D.F. - La Photothèque.)*

248 *Venetian art.* Venice, SS. Giovanni e Paolo. GIROLAMO MOCETTO. *Four Saints. Beginning of 16th century* (signed). *In situ.* Window. *(Photo: Zanipolo.)*

249 *Florentine art.* Florence, Signoria. FILIPPINO LIPPI. *The Virgin and Child between Saints. c. 1486.* Florence Uffizi. Painted on panel; 3.55×2.25 m. *Photograph shaded to emphasize the niche with the Madonna. (Photo: Anderson.)*

250 *Ferrarese art.* ERCOLE DE' ROBERTI. *Ravenna Altarpiece. 1480.* Milan, Brera. Painted on panel; 2.40×3.25 m. *Photograph shaded to emphasize throne with Madonna. (Photo: U.D.F. - La Photothèque.)*

251 *Umbrian art.* PERUGINO. *Polyptych. 1491* (signed). Rome, Villa Albani. Painted on panel; overall size 1.40×1.60 m. Below, left to right: *Saint John the Baptist and the Archangel Gabriel, Adoration of the Child Jesus, Saint Jerome and the Archangel Michael.* Above, left to right: *Angel of the Annunciation, Crucifixion, Virgin of the Annunciation. Photograph shaded to emphasize the Frame. (Photo: Alinari.)*

252 *Umbrian art.* PERUGINO. *Polyptych* (detail): *Virgin of the Annunciation. 1491* (signed). Rome, Villa Albani. *Cf. ill. 251. (Photo: Alinari.)*

253 *Lombard art.* Treviglio, San Martino. BERNARDO BUTINONE and BERNARDINO ZENALE. *Polyptych. 1485. In situ.* Painted on wood: overall size 4.10×3.80 m. *(Photo: Wellsfoto, Bergamo.)*

254 *Lombard art.* Treviglio, San Martino. BERNARDO BUTINONE and BERNARDINO ZENALE. *Polyptych* (detail): *Saint Martin dividing his cloak. 1485. In situ.* Central panel of lower part of polyptych. *Cf. ill. 253. (Photo: Wellsfoto, Bergamo.)*

255 *Art of northern Italy.* Mantua, Santa Maria della Vittoria. ANDREA MANTEGNA. *Madonna della Vittoria. 1495.* Paris, Louvre. Canvas; 2.80×1.60 m. Commissioned by Francesco Gonzaga to commemorate the victory of Fornovo in 1495. *Photograph shaded to emphasize the Madonna's throne. (Photo: U.D.F. - La Photothèque.)*

256 *Venetian art.* GIAMBATTISTA CIMA DA CONEGLIANO. *Altarpiece. 1489.* (signed and dated). Vicenza, Museo Civico. Tempera on canvas; 2.14×1.79 m. *Photograph shaded to emphasize the Madonna's throne. (Photo: U.D.F. - La Photothèque.)*

257 *Venetian art.* Castelfranco Veneto, San Liberale. GIORGIONE. *The Virgin and Child between Saint Francis and Saint Liberale. c. 1504. In situ.* Painted on panel; 2×1.52 m. *Photograph shaded to emphasize the Madonna's throne. (Photo U.D.F. - La Photothèque.)*

258 *Ferrarese art.* Bologna, San Petronio. FRANCESCO DEL COSSA. *Griffoni Altarpiece* (detail): *Saint Vincent Ferrer. 1472-1473.* London, The National Gallery. Painted on panel; 1.535×0.60 m. This is the central panel of the lower section of this altarpiece, which has been dispersed. *(Photo: U.D.F. - La Photothèque.)*

259 *Venetian art.* Venice, San Giovanni in Bragora. BARTOLOMMEO VIVARINI. *Polyptych. 1478. In situ.* Painted on panel; the central panel measures 1.30×0.48 m., the lateral panels 1.30×0.45 m. This work is signed and dated on the central panel. *(Photo: U.D.F. - La Photothèque.)*

260 *Venetian art.* Ascoli Piceno, cathedral. CARLO CRIVELLI. *Polyptych* (detail). *1473* (signed and dated). *In situ.* Painted on panel; overall size 3.64×2.80 m. Lower part of the great polyptych in ten panels commissioned by the bishop Prospero Caffarelli in 1472. *(Photo: U.D.F. - La Photothèque.)*

261 *Florentine art.* Sandro Botticelli. *Adoration of the Kings. c. 1481.* London, The National Gallery. Painted on panel; diameter of the *tondo* 1.315 m. *(Photo: U.D.F. - La Photothèque.)*

262 *Florentine art.* SANDRO BOTTICELLI. *Portrait of a Woman. c. 1475. Florence, Palazzo Pitti.* Painted on panel; 0.61×0.40 m. *(Photo: U.D.F. - La Photothèque.)*

263 *Florentine art.* SANDRO BOTTICELLI. *Portrait of Giuliano de' Medici. 1478.* Washington, National Gallery of Art, Kress Collection. Painted on panel; 0.76×0.526 m.

Of the four portraits of Giuliano de' Medici, that in Milan is said to have been painted during his lifetime and the three others, including this one, are said to have been taken from a death-mask. *(Photo: National Gallery of Art.)*

264 *Florentine art.* Florence, Ognissanti. SANDRO BOTTICELLI. *Saint Augustine in Meditation* (detail). *1480. In situ.* Fresco; 1.52×1.12 m. According to Vasari, Botticelli intended this picture to compete with Ghirlandaio's *Saint Jerome*, painted in 1480. *(Photo: U.D.F. - La Photothèque.)*

265 *Florentine art.* Castello, Medici Villa. SANDRO BOTTICELLI. *Primavera* (detail). *1478.* Florence, Uffizi. Painted on panel; 2.03×3.14 m. *(Photo: U.D.F. - La Photothèque.)*

266 *Ferrarese art.* Ferrara, San Luca in Borgo. COSIMO TURA. *Saint James. c. 1480-1485.* Caen, Musée. Oils on panel; 0.73×0.32 m. Central panel of a polyptych in six sections which are now in galleries in Caen, Paris, Bergamo, Florence and Berlin. Reconstructions have been suggested by R. Longhi (*Cf.* bibliography, no. 192) and M. Salmi (*Cf.* bibliography, no. 339). *(Photo: U.D.F. - La Photothèque.)*

267 *Ferrarese art.* Bologna, San Petronio. ERCOLE DE' ROBERTI. *Griffoni Altarpiece* (detail): *Saint Michael. c. 1473.* Paris, Louvre. Painted on panel; 0.26×0.11 m. From one of the small side-panels or *lateralie*. *(Photo: U.D.F. - La Photothèque.)*

268 *Florentine art.* Florence, Santa Maria Novella, Strozzi Chapel, left wall. FILIPPINO LIPPI. *The Miracle of Saint Philip* (detail). *1502. In situ.* Fresco. *(Photo: Alinari.)*

269 *Art of Central Italy.* Urbino, San Bernardino. PIERO DELLA FRANCESCA. *Montefeltro Altarpiece. 1475.* Milan, Brera. Painted on panel: overall size 2.48×1.70 m. *(Photo: U.D.F. - La Photothèque.)*

270 *Art of Central Italy.* Urbino, San Bernardino. PIERO DELLA FRANCESCA. *Montefeltro Altarpiece* (detail). *1475.* Milan, Brera. *Cf. ill. 269.* *(Photo U.D.F. - La Photothèque.)*

271 *Art of Northern Italy.* Aigueperse, Notre-Dame. ANDREA MANTEGNA. *Martyrdom of Saint Sebastian. c. 1467.* Paris, Louvre. Canvas; 2.60×1.47 m. Sent to Aigueperse in 1481 on the occasion of the marriage of Clara di Gonzaga to Gilbert de Bourbon, comte de Montpensier. The date of the painting itself is a matter of controversy. Some writers suggest 1475-1480, while Tietze-Conrad and others consider it to be a youthful work dating from about 1476. *(Photo: U.D.F. - La Photothèque.)*

272 *Art of Southern Italy.* ANTONELLO DA MESSINA. *Martyrdom of Saint Sebastian. 1475-1476.* Dresden, Gemäldegalerie. Painted on panel, transferred to canvas; 1.71×0.855 m. *(Photo: Deutsche Fotothek.)*

273 *Art of Southern Italy.* Venice, San Cassiano. ANTONELLO DA MESSINA. *San Cassiano Altarpiece.* Reconstruction by J. Wilde. *1475-1476.* Classic example of *sacra conversazione.* The altarpiece showed the Virgin and Child surrounded by saints: Saint Nicholas, Saint Mary Magdelen, Saint Liberale, Saint Cecilia and Saint Ursula, Saint Dominic, Saint Sebastian and Saint Helena. It was broken up in 1659. Three fragments went to the gallery of Archduke Leopold in Brussels, where they were attributed to Giovanni Bellini, and then passed to Vienna. In 1929 Bernard Berenson recognized them as part of the *San Cassiano Altarpiece.* The discovery of other elements of the picture has made a reconstruction possible. *Cf.* bibliography, no. 409. *(Photo: Kunsthistorisches Museum, Vienna.)*

274 *Art of Southern Italy.* Venice, San Cassiano. ANTONELLO DA MESSINA. *San Cassiano Altarpiece* (detail): *Saint Nicholas and Saint Mary Magdelen. 1475-1476.* Vienna, Kunsthistorisches Museum. Painted on panel; 0.555×0.35 m. *Cf. ill. 273.* *(Photo: Kunsthistorisches Museum.)*

275 *Art of Southern Italy.* ANTONELLO DA MESSINA. *Pietà with Angels. 1475.* Venice, Museo Correr. Painted on panel; 1.17×0.85 m. This painting, which had badly deteriorated, was restored in 1940. *(Photo: U.D.F. - La Photothèque.)*

276 *Art of Southern Italy.* ANTONELLO DA MESSINA. *Annunciation* (detail). *1474.* Syracuse, Palazzo Bellomo. Painted on panel, transferred to canvas; 1.70×1.70 m. *(Photo: Villani e Figli, Bologna.)*

277 *Art of Southern Italy.* ANTONELLO DA MESSINA. *'Salvator Mundi.' 1465* (signed). London, National Gallery. Painted on panel; 0.39×0.295 m. *(Photo: U.D.F. - La Photothèque.)*

278 *Venetian art.* GIOVANNI BELLINI. *Stigmatization of Saint Francis. 1479-1485.* New York, Frick Collection. Painted on panel. *(Photo: Frick Collection.)*

279 *Ferrarese art.* ERCOLE DE' ROBERTI. *Ravenna Altarpiece* (detail). *1480.* Milan, Brera. Painted on panel; 2.40×3.25 m. *(Photo: U.D.F. - La Photothèque.)*

280 *Flemish art.* Urbino, guild of Corpus Domini. JUSTUS OF GHENT *Institution of the Eucharist. 1470-1475.* Urbino, National Gallery of the Marches. Oils on panel; 2.87×3.12 m. *(Photo: U.D.F. - La Photothèque.)*

281 Urbino, Ducal Palace. PEDRO BERRUGUETE. *Aristotle. c. 1476.* Paris, Louvre. Painted on panel; 1×0.60 m. One of a series of 28 portraits of 'illustrious men' which appeared above the marquetry panels on the walls of the *studiolo* of the Duke of Montefeltro. The decor of the *studiolo* was broken up in the 18th century and is now divided between the Louvre and the palace at Urbino. The attribution to Justus of Ghent seems less likely than that to Berruguete. *(Photo: U.D.F. - La Photothèque.)*

282 Urbino, Ducal Palace. PEDRO BERRUGUETE. *Solon. c. 1476.* Paris, Louvre. Painted on panel; 1×0.60 m. *Cf. ill. 281.* *(Photo: U.D.F. - La Photothèque.)*

283 *Venice,* Santa Maria della Carità. PEDRO BERRUGUETE. *Pietà with Angels. End of 15th century.* Milan, Brera. Canvas, 0.62×0.71 m. *(Photo: U.D.F. - La Photothèque.)*

284 Urbino, Palace Library. UNIDENTIFIED MASTER. *Allegory of Music. 1474-1508.* London, The National Gallery. Painted on poplar-wood panel; 1.56×0.976 m. One of a series of *Allegories of the Liberal Arts,* of which there were probably seven (the *trivium* and the *quadrivium*). These paintings are exceptionally hard to attribute to any one painter. Names suggested include Giovanni Santi, Bramante, Melozzo da Forlì, Berruguete and Justus of Ghent. *(Photo: U.D.F. - La Photothèque.)*

285 Urbino, Ducal Palace. PEDRO BERRUGUETE (attr.). *Federico da Montefeltro and his son Guidobaldo. c. 1477.* Urbino, National Gallery of the Marches. Painted on poplar-wood panel; 1.36×0.82 m. This panel was among the portraits of illustrious men painted for the *studiolo* of the duke by Justus of Ghent and Pedro Berruguete. *(Photo U.D.F. - La Photothèque.)*

286 *Tuscan art.* PIERO DELLA FRANCESCA. *Nativity c. 1475.* London, The National Gallery. Painted on panel; 1.245×1.23 m. *(Photo: U.D.F. - La Photothèque.)*

287 Urbino, Ducal Palace, library. UNIDENTIFIED MASTER. *Lecture at the Court of Urbino. Federico da Montefeltro and his court listening to a humanist. c. 1480.* Windsor Castle, Royal Collection. Painted on chestnut-wood panel; 1.30×2.12 m. Attributed variously to Melozzo da Forlì and to Berruguete; Justus of Ghent seems to have been ruled out. *(Photo: National Gallery.)*

288 *Florentine art.* ANTONIO POLLAIUOLO. *The Rape of Deianeira. c. 1475.* New Haven, Yale Gallery of Fine Arts, J. Jackson Jarves Collection. Painted on panel, transferred to canvas: overall size 0.54×0.80 m. *(Photo: Yale Gallery of Fine Arts.)*

289 *Florentine art.* ANTONIO POLLAIUOLO. *The Rape of Deianeira* (detail). *c. 1475.* New Haven, Yale Gallery of Fine Arts, J. Jackson Jarves Collection. *Cf. ill. 288. (Photo: Yale Gallery of Fine Arts.)*

290 *Florentine art.* STUDIO OF VERROCCHIO. *Tobias and the Archangel Raphael. c. 1467.* London, The National Gallery, Painted on panel; 0.84×0.66 m. *(Photo: National Gallery.)*

291 *Florentine art.* STUDIO OF PIERO POLLAIUOLO. *The crucified Christ between Saint Jerome and Saint Anthony. End of 15th century.* Argiano (Val di Pesa), Santa Maria e Angiolo. Painted on panel, in very bad condition. *(Photo: U.D.F. - La Photothèque.)*

292 *Florentine art.* Florence, San Salvi. Vallombrosian monastery. ANDREA VERROCCHIO with LEONARDO DA VINCI. *The Baptism of Christ* (detail). *c. 1470-1475.* Florence, Uffizi. Oils and tempera on panel, continued in oils by Leonardo; 1.77×1.51 m. overall. As early as 1510, Leonardo's work on this painting is mentioned by Albertini in his description of Florence. Vasari writes: 'When Andrea was painting a picture of the *Baptism of Christ,* Leonardo painted an angel holding garments, and although he was very young he made it infinitely superior to the figures painted by Andrea.' *(Photo: U.D.F. - La Photothèque.)*

293 *Florentine art.* ANDREA VERROCCHIO. *The Baptism of Christ* (detail): *Saint John the Baptist. c. 1470-1475.* Florence, Uffizi. *Cf. ill.* 290. *(Photo: U.D.F. - La Photothèque.)*

294 *Florentine art.* Villa di Castello. SANDRO BOTTICELLI. *Primavera* (detail). *1478.* Florence, Uffizi. Painted on panel; 2.03×3.14 m. *(Photo: U.D.F. - La Photothèque.)*

295 *Florentine art.* Milan, San Francesco. LEONARDO DA VINCI. *The Virgin of the Rocks. 1483.* Paris, Louvre. Painted on panel, transferred to canvas: 1.99×1.22 m. There are two versions of the *Virgin of the Rocks;* this one was acquired very early by Francis I. The other, a copy by the master and his studio, is considered by some recent experts to be the original of 1482-1483. It is in the National Gallery in London. *(Photo: U.D.F. - Draeger.)*

296 *Umbrian art.* PERUGINO. *Apollo and Marsyas. c. 1483-1497.* Paris, Louvre. Painted on panel; 0.39×0.29 m. *(Photo: U.D.F. - La Photothèque.)*

297 *Umbrian art.* Florence, Santa Chiara. PERUGINO. *The Lamentation. 1495* (signed and dated). Florence, Palazzo Pitti. Painted on panel; 2.16×1.94 m. *(Photo: U.D.F. - La Photothèque.)*

298 *Umbrian art.* Florence, Santa Maria Maddalena de' Pazzi. PERUGINO. *The Crucifixion* (detail). *1496. In situ.* Fresco; 4.80×8.12 m. overall. In the form of a triptych with Saint Bernard and the Virgin on the left, Christ crucified and Saint Mary Magdalen in the centre and Saint John the Evangelist and Saint Benedict on the right. *(Photo: Alinari.)*

299 *Umbrian art.* Perugia, San Lorenzo. PERUGINO. *The Marriage of the Virgin. c. 1503-1504.* Caen, Musée. Painted on panel; 2.34×1.85 m. *(Photo: U.D.F. - La Photothèque.)*

300 Rome, San Francesco de' Padri Minori. RAPHAEL. *The Marriage of the Virgin. 1504.* Milan, Brera, on poplar-wood panel; 1.18×1.70 m. On the frieze of the temple portico is the inscription *Raphael urbinas,* and on the spandrels of the arch the date *MDIIII. (Photo: U.D.F. - La Photothèque.)*

301 *Florentine art.* PIERO DI COSIMO. Cassone panel: *The Legend of Prometheus* (detail). *c. 1500.* Strasbourg, Musée. Painted on panel; 0.68×1.20 m. overall. *(Photo: U.D.F. - La Photothèque.)*

302 *Florentine art.* PIERO DI COSIMO. *The Death of Procris* (detail). *End of 15th century.* London, The National Gallery. Painted on panel; 0.65×1.83 m. overall. M. Davies says that this is not a *cassone* panel but was incorporated into a panelled wall. *(Photo: U.D.F. - La Photothèque.)*

303 *Florentine art.* PIERO DI COSIMO. *Hunting Scene* (detail). *End of 15th century.* New York, The Metropolitan Museum of Art. Tempera and oils on panel; 0.705 × 1.695 m. overall. *(Photo: Metropolitan Museum of Art.)*

304 *Florentine art.* PIERO DI COSIMO. *The Virgin and Child with a pigeon. End of 15th century.* Paris, Louvre. Painting: 0.87 × 0.58 m. *(Photo: U.D.F. - La Photothèque.)*

305 *Tuscan art.* Prato, 'Canto al Mercatale.' FILIPPINO LIPPI. *Tabernacle* (detail): *The Virgin and Child. 1498. In situ.* Fresco. *(Photo: U.D.F. - La Photothèque.)*

306 Florence, Santo Spirito. RAFFAELLINO DEL GARBO. *Pietà and Saints. c. 1505.* Munich, Pinakothek. Painted on panel. *(Photo: U.D.F. - La Photothèque.)*

307 *Umbrian art.* LUCA SIGNORELLI. *Two Nudes. 1498.* Toledo (Ohio), The Toledo Museum of Art. (Gift Edward Drummond Libley.) Painted on panel; 0.68 × 0.42 m. *(Photo: Musée.)*

308 *Florentine art.* Florence, San Paolino. SANDRO BOTTICELLI. *Pietà and Saints. c. 1490-1500.* Munich, Pinakothek. Painted on panel; 1.10 × 2.07 m. *(Photo: U.D.F. - La Photothèque.)*

309 *Florentine art.* SANDRO BOTTICELLI. *The Divine Comedy: Paradise, Canto XXVIII. 1479-1503.* Formerly in Berlin, Kupferstichkabinett. Silverpoint and lead; 0.47 × 0.32 m. *(Photo: Bibliothèque Nationale, Paris.)*

310 *Florentine art.* SANDRO BOTTICELLI. *The Story of Virginia. c. 1490.* Bergamo, Accademia Carrara, Morelli bequest. Painted on panel; 0.86 × 1.65 m. It seems that this is one of the small panels mentioned by Vasari. *(Photo: U.D.F. - La Photothèque.)*

311 Modena, Capuccini. FRANCIA. *Madonna in a Rose Garden. End of 15th century.* Munich, Pinakothek. Painted on poplar-wood panel; 1.745 × 1.315 m. *(Photo: U.D.F. - La Photothèque.)*

312 *Venetian art.* VITTORE CARPACCIO. *Meditation on the dead Christ. 1505-1510.* Berlin-Dahlem, Staatliche Museen, Gemäldegalerie. Canvas: 1.45 × 1.85 m. *Shaded to emphasize landscape and vegetation. (Photo: Staatliche Museen - Walter Steinkopf.)*

313 *Venetian art.* GIOVANNI BUONCONSIGLIO. *Pietà. End of 15th century.* Vicenza, Museo Civico. Painted on panel; 1.60 × 1.80 m. *(Photo: U.D.F. - La Photothèque.)*

314 *Lombard art.* Milan, Santa Maria di Brera, sacristy. VINCENZO FOPPA. *The Virgin and Child between Saint John the Baptist and Saint John the Evangelist. 1485* (dated). Milan, Brera. Fresco; 1.70 × 1.90 m. *(Photo: U.D.F. - La Photothèque.)*

315 *Piedmontese art.* Ivrea, San Bernardino. GIAN MARTINO SPANZOTTI. *The Life of Christ: Christ before Caiaphas. End of 15th-beginning of 16th century. In situ.* Fresco. *(Photo: Chomont Perino, Turin.)*

316 *Venetian art.* VITTORE CARPACCIO. *Sacra Conversazione. c. 1502.* Caen, Musée. Painted on panel; 0.96 × 1.25 m. A typical *sacra conversazione*, with the Virgin and Child surrounded by the child John the Baptist, Saint Joseph, Saint Anne, Saint Elizabeth and Saint Zacharias (or Joachim). In the background can be seen episodes from the life of Saint Jerome. *Photograph shaded to emphasize the rocky setting. (Photo: U.D.F. - La Photothèque.)*

317 *Mantuan art.* ANDREA MANTEGNA. *Madonna of the Quarries. c. 1466.* Florence, Uffizi. Painted on panel; 0.29 × 0.215 m. This small painting was in the possession of the Medici when Vasari mentioned it in the second edition of his *Vite* (1568), but it is not included in the 1494 inventory. A. Venturi gives the date as 1466, Tietze-Conrat as 1484. *Photograph shaded to emphasize the background of rocks. (Photo: U.D.F. - La Photothèque.)*

318 *Ferrarese art.* Bologna, San Petronio. FRANCESCO DEL COSSA. *Griffoni Altarpiece* (detail). *1473.* Milan, Brera. Oils on panel. This is the lower left-hand panel of the polyptych, which is now dispersed. *(Photo: U.D.F. - La Photothèque.)*

319 *Lombard art.* BERNARDINO ZENALE. *The Virgin and Child between Saints. End of 15th century.* Denver, Art Museum, Kress Collection. Painted on panel; 1.815 × 1.246 m. Formerly attributed to Master X.L. on the basis of the monogram found on the picture. *Cf.* Bibliography, no. 381. *(Photo: Art Museum.)*

320 *Florentine art.* LEONARDO DA VINCI. *The Virgin and Child with Saint Anne* (detail). *c. 1506-1510.* Paris, Louvre. Painted on panel; 1.685 × 1.30 m. There are several versions of this picture: (a) Milan version, *c.* 1499 (cartoon in London), (b) Florence version, 1501 (cartoon lost), (c) second Milan version, now in the Louvre, painted between 1506 and 1511 (cartoon lost). *(Photo: U.D.F. - Draeger.)*

321 *Florentine art.* PIERO DI COSIMO. *Allegory. End of 15th century.* Washington, The National Gallery of Art, Samuel H. Kress collection. Painted on panel; 0.56 × 0.44 m. *(Photo: National Gallery of Art.)*

322 PIERO DI COSIMO. *Portrait of Giuliano da Sangallo. c. 1505.* The Hague, Mauritshuis. Oils on panel; 0.47 × 0.34 m. Vasari mentions this as one of the pictures by Cosimo in the possession of Francesco da Sangallo. *(Photo: Haufstaengl-Giraudon).*

323 *Florentine art.* Florence, Santa Maria Novella. SANDRO BOTTICELLI. *Adoration of the Magi* (detail): *portrait of the artist. c. 1476-1477.* Florence, Uffizi. Painted on panel; 1.11 × 1.34 m. overall. This work includes several Medici family portraits as well as this self-portrait on the extreme right. *(Photo: Alinari-Giraudon.)*

324. *Florentine art.* LORENZO DI CREDI (attr.). *Portrait of Andrea Verrocchio* (?). *c. 1488.* Florence, Uffizi. Oils on panel; 0.50 × 0.36 m. According to Vasari, Lorenzo di Credi painted many portraits, including one of Andrea Verrocchio, whose principal pupil he was

Some authorities consider that this is not a portrait of Verrocchio but of Perugino. *(Photo: Anderson-Giraudon.)*

325 *Art of the Romagna.* Loretto, sanctuary of the Santa Casa. MELOZZO DA FORLÌ. *Palm Sunday* (detail): *self-portrait. 1486. In situ.* Fresco. *(Photo: Alinari-Giraudon.)*

326 *Umbrian art.* The Vatican, Sistine chapel. PERUGINO. *Christ giving the Keys to Saint Peter* (detail): *self-portrait. 1481-1483. In situ.* Fresco. *(Photo: Alinari-Giraudon.)*

327 *Florentine art.* Florence, Santa Maria Novella, choir. DOMENICO GHIRLANDAIO. *Saint Joachim expelled from the Temple* (detail): *self-portrait. 1486-1490. In situ.* Fresco. Part of the cycle *The Life of the Virgin.* Left wall. *(Photo: Anderson-Giraudon.)*

328 *Florentine art.* LEONARDO DA VINCI. *Double spiral staircase and bastions of a fortress. End of 15th century.* Pen drawing. (Manuscrit B, f. 69 *recto*). Paris, Institut de France. From A. Sartoris, *Léonard architecte*, Paris, 1952, p. 40.

329 *Florentine art.* LEONARDO DA VINCI. *Façade of church. 1490.* Milan, Biblioteca Ambrosiana. Drawing 238 *verso.* From J.P. Richter, *The Literary Works of Leonardo da Vinci*, II, Oxford University Press, 1939, 2nd ed., pl. XCIV, 4.

330 *Sienese art.* FRANCESCO DI GIORGIO MARTINI. *Reconstruction of the 'colonnacce' of the forum of Nerva. c. 1470.* Turin, Biblioteca del Re. One of the collection of architectural drawings entitled *Codice architettonico di monumenti antichi di Roma e d'altri luoghi.* From R. Papini, *Francesco di Giorgio architetto*, II, Florence, 1946, pl. 11.

331 *Certosa di Pavia.* Reconstruction of the façade as it must have looked at the end of the Quattrocento. Sketched by the author.

332 Ferrara, Palazzo dei Diamanti. Schematic elevation. *1492-1565.* From B. Zevi, *Biagio Rossetti, architetto ferrarese, il primo urbanista europeo.* Turin, 1960, pl. 25.

333 Florence, Palazzo Gondi. Schematic elevation. After GIULIANO DA SANGALLO. 1480. From C. von Stegman and H. von Geymuller, *The Architecture of the Renaissance in Tuscany*, New York, p. 127.

334 Architectural drawing. After FRANCESCO DI GIORGIO MARTINI: *Town Square* (detail). *End of 15th century.* The original is in the National Gallery of the Marches at Urbino. From R. Papini, *Francesco di Giorgio architetto*, II, Florence, 1946, pl. 79.

335 Diagram of villa. After BENOZZO GOZZOLI: *Childhood and first prodigies of Moses* (detail) . 1468-1484. Pisa, Campo Santo. Sketched by the author.

336 Diagram. Tomb, Type 1. Raised slab. After ANTONIO POLLAIUOLO: *Tomb of Sixtus IV. 1493.* Vatican. Sketched by the author.

337 Diagram. Tomb, Type 2. Wall-tomb in a niche. After ANTONIO ROSSELLINO: *Tomb of the Cardinal of Portugal. 1459-1460.* Florence, San Miniato. Sketched by the author.

338 Diagram. Tomb, Type 3. Aedicular tomb. After GIAN CRISTOFORO ROMANO: *Tomb of Gian Galeazzo Visconti. 1491-1497.* Certosa di Pavia. *Cf. ill. 139.* Sketched by the author.

339 Padua, Eremetani, Ovetari chapel. ANDREA MANTEGNA: *Frescoes.* Perspective view and diagram of walls opened out to show position of frescoes. From G. Fiocco, *La Chapelle Ovetari dans l'église des Eremétiques*, Milan, n.d., fig. 7, and sketched by the author.

340 Ferrara, Palazzo Schifanoia, Sala dei Mesi. ERCOLE DE' ROBERTI and FRANCESCO DEL COSSA. Perspective view and diagram of east and north walls opened out to show position of frescoes. Only these two walls retain their decoration intact. On the east wall are May, April and March: on the north wall, September, August, July, June. *Cf. ill. 209* (detail). From P. d'Ancona, *Les Mois de Schifanoia à Ferrare,* French translation, Milan, 1954, and sketched by the author.

341 The Vatican, Borgia apartments, Sala dei Santi. PINTURICCHIO. Perspective view, ceiling, and diagram of walls opened out to show position of frescoes. *1492-1494.* From M. Calvesi, *Les Trésors du Vatican*, Geneva, 1962, pp. 83 and 85, and sketched by the author.

342 Diagram. Altarpiece, Type A: *pala.* After GIOVANNI BELLINI: *San Giobbe altarpiece.* Painted on panel; 4.68×2.55 m. *1488.* Venice, Accademia. Sketched by the author.

343 Diagram. Altarpiece, Type A¹: *pala* +predella'+ *lateralie.* After DOMENICO GHIRLANDAIO: *The Coronation of the Virgin.* Painted on panel; 3.30×2.30 m. *1486.* Narni, Municipio. Sketched by the author.

344 Diagram. Altarpiece, Type B: triptych. After ANTONIO DA FABRIANO: *The Virgin and Child.* Painted on panel; 2.10×1.72 m. 1474. Genga (Marches), San Clemente. Sketched by the author.

345 Diagram. Altarpiece, Type B¹: double triptych+predella+pediment. After BERNARDINO BUTINONE and BERNARDINO ZENALE: *San Martino Altarpiece.* Painted on panel; 4.10×3.80 m. *1485.* Treviglio, San Martino. *Cf. fig. 253.* Sketched by the author.

346 Diagram. Altarpiece, Type C: single-tier polyptych in five sections. After BARTOLOMMEO VIVARINI: *Altarpiece of Scuola dei Tagliapetra.* Painted on panel: 1.25×1.91 m. *1477.* Venice, Accademia. Sketched by the author.

347 Diagram. Altarpiece, Type C¹: polyptych in several tiers. After CARLO CRIVELLI: *Altarpiece of Ascoli Piceno.* Painted on panel; 3.64×2.80 m. *1473.* Ascoli Piceno, cathedral. *Cf. ill. 260.* (detail). Sketched by the author.

348 Diagram. Altarpiece, Type D: mixed (sculpture and painting). After VINCENZO FOPPA and LODOVICO BREA: *Della Rovere altarpiece*. Painted on panel: 6.70 × 3.80 m. *1490*. Savone, Santa Maria di Castello. Sketched by the author.

349 *Ferrarese art*. Bologna, San Petronio. FRANCESCO DEL COSSA and ERCOLE DE' ROBERTI. *Griffoni altarpiece* (reconstruction). *c. 1473*. Now dispersed. Painted on panel. From R. Longhi, *Officina ferrarese*, Florence, 1934 and 1940, *ill.* 98.

350 *Venetian art*. Ascoli Piceno, San Domenico. CARLO CRIVELLI. *Demidoff Altarpiece* (reconstruction). *1476*. Painted on panel. The panels showing the Virgin and saints, now in the National Gallery, have been assembled in an imaginary frame. Sketched by the author.

351 *Umbrian art*. Perugia, San Pietro. PERUGINO. *San Pietro Altarpiece* (reconstruction). *1495-1500*. Now dispersed. Painted on panel. From E. Camesasca, *Tutta la Pittura del Perugino*, Milan, 1959, p. 72.

352 *Umbrian art*, Siena, Sant' Agostino. LUCA SIGNORELLI. *Bichi Altarpiece* (reconstruction). *1498*. Carved and painted wood. Sketched by the author.

353 Map showing the principal fortifications and castles at the end of the 15th century.

354 Map showing the principal churches built on a central plan by the end of the 15th century.

355 Map showing the principal tiered wal-tombs at the end of the 15th century. The original sites of the tombs are given.

356 Map showing the principal tiered altarpieces. The original sites of the altarpieces are given.

357 Map of Italy at the end of the 15th century.

358 Map of Northern and Central Italy at the end of the 15th century.

MAPS

353 - CASTLES, VILLAS AND PALAZZI

354 - CHURCHES ON A CENTRAL PLAN

355 - TIERED WALL TOMBS

356 - TIERED ALTARPIECES

CASTLES, VILLAS AND PALAZZI

CHURCHES ON A CENTRAL PLAN

TIERED WALL TOMBS

TIERED ALTARPIECES

Acknowledgements

Works such as THE GOLDEN AGE OF THE RENAISSANCE and STUDIOS AND STYLES OF THE RENAISSANCE involve a great number of debts of every sort, and I must express my gratitude to the friends and colleagues who have given help in compiling these volumes. An historian can never fully acquit himself of his obligation to all those whose example or knowledge have made possible a work in which any lacunae, imperfections or daring opinions are bound to remain entirely his own responsibility. But I wish to express my particular gratitude to Mmes A.M. Brizio, G. Sinibaldi, B. Canestro-Chiovenda; to Professors R. Longhi, G. Fiocco, U. Procacci, S. Bettini, S. Bottari, P. Rotondi, D. Redig de Campos, E. Castelnuovo, F. Zeri, C. Gnudi, C. Volpe, R. Palluchini, P. Zampetti, M.A. Muraro; to Dottori G. Marchini, G. Mazzini, M. Rosci, L. Castelnovi, G. Perocco, S. Bettagno; to Professors E. Panofsky, M. Meiss, U. Middeldorf, C. de Tolnay, A. Blunt, E.H. Gombrich, E.K. Waterhouse, J. Ackerman, W. Paatz, L.H. Heydenreich, W. Lotz, S. Lorentz, J. Bialostocki, J. Pope-Hennessy; to Messrs Denys Sutton, Humphrey Brooke; to Dr. C.L. Frommel; to Mme S. Béguin, to C. Sterling, R. Jullian, R. Ternois; to my friends J. Thuillier, M. Laclotte, H. Zerner, R. Klein. To these names must be added those of Mme C. Lorgues and Mlle R. Plouin for their devoted assistance. Thanks are also due to all private collectors who have permitted us to use important works of art from their collections. I also wish to record my appreciation of the enjoyable collaboration of the team engaged on 'The Arts of Mankind'.

André Chastel

THIS, THE EIGHTH VOLUME OF 'THE ARTS OF MANKIND' SERIES, EDITED BY ANDRÉ MALRAUX AND GEORGES SALLES, HAS BEEN PRODUCED UNDER THE SUPERVISION OF ALBERT BEURET, EDITOR-IN-CHARGE OF THE SERIES. THE BOOK WAS DESIGNED BY ROGER PARRY, ASSISTED BY JEAN-LUC HERMAN AND THE MAPS WERE DRAWN BY JACQUES PERSON. THE TEXT, THE PLATES IN BLACK AND WHITE AND IN SEPIA WERE PRINTED BY L'IMPRIMERIE GEORGES LANG, PARIS; PLATES IN COLOUR BY L'IMPRIMERIE DRAEGER, MONTROUGE. THE BINDING, DESIGNED BY MASSIN, WAS EXECUTED BY BABOUOT, GENTILLY.